SLEEPWALKING INTO WOKENESS: HOW WE GOT HERE

JOHN O'SULLIVAN

To Graham
With thanks and
[illegible]

SLEEPWALKING INTO WOKENESS: HOW WE GOT HERE

JOHN O'SULLIVAN

ACADEMICA PRESS
WASHINGTON~LONDON

Library of Congress Cataloging-in-Publication Data

Names: O'Sullivan, John (author)
Title: Sleepwalking into wokeness : how we got here | O'Sullivan, John.
Description: Washington : Academica Press, 2024. | Includes references.
Identifiers: LCCN 2023950194 | ISBN 9781680533293 (hardcover) |
9781680533316 (paperback) | 9781680533309 (e-book)

To my wife, Melissa, without whose love
—tough as well as tender—this book would only have been started.

Contents

Preface

What follows is a selection of forty-one essays from nine magazines, three websites, two books, and one monograph written over a period of thirty-eight years one a wide variety of topics. I am grateful to the editors of *National Review*, *Quadrant*, the *Hungarian Review*, *The National Interest*, *The New Criterion*, the *Claremont Review of Books*, *Commentary*, *Országút*, *The Critic*, *Conservative Home*, *National Review Online*, and *Quadrant Online* for their kindness in supporting their publication here, and still more for their earlier willingness to commission the articles and to improve them with skillful editorial suggestions.

My gratitude is due in particular to my colleagues at *Hungarian Review*—in particular Gyula Kodolányi, Ildikó Geiger, and Éva Eszter Szabó—who urged me to embark on the project of republishing these essays. Nor should I omit praise for their steel nerves as the deadlines loomed.

To their names, I must gratefully add two more. Paul du Quenoy and his colleagues at Academica Press have added their own helpful criticisms and amendments and ensured that my essays appear in an impressively readable form. And Rod Dreher, himself one of America's finest and most insightful writers on social, religious, and political themes, has given the book a sparkling foreword of great wit and generosity.

In the end, of course, the articles must anyway speak for themselves. I would add only two points the reader might bear in mind. The first is that because they are articles on public affairs, they often conclude with predictions either explicit or implicit. Now, it is not possible to foretell the future, and inevitably, some predictions prove to be erroneous. Almost all the pieces appear as originally published. Some have been adapted for length or other reasons. In all cases, though, my editors and I have left any predictions intact. It is for the reader to judge which failed and which were borne out, and sometimes only God knows that.

The second point is that given the essays stretch over thirty-eight years—'Britain under the Iron High Heel' appeared in 1985 and 'Still the Best of Enemies' in 2023—and cover a wide range of topics, they were not selected to make a single political or moral point. Each article deals with a particular question, and if it offers a particular explanation or remedy to it, that cannot be extended to explain all the other questions. That said, if there is one general theme that emerges from some or most of the essays, it is that the revolution of 'Wokeness' that currently assaults us is not a complete novelty but a fusion of earlier 'movements' rooted in similar or related ideological beliefs and often, alas, fallacies. We have seen all these things before but as separate movements or ideas. Now we are seeing how they have all combined and blended into a single revolution; in the future, we shall likely see how they diverge and clash under the pressure of contradictions and events.

My reaction to Wokeness, therefore, is that of an insomniac. I have been there before, too many times in fact, and I know how it turns out.

Foreword
Rod Dreher

'The thing about John O'Sullivan,' a young conservative English writer said to me, 'is that he has no natural enemies.' It was both true and a compliment, but if I did not know John myself, I might not have taken it that way. After all, that line might mean that the man described was so bland and inoffensive as to not be worth hating. That emphatically is not John O'Sullivan, who is one of the sagest and most acute observers of contemporary politics and culture in the English language, as well as a writer of remarkable effervescence and verve, even late into his long and productive career. My interlocutor was paying tribute to John's deep humanity, to his charity, and to his capacity for friendship.

All of these qualities come through in the essays compiled in this volume, which cover a period of over thirty years – an eternity in the life of a culture as accelerated as ours. It has been a period in which the decline of the West became impossible to deny. The advent of the feverish form of semi-totalitarian identity politics we call 'Wokeness' has increased the velocity of our race to the bottom.

Remarkably, John has a conservative's capacity to perceive the severity of the problems about which he writes, with an Englishman's ability to maintain good humour and sound judgment when everyone else around him wallows in despondency. On second thought, not every Englishman has that gift. Only one in John O'Sullivan's league comes to mind: G. K. Chesterton, a fellow English Catholic. Perhaps there is something in that.

It will not surprise you to learn that the *eminence grise* of Anglophone conservative journalism has a peerless knack for discerning what is wrong with the world. It helps to have lived such a long life at the centre of world affairs, and to have kept your eyes wide open while doing so. For instance, in a 2020 dissection of that year's 'metastasizing directionless anarchy' of the George Floyd race riots, John cited lessons from Mao Zedong's Cultural Revolution to explain what was happening throughout the Woke West. Trenchant analyses of public affairs are a dime a dozen, but it is hard to find ones that are as smart, well-written, and as historically informed as John's consistently are.

Many writers can inform and enlighten, but few can do so while also entertaining. John O'Sullivan can. He has throwaway observations that could form the thesis of entire books. For example, in 'Does the West Still Exist?,' a 1999 review of a book about the historical meaning of the West, he sums up a late eighteenth-century battle thus: 'What this scene signifies for our purposes is the change from the history of events to the history of ideas.'

Blessed is the public figure in whose defence John O'Sullivan's pen rises. He deploys gentle mockery of overwrought left-wing critics of Prime Minister Margaret Thatcher ('Britain under the Iron High Heel,' 1989) to build a persuasive case that the dreaded Mrs T's supposedly illiberal policies were thoroughly reasonable, and indeed the kind of thing that any other British government would have done. You reach the end of the piece wondering how anyone could have thought otherwise. In a short, wonderfully observed piece criticizing a negative view of his late friend and employer William F. Buckley, John delivers this masterpiece of condensed wisdom:

> It sounds extravagant to say so, but this second Buckley was an Antonio Gramsci for the television age who transformed the fool's gold of celebrity into the real gold of conservative votes. The first Buckley, no less extravagantly, was a Diaghilev of opinion journalism, determined to shock and entertain, turning to a succession of editorial Cocteaus and demanding: 'Astonish me, Jean!'

Verily, the man can write.

What John does better than anybody else in his field is to discern what is *right* with the world—and to celebrate it. Try to get through his obituary for Mrs Thatcher without tears, would you? Once I sat with John at a small dinner table in a pocket-sized square in an Adriatic seaside village, awaiting a bottle of wine and menus. John raised his sparkling eyes to the early evening sky, lowered them to survey the balconies on the decaying but dignified townhouses surrounding us, and pronounced, 'This is *marvellous*!' He was eighty years old then, but still had a young man's capacity for appreciative wonder.

We live in a world where conservative politics, like politics on the Left, has curdled into emotive contempt. Though these essays read as fresh as the day they were published, there is one sense in which John O'Sullivan is out of step with his time: his inability to sneer and to despair. Though a devoted servant of Margaret Thatcher, the sunny Catholic from Liverpool is temperamentally the last Reaganite. John's line about Mrs Thatcher could equally be applied to him: that she was 'a walking reproach to a certain kind of cynical worldview.'

Reading this book left me feeling as I did when I read Clive James's similar essay collection, titled *Cultural Amnesia*: as if I had gone on a tour of recent cultural history guided by a witty and learned companion. In these pages you will revisit the fall of communism, the crisis of liberal democracy, Wokeness (of course), racism, the Sexual Revolution, Brexit, COVID, Donald Trump, migration, books, movies, and fond remembrances of great lives lived. Worldly, witty and wise, John O'Sullivan has seen it all, done it all, loved most of it, and forgiven the rest.

No matter what your own political persuasion, you will journey through these pages accompanied by a cherished friend. John being John, it could not be otherwise.

Where Wokeness Leads the Way:
A Brief History of Cultural Revolutions
13 July 2020

As far as the great British public was concerned, the Chinese Cultural Revolution began in London in 1966 when Chinese diplomats rushed out of their embassy in Portland Place (conveniently close to Broadcasting House) and attacked the police stationed there to guard them. A picture of one "diplomat" threatening a policeman with a hatchet made it onto the front pages, and the next day crowds gathered on the opposite side of the Place shouting anti-Chinese slogans. Drunken British hooligans—less of a cliché in 1966 than today—were patriotically inspired to ransack a few Chinese restaurants across the country. Their owners defensively placed in their windows signs that proclaimed 'We Are Hong Kong Chinese and British'—sentiments that were interestingly echoed in Hong Kong in recent days. And the British end of China's Cultural Revolution rumbled on for a while until eventually it ran out of steam and the news.

The Battle of Portland Place, though apparently irrational, was probably a calculated Chinese response to restrictions placed on the movements of their diplomats by Harold Wilson's government which itself was reacting (much more reasonably, you may think) to the burning of a UK mission and the roughing-up of UK diplomats by 'Red Guards' in China. Both governments had no interest in prolonging the crisis, however, and when Mao and his faction re-imposed control over both their rivals and their student revolutionary supporters, they embarked on long negotiations that, among other results, tacitly accepted postponing the return of Hong Kong to China until 1997.

At the time, however, the Brits had become fascinated by the anarchic disorders that were sweeping China as students paraded their teachers in dunces' caps, local authorities sent lawyers to spread night soil over the fields in forced labour, and precious artefacts of Chinese culture were seized from museums and destroyed in the streets. Young Red Guards, waving Mao's 'Little Red Book' were licensed to imprison, beat, torture, and even kill people in positions of authority who supposedly represented the obstacles that traditional culture presented to the achievement of a true Marxist proletarian revolution.

It was hard to see such crude atrocities as having much to do with ideas or culture. Mao's 'Little Red Book,' which I bought in a Marxist bookshop in London, proved to be a dull collection of improving maxims addressed to young Communists who wanted to succeed under socialism. It had the same intent as—but none of the wit of—Victorian maxims like 'The man who watches the clock will always be one of the hands.' And how could a revolution that brutalized and killed its victims almost at random, murdering Communist apparatchiks as readily as distinguished historians or scientists, be interpreted as advancing any serious social goal? What was mystifying then—and to some extent still is—was the seeming pointlessness of the whole enterprise. Were these horrors the results of anarchy or dictatorship? The exiled Hungarian historian, Tibor Szamuely, told a Tory audience in Yorkshire's Swinton Conservative College, only partly tongue in cheek, that all the sources of information about the revolution seemed to be Maoist ones: 'One radio station will say "In our province the reactionaries have killed 1,000 people" only for another to reply "That's nothing. In our province the reactionaries have killed 10,000 people."' Was the entire Cultural Revolution an exercise in power politics to destroy Mao's enemies or a kind of revolutionary fiesta that would ensure the loyalty of an entire generation of young Chinese to his scorched-earth version of revolution?

Historians now seem to agree that it was both. Mao launched it to attack his enemies in the communist power structure at a time when his authority had been weakened by the catastrophic failure of his Great Leap Forward programme. Once launched, however, it developed an anarchic energy of its own as Mao's youthful followers beat, humiliated, and murdered anyone who held any kind of authority, and many who had none. In the end, almost three million people died in the course of the great anarchy; many more lives were permanently ruined. Its other results were, as theatre critics say, 'mixed.' Mao emerged from the Cultural Revolution supreme in China, a kind of God-Man, with his party rivals dead or imprisoned. But after his death, the Maoists were purged and the politics of revolutionary egalitarianism abandoned. Deng Xiaoping introduced his capitalist-roader economic reforms about the time Margaret Thatcher arrived in Downing Street, and China's power and prosperity have grown rapidly ever since. As for the Red Guards, they plainly failed to impose a permanent revolution on China or even on themselves. Those who survived their own atrocities, as many have since testified, now look back with shame and horror at the way they inflicted brutality on people who had done them no wrong and, in some cases, had been their kindly mentors or even their parents. Whatever criticisms the Chinese people have of their government today, they show no nostalgia for Mao or his ism.

It was only outside China that enthusiasm for Maoism survived among left-wing politicians like Britain's Tony Benn, academic revolutionaries like Malcolm Caldwell (who was murdered while enthusiastically touring an even more primitivist revolution in Cambodia), and Hollywood celebrities with a taste for exotic radical politics safely distant. Some Western Maoists saw Maoism admiringly as the most complete rejection ever attempted of the seductive but alienating Western liberal capitalism they despised. Others were simply naive utopians ignorant as to what it was like to live under Maoism. Both schools of radical thought were effectively refuted by Deng Xiaoping's response to Shirley MacLaine in a White House receiving line when she said that a doctor sent to hard labour in the fields to overcome his sense of bourgeois privilege had told her it was the most uplifting experience of his life.

'He told you that, did he?' replied the plain-speaking Deng. 'He was lying.'

As for almost all other Westerners in 1966 and later, we looked at the theory-intoxicated antics of the cultural revolutionaries with amazement and thought, 'it could never happen here.'

Well, it is happening here now, of course, at least in Britain and the United States, and even in parts of Western Europe and the Anglosphere, though less aggressively. The scenes of crowds burning cities, attacking the police, looting small businesses, and then in an illogical but somehow understandable progression, pulling down statues, destroying national symbols, and doing their best to erase familiar signposts and symbols of their (and our) own past leave little doubt about what is going on. It is a revolution against our culture, our history, our countries, and ourselves. Its immediate cause was the brutal murder of George Floyd by a Minneapolis police officer. That immediately became the worldwide symbol of racism against Black Americans, especially at the hands of the police, and it led in turn to a metastasizing directionless anarchy.

We can explore many speculations about why this spread was so swift, dramatic, and largely un-resisted. People are bored and angry after eight weeks of lockdown. They are afraid of the economic consequences of COVID-19, which may bring about a sharp fall in their own standard of living when the pandemic finally ends. They want to blame someone for their own anxieties, preferably the government which, as it happens, really deserves blame for its handling of the pandemic. A large body of unemployed graduates, some unemployable, others employable only in non-graduate jobs—in other words, the traditional cannon fodder of revolution—already existed and will inevitably soon be joined by others as the post-COVID economy sheds jobs made uneconomic by the lockdown. All of these things have combined to foster a climate of febrile discontent, free-floating anxiety, and distrust of authority that coincidentally distrusts itself.

All these help to explain the spread of anarchy once it has started. None explains why the murder of one man, George Floyd, in one country should start a revolution against the cultural symbols and identities of several nations which do not have the social evils that the murder supposedly symbolizes. It is not as if the murder is being justified or covered up. On the contrary, it is universally condemned; it seems likely to be punished with remarkable speed (by the standards of American justice); and it is not even one particular example of a general war on

Black America by racist police because, though it is dangerous to say so, there is no such war.

Black Americans suffer many serious social disadvantages, but they are the result of many causes most of which are unrelated to the racism of cops and other Americans. The figures for fatal shootings of men by the police show that about two thirds of such victims are white and one third black—amounting to nine people last year. In addition, such shootings have been falling for several years. Admittedly, police shootings of black men are disproportionately high in relation to the Black percentage of the population, but they are disproportionately low in relation to Black involvement in crime. And they are very few in comparison with the overwhelming majority of murders of Blacks committed by other Blacks. Even though racism plays a part in the social problems of Black America, it is not the main explanation of those problems, let alone a complete one.

As the conservative Black columnist Larry Elder recently wrote: 'Assume there's a vaccine against white racism. Would 70 per cent of black kids STILL be raised in fatherless homes? Would 50 per cent of blacks STILL drop out of many urban high schools? Would 25 per cent of young black urban men STILL have criminal records? Would blacks STILL kill 7,000 blacks every year?' The implied answer, alas, is that probably things would improve only slightly, if at all. And if the solutions to such problems proposed by progressive elites were adopted, for instance defunding the police, they would almost certainly make the lives of ordinary Americans, Blacks in particular, much more dangerous as well as poorer.

Suppose, however, that you think Elder is wrong about America and Black lives. Even so we are left with the mystery of why the murder of someone in Minneapolis—a city ruled by progressive Democrats with Black officials at all political levels for two generations—should be a legitimate excuse for riots in London and other British cities where the police bend over backwards in order to maintain good 'community relations' with all races? Why too should some of the protests rapidly become violent riots against the symbols of national life and *British* history? My answers to those questions, drawing on the experience of the Chinese Cultural Revolution, would stress five broad similarities:

The first is that, as in the China of 1966, there is a deep political conflict between different political and cultural elites in both Britain and America, which is now being fought out on the terrain of constitutional patriotism versus multiculturalism. It was a subterranean and unacknowledged conflict for a long time. But as Christopher Caldwell has demonstrated in his recent book, *The Age of Entitlement*—more or less irrefutably as the respectful criticisms of his opponents covertly admit—the passage of the 1964 Civil Rights Act and its later expansions by the courts have created a second US Constitution that is at odds with the US Constitution ratified in 1788. By making the outlawing of discrimination the central criterion of a large and expanding portion of American life, the second constitution has undermined and increasingly negated the constitutional protections of the first one. Initially, it powered the massive federal legal regulation of economic life on such matters as hiring, promotion, salaries, the ethnic composition of the workforce and college entry, and the re-writing of tests and standards to weaken meritocratic criteria for appointments at all levels; more recently, it has inspired claims that constitutional rights such as free speech and majoritarian democracy should be regulated constitutionally to ensure that they do not disadvantage racial or other minorities. Britain has undergone a less severe version of this constitutional transformation which has taken place (and thus been more visible) largely under the auspices of the European Union and its legal supremacy over UK law.

Many US and UK citizens, including some Black and minority citizens, have experienced this slow constitutional revolution as the imposition of undemocratic and 'unjust' rules where EU law, federal regulations, court decisions or 'social justice' arguments trump earlier understandings of fairness and common sense. As they have become increasingly aware of this de facto constitutional change, they have grown more and more resistant to it. Conservative parties and organizations have been forced by their electorates into becoming the defenders of the original constitutions, while their radical left counterparts have adopted the new constitutions as their enthusiastic partisans. Remember President Obama's 2009 promise that America would be 'fundamentally' changed by his victory. These subterranean discontents exploded into clear national view in both countries when President Trump won the 2016 election and Brexit was ratified by a referendum in the same year. These battles not only continue; they grow fiercer and more bitter.

The second similarity is that this constitutional conflict has been increasingly one of 'identity politics' even as it has become more a matter of everyday partisan controversy. A comparison with the Chinese cultural conflict is inexact here because almost everyone involved in it was Han Chinese. But Mao's Communist enemies were denounced as class enemies and capitalist roaders. In communist thought, as Solzhenitsyn has pointed out, those identities possess immutable characteristics akin to those of race. The children of aristocrats and the bourgeoisie in the Soviet Union and East Central Europe were deprived of good education and other social opportunities because they had inherited the status of their parents. That kind of categorization divides people more than just politically. It means that your political opponents belong almost to a different tribe which cannot legitimately claim the same rights as loyal citizens and may even deserve to be shunned, denied employment, shamed, or beaten. In China, it justified such extreme measures as the murder of Mao's opponents; in Cambodia, wearing spectacles was grounds for imprisonment, torture, and execution.

In Anglosphere politics, "tribes" already existed in the form of racial, ethnic, and other groups. But the original constitutions promised them and all citizens legal equality and political rights. That promise was grotesquely violated by slavery and gravely compromised by continuing racism afterwards. It was an ideal confined to legal and political equality, moreover, that neither promised substantive economic equality nor could honestly do so in a free competitive society. Nonetheless, it moved steadily towards greater fulfilment until it reached the Civil Rights Act of 1964, which implicitly *did* promise greater substantive equality. That promise was made explicit in later court interpretations that, for instance, treat inequalities not obviously justified by a third factor as deriving necessarily from discrimination. On that justification, a vast engine of federal bureaucratic intervention guided by court decisions was built to root out discrimination and to move towards the equality of racial, ethnic and other groups. Real progress towards that goal has been made—Black and minority Americans occupy leadership roles throughout American society—but for a variety of reasons inequalities continue to exist, and will continue to do so. These are now blamed by self-styled 'anti-racists' on a shadowy 'systemic racism' in public debate. Liberal-left and radical movements preach a "narrative" that treats America as a fundamentally racist society in which Black people and other minorities are the victims of 'white supremacy' institutions that must therefore be torn down and replaced by multicultural ones—possibly elected on racially proportionate lines as Hudson Institute scholar John Fonte has predicted—consistent with the post-1964 second constitution.

It is, of course, absurd to claim that the nation that twice elected Barack Obama is a fundamentally racist nation governed on white supremacist lines. That is a wicked lie. But there are practical reasons for the support these anti-racist fantasies get. Anti-discrimination laws in the post-1964 constitution, for instance affirmative action preferences, give some racial and gender identities significant social and economic advantages and give other identities significant disadvantages. The electoral strength of the Democratic Party—and of the Left within the party—is rooted in Black, minority, and migrant communities. Defending racial preferences has therefore become an organizing principle of Left-Democratic politics with the intended effect of herding all 'minorities' into a single majority bloc. In effect all politics has been 'racialized' as a struggle between white majority and ethnic minorities. To be sure, racial politics are in reality more blurred than this narrative allows—recent polls show that 'white liberals' (about 20 per cent of white voters) are angrier about white racism than are most Black voters. Majorities of all races would still probably reject the argument that America is a white supremacist country. That is why much electoral propaganda from the Left is aimed at arousing and aggravating racial and other resentments in order to discourage their ethnic constituencies from assimilating into the great multi-ethnic American majority (stigmatized falsely as "white") and reducing the power of their coalition of minorities.

That explains half of the significance of the slogan 'Black Lives Matter' (BLM). The words in themselves are true and inarguable. But when people are dismissed because they refuse to mouth a formula they feel to be racist, when people are investigated by the police as racists for responding 'All Lives Matter' when asked, and when the authorities allow mobs to tear down statues on the grounds that they are a denial of the slogan in marble, then the slogan becomes other than truth. It becomes a demand for compliance. Compliance to what, however? The BLM movement's actual political programme goes beyond racial fairness and legal equality to resemble a catchall for anything the quasi-Marxist Left can force moderate Democrats to swallow for the sake of office. That was quite a lot in the early stages of this revolution, but progressive politicians with an eye on public opinion are already sliding away from its stronger commitments such as 'Defund the Police.'

But the vaguer compliance that BLM demands and gets may be more dangerous. This is a public endorsement of the broad BLM analysis that America is a fundamentally racist society governed by white supremacy. Left politicians, corporate America, the mainstream media, and much of the establishment have shown that they will happily assent to this broad analysis, some (in the media) maybe sincerely, others on the ground that talk is cheap. In making that concession, however, they are assenting to the Lie.

That is how Václav Havel described (in a famous essay, *The Power of the Powerless*) the way in which totalitarianism extends its control of the citizenry under communism. A greengrocer might enjoy a quiet life if he were to place a sign in his window alongside the beets and white carrots that read 'Workers of the World—Unite!' It signifies his support or acquiescence to the regime. It does not, of course, stop there. Having assented to the regime's central lie—in the present case the lie of white supremacy—the corporate CEO or university vice-Chancellor will find himself assenting to a succession of subordinate lies. That will require assent to such nonsensical notions as: that racism is whatever anyone perceives as racism; that only white people can be guilty of it because only whites have power; that women must always be believed, whatever the evidence; that statistics should not be collected if they undermine leftist preconceptions; that children prosper equally in all kinds of family structures; that all cultures are equal, including those cultures that deny human equality in both theory and practice; and that all group differences are the result not of their different attitudes and aptitudes but of unlawful discrimination.

Every time assent is given to such a lie, another set of regulations will be imposed to "correct" the accusation embedded in it. While this continues, the revolution has a strong moral advantage over its subjects who have given public assent to an entire ideological structure of ideas of which some new demand is simply its latest expression. Were they lying hypocrites when they affirmed Black Lives Matter but now refuse to endorse racial quotas in employment, university admissions, prison numbers, or examination results? Are they traitors now when they question such obvious measures to attain social justice? It is not hard to judge. Their crimes are proved by their failure to subscribe to the ruling Lie. Are they, maybe, white supremacists? Or class enemies? Or capitalist roaders? Whichever it is, they have no standing in a socially just society, no right to speak, no claim to exercise authority even if their claim to it rests firmly on a democratic mandate. Most submit for the sake of a quiet life.

This coward's progress continues until the system becomes so oppressive that the greengrocer rebels. He removes the Marxist slogan from the window and with it his assent to the lie and to the regime. But that can take a long time, and until then the revolutionary System—which unlike liberal democracy really *is* a system in how it imposes its "truths" on dissenters—grinds on. How it does so, can be seen in the final three of the five similarities it shares with the Chinese Cultural Revolution.

The third such similarity is that progressive elites in the West have their own Red Guards—in Antifa, BLM, and other groups—who enforce the BLM analysis on those who resist or even show reluctance in assenting to it. The Red Guards' methods include burning the property of resisters, beating them up, forcing them to contribute to BLM funds, preventing them speaking for themselves, and of course murdering them. It is the most striking similarity with what happened in China in 1966.

But how are these Red Guards able to do so in a democratic society based on law?

That is explained by the fourth similarity: in a society divided between two governing elites—the Maoist versus the Communist, the progressive versus the elected, those enjoying the Mandate of Heaven versus those holding office—the lawful authorities apply the law selectively. They try to accommodate the protests, even violent ones, of the side that incarnates the revolutionary idea while cracking down hard on those who foolishly breach the law in resisting anti-racist protesters who pull down statues. Some authorities do so from sympathy for the protesters, others from cowardice and fear of being attacked as racist. An illustration of this, both symbolic and real, was the decision by British police and the Premier League soccer body to instruct policemen and footballers to 'take the knee' (i.e., kneel) in acceptance of the truth and authority of Black Lives Matter. That was the moment in Britain when the greengrocer put the sign in his front window. It has been followed also by the Mayor of Seattle, who tolerated the establishment of a "liberated" zone in her city until murders began to occur and the mob encroached on her own neighbourhood. And there have been many other examples of this violent lawlessness being tolerated.

If you are unaware of the extent of this anarchy, that is probably because of the fifth similarity. Since the central claims of the revolutionary cause are false, notably those that include the phrase 'white supremacy,' and since many of its actions are violent as well as unlawful, and since both would be unpopular if accurately reported, those media outlets sympathetic to the BLM revolution have to lie and obfuscate in their accounts of its excesses. Here is how BBC news reported the first London protests: '27 police officers injured during largely peaceful anti-racism protests in London.' And there have been many other examples of this violent lawlessness going unreported or being sugar-coated.

All in all, this late flowering of Anglo-American revolutionary instability is a grim picture, but we should be wary of assuming that it will succeed in overturning or transforming either society. The revolution is in its earliest stages. We cannot know how it will turn out. Such upheavals generate opposition as their true oppressive character becomes clearer. And already there are signs that it is running out of steam in Britain as the extreme opinions of the organizers of Black Lives Matter get more attention and their movement's directionless destruction alienates people.

In America, the revolutionaries face the obstacle of a presidential election. They must know that the 1968 Paris manifestations collapsed when President de Gaulle called an election and won it handsomely with the party that backed the students winning about four per cent of the vote. Elections trump revolutions in the game of politics because they have a much stronger claim to popular consent. If Trump wins re-election, especially if his party also keeps control of the Senate, that will shift the political initiative back to him; if the Democrats win, they will try to recruit and control the revolutionary Left and to dilute their policies. Either way revolution will be off the agenda for four years.

As for the Hungarian Revolution of 1956, that too demonstrated the limits of revolution. For it was in truth a counter-revolution against the kind of Marxist revolution enforced then by Mátyás Rákosi and espoused today by Black Lives Matter. Between late 1948 and mid-1953, Hungarians, under Soviet arms, were forced to emulate Rákosi as 'the wise father of the Hungarian people,' and 'the best disciple of Comrade Stalin.' During that period, about 600,000 police and court actions were enacted, including the death penalty, in a nation of hardly more than nine million, on charges of bourgeois and reactionary activities, spreading false rumour, and 'sabotaging production' in a revolutionary communist regime that steered Hungary, one of the richest pantries of Europe, to the brink of famine. Examples of horrendous abuses by the systemic hatred of Soviet communism (against religion and against ethnic groups) abound in the testimonies in this July issue of *Hungarian Review*.

Though the 1956 Revolution did not succeed in its main objective of liberating Hungary from Soviet communism for more than thirty years, it convinced the Soviets that they could not govern Hungarians as Rákosi had done. Kádár would have to win their acquiescence if not their consent. And communism cannot survive long on consent.

Nor, finally, should we underestimate the appeal of our own democratic culture to refugees from its revolutionary opposite. In response to the crackdown on Hong Kong's civil liberties by a cheap imitation Mao knock-off, Britain announced last month that it will admit more than three million Hong Kong UK passport-holders to the UK and give them a path to UK citizenship. A poll shows this proposal was welcomed by 57 per cent of all voters and majorities in all political parties—a sharp corrective to the media and progressive narrative of British racism. Moreover, the new Brits are likely to have a sceptical attitude to cultural revolutions anywhere and some knowledge of where they lead. Only recently, some Hong Kong demonstrators were waving Union Jacks rather than burning them and singing 'God Save the Queen' in preference to 'The Internationale.' Their fathers and mothers thirty years before were building a replica of the Statue of Liberty in Tiananmen Square rather than erecting a monument to the Unknown Red Guard. We should never forget that we have good clear-sighted people of all races on our side of these barricades. And their numbers grow whenever the next revolutions lumber into view.

For there is one sure and certain cure for believing in revolutionary Marxist socialism: living under it.

Originally published in Hungarian Review, *Vol. XI, No. 4, July 2020,* *www.hungarianreview.com/article/20200713_cultural_revolutions_then_* *and_now.*

Does the West Still Exist?

A Review of *From Plato to NATO* by David Gress, and *Twilight of the West* by Christopher Coker
1 March 1999

Is the West an idea? A civilization? Or a set of political arrangements? Plainly it is all three and, as a result, difficult to pin down between hard covers. For if we talk about the decline of the West, we may be discussing the difficulties that NATO encounters in formulating policy toward the Balkans, or the rise of ideologies such as environmentalism that blame the problems of the world on Western science and capitalism, or the debasement of Western (and other) cultures by Hollywood's entertainment industry. Or ten other topics.

So both David Gress and Christopher Coker have set themselves a formidable task when they attempt to chart the West's progress. Although they are fairly near to each other on the political spectrum—Gress being a judicious Danish neoconservative and Coker a pessimistic English conservative—they have written very different books. To oversimplify, Gress is inclined to stress the concept of the West as an organic civilization—though one repeatedly riven by civil and cultural wars—and therefore to believe that its political structures are natural and likely to survive. Coker tends to see the West as an idea in the minds of poets and philosophers, and he therefore envisages its political links being gradually eaten away by the intellectual acids of Europeanism, multiculturalism, and postmodern scepticism.

Yet it is Gress who opens his book on a note of strong scepticism about the idea of the West—or, rather, that particular idea of the West he calls the 'Grand Narrative.' This was the account, promulgated in such forums as the contemporary civilization course at Columbia and the 'Great Books' programme at the University of Chicago, that depicted Western history as the progress of liberty from the ancient Greeks to modern America. Gress concedes that these were great educational enterprises in their day, but he skilfully deconstructs their claim to be an adequate account of the actual social and intellectual history of the West.

Their essential error was to treat liberty as a moral abstraction, invented by the Greeks and passed on to the modern age, almost outside of history, by a series of great thinkers and great books. This involved a number of distortions. It blurred the serious differences between the Greek concept of liberty as the right to participate in government, and the Western idea of liberty as, in Benjamin Constant's phrase, 'the individual's right to his own pursuits.' It leapt nimbly over those lengthy historical interludes that did not lend themselves to a buoyant account of liberty's progress—i.e., the Roman Empire, the Dark Ages and indeed most of the period from the Greeks to 1776. It downplayed crucial elements in Western history, such as the specifically religious aspects of Christianity, which had helped to form Western ideas of liberty, but which did not conform to the political sympathies of its liberal authors, and such as the importance of the Germanic tribes in the Dark Ages (because of possible confusion with a modern nation state of the same name). In addition, it exaggerated the role that (admittedly important) philosophers, such as Locke and Rousseau, had played in making Western freedom a practical possibility. In other words the 'Grand Narrative' saw the whole of Western history 'from Plato to NATO' as a teleological process leading up to moral perfection in the form of the modern American liberal circa 1955.

In the words of *Private Eye*: Shome misthtake, surely. Neither the West nor any real-world civilization could possibly live up to this idealized picture of inevitable progress punctuated by what Gress calls 'Magic Moments': Magna Carta! The Copernican Revolution! 1776! The Atlantic Charter! The actual history of the West has included such unpleasant features as war, slavery, social oppression, religious bigotry and torture, economic inequality, and racial arrogance. These evils were not confined to the West, of course, and a case could easily be made that Western civilization has acted to correct them sooner and more thoroughly than any other civilization. Their mere existence, however, undermined the 'Grand Narrative.' Western civilization was more—and worse—than a history of liberty. It was not even the story of liberty triumphing over these evils, since, in greater or lesser form, they still exist. Might it not be, then, that the West was the story of these evils triumphing over liberty—and then hypocritically donning the red cap? Indeed, that was the judgment of anti-Western radicals (themselves usually Western) in the sixties and, after the briefest possible resistance, the verdict accepted by the very liberals whose story the 'Grand Narrative' had been.

Having demolished the Authorized Version, Gress sets down his own account of how liberty actually developed—not as an isolated abstraction but intertwined with slavery, war, and oppression, and flourishing especially in the interstices of Western history. He quotes Montesquieu to the effect that freedom and prosperity occur 'in societies where several govern,' as when the clashes between the Holy Roman Empire and the Papacy enabled not only kings but also self-governing cities to demarcate some autonomy. And because liberty produced prosperity when it was allowed to do so, intelligent rulers often left its accidental occurrences alone or, more rarely, deliberately instituted limited editions of it. 'Liberty grew because it served the interests of power,' says Gress in the first sentence of his book. As the West took on distinctive shape, however, Power increasingly found that Liberty had either slipped from its control or that its benefits were too valuable to risk losing.

But this is to summarize brutally what is a tour de force of historical argument and criticism. In search of changing concepts of the West, Gress guides us through the Roman Empire, late Antiquity, the Middle Ages, the Renaissance, the Age of Liberalism, and our own century. He deals exhaustively with an extraordinary range of topics, from the political institutions of the Germanic tribes to the emergence of romantic love, that have helped shape a distinctive Western identity. And he presents the theories of scholars from Gibbon to Samuel Huntington on all of these matters as he goes along, subjecting them to a judicious and generally persuasive criticism.

The Radical and Sceptical Traditions

What emerges from this large survey is that there are several 'Wests.'

Emperors, popes, kings and revolutionaries fought for different international orders, and philosophers disputed over what the outcomes of these struggles signified. 'The West' is what emerged, either victorious or persuasive, at any one time. And such struggles continue in our own day.

Nonetheless, Gress selects two such 'Wests' as sailing along—and by their drift revealing—the main currents of Western civilization. What he calls the 'Old West' was the medieval synthesis, achieved around 1000 A.D., of three powerful civilizational forces: Roman imperial order (the memory of which inspired attempts to construct international polities like the Holy Roman Empire); the 'aristocratic freedom' of the Germanic tribes (which evolved into consultative, if not democratic, methods of government); and Christianity, or what Gress calls 'Christian ethnicity' (which provided otherwise different peoples with a common underlying moral and psychological outlook). Until the Reformation and the nation state jointly overthrew it, this medieval synthesis gave rise to a broad sense of Western identity in certain classes across Europe. Paradoxically, the religious wars confirmed this, for people on both sides shared a common view of what was at stake.

If the wars of religion helped destroy the 'Old West,' what emerged from them was what Gress calls the 'New West' of science, democracy and capitalism, which is essentially the same modern West that recently won the Cold War. But was this New West an outgrowth of the Old? Or was it, to coin a phrase, a *novus ordo seculorum*, a historical caesura and something new under the sun? Gress argues forcefully that it grew directly out of the Old West; that, for instance, the green shoots of capitalism and democracy could be detected beneath the melting snows of the late Middle Ages.

This is a crucial dispute; even the Enlightenment—which is in effect the intellectual crystallization of the New West—expressed divided opinions on this very point. The 'radical Enlightenment' of Voltaire, Rousseau and the French revolutionaries conceived modernity as something to be achieved against the past. The philosophes, for instance, saw institutional Christianity as an obstacle to political and intellectual freedom, to be either overthrown or exiled from the public square into private life by the secular power. The 'sceptical Enlightenment' of Hume,

Locke, and Montesquieu, on the other hand, saw freedom as emerging, however imperfectly, from the practices, traditions and institutions of the Old West, including the Christian religion. 'Superstition,' said David Hume, 'is an enemy to civil liberty, and enthusiasm a friend to it.' By which he meant that evangelical Protestant sects had nurtured the kind of personality that not only demonstrated economic enterprise but also thought for itself—a truth still wreaking progress in Latin America. As David Martin's *Tongues of Fire* reminds us, Wesleyism may be the most profound, because the most personal, revolutionary force of the last three hundred years. It is, however, a revolution within tradition rather than against it.

From this point on, the battle lines were drawn between two intellectual armies defending different versions of the New West. The heirs of the sceptical Enlightenment—conservatives or classical liberals, according to taste—defended the imperfect, partial and compromised versions of democracy, science, and capitalism as they emerged from history. Their opponents—radical liberals or socialists, again according to taste—demanded mint-fresh institutions of freedom that would liberate man from historical oppression (including the oppression of his own customary beliefs and practices). And because they were asking for institutions untainted by history, the latter inevitably became disenchanted with the actual institutions that stood before them and refined their aim into such a triad as science, equality, and planning. The first clash between these two forces outside the printed page and the lecture room was the French Revolution.

Who Is in? Who Is out?

It is at this point that Coker appears on the scene, rather like Pierre at the Battle of Borodino. For he opens his book with Goethe's account of his experience at the Battle of Valmy, where a professional Prussian Army was soundly beaten in short order by France's revolutionary peasants. Goethe's comment on this, given to the soldiers on the evening of their defeat, was:

'From this place and this time forth commences a new era in world history and you can all say that you were present at its birth.' What this scene signifies for our purposes is the change from the history of events to the history of ideas.

For as well as the French Revolution, two events on either side of 1789 had raised questions about the proper limits of the West: namely, the American War of Independence and Russia's full entry into the European system (courtesy of Bonaparte). Were America and Russia genuinely Western nations? Or were they peripheral to the main plot of Western history? On top of that, the American democracy born in 1776 not only raised questions about the West's political character but initially gave misleading answers about it as well. For the American Revolution, though inspired and guided by the ideas of the sceptical Enlightenment, was widely seen at first as precursor and brother to the French Revolution, which was really the radical Enlightenment in arms. It seems clear in retrospect that 1776 was the universalization of Britain's liberal Glorious Revolution of 1688, to which both 1789 and 1917 were radical counter-revolutionary responses—with the liberal revolutions of 1989 deciding the contest, at least for the moment, in favour of 1776. But history had not clarified that in 1815. And there was one further entrant into the ideology stakes. German reactions to the French Revolution included the rise of a romantic cultural nationalism that tended to despise both Enlightenments—Anglo-American Whiggery and the French Revolution—as equally rootless and dehumanizing.

As a result, whereas the European sense of the Old West was largely unconscious insofar as it existed at all, reactions to the French and American Revolutions in Germany and elsewhere consisted inter alia of highly self-conscious reflections on such questions as the meaning of history, the world spirit, the distinction between a civilization (French, superficial) and a Kultur (German, profound), and the legitimate boundaries and spiritual character of the West. In the 140 years after 1815, as Coker recounts it, the poets and philosophers of Europe devoted much thought and imagination to what the West was and what the West meant.

Clearly the West was more than Metternich's 'geographical expression.' But agreement ended there. And when these debates moved on to questions of power politics and cultural authenticity, these were not always clearly distinguished. Was Germany a part of the West, for instance? An influential school of German cultural nationalists, including even Thomas Mann at the time of the First World War, thought not; Germany was a community offering deeper solace to its people than the bourgeois internationalism of either the French or the Anglo-American variety. But other Germans no less concerned with cultural values, notably Nietzsche, had seen Germany as the West's central power, the one which, because of France's spiritual exhaustion, would have to take the lead in resisting czarist authoritarianism.

Was, then, Russia a part of the West? It was certainly threatening to become so by virtue of its growing power. But as early as the 1850s, the German philosopher Bruno Bauer, seeing Russia as a barrack-square society bereft of ideas and Reason, was advocating a European coalition to resist it. A century later, as we know, America was to lead such a coalition.

But, then again, was America itself a part of the West? Goethe believed so. Indeed, he thought it was the future of the West, in one of his novels dispatching as emigrants to the United States those of his characters who did not commit suicide. And slightly less far-sightedly, Hegel thought that America might eventually become a decisive part of the West, but that for the foreseeable future it was on the edge of history. Spengler, however, took the common view still found among European elites that America was not a country but a mere place, 'a barren field and a population of trappers drifting from town to town on the dollar hunt.'

As is their wont, the Germans made a disproportionate contribution to these lofty discussions. The Anglo-Americans were still living in a splendid philosophical isolation: Americans following a destiny too manifest to debate, and the British ignoring the world spirit in their pursuit of world power. It was the French, on this occasion given foresight by their fading power, who anticipated that the United States would have to infuse cultural and political energy into a declining Europe. Coker quotes Henri Martin as fearing in the 1870s that a Russian-dominated Europe would leave America to preserve 'all the higher human elements of civilization,' and Jules Michelet as forecasting an 'Atlantic Union' to prevent this melancholy outcome. In the event, these debates were conclusively settled in Michelet's favour by two world wars that dragged America willy-nilly into Europe, and by the Cold War, which detained her there for another fifty years. If any single moment was the West's rendezvous with destiny, it was the signing of the Atlantic Charter by Churchill and FDR on a British warship in Placentia Bay, Newfoundland, in August 1941—as both our authors agree.

Interpreting Atlanticism

Or do they? Both Gress and Coker attach great importance to the Atlantic Charter, but they differ seriously on its significance. In Coker's eyes, it initiated an essentially Anglo-American view of the West, which began to decay in the sixties with the growth of a specifically continental Europeanism; in Gress' opinion, it was one important episode in the long struggle between Western traditionalists and 'the children of the French Revolution'—a struggle in which the traditionalists have recently scored a great victory with the collapse of communism.

Because Coker's judgment is the more familiar one, I shall deal with it more briskly than his shrewd and sardonic argument deserves. The Atlantic Charter, in his view, was 'a historical turning-point' and 'a change of consciousness,' but mainly for the British, less so for the Americans, and only briefly and pragmatically for the continental Europeans. France, the most independent of the European wartime allies holed up in London, did not even sign it until late in 1944. The Soviet threat ensured that Atlanticism remained a military necessity for Europe until recently. But as *détente* and *Ostpolitik* took hold in the sixties, the concept of Europeanism advanced in tandem with them—fuelled by a French intellectual tradition of anti-Americanism, growing European economic integration, and the political reality that European social democracy never felt entirely comfortable with American capitalism. By the late 1980s, as John Laughland pointed out in *The Tainted Source: The Undemocratic Origins of the European Idea* (1997), the rhetorical attacks of French politicians on the 'Anglo-Saxons' and their liberal system of trade and capital movements bore a curious resemblance to what Vichy politicians were saying in the early forties.

It is a mystery why American statesmen were so slow to see the Europeanist threat to Atlanticism, and Coker has some fun reversing the usual finger pointing. Instead of blaming the British for missing the European bus, he argues that they accurately divined its anti-American (or at least its Americo-sceptical) implications early on. It was successive American leaders—including such respected figures as George Ball—who rashly pooh-poohed these warnings in their eagerness to shovel Britain into what is now the European Union. (Only Henry Kissinger expressed serious public anxieties on that score.) Their calculation was that British membership would ensure that Europe became a more reliable US ally; but at present it looks more likely that Europe will make Britain a less reliable US ally.

That may not matter to Americans overmuch, Coker speculates, since the United States itself is losing its eighteenth-century Western identity as a result of mass immigration from Third World countries, the spread of bilingualism and multiculturalism, and the failure or refusal of America's elites to insist on assimilation. It is therefore losing also the sense that its primary defence and diplomatic commitment must be to Europe. Even the prospect of European protectionism is dismissed as unimportant by Coker since America has already forged strong trade links with the rest of the world—though the 'Asian contagion' may upset that particular calculation. On this view America is becoming, or may have already become, a different civilization from that of Europe—what James Kurth in these pages has called 'the post-West'—and so the two sides of the Atlantic are increasingly likely to part company politically too.

Gress has a very different, and original, interpretation of the Atlantic Charter. He sees it as an amalgam: an expression of the values of the New West as represented by the sceptical Enlightenment and as influenced by the circumstances of 1939–41. It proclaimed national self-determination, democracy, free trade, and collective security—the causes that the interwar years were thought to have neglected or betrayed. And although the Charter was signed two months after Hitler's invasion of Russia, this was also the political programme that the Western democracies had formulated in opposition to both totalitarian dictatorships, united after 1939 by the Nazi–Soviet pact. What would later be fully articulated as 'anti-totalitarianism' was implicit in the principles outlined at Placentia Bay. Moreover, by bringing America into the contest, at least in spirit, the Atlantic Charter was giving new energy to this traditional West, since the Americans still had that confidence in freedom, democracy, capitalism, and the future that had begun to wither in Europe.

However, once the alliance with the Soviet Union was entrenched, it inevitably transformed the West's view of 'what we are fighting for.' Christianity and capitalism, for instance, could hardly be the war aims of an alliance that included the Soviet Union, and capitalism was at least seen at the time as compatible with the genocidal West represented by Hitler. Indeed, the very notion of the West was compromised, because Hitler claimed to be fighting for it against our new Soviet allies. So anti-totalitarianism was replaced by what Gress calls 'the anti-fascist mindset.' In place of the now compromised triad of science, democracy, and capitalism, for instance, the Soviets proclaimed science, equality, and rational planning, a substitution designed to delight the 'children of the French Revolution' in Europe. Indeed, as the 'anti-fascist mindset' spread during the war, it seemed to many that the true West must include the Soviets and exclude capitalism and Christianity. A West that made the opposite choices would be plainly tainted with fascism. The result is described by Gress:

> The argument over Western identity was thus between those who identified the West with America—the commercial republic with its Christian foundations—and those whose idea of the West rejected Christianity and capitalism and looked rather to the ideals of progress and social transformation that they believed had been at least partly realized in the Soviet Union.

Admittedly, there were socialist factions and individual intellectuals—the Bevanite Labour Left, George Orwell—who urged an early Third Way, arguing that either Britain or a new united Europe should pioneer the combination of socialism and democracy as a civilized alternative to totalitarian Scylla and capitalist Charybdis. But even the Attlee government, which might theoretically have favoured it, saw this as a distraction from the urgent tasks of rebuilding the post-war European economies and organizing resistance to the Soviets. As the illusory nature of this Third Way became clear, its supporters either gave their backing to the American-led democracies, like Orwell, or became "neutralist" with a bias toward the "socialist" world.

Thus began what might be called a cold civil war in the West, in which anti-Americanism always enjoyed substantial support among West European intellectuals. From 1941 to 1947, admiration for Soviet wartime heroism ensured that the anti-fascist version of the West was largely dominant. Between 1947 and 1968, fear of the Soviet Union became a paramount factor in Western opinion, the concept of anti-totalitarianism was dusted off, and the West united politically and to an extent even intellectually under American leadership. Then, the Vietnam War concentrated attention on America's flaws, and for twenty years after 1968, there was a sustained campaign against America, and later the West generally, represented as the enemies of humankind politically, economically and ecologically.

Finally, without this campaign having abated even slightly, the Soviet Union suddenly collapsed. This discredited for the moment the economic and political claims of the radical Enlightenment, installed America as a hegemonic power in both the West and the world, and gave immense prestige to the New West ideals of democracy, science and free markets. By any standards this was a world-historical victory—yet one, as Gress concedes, that was curiously muted by the West's own moral self-doubt, and in danger of being drowned out by the unabated cries of environmentalists, multiculturalists, and fifty-seven varieties of anti-Western criticism.

These are very different analyses and they dictate very different prescriptions. Coker, suspecting that the West is losing its internal cultural coherence and is doomed to split politically into rival continents, thinks that in this weakened condition it had better reach some kind of multicultural bargain with other civilizations. Gress sees America as the heartland of a New West with an irreducible minimum of cultural identity that cannot and ought not to be dissolved into a vague multicultural universalism. And so he concludes that in a world of clashing civilizations, it has an unavoidable interest in maintaining the habits and structures of political cooperation.

Alternative Futures

Neither line of argument is entirely satisfactory. Coker claims that none of the usual suspects—China and fundamentalist Islam, for example—in the police line-up of anti-Western challenges is likely to be sufficiently threatening to persuade the West to rediscover its sense of common purpose. But the chapter discussing such vast subjects is too sketchy to be persuasive, and Coker is forced to leave extremely important questions hanging in the air. For instance, 'China may emerge as a fully modern state or dissolve into a vast Third World country.' True enough, but the West will hardly be unaffected by which it is. If Coker seems unaffected himself, it is because he thinks that the world has moved beyond old-fashioned power politics, making a revived Western coalition an inappropriate, if not unavailable, form of geopolitics. The West's next task is to engage in a constructive dialogue with other civilizations in order to help construct a new world culture.

It is hard to know what to make of this. To begin with, it is largely unnecessary to instruct the West to act in the wider international interest. Except in occasional articles and speeches by some over-muscular neoconservatives, the West has not displayed any marked civilizational egoism in recent years. At least as led by the United States, it has sought in its policies on trade and international economics to accommodate, and even advance, the legitimate interests of other parts of the world. One large exception and one important qualification must be attached to this general rule. The exception has been Europe's Common Agricultural Policy; but that has ignored the interests of the United States, Australia, and New Zealand as much as it has those of the Third World, and is therefore a factor in the dissolution rather than the expansion of the West. The qualification is that while the West may have accommodated other interests, it has done so in the light of its own values—notably free trade and human rights.

A new world culture would presumably correct that bias, would it not? Again, however, what would such a culture look like? Cultures are made up of such intractable components as language and religion. Always a magpie civilization itself, the West has been happy to appropriate religious styles, foreign words and all kinds of ambient cultural bric-a-brac. But more than that is unlikely. It is hard enough to interest many Westerners in their own religions, let alone Asian or African ones, and with the rise of Christian and Muslim "enthusiasm," religion is more likely to be a source of cultural conflict than of accommodation. As for language, the tongue most likely to be the basis of any world culture is English, which, even granting such developments as the "post-colonial novel," implies the opposite of a Western retreat. Is Coker, then, more concerned with strictly political and economic values? If so, the problem becomes still more perplexing. Strip political authoritarianism from 'Asian values' and what is left sounds suspiciously like the 'Victorian values'—hard work, law and order, good schools, and a decent family life—of no less Western a figure than Lady Thatcher.

However, political authoritarianism, having just been defeated after a long struggle within the West, is unlikely to be openly embraced by even the most masochistic multiculturalist. Its inconsistency with the liberty at the heart of the West is too blatant. What follows, surely, is that any halfway realistic prescription for a world culture must avoid the cultural fundamentals derived from the Old West, and stick instead to the New West's outward signs of inward grace—democracy, free markets, and the scientific method—which can be represented as the heritage of all humankind.

The resulting paradox we might call "Western universalism," and this turns out to be one of the main targets against which Gress aims the last rounds in his Maxim gun. Indeed, he directs devastating fire at a bewildering variety of targets in his final two chapters: postmodernists, multiculturalists, environmentalists, communitarians, post-materialists, transcendental humanists, Islamists, the Singapore school, and several others besides. Most of these schools of thought come under the heading of anti-Western Westerners, the great-grandchildren of the French Revolution, who have adopted the intellectual methods of Marxism but abandoned social class for the environment, race or gender as the grounds for attack on the West. Gress demolishes their arguments with a fine painstaking zest. His comprehensive diligence reminds me of the British Conservative Party's Campaign Guide, which used to be issued to canvassers and which contained full and complete answers to every possible question that might be posed on the doorstep. But this comprehensiveness sometimes risks obscuring the outlines of his main argument: a critique of so-called Western universalism.

He argues that it is in the first instance a kind of hallucination. Other civilizations may seem to have adopted Westernization, but the likelihood is that unless they actually cease to be themselves, they have merely taken over the technical knowledge and procedural rules of Western culture. They may institute free-market capitalism, and do so successfully, but will they prove as capable of habitual innovation? They may have procedures for voting, but will that result in a routine transfer of power from government to opposition? He concludes that the world outside the West is likely to see the spread of capitalism but not of democracy, and that this process should therefore be called modernization rather than Westernization.

Even this limited adoption of Western institutions will make other civilizations richer and stronger. But as Samuel Huntington points out, that will have the perverse result of making them more anti-Western as well. They will certainly be more resistant to Western cultural hegemony. Already, many Muslims believe that they have learned to combine Western techniques with the greater spiritual and civilizational powers of Islam. Far from converging, therefore, civilizations will tend to grow apart, with the rest becoming 'more modern and less Western,' in Huntington's words. The end result will be a world of five or six major civilizations, all of which are rich and powerful in varying degrees, but which remain foreign, mysterious, and even suspect to each other.

That being so, the West will have a strong incentive to retain some sort of organizational unity and to remain distinctively Western in spirit and culture. As Gress says exasperatedly at one point, in what might almost be a direct reply to Coker, 'A multicultural West is a contradiction in terms; the only West that can be accommodating to other cultures is a West that knows itself and, on the strength of that understanding, encounters others.'

What would such a West be like? It would recognize itself, in Gress's words, as 'the obedient child of the Old West.' Among other qualifies, it would have a place for religion, above all Christianity, in its self-image; it would understand that capitalism was not democracy's antagonist but that they were mutually dependent; and it would know that liberty was safest in pluralistic societies 'where several govern.' As at the signing of the Atlantic Charter, this unmistakably describes a West that includes— and indeed is led by—America, the strategic heartland where Christianity and capitalism still retain considerable, if reduced, self-confidence and popularity.

There could hardly be two more contrary conclusions. Coker thinks that the Western Brothers have quarrelled so irrevocably that there is nothing for it but for them to divide the estate and go out to seek profitable alliances with their former retainers. Gress thinks that the hostility of those beyond the Pale will force the family to stick together under the slightly austere Uncle Sam, who, culturally if not fiscally speaking, has saved and invested more, and partied less, than his improvident relatives. And although both writers concede that the future is unknowable, that will not go far in reconciling their differences.

Nevertheless, perspective may lend a hand here. Coker is pessimistic about a West that began to be imagined about the time of Valmy, was realized in 1941, and started to break apart in the sixties with the establishment of "Europe." Gress's Europe started to coalesce in the Dark Ages, emerged in its modern divided self at about the time of Valmy, and has been both growing in power and wracked by civil wars ever since. It is understandable that Coker should look at present political trends and conclude that they point clearly to the West's dissolution, and equally reasonable that Gress should see them as yet another, perhaps extended, episode in the long struggle between the mainstream Western tradition and its internal enemies. And in the timescale in which they pitch their forecasts, both may even be right.

The case for Coker's predictions makes itself. The evidence is before our eyes in such signs as the boasts of European politicians that the euro will shortly rival the dollar as top currency; the spread of multiculturalism, bilingualism, and a deracinated history in the schools;

the drive for a militarily pointless but politically significant 'European defence identity' in NATO; the divergence between the United States and the European Union over American sanctions on Cuba and Iran; the EU's restrictions on American cultural imports; and much else. *National Interest* readers have already seen the case that Atlantic arrangements are destined to erode in the post-Cold War world argued ably and briskly by Stephen Walt in 'The Ties That Fray: Why Europe and America Are Drifting Apart' (Winter 1998/99). Coker's additional point is that these ties began to fray while the Soviet threat was still an incentive for cooperation and that they therefore signify a much deeper civilizational divide. If Gress is to convince us otherwise, he has to point to less obtrusive trends that are likely to draw America and Europe together over the long haul.

These are not hard to find. To begin with, the West, which was linguistically Balkanized one generation ago, is now increasingly united by a single language. English is the language of business, the airline industry, practical diplomacy, Hollywood, and the internet. It has even been given official status by the European Union. To be sure, English is also shared with many non-Westerners, but that does not diminish its force as a factor fostering Atlantic cultural unity. Cultural unity does not, of course, preclude passionate disputes; indeed, it practically guarantees them, as Shaw's remark about Americans and British being divided by a single language recognizes. The quality of Atlantic culture, especially its pop-cultural side, is one indictment in Europe's charge-sheet against the United States. But these atrocities are of concern to Americans as much as to Europeans, and the official European response—to subsidize even worse local imitations of American trash—hardly improves matters. Moreover, the concept of Atlantic culture is not exhausted by television sitcoms and Hollywood "slasher" movies. English also fosters the development of an Atlantic public opinion and consciousness. Through magazines like *The Economist* and newspapers like the *Financial Times*, we are all aware of the same information and all concerned about the same controversies. Inevitably, this political culture is often superficial, but that is in part because Atlantic cultural unity is in its early stages.

Religion is another source of Western unity—or at least no longer a barrier to it. Most commentators focus on such obstacles to a strong West as growing secularism, the divide between secular elites and the Religious Right, and the allegedly similar divide between a post-Christian Europe and a still-Christian America. But these are emotionally mild conflicts compared to those between different Western religions in the recent past. Even as late as the forties, there were deep and bitter divisions between different Protestant denominations, let alone between Catholics and Protestants and Christians and Jews. And these translated into significant national religious differences between, say, Protestant England and Catholic France. But movements like Christian ecumenism and the Jewish–Christian dialogue have healed these divisions to an extent that would have astonished our grandparents.

Nor does secularism enjoy a settled victory either in Europe or among America's elites. 'Modern man' is a creature shaped largely by agnostic philosophers and liberal theologians who created him in their own image. Church attendance may be down in most countries, but opinion polls show a large residue of Christian and other religious beliefs in European populations. The United States is experiencing a religious revival that some observers compare to the Great Awakenings. Above all, the supposed link between modernity and secularism is a fragile one. It may apply, for instance, to the liberal humanities, but it does not seem to hold for the physical and technical sciences. Evangelical Christians are apparently found in large numbers at the cutting-edge of science and technology, and America is not only more religious than Europe, it is also more advanced in the new applied sciences. It would not be surprising if even agnostic sectors of society were to be influenced over time by this evidence of worldly accomplishment—which would soothe another cultural tension in Euro–American relations. But in any event secularism seems unlikely to divide the West in the way that earlier religious differences did.

Political divisions are, of course, more eternal than religious ones. And the division between American capitalism and European social democracy, though largely a matter of degree, is now of fifty years standing. But it must be qualified by three new divisions that currently fracture Western politics. The first of these is the latest incarnation of the conflict between the sceptical and radical Enlightenments; let us call it the battle between the West and the post-West. This is a struggle over, among other things, the meaning of democracy. As the scholar John Fonte has pointed out, the traditional Western view of liberal democracy is now being challenged by advocates of 'cultural democracy,' who would replace individual rights with group rights, majority rule with 'fancy franchises,' and individual merit with ethnic proportionalism. Indeed, gender proportionalism would trump even popular democratic elections, since the voters would have to choose a parliament composed 50 per cent of women.

Supporters of cultural democracy are now entrenched in national and international bureaucracies, and are the main source of activist energy in parties of the Left. But they are as likely to be found in Washington as in Paris; this is a conflict within Western nations rather than between them. It is also a fairly mild conflict compared to the murderous ideological battles that have disfigured this century. If cultural democrats are Bolsheviks, they are Bolsheviks acting within the restraints of formal democracy. But then—to borrow from Marx—socialism repeats itself: the first time as genocide, the second time as therapy.

The second division has opened up because cultural democrats are opposed, or at least hampered, by their allies in social democratic parties who retain, or have recovered, a faith in the New West triad of democracy, capitalism and science. These are the advocates of the Third Way, which, when it is not mere blather (which it is most of the time), is an attempt to reconcile the social democratic parties with the West, correcting the mistaken policy of the post-war Left of maintaining a high-minded neutrality between Western freedom and Soviet socialism. This task is made much easier by the economic and social progress of the last fifty years. The original advocates of a Third Way, like Orwell, could point to real hardship in capitalist societies that had very modest nets of social welfare. By the end of the Cold War, the conservative parties in America and Western Europe were advocates and custodians of extensive welfare arrangements. Indeed, one reason why the Blairite Third Way sometimes seems so thin is that it claims to occupy a distinctive position on the ideological spectrum (free markets plus state safety nets) where in fact even the Thatcherites perched quite comfortably. But admittedly, what is bad argument may be good politics.

Indeed, the third division is that between the post-war West and the new democracies of Central and Eastern Europe. As Gress points out, the end of communist rule led to a revival of classical liberal thought in the new democracies. The need for new constitutions led to politicians reading Burke, Montesquieu, Constant, and the Federalist Papers for the first time, and drawing on such ideas as the separation of powers. The experience of the planned economy persuaded them of the virtues of free-market capitalism. Although these countries all want to be part of "Europe," their leaders also look for guidance, example, and protection to the United States. And they have not had their freedom long enough to become disenchanted with the future. They may be closer geographically to Western Europe, but politically and philosophically they are America's natural friends. So their entry into the Western community, far from introducing a difficult cultural challenge as Coker seems to suggest at one stage, is likely to strengthen the West by reducing the net amount of anti-Americanism in Europe.

On balance these new political trends seem likely to moderate rather than aggravate existing tensions between America and Europe. But these may look more threatening at present than over the long run because they are the result in part of the West's overwhelming dominance in the world. It is, after all, the bloc led by the world's only superpower, and as such plainly feels that it can enjoy the luxury of internal rivalry and dissent, just as the variations on postmodernism within the academy testify to a society that is rich and secure enough to afford almost any frivolity.

Nevertheless, this present dominance is an extraordinary and probably temporary state of affairs. No one can forecast the precise coalition of civilizations, nations or sub-national forces that might pose a serious threat to Western interests in the future. Such a coalition is, however, a moral certainty at some time. And when it arrives, the West is likely to exist as a civilizational, economic, and political coalition, and as at least a potential military one. That is not everything of course; but it is quite a lot.

This review of David Gress's, From Plato to NATO *(New York: Free Press, 1998), 592 pp., and Christopher Coker's,* Twilight of the West *(Boulder: Westview Press, 1998), 203 pp., was originally published in* The National Interest, *1 March, 1999, https://nationalinterest.org/bookreview/how-the-west-was-spun-837.*

Global Governance or National Democracy: Who Rules?

A Review of *Sovereignty or Submission: Will Americans Rule Themselves or Be Ruled by Others?* by John Fonte
1 March 2012

For some years John Fonte has enjoyed an odd and slightly enviable reputation. He is the scholarly defender of democratic sovereignty most likely to be invited to debate the matter by and with his opponents in the academic school of global governance. This is partly explained by the fact that, as the reader of this book will discover, Dr Fonte is a courteous, well-informed, logical, and above all honest debater. That also happens to be true of his better antagonists, such as Peter Spiro, on the global governance side. For reasons we shall soon encounter, however, it is not true of all of them.

The second explanation of Dr Fonte's reputation is that he is one among very few scholarly defenders of sovereigntist ideas. In the academy, the media, the law, the foreign policy establishment, the corporate world, the wider political elite, and—almost inevitably—the bureaucracies that serve international institutions and non-governmental organizations, the ideology of global governance is the prevailing intellectual orthodoxy. Those scholars who adopt a hostile attitude—or even a sceptical one—to its doctrines are in a distinct minority. And because academic tenure and research funding follow intellectual orthodoxy, they even resemble an endangered species in the academy.

This disparity of scholarship has thus had a remarkably rapid and thorough impact on institutional innovation, diplomacy and political debate. Although global governance in its current form is a relatively new idea—dating roughly from the end of the Cold War—it is increasingly the basis of government decisions, bilateral agreements, and international treaties such as the Kyoto Protocol or the treaty establishing the International Criminal Court. There has been little organized and systematic opposition to its advance comparable to, for instance, the resistance of the Western liberal democracies to Soviet communism after 1947. Accordingly, books, op-eds, law journal articles, proceedings of international conferences, and think tank reports advocating different aspects of global governance appear almost daily in the print and electronic media.

There are countless blasts but almost no counterblasts. *Sovereignty or Submission* is the first major counterblast from the sovereigntist side of the debate. It is a late but welcome exception.

It is also an example of a disturbingly familiar paradox: the lone voice speaking out on behalf of multitudes. As Dr Fonte illustrates again and again (and as opinion polls repeatedly confirm), the concept of democratic national sovereignty and the nexus of ideas and institutions built upon it reflect the beliefs of the overwhelming majority of citizens in the United States and other advanced democracies. Americans, Australians, Brits, Italians, and the citizens of other free nations imagine they are self-governing peoples who settle domestic political issues—such as the limits of free speech or an adequate level of welfare provision—by democratic debate and majority voting. Despite occasional grumbling about politics and politicians, they like it that way. All the evidence suggests that they would oppose any open attempt to replace their democracies with another political system.

'Global governance' *is* another political system or regime. It seeks to take ultimate political power (sovereignty) from democratic parliaments and congresses accountable to national electorates in sovereign states and vest it in courts, bureaucratic agencies, NGOs and transnational bodies that are accountable only to themselves or to other transnational bodies. In the international system that prevails under our existing system, legitimacy flows upwards from the voters in elections through sovereign governments via treaties to international institutions that enjoy specified and limited powers agreed in advance. Under global governance, however, legitimacy flows from post-national elites in transnational institutions via open-ended treaties downwards to post-sovereign governments enjoying powers regulated by transnational bureaucrats and lawyers to—finally—the voters.

Advocates of this second system argue that the voters enjoy more real power as a result of 'pooling' (that is, surrendering) their sovereignty to transnational bodies carrying greater clout in international affairs. But they are curiously unable to describe how the voters can actually use this greater power. How can they, for instance, amend an international law? Or vote the European Commission out of office? Or appeal against a decision of the International Criminal Court? Or influence the diplomatic campaigns of the European Union such as its attempt to outlaw capital punishment? The voters can do none of these things—and fewer of the things they used to be able to do—because they lack the ultimate democratic sanction: they cannot throw the (transnational) rascals out. It is not the voters but the elites running the courts, the NGOs and the transnational bodies who exercise this augmented sovereign power in a wilderness of committees. In short, global governance is yet another attempt (the third major one since 1917 by my counting) to sell elite rule in democratic disguise—in this case, very light disguise.

Or, to put it metaphorically: a bachelor is a sovereign power; a married man enjoys the benefits of pooled sovereignty. That is a hard sell—especially to married men. So it is hardly surprising that the attempt to impose it on liberal democracies has been a decidedly covert one.

Here is how it is done. Global governance begins as the ideology of small but influential transnational elites operating just outside the spotlight of national politics. Its voice is loud in academic seminars but muffled to the point of being dumb in national political debates and in the non-specialist media. Its academic, legal, corporate and political supporters spread their ideas in the obscurity of learned journals, international conferences and legal judgments. When these notions have sufficiently permeated the domestic bureaucracies of governments, then politicians and bureaucrats travel to pleasant foreign cities to negotiate treaties and covenants that reflect the new orthodoxy. On rare occasions—as when Hillary Clinton led the US delegation to the Beijing conference on women's rights—these treaties are openly arrived at and fiercely debated at home. That slows the process down. So, most of the time, they take place in smokeless rooms in Geneva between faceless diplomats watched only by the lobbyists of left-wing NGOs and self-interested multinational corporations.

When they finally emerge from the long process of multilateral negotiation, moreover, these global treaties have only begun their careers. They have irreproachable titles signalling noble aspirations such as protecting women or opposing genocide. But they are subject to extravagant re-interpretation by international courts, national courts, and even—under the rubric of the new customary international law—conferences of law professors claiming transnational legislative force for their law review articles. Even un-amended, these treaties contain provisions that go well beyond a commonsense interpretation of their headline aims. They incorporate monitoring and enforcement mechanisms that transfer authority over the issues covered from national governments to UN agencies and other transnational bodies. And they intrude into the most domestic of domestic policies—an intrusion often sought or welcomed by the courts, the bureaucracies, NGOs, and other local bodies anxious to reverse a policy on which they suffered a defeat in the nation's democratic debate. Indeed, a major impetus behind global governance is the desire of elites to insulate themselves against the possibility of such defeat.

Much of this takes place in the political twilight inhabited by NGOs, lobbyists and pressure groups. The wider national public often learns of it only at the point that a UN monitoring body arrives to argue that the treaty requires changes in the law, welfare or the national constitution.

A few examples chosen at random from many such in Dr Fonte's book:

1. The UN committee monitoring the UN Covenant on Eliminating Racial Discrimination told the USA in 2001 to overturn the First Amendment of the USA Constitution—the one that protects free speech—because it was an obstacle to outlawing what the committee regarded as hate speech. (US diplomats negotiating a treaty routinely insist on laying down 'reservations' when they suspect that some of its

provisions might be incompatible with the Constitution. This greatly irks the UN and other global bodies.)

2. In 1997 UN monitors of the Convention on the Elimination of Discrimination against Women complained that 'only 30 per cent of Slovenia's children were in day care centres.' Too many children were being raised at home by their parents because the elected Slovenian government was providing government benefits to stay-at-home mothers. In the monitors' view, this reinforced old stereotypes and deprived children of the educational and social opportunities of the day care centres.

3. The UN committee monitoring the Convention for Civil and Political Rights complained to Australia in 2000 about its detention of illegal immigrants. It also chastised the United States for the 'increased level of militarization on the south-west border with Mexico.' And, finally, the committee was troubled by the American federal system itself because 'the states of the union retain extensive jurisdiction over ... criminal and family law,' which 'may lead to a somewhat unsatisfactory application of the Covenant throughout the country.'

Such intrusions into the domestic politics of sovereign liberal democracies are catnip to the tabloid press. Once it emerges that a country like Canada has agreed to submit its welfare budget for approval by a UN treaty rapporteur who is also the diplomatic representative of a notorious dictatorship, this becomes an instant political scandal. The public reacts along the lines of 'What the hell is going on here?' Advocates of global governance respond with variations on 'Nothing to see here, folks; move along please. Just a small earthquake in theory; not many disenfranchised.' A brief controversy ensues until the next "shock horror" story edges it out of the headlines.

But such stories cannot keep appearing in the mass media without arousing popular concern. The soft soap of global governance eventually fails to soothe. After a long period in which a revolution has been occurring either unnoticed or with general mild approval, those attached to the status quo—in this case, liberal democratic governance—notice that this new revolution is incompatible with their sovereign rights and established institutions. And a genuine debate bursts forth, often passionately.

When serious and sustained debate does eventually break out, early opponents of such revolutions are often disdained by their natural allies. In his 1968 introduction to Burke's *Reflections on the French Revolution*, Conor Cruise O'Brien points out that his students almost always assumed that Burke was writing during and after the Terror. In reality some of his most passionate philippics were written several years beforehand. Most well-informed Englishmen, including Burke's closest political friends, thought that his early hostility to the French Revolution was excessive and unbalanced. They imagined that France was imitating their own constitutional liberalism. They did not see the radical implications of the Revolution's ideology and therefore they missed the bloody and anarchic direction in which it was heading. Burke's predictions of the Terror were prescient because his analysis of the Revolution's early liberalism was profound. Only when his predictions were confirmed by events, however, were conservative and liberal Englishmen converted to his scepticism. Is something similar about to happen to the quiet revolution of global governance?

Until quite recently Dr Fonte and other democratic sovereigntists— an unlovely term coined to describe supporters of liberal democracy at home and sovereign statehood abroad—have been in the same position as the early Burke. They have found it hard to persuade their fellow citizens that there is anything to worry about. That is partly because global governance needs a deal of explaining. Like Marxism it presents itself as the fulfilment of liberalism, democracy and internationalism rather than as their negation. It lacks the appalling frankness of Marxism, Nazism and jihadism—their willingness to state without blinking that their rule will brook no fundamental opposition. Instead, it uses many of the same terms—human rights, peace, international law—as democrats and internationalists to describe its aims. These clouds of ink deceive and pacify many.

But Dr Fonte is a pioneer in the trade of de-mystifying ideologies. He was the first anthropologist to classify and analyse the early primitive 'transnational progressives.' He is accordingly well-equipped to extract the real meaning from global governance's later sophisticated euphemisms. (The first half of his book, indeed, is a Cook's tour of political theory over the past four hundred years—and as such a highly readable introduction to political ideas outside its main context.) So he has little difficulty in demonstrating that to 'pool sovereignty' is to lose it since the pooling creates a new sovereign authority above and over the nations who did the pooling. In the next breath he shows that to sign a treaty with clearly defined obligations to other nations (even major obligations such as Article Five's declaration of war under NATO) is to exercise sovereignty; to sign a treaty with a post-national entity obliging you to do whatever it demands, however, is to surrender sovereignty. The former treaty is a case of internationalism; the latter one of transnationalism. Transnationalism, far from being a kind of super-charged internationalism, is in fact hostile to it. Internationalism rests on cooperation between sovereign nation-states which transnationalism first imprisons and then gradually eliminates in a euthanasia of regulations. Of the two structures, significantly, only internationalism is compatible with democracy in national domestic politics. Transnationalism boasts unwisely of its 'irreversible' nature whereas democracy is a system of second thoughts in every election.

Again and again Dr Fonte traces where the logic of these ideas leads—and invariably it is to a massive, remote, undemocratic, regulatory Leviathan.

But why tap the thermometer when you can see the weather—especially if you have just been struck by lightning? Theory need no longer be our only guide. In Europe global governance advocates have already established an institution that embodies and illustrates some of their fondest beliefs, namely the European Union. It provides us with a trailer of what a system of global governance would look like in practice, as Walter Russell Mead points out:

> Think of the European Union blown up to a global scale; in the Global Union nations would have their own governments and their own laws, but an increasingly dense framework of commonly agreed-upon laws and norms, and an increasingly complex and effective web of global institutions would

supplement and in many cases replace the authority of national governments.

And that is putting it mildly. The current crisis of the euro demonstrates two additional and glaring dangers in such a structure: the first is that unwise and unpopular policies tend to be adopted in the absence of democratic accountability; the second is that even when they have manifestly failed, such policies tend to continue unchanged in the absence of democratic accountability. Further, the long-running failure of the Common Agricultural Policy—which ruins the export prospects of small Third World farmers in order to sustain high food prices for European consumers at a cost equal to 40 per cent of the EU's entire budget—shows that such folly can be maintained more or less indefinitely (or until the entire structure runs out of cash and thereby collapses). Elites are far more unwilling to give up their fantasies than are practical-minded ordinary voters (in part because the elites do not have to suffer the negative aspects of utopia). The triumph of global governance would therefore risk repeating the unpopular failures of the EU on a world scale and at Brobdignagian expense.

Global governance is not, fortunately, an inevitable destiny for Americans or anyone else—though its advocates, like those of Marxism, like to present it as such. It is one possible future among several. In the second half of his book, Dr Fonte examines the likely geopolitical choices available to political man in a world where history has ended in Francis Fukuyama's sense. He sees four ideological contenders for the title of dominant global governing philosophy.

The first is that of internationalism resting on cooperation between sovereign democratic nation states. That is the system which still provides the United States with its regime and which, until very recently, was the prevailing constitutional doctrine of Western Europe. It received a marked fillip, indeed, when the nations of Central and Eastern Europe threw off communism and joined "the West." They thought they were joining a structure built along liberal democratic lines, but they found themselves instead in a halfway house to global governance. Like the British, though for a slightly different reason, they are uncomfortable in such a structure; it reminds them (in more relaxed moments) of the

Habsburg Empire and (in moods of bitter despair) of the Soviet Empire. If liberal democratic internationalism—'Philadelphian sovereignty' in Fonte-esque language—emerges finally as the hegemonic ideology of international affairs, then most European states will presumably abandon their flirtation with post-nationalism and post-democracy and recover some of their democratic authority from Brussels.

Also, in these circumstances, there would be a tendency throughout the world for states throwing off authoritarian systems of government to model themselves along liberal democratic lines. Such states, of course, like all democracies, would increasingly reflect the nature of their own societies especially as concerns religion. Thus, we should expect states emerging from the 'Arab Spring,' if they develop along democratic lines, to look more like Turkey than like America. That should neither surprise nor discomfit supporters of democratic sovereignty; rather it should confirm their commitment. As Dr Fonte points out, America and France are two democratic nations committed to the division of church and state, yet they have opposite views on 'banning the burka' because their traditions of secularism are subtly different. A democratic world would be far from uniform, but its diversities would be the result of popular choice rather than of centralized ideological-cum-legal prescription.

Two other rising competitors for ideological dominance worldwide are jihadism and sovereign authoritarianism—the respective ideologies of Al Qaeda (and others) and China (and others). When Fukuyama wrote about the end of history, he meant not that history in the sense of wars, royal successions, election victories and similar "events" would come to a halt, but that no plausible alternatives would emerge to challenge Western democracy as the dominant ideology of governing. Neither of these doctrines seems likely to refute his thesis. Both can cause a great deal of damage in the world—through terrorism, military competition and general trouble-making; neither looks able to gain sufficient acquiescence, let alone support, from others to allow it to shape international relations and global institutions in its own image. Jihadism proposes a world theocracy that would be deeply unacceptable to the 80 per cent of the world population that is non-Muslim—and hardly less so to most of the remaining Muslim 20 per cent. Sovereign authoritarianism, even when most materially successful as in China, has a legitimacy problem such that Chinese spokesmen justify their system as offering the practical benefits of democracy in other ways. Neither inspires outside a narrow ambit drawn mainly from co-religionists or the authoritarian ruling class. Both live under a delayed death sentence—Al Qaeda literally, sovereign authoritarianism metaphorically. If these are the main challenges to Western democracy, then Fukuyama is right to maintain that they are implausible.

What Fukuyama did not sufficiently foresee, as Dr Fonte points out, was that a plausible challenge to Western liberal democracy might come from within the West itself—indeed, from within Western liberal democracy itself. Like Marxism, however, global governance is just such a challenge. It emerges from the leading social classes in Western society. It affects to solve the global problems that—allegedly—democratic sovereign states cannot solve through international cooperation (or as the phrase has it, 'on their own'). It presents itself as the fulfilment of democracy—a deeper and truer democracy than the discredited partisan bickering of political parties. Yet it subverts democratic accountability and the consent of the governed at every turn, and it seeks to transfer ever-increasing powers from democratic institutions to global bodies and NGOs that reflect elite opinions and priorities. A kind of sublime post-democratic ecstasy was surely reached in the conception of GONGOs—NGOs created and financed by transnational bodies to urge that they take more powers from government in order to implement the reforms that voters and governments have 'failed to take' (that is, voted against).

The intellectual quadrille danced by these four competitors for diplomatic hegemony is complicated. Day to day, the doctrines of global governance are a useful tool for jihadist sympathizers and authoritarian governments as they embark on, for instance, 'lawfare' to hobble US efforts to fight terrorism and to restrain America generally. But rising nation states, whether democratic or undemocratic—such as China, India, Brazil, and Indonesia—are unlikely to accept that their foreign and domestic policies should be determined, or even vetoed, by a UN agency on the basis of some imaginative interpretation of a treaty signed by a party now in opposition. The slow-motion train-wreck of the Kyoto process—an allegedly irresistible force that met a genuinely immovable object in the form of Sino–Indian opposition—is probably the first of many such reverses for the advocates of global governance. As the sovereign powers of Asia, Africa and Latin America complete their rise into the international community, global governance will look increasingly provincial—a last effort by a fading postmodern Europe to extend its power in the guise of transnationalism, a form of neo-colonialism waged by lawyers rather than soldiers and administrators.

So it is unlikely that the forces of global governance will succeed in establishing some form of global authority or their version of a 'global rule of law.' On the other hand, these forces, assisted by the material interests of transnational pragmatists in multinational corporations might attain considerable influence, even a critical mass, over opinion makers and statesmen in Western democracies (including the USA). This influence might even become the conventional wisdom of elite opinion, achieving what the Italian Marxist thinker Antonio Gramsci called 'ideological hegemony.' It has already gone a long way in that direction.

If that were to continue—if the mind of the democrat were to be captured by the arguments of the globalist—then the result could well be not the triumph of global governance but the suicide of liberal democracy, regarding both domestic self-government and self-defence against terrorists and sovereign but undemocratic states. Thus the global governance project, although unable to achieve success on its own terms, would essentially disable and disarm the democratic state. Fukuyama's scepticism notwithstanding, if liberal democracy drinks deep from the cup of global governance it will poison itself.

Such a suicide of liberal democracy would likely happen gradually over a long period. In Chapter Six, Dr Fonte analyses the slow-motion suicide of the liberal democratic nation states of Western Europe, as they transform themselves into subordinate states within the supranational legal regime of the European Union. That still continues. Among the chief facilitators of this "suicide," moreover, are the national judges of the various European nations. In the construction of a global legal regime, judges at the highest levels within nation-states would also play a crucial role.

Some serious comfort is to be found therefore in the growing resistance within Europe to the not-quite-completed project of undemocratic European governance. Voters and taxpayers are rebelling, both in the polling booths and in the streets, against structures of unaccountable power that deliver currency crises, high unemployment and massive policy failures. If global governance remains controversial and contested in its heartland—and it does at several levels—then there is every reason to believe that it can be halted and reversed more generally.

The forces of scepticism everywhere, moreover, enjoy one potentially decisive advantage: global governance is the ideology that dare not speak its name. It has to deny on television the doctrines that it boasts about in the seminar. It has to conceal its achievements such as the Common Agricultural Policy. It has to engage in verbal tricks to justify its rules and institutions as liberal and democratic when in fact they are their opposites. In general global governance has to lie and dissemble incessantly.

That was fine when no one was paying attention. Global governance could apparently survive anything but discussion. With the publication of this book, however, that qualification no longer applies. Dr Fonte has ensured that there will finally be a full national and international debate on the sovereignty issue. He has removed the veils of euphemism and legal circumlocution that surrounded it. He has given us an intellectual armoury to defend our constitutional liberal democracies against internal subversion or external attack.

He has done everything that can be done by a political writer. His readers must now do the rest.

This review of John Fonte's Sovereignty or Submission: Will Americans Rule Themselves or Be Ruled by Others? *(Encounter Books, 2011), 449 pp, was originally published in* Quadrant Online, *1 March 2012, https://quadrant.org.au/magazine/2012/03/global-governance-v-democratic-sovereignty/.*

Misunderstanding
the 2008 Crash to Strengthen the State
2014

More than eighty years after the Wall Street Crash, economic historians are still debating the causes and consequences of the Great Depression. Within a day or two of the fall of Lehman Brothers in September 2008, however, a full-fledged consensus had emerged among political and media elites throughout the Western world on the causes and consequences of this new financial crisis. It is perhaps the only world crisis to have been fully explained to the public while it was still occurring.

This consensus was seductively simple. Weak or non-existent regulation—introduced by Ronald Reagan and Margaret Thatcher two decades before—had allowed the US banks, other financial institutions, and 'Wall Street' to finance the sale of mortgages to low-income borrowers with little or no collateral; to package this dodgy debt together with high-grade securities in new financial instruments no one really understood; to get top-grade ratings for these suspect packages from the rating agencies; to sell them onto other unsuspecting banks around the world; and thereby to build up a tower of trillions in bad debt throughout the financial system that could only be paid off by a prolonged worldwide economic recession.

This verdict, delivered even as the crime was being committed, was greeted with almost instant acceptance across a wide swathe of elite opinion. Cardinal Cormac Murphy O'Connor, then Britain's Archbishop of Westminster, declared in January 2009 that capitalism was 'dead.' He told at a fundraising dinner for Catholic charities that communism had died in 1989 and that capitalism had been killed in 2008 by the credit crisis. Joseph Stigler, the Nobel Prize-winning economist, had employed exactly the same analogy four months previously: 'the fall of Wall Street is for market fundamentalism what the fall of the Berlin Wall was for communism—it tells the world that this way of economic organization turns out not to be sustainable.' ('Market fundamentalism' sounds like some new and sinister phenomenon, but it is merely a way of describing global free markets that slyly links them to jihadist terrorism and, worse, to American Evangelical Protestantism.) President Sarkozy of France announced 'laissez-faire capitalism is over.' And introducing its 2008 instant series, 'The Future of Capitalism,' the *Financial Times* asked with headline eagerness: 'The credit crunch has destroyed faith in the free market ideology that has dominated Western economic thinking for a generation. But what can—and should—replace it?'

The ready answer from the same kind of elite voices was more extensive and stronger government regulation—and, given the international nature of the crisis, even global governance—of world financial markets. George Soros, perhaps the world's most famous financier and hedge fund manager, placed the blame squarely on two retired politicians in an interview with *Der Spiegel*: 'Everything was based on self-regulating markets, which by the way was not an American invention. It started with Margaret Thatcher in the UK and was further promoted and pushed here in the US by then President Ronald Reagan.' He thus proposed a whole raft of new regulations. Similarly, President Sarkozy of France, having already railed against the 'dictatorship of the market,' now declared, 'No financial institution should escape regulation.' He told the European parliament that greater regulation on a European and even global basis should cover private equity and hedge funds, the rating agencies, such as Moody's, derivatives, tax havens, sovereign wealth funds, and the compensation packages of bankers. A series of European Union, G2, G8, and G20 summits followed at which plans for such extensions of regulation were discussed and occasionally agreed. President Sarkozy even asked, 'Am I a socialist?,' and replied, with uncharacteristic uncertainty, 'Perhaps.'

Six years later this analysis seems simplistic, exaggerated, and largely (though not wholly) false. Its ready adoption by so many influential people reflects not the economic crisis it supposedly addressed but anti-capitalist beliefs and statist interests that they had suppressed or downplayed in the face of globalization's apparent success. Specific new regulations introduced on the basis of this analysis have not been in effect long enough for a judgment to be made about their long-term effects. Some seem prudent corrections to previous banking laxity on risk capital requirements; others may restrict innovation unduly such as the EU's oversight of hedge-funds; still others, notably the new US legislation on financial services, may delegate too much regulation-writing authority to bureaucratic agencies (with similar effects on innovation). We must wait and see.

But the overall theory that free market capitalism had failed as communism had failed, thereby inflicting a massive long-term global recession equivalent to the economic wasteland produced by communist planning, has plainly been shown to be nonsense. To be sure, America still struggles with recession. Some European countries, such as Spain, Greece, and Ireland are mired in economic difficulties that are in large part self-inflicted (including the euro.) Others, notably Germany, France, and even Britain, are already recovering from recession—Poland is one of a few countries that never experienced it. And Asia is booming. Jagdish Bhagwati, a colleague of Joseph Stigler's at Columbia University, summed up the real contrast:

> When the Berlin Wall collapsed, we saw the intellectual bankruptcy of both the authoritarian politics of communism and the economics of extensive, almost universal, ownership of the means of production and of central planning. We saw a wasteland. But, when Wall Street and Main Street were shaken by crisis, we were witness to a pause in prosperity ... We had enjoyed almost two decades where the liberal reforms undertaken by nearly half the world's population, in China and India, had produced unprecedented prosperity and ... finally made a significant impact on poverty.

That is not to deny that the financial crisis was a severe one with damaging consequences in negative or lower growth, higher unemployment, loss of wealth, and—more insidiously—loss of self-confidence in Western elites. It was all of these things. Let me also set aside the secondary causes and/or crises that followed the US financial implosion but that were analytically distinct from it—crises in Greece, Spain, Ireland, and Eastern Europe that flowed from reckless budgeting, wildly over-generous transfer payments, the evident fact that the eurozone was not an optimal currency area, and other non-American causes—and concentrate on the financial and economic turmoil resulting from the American sub-prime mortgage crisis. What caused *that*? Was it mainly or wholly the absence of regulation? To find out, let us look at where, when, and how it began.

As it happens, I was present at the scene of the crime. In 1993, I was editing a magazine, *National Review*, in New York when two journalists next door on the magazine *Forbes*, Peter Brimelow and Leslie Spencer, noticed that a Boston Federal Bank study showing discrimination against minorities in mortgage lending had a crucial flaw. *National Review* (where Brimelow later moonlighted as a senior editor) noticed the criticism and ran an editorial supporting it. But let Brimelow take up the story:

> When my brilliant co-author, Leslie Spencer, asked the Boston Fed's research director, Alicia H. Munnell, what minority default rates were, she said proudly that census tract data showed that they were equal to whites. When Leslie pointed out that this actually proved there was no discrimination, because the lenders had somehow weeded out the credit risks down to the same acceptable level, Munnell was dumbfounded and had to concede (on tape) that she did not, in fact, have definitive proof of discrimination at all.
>
> We had discovered a fundamental technical flaw. We sat back and waited for our Pulitzer Prizes.
>
> Nothing happened. The Boston Fed study continued to be cited by press and politicians. Alicia Munnell was apotheosized into the Clinton administration.

Nothing happened because this criticism had uncovered, ahem, an 'inconvenient' fact and had to be ignored. Both American political parties were committed—both for praiseworthy social reasons and for selfish political ones—to expanding home-ownership by minorities. If the banks could be shown to discriminate against minority lenders, then they could be compelled to lend to them. But since minority borrowers were disproportionately poor, they could not afford the down payments or repayment schedules which the banks required to the same extent as other Americans. So the banks were encouraged by legislation, by pressure from Housing and Urban Development officials, and by regulatory agencies to reduce their deposit and other requirements to minority and low-income borrowers. By the mid-1990s, mortgage banks were offering mortgages in return for 3 per cent deposits—and later for no deposits at all. Millions of new borrowers now had to make monthly mortgage payments that were large in relation to their incomes. And if Brimelow and Spencer were correct—and they were—many of those borrowers would eventually default.

So the banks now had to find ways of passing on a stock of dodgy loans in order to reduce their own risks. They did so by 'securitizing' them—that is, by putting the dodgy loans in a package with AAA-rated ones and selling the resulting securities to the secondary mortgage market. In effect they were selling the stream of income derived from the payments made by the holders of different quality mortgages. In principle, securitization is a reasonable method of spreading the risk by diluting it. For it to work fairly, however, the overall risk has to be accurately assessed and described. That did not happen. The rating agencies—a government-enforced private cartel not subject to competition from more sceptical observers—gave high marks to mortgage-based securities that seriously understated the risks of default.

They could do so because there were sure-fire buyers in the secondary mortgage market for them in the form of the semi-government agencies: Fannie Mae (the Federal National Mortgage Association) and Freddie Mac (the Federal Home Loan Mortgage Corporation). As Steven Horwitz and Peter Boettke point out in *The House That Uncle Sam Built*, these two agencies owned or controlled half of the mortgage market by the time they were nationalized in 2008. They had the implicit support of the taxpayer, the mission to make housing more affordable, and seemingly the belief that house prices would rise indefinitely. So they were willing and able to buy the mortgage products originated by the banks, repackage them, and sell them onto other purchasers in an expensive game of 'pass the parcel.' Once the banks realized that they could not only make money from dodgy mortgage loans but also transfer their risks to government-backed purchasers, they naturally originated more and more of them.

Banks began actively to recruit low-income purchasers with offers requiring no collateral to purchase homes of dubious long-term value. This process began under the Clinton administration, but it gathered steam under the second Bush administration, which wanted to turn Mexican immigrants into Republican voters by making them homeowners along the way. As Wall Street realized that this was a money spigot, these loans fuelled the issue of more and more exotic financial instruments, such as mortgage-based collateralized debt obligations, until Wall Street managed hundreds of billions of assets in the secondary mortgage market. As the high levels of risk involved became increasingly apparent, Wall Street developed offsetting financial instruments, notably credit default swaps, to act as a form of insurance against a stalling of house prices and a market collapse. These instruments, though largely opaque, were estimated to run into unimaginable levels of multi-trillions. Yet the whole edifice rested on a few million dodgy mortgage loans, mainly in the 'sand states' of the American Southwest—and eventually the inverted triangle of debt collapsed along with Lehmann Brothers.

That, however, raises a further question: how was a relatively small cancer in a relatively small section of the US economy allowed to metastasize into a world-class financial disease. To that question there are four answers:

First, what shaped the wider crisis was less the absence of regulation, as the initial critics argued, than the perversion of regulation. In the first instance government employed regulatory and other powers to compel the banks to make risky loans for little or no collateral. Later, when securitized mortgages carrying essentially unknown levels of risk were available, international banking regulations on capital reserves made them artificially attractive. It is scarcely credible but, as Horwitz and Boettke point out, if a bank sold a mortgage to Fannie Mae and bought it back in a securitized package, it was required to hold 40 per cent less capital in reserve than if it had simply kept its own original mortgage. Yet, it would have less information than about its own original mortgage (and the likelihood was that its value would be less). In other words, regulatory rules actually encouraged reckless financial speculation.

When it was not perverse, regulation seems to have been myopic. Fannie and Freddie, responsible for about half of the mortgage crisis, as we have seen, were regulated by a body called OFHEO. In testimony to Congress, America's most famous investor, Warren Buffet, delivered the following verdict on its competence:

> Something called OFHEO was set up in 1992 by Congress, and the sole job of OFHEO was to watch over Fannie and Freddie ... OFHEO has over 200 employees now. They have a budget now that is $65 million a year, and all they have to do is look at two companies. I mean, you know, I look at more than two companies.

> And they sat there, made reports to the Congress, you can get them on the Internet, every year. And, in fact, they reported to Sarbanes and Oxley every year. And they went—wrote 100-page reports, and they said, 'We've looked at these people and their standards are fine and their directors are fine and everything was fine.' Then all of a sudden, you had two of the greatest accounting misstatements in history. You had all kinds of management malfeasance, and it all came out. And, of course, the classic thing was that after it all came out, OFHEO wrote a 350–340 page report examining what went wrong, and they blamed the management, they blamed the directors, they blamed the audit committee. They did not have a word in there about themselves, and they are the ones that 200 people were going to work for every day with just two companies to think about. It just shows the problems of regulation.

Regulatory failure, however, is but a specific version of the wider second answer—namely, the agency principle—that concerns people in both government and the free market. Agents are indispensable in a complex society. How can we ensure that an agent acts in the interest of his ward, or his shareholders, or his client, or the public? We can have criminal laws to prevent the worst fiduciary abuses, of course, but these will not catch sophisticated managers. So we design incentives to ensure that the interest of the agent and the client are as identical as possible. In recent years, these incentives have included linking the manager's income with the value of the stock. As we know, however, managers responded by briefly manipulating the value of the stock to increase their income. Similarly, as several authors (but most notably Michael Lewis of *Liar's Poker*) have shown, Wall Street investment houses down to far humbler advisers gave advice to customers that ignored or was even detrimental to their interests. Lewis cites a case of two women of modest income who, on the advice of their estate agent, bought five houses that they lost when house prices fell and they could no longer afford to make the mortgage payments. Self-dealing is in no way confined to Wall Street or finance, however. It today compromises almost all the professions, not excluding law and accountancy, and could hardly be extirpated even if regulatory bodies were free of it. What explains this?

That brings me to the third answer: the decline of Christian morality and the absence of any likely replacement for it. Commercial morality and professional ethics are unlikely to flourish in a society where truth, honesty, and the other virtues are not encouraged and are even disparaged in everyday life. As Pope Benedict XVI said recently in his speech in Westminster Hall: 'There is widespread agreement that the lack of a solid ethical foundation for economic activity has contributed to the grave difficulties now being experienced by millions of people throughout the world.' In the absence of such a foundation, people will inevitably follow other powerful incentives. And they did so.

That brings me to the fourth answer: the false signals of monetary laxity. Even if self-dealing individuals and corrupt institutions, unconstrained by morality or regulation and following perverse incentives, had sought to enrich themselves ruthlessly in the property market, they simply could not have inflicted such severe financial and economic damage on the US and the world as the 2008 crash actually did. Banks selling dodgy mortgages and Wall Street institutions selling derivatives based on them would have gone bankrupt much earlier and with far less collateral damage. Assets would have been re-distributed with less pain. The world would have returned to financial stability without a major recession. What made this crisis far worse was that the

Federal Reserve had supplied massive amounts of money to the market in order to keep recession at bay and the housing market aloft.

In the five years from 2001 to 2005, there was a sharp rise in the money supply and interests were held down to historically low and (at times) negative figures. People, in other words, were being paid to borrow and spend—and so naturally they did. The consequent inflation was disguised for a time because the excess money did not show up in higher wages or retail prices. Low-wage competition from Asian workers in a globalized world kept the prices of everyday goods down. Inflation of assets—such as Old Masters, fine wines, and, yes, houses—rose in price instead. Investment therefore poured into the housing market, the various mortgage markets, and the derivative markets in a classic inflationary boom.

This boom lasted far longer than most (and thus proved ultimately more damaging), however, for two reasons. First, the Chinese refusal to revalue the Renminbi upwards meant that they built up massive currency reserves that they then had to spend in Western capital markets. Wall Street was awash in cash. Its financial innovations in the housing market were born partly of the need to invest these billions somewhere. Second, Alan Greenspan at the Fed made it clear that the Fed would step in to supply the necessary extra liquidity if ever the bubbles threatened to burst and send financial markets crashing. That put a floor under the widespread myth that real estate prices would rise indefinitely until, suddenly, one day they stopped doing so.

Whatever else it is, this combination of a lax domestic monetary policy with the destabilizing secondary effects of a fixed currency cannot be fairly described as a self-regulating market. Nor can the eventual collapse of this combination be ascribed to the absence of regulation. And, ironically, it is George Soros who in his *Der Spiegel* interview exonerates Thatcher, Reagan, and self-regulating markets from responsibility for the 2008 crash:

> Whenever a crisis endangered the prosperity of the United States—as for example the savings and loan crisis in the late 1980s, or the collapse of the hedge fund Long Term Capital Management in 1998—the authorities intervened, finding ways

for the failing institutions to merge with others and providing monetary and fiscal stimulus when the pace of economic activity was endangered. Thus the periodic crises served, in effect, as successful tests that reinforced both the underlying trend of ever-greater credit expansion and the prevailing misconception that financial markets should be left to their own devices.

In other words, as I have argued elsewhere in a defence of Thatcher and Thatcherism, what Soros calls 'market fundamentalism' was very far from anything like a system of self-regulating markets (whether or not one regards that as possible or desirable). It was a covert attempt by the regulatory authorities to sustain artificially high asset prices resting on irresponsible credit expansion by arbitrary interventions in the market to save favoured financial institutions from the results of their own folly. It would be hard to invent a system that was more completely at odds with what Thatcher, Reagan, Friedman, Hayek, or any other 'neo-liberal' believed, did, or represented.

So, as Jagdish Bhagwati has repeatedly argued, there is no need to re-think the dismal science of economics, merely to remember that it is dismal rather than optimistic. And those commentators who demand that the economics profession produce a new Newton, Darwin, or Einstein to discover a new economics—rather as Diaghilev ordered Cocteau 'Astonish me, Jean'—merely reveal that they confuse discovery with invention.

To sum up, truly earth-shaking events like the financial crisis of 2008 are almost never the product of a single major cause or even of several minor causes. They are perfect storms produced by the concatenation of several major events. The rise of Nazism, for instance, required Germany's defeat in 1918, the 'stab in the back' legend, the harshness of the Versailles Treaty towards the Central Powers, the perceived illegitimacy of the Weimar regime, the fear of Bolshevism after the 1919 revolts, the alienation of the Wilhelmine bureaucracy, the catastrophic inflation of the 1920s that destroyed the savings of the middle class, the catastrophic unemployment of the 1930s that ruined the working class, a strong, but wounded tradition of German nationalism, and not least the extraordinary power of Hitler's own personality. The perfect financial storm of 2008 had almost as many causes: the prolonged attempt under two administrations to increase minority home ownership; innumerable official measures to achieve this by pressuring banks to soften down-payment requirements and repayment schedules for low-income borrowers; attempts to spread the higher risks of these sub-prime mortgages by securitization packages that blended them with lower-risk ones; the perverse encouragement of bad debts and moral risks by regulators and rating agencies that gave such packages a higher rating than they merited; a widespread belief, shared by investors and regulators alike, that house prices underpinned by Uncle Sam would never fall; financial innovations that exploited this artificial market by enabling investors to bet both that it would collapse and that it would rise indefinitely; a flood of cheap credit financed by a lax monetary policy designed to keep a recession at bay and the housing market buoyant; large additional infusions of cash into the market owing to China's refusal to raise its currency and thus its need to spend reserves on US bonds; the repeated failure of the agency principle both in private investment and in official regulation so that neither protected the interests of investor clients; and the decline of professional ethics and commercial morality in everyday life.

All of these factors were required to produce a towering inferno of financial speculation from a relatively modest problem of risky mortgages. Not all of them were financial or economic in nature; some were social or political. Only one—financial innovation—derived originally from the financial markets. But some of the worst financial excesses occurred in regulated markets. And some of the unregulated innovations, notably hedge funds, were innocent of the crash. None of these factors contradicted the basic findings of free market economics (though they may have surprised some free market economists) since it has accommodated and explained crashes and instability from the Dutch Tulip craze onwards. They have not even disproved the neo-liberal belief that individuals know their own interests better than governments do—which was confirmed by the multiple failures of regulators in the long run-up to the crash.

The fox knows many little things, the hedgehog one big thing, writes Isaiah Berlin quoting Archilochus. On this occasion, the one big thing that the hedgehog knows happens to be wrong.

Originally published in Gerald Frost, ed. Understanding the Crash. The Financial Crisis of 2008: Causes, Consequences, Cures *(Budapest: Danube Institute, 2014), 94 pp.*

When Liberal Democracy Becomes an Ideology

Foreword to *The Demon of Democracy* by Ryszard Legutko
12 May 2016

In the first few pages of this important book, Ryszard Legutko describes the oddity whereby former Communists adapted far more easily and successfully than former dissidents and anti-communists to the new liberal-democratic regimes established in Central and Eastern Europe after the fall of the Berlin Wall in1989. Others have noticed this phenomenon too, but they have usually attributed it to such reasons as that the former Communists had greater administrative experience, or that the rules of "transition" protected their power temporarily, or that having privatized state enterprises into their own hands, they brought more resources to playing the game of politics in media and government.

These practical factors were certainly important. However, they did not explain why there was so little *moral* resistance to the continuing dominance of the old nomenklaturas in post-communist democracies. Quite the contrary. Lightly re-baptized as social or liberal democrats, they dominated debate and formed governments. In Western Europe, public and private institutions, including European Union bodies, seemed to find former Communists more congenial than former dissidents as partners in politics and business. On the rare occasions when resistance did erupt, it was usually in response to official efforts to expose still influential communist networks, notably in intelligence agencies, or to restore state property to its original and rightful owners. It was almost as if anti-communist democrats were seen as a greater threat to the new liberal-democratic regime than those who had been its open enemies only yesterday. In addition to their practical advantages, therefore, the former Communists enjoyed a mysterious ideological edge.

Professor Legutko is both a prominent Polish and European statesman and a distinguished philosopher who, in addition to more conventional credentials, was once the editor of *Solidarity*'s underground philosophy journal—a position that would have delighted G. K. Chesterton as well as demonstrating the professor's devotion to truth and freedom. So he is ideally equipped to analyse the mystery of this ideological edge. He finds it in an unexpected place, namely in the structure and practices of the dominant political philosophy of the modern West: liberal democracy. This is a startling discovery. It surprised Legutko himself, and he is pains to point out that even with all the flaws he identifies, liberal democracy is manifestly superior humanly and politically to all forms of totalitarianism.

That said, he is able to demonstrate that liberal democracy, as it has developed in recent decades, shares a number of alarming features with communism. Both are utopian and look forward to 'an end of history' where their systems will prevail as a permanent status quo. Both are historicist and insist that history is inevitably moving in their directions. Both therefore require that all social institutions—family, churches, and private associations—must conform to liberal-democratic rules in their internal functioning. Since that is not so at present, both are devoted to social engineering to bring about this transformation. And as such engineering is naturally resisted, albeit slowly and in a confused way, both are engaged in a never-ending struggle against enemies of society (superstition, tradition, the past, intolerance, racism, xenophobia, bigotry, etc., etc.). In short, like Marxism before it, liberal democracy is becoming an all-encompassing ideology, which behind a veil of tolerance brooks little or no disagreement.

That must strike a newcomer to the argument as absurd. But in chapter after chapter—on history, politics, religion, education, and ideology—the author lays out strong evidence that this transformation is taking place. Transformation is the correct term. The regime described here by Legutko is not liberal democracy as it was understood by, say, Winston Churchill, or FDR, or John F. Kennedy, or Ronald Reagan. That was essentially majoritarian democracy resting on constitutional liberal guarantees of free speech, free association, free media, and other liberties needed to ensure that debate was real and elections fair. Legutko hyphenates 'liberal-democratic' as an adjective in the book; maybe he should do the same with the noun 'liberal-democracy' to distinguish it from the liberal democracy of the nineteenth and twentieth centuries.

One of the most crucial differences between these two regimes is openness. Liberal democracy is a set of rules designed to ensure that government rests on the consent of the governed. Except within the broadest limits, it does not inherently dictate what policies should emerge from government, or what social arrangements should be tolerated, or prohibited. It is open to a wide range of policy outcomes and willing to accept a genuine diversity of social arrangements, including traditional ones. Here the people rule both as voters and as citizens making free choices. Liberal-democracy, however, has policies and prohibitions built into its ideological structure. It is not really open to institutions and policies that run counter to its "liberationist" instincts. It increasingly restricts their freedom of manoeuvre on anything from parental rights to national sovereignty. It is even hostile to some fundamental values of liberalism such as free speech. Accordingly, it sometimes comes up against the wishes of the voters expressed in elections and referenda.

That is where the second crucial difference between liberal democracy and liberal-democracy enters the equation. In the former the wishes of the majority, albeit qualified by negative constitutional restraints, ultimately determine law and policy. In the latter policy is determined both by electoral majorities in accountable bodies and by a range of non-accountable institutions such as courts that make laws rather than interpret them, transnational institutions such as the EU, UN treaty-monitoring bodies, and domestic bureaucracies with wide regulatory powers under delegated legislation. Increasingly, power has drained from elected bodies to courts and other non-accountable institutions; the former have lost confidence, and the latter have become bolder, not merely restraining the majority but also dictating law and policy. The imperfect balance that has always existed within liberal democracy between democracy and liberalism has tipped heavily in favour of liberalism. Liberal-democracy is the result.

Paradoxically it is both less liberal and less democratic than liberal democracy. The range of acceptable political expression and the ability of voters to choose between different policies have both been greatly narrowed. In return, the voters have become increasingly alienated and inclined to rebel against the new structures of power. As all these outcomes become clearer, there will be a major debate in the Western democracies on the legitimacy of their governing institutions. When that debate happens—and it is already in train—this culturally rich, philosophically sophisticated, and brilliantly argued book will be an essential guide to understanding where we went wrong and how we can go right.

Originally published in Hungarian Review, *Vol. VII, No. 3, May 2016,* *www.hungarianreview.com/article/20160512_foreword_to_the_* *demon_in_democracy.*

Conservatism, Populism, and Liberalism in the Post-Democratic Age
23 November 2017

There is a quiet civil war among historians as to whether Robert Menzies or John Howard is the greater prime minister. John Howard has more or less committed himself to the view—in his fine two-part documentary on Menzies produced by the Menzies Research Centre—that Menzies was Australia's greatest leader. And that might seem to settle things. But last week I was present in Sydney at an IPA event when John Roskam, introducing Mr Howard, firmly disagreed and nominated him for the title. There was loud applause for this judgment which was joined, if not led, by John Stone who was, I think, the first credentialed observer to hand this palm to Australia's premier battler, in the March 2008 issue of *Quadrant*.

I have to say that I like this Menzies–Howard contest. It cannot really go wrong, can it? It is something like the opposite of Henry Kissinger's verdict on the Iran–Iraq War: it is a pity they cannot both win. Of course, it is not my place, as a foreigner who discovered Australia about forty years too late, to presume to offer a verdict. But I would like to suggest that something to bear in mind when judging political greatness is the question: What opportunities for greatness did history offer that leader? What were the challenges, the opportunities, and the risks? What happens if the Man cometh but the Hour does not? President Clinton regretted that he had not been faced by a really serious challenge like the Second World War. He felt it would really have stretched him.

John Howard did have a rare opportunity for a conservative statesman, which was that his opponents in the Australian Labor governments of Hawke and Keating understood the need for economic reform as he did. Both Labor and Coalition governments then implemented what was in effect a rolling programme of reform. That was important because the bipartisan foundation of Australia's reform programme made it more likely to endure and in fact gave it more than three decades of implementation. But there is more to be said—a little pre-history—on this. The beginnings of that reform were laid down in the Campbell Report that Mr Howard had commissioned as Treasurer in the Fraser government. That report influenced the nation, the realists in the Labor Party—and, I dare say, it may have influenced the Liberal Party too. Chance favours the prepared mind—in this case the national mind—and the national mind was prepared by the Campbell Report. And it was John Howard who appointed the Campbell Commission.

That little pre-history underscores the vital importance of serious intellectual investment in ideas and policies in and out of government. If the ideas of the Right are not explored and advanced, those of the Left will triumph effortlessly. That is why the role of the Menzies Research Centre, as a kind of intellectual scout of liberalism and conservatism foraging ahead of the body of MPs and activists, is so vital to the future success of Coalition governments.

And that brings me to my final comparison. If one of the attributes of political skill is to convert the Opposition to one's point of view, then the obvious comparison for John Howard is with Margaret Thatcher. I certainly see the likeness, and so did she. Both converted their opposition labour parties to economic realism to the benefit of the country. Unfortunately, it is starting to look as if both conversions were temporary and both UK and Australian labour parties are today whoring after doctrines that do not even have the benefit of being strange but are all too familiar as the oft-trodden road to perdition.

All Is Flux

That is merely one development, however, in the politics of the advanced democracies of the West, which are almost all in an extraordinary degree of movement, confusion, even chaos. As the Greek philosopher said: All is flux.

Consider merely a few random examples of dramatic political change across the globe.

There is the decline of mainstream parties of the Left. French socialists went from being the governing party to getting seven per cent of the total vote in the recent elections. Poland's post-communist socialists have all but disappeared in the last three elections, to be replaced by competition between an urban liberal party and a rural conservative one. There are now three Spanish parties competing for the votes that only recently went to the Socialists. And though Jeremy Corbyn staged a surprise recovery for Labour in the UK, the party has lost its reliable Scottish redoubt that gave it upwards of fifty seats at Westminster.

The mainstream Right is a little better off, but not enjoying the dominance it might have expected from the decline of the Left. The French Right, the latest incarnation of a Gaullist-accented centre-right, expected to be the major party in Parliament this year. It is now an opposition of honourable size to Emmanuel Macron's new "centrist" majority. The Right is also out of power in Italy, Greece, Sweden, Ireland, Canada, and elsewhere, but its overall condition is mixed: it is either in power or a realistic contender for power but uncertain, fumbling, doubting its own ideas but nervous of new ones, and often plagued by new rivals that are winning over its own base with policies that the mainstream parties shunned as old-fashioned some time ago. Often its internal debate is whether to co-opt these rivals or condemn them.

This flux reflects the underlying demographic reality that the class composition of the mainstream parties has been changing for some time. Almost everywhere one finds that the mainstream Left is losing its traditional base in the blue-collar working class as it designs its policies to attract the middle-class urban professionals with progressive views, especially those working in the public sector and in the "third" sector of the media, NGOs, and the academy. The Australian Labor Party in particular has been distracted by the contortions of trying to woo and destroy the Greens simultaneously. Mr Howard was the first major Western politician to act upon the insight that the blue-collar voters could now be won, in an election in which he was cheered by miners and loggers.

Recent elections in the United States and Britain have shown that the Republicans and the Tories now win substantially more votes from the lesser-educated and fewer from the highly-educated. And as we shall see later, this crossover trend seems to be consistent with a new division in electorates across Europe—that identified by the English social democrat David Goodhart in his recent book *The Road to Somewhere* as being between the 'Somewheres' who are firmly attached to their home, district, nation, and identity, and the 'Anywheres' who have the skills to live and work anywhere and a correspondingly weaker attachment to home and nation.

There are some worrying aspects of these trends for conservatives and non-progressive liberals. But we should recall Lord Northcliffe's reply to a deputation of capitalists who asked for his papers' support in a strike: 'Gentlemen, the pennies of the working class are quite as good as yours—and there are a damn sight more of them.' The same applies to votes—not as much as in Northcliffe's day but still substantially in net terms.

And, finally, there is the *spectre de jour*, the rise in "populism," or what the media and the political classes call populism—namely, the emergence of new parties, some Left, some Right, some a blend of the two, that challenge the mainstream parties, that campaign on issues that the existing parties have neglected, and that become a serious and perhaps permanent part of the political system.

A recent issue of the *Journal of Democracy*, published by America's National Endowment for Democracy, provided a handy compendium of Europe's populist parties. Takis S. Pappas, a Greek political theorist living in Hungary, listed twenty-two different parties he cautiously calls 'challengers to liberal democracy.' Seven have held power in coalition and another four alone. I was surprised by those high numbers, and that may be because Professor Pappas includes parties—such as the socialist Pasok, which governed Greece for twenty-two years, UKIP, Italy's main opposition party, and the present governing parties of Hungary and Poland—as "populists" when some of them look to me more like conservative parties, sometimes headed by charismatic leaders. These parties are undoubtedly taking votes from the mainstream parties. The question that we should be asking about them is this: Have the populists taken these votes for the foreseeable future, thus becoming permanent contenders for power in our existing political system? Or are they merely temporary custodians of these votes that will return to the mainstream parties when their voters have completed their own transitions to different political identities with different sources of political support?

That is not, of course, the way that political establishments, existing parties, or the media, or indeed Professor Pappas want us to think about populism. As the professor sees it, these parties are not participants in democracy but challengers to it. He fears that once in power they will turn against democracy and override its constraints if they become an obstacle to the achievement of their visions. He tacitly assumes that mainstream parties can be trusted not to betray democracy in this way—the European Union's well-known 'democracy deficit' almost never strikes respectable opinion as such an infringement. And he is echoed on all these points by most other political commentators who instruct us as follows: the main choice before us today is between populism and liberal democracy. Once examined sceptically, however, that hardly seems like a choice at all. It sounds more like a slogan to conscript the voters into shunning populists and continuing to vote for what are called the 'legacy parties' without thinking too much about it.

Populism, Liberalism, and Democracy

Yet thought is required here. As we shall see, populism and liberal democracy, though common terms in the higher journalism, are slippery ones. Consider the textbook accounts of populism. Among other things, it supposedly describes a movement that is personalist, rooted in a leader-principle, hostile to the 'regime of the parties,' and based on blending Left and Right in a vague new synthesis. If that is the case, then the most successful populist leader in Europe today is Emmanuel Macron, President of France. He denounced the existing parties as corrupt and incompetent (not without some evidence). He founded a new party based around himself—EM standing for both En Marche and

Emmanuel Macron. He carefully selected parliamentary candidates and cabinet members on the basis of their loyalty to him and of their being untainted by the past. He advanced a set of policies that blended 'pro-business' economic reforms with extreme social liberalism in identity politics—combining Left and Right politics in the French context. And finally, since his election, he has sought to present himself as a national leader above politics, at one point summoning all the legislators to Versailles where he addressed them for about ninety minutes. (He got bad reviews from them and, more recently, from the voters.) Altogether Macron's performance has been, if anything, an exaggeration of what populism traditionally means.

Yet Macron is never described as populist. Quite the contrary: the EU Commission President, Jean-Claude Juncker, hailed his election as the beginning of the end of populism, and a *New York Times* analysis on Macron's recent reverses pointed to his defeat of populism as one rare success. That is because Brussels and establishment opinion generally approve of his broad ideological tendencies, which embrace such familiar policies as multiculturalism, open borders, a banking union to underpin the euro, and a kind of militant born-again Europeanism. They regard populism as a threat to these policies and so they ignore the populist aspects of the Macron victory. As generally used, therefore, populism is not a neutral dispassionate description but a "boo" word employed to discredit those called populist or at least to indicate disapproval of them. This definition of populism seeks to end debate before it begins rather than to advance or clarify it.

Liberal democracy too is a protean concept that today needs a considerable amount of clarifying. In the relatively recent past—the days of FDR and Churchill, JFK and Macmillan, Reagan and Thatcher—liberal democracy meant free competitive elections in an atmosphere of free speech, free assembly, and a free press. How could an election be free without free speech to allow full discussion of the issues? We fought the Cold War under this sign. To be sure, there were some additional liberal restraints on majority rule even then but they were modest and few in number.

In recent years, however, liberalism has come to mean the proliferation of liberal institutions—the courts, supra-national bodies, charters of rights, independent agencies, UN treaty monitoring bodies—that increasingly restrain and correct parliaments, congresses and elected officials. This shift of power was questionable when these bodies merely nullified or delayed laws and regulations. But more recently they have taken to instructing democratically accountable bodies to make particular reforms and even to impose them on the entire polity through creative constitutional and treaty interpretation. Their decisions have concerned a wide range of official powers from welfare rules through gay marriage to regulations on migration and deportation (of, among others, convicted terrorists). Liberal democracy under this dispensation becomes the undemocratic imposition of liberal policies—which, incidentally, is the core of truth in Viktor Orbán's somewhat misleading advocacy of 'illiberal democracy.'

This transfer of power has happened in part because progressive elites at the top of mainstream political parties have happily gone along with it. They did so by the simple expedients either of not discussing these issues—in the common phrase, by keeping them out of politics—or in the case of measures they favoured, by leaving the courts or regulatory agencies to carry them out and then treating their passage as a *fait accompli*. Their justification in these latter cases was that since Parliament or Congress had "failed" to pass some urgent reform, it was the duty of the courts to step in and do so. In fact legislatures had not "failed" but *refused* to pass these measures. The courts, in stepping in to do so, were therefore arrogating legislative powers to themselves and hoping to get away with it, as they usually did, by rhetorical sleight of hand.

Immigration control is one example of policies excluded by silence in many countries; European integration is an example, especially in Britain, of a policy that has been pursued in silence or behind a veil. This shift of power is almost a constitutional convention by now. The longer it continues unnoticed, the more it will determine laws and regulations, the more that electoral or parliamentary majorities will cease to be the decisive decision-makers, and the more they will become one among several stakeholders around the table. Majoritarian democracy in these conditions mutates into a system that the Hudson Institute's John Fonte calls post-democracy, in which elites and the institutions they control exercise more power than the voters and their elected representatives.

Let me illustrate this further—and by a novel route. As a journalist I have always envied social scientists because whereas the rest of us are only as good as our arguments, they enjoy the benefit of opinions that have been scientifically validated. So I am borrowing one of their techniques and expressing this stage of my argument in the form of an impressive social science diagram.

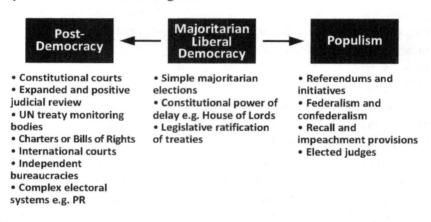

Post-Democracy	Majoritarian Liberal Democracy	Populism
• Constitutional courts • Expanded and positive judicial review • UN treaty monitoring bodies • Charters or Bills of Rights • International courts • Independent bureaucracies • Complex electoral systems e.g. PR	• Simple majoritarian elections • Constitutional power of delay e.g. House of Lords • Legislative ratification of treaties	• Referendums and initiatives • Federalism and confederalism • Recall and impeachment provisions • Elected judges

Liberalism versus Democracy?

What does the diagram tell us? It is a spectrum of constitutional powers in which the central point is liberal majoritarian democracy as it would have been understood by FDR, Churchill, JFK, Reagan, and so on. At one end of the spectrum you have post-democracy; at the other end, populism. As liberal restraints on democratic majorities increase in number and importance, the system moves towards post-democracy. As they decrease in number—or even as moves in the opposite direction towards direct democracy occur—the system moves towards populism. But every action stimulates a reaction. So as more power has shifted to liberal institutions in recent years, and as democratic majorities have become weaker as a result, the more populism has emerged to complain that the will of the voters is being ignored, and to demand it be respected, and the restraints on it removed.

That is what the recent surges of populism represent—and theorists have come to understand the fact. It was a Dutch political scientist of liberal views, Cas Mudde, who pointed out some years ago that 'populism is an illiberal democratic response to undemocratic liberalism. It criticizes the exclusion of important issues from the political agenda by the elites and calls for their re-politicization.'

But there is an equal and opposite truth to this. If majority rule remains the driving force of democracy, then populism and populist issues will be absorbed within traditional democratic debate and made subject to its conventions. The UK referendum on Brexit achieved exactly that. Once the voters had made their decision, and once the government had accepted and promised to implement it, Brexit became an orthodox part of the political debate, with the government proposing measures to implement it, the Opposition suggesting amendments to those measures, the courts hearing cases to ensure that Brexit was pursued within the rules of the political game, and so on.

It is also significant that UKIP has seen its support drain away since one mainstream party—and arguably both—adopted its signature issue and began carrying it into practical effect as the small and relatively powerless UKIP simply cannot do. This is important. As you may recall from a few minutes ago, I asked if populist parties were here for good—a permanent entry into the competition of parties—or if they were likely to fade away as other parties took up their issues. Either may happen, of course. But the UKIP case suggests that populist parties may be way-stations for discontented voters who may not know it but who are on their way to adopt new political loyalties and to join new political parties, as for example the blue-collar workers moving right.

Once we take these (fairly major) developments into account, it becomes possible to craft a definition of populism that is not simply a way of abusing a political party or jeering at its arguments without meeting them honestly and seriously. Professor Mudde has given us one such definition above: populism is an illiberal democratic response to undemocratic liberalism. Another was revealed unintentionally by

Professor Pappas when he said: 'Populist parties embrace democracy but not liberalism. Liberalism without democracy is not a combination found in real-life polities today.' It is his second sentence that discloses the definition we need. For 'liberalism without democracy' is an apt description of the system of government towards which the West has been moving since 1989, and populism is the resistance to it. And however we juggle things, the main choice facing the voters seems likely to be between some sort of democratic populism and some form of liberal or, in less deceptive language, some form of progressive elitism.

That is not formally the choice in many countries at present. But it is a choice towards which post-industrial voters and countries seem to be tending, as we saw earlier when looking at the fates of Left and Right around the world. Perhaps because of the extraordinary Macron phenomenon, French intellectuals have been examining the significance and likely results of this and other trends, and they are coming up with some persuasive, if challenging, interpretations. In particular Pierre Manent, director of studies at L'École des hautes études en sciences sociales (EHESS) in Paris, in an article translated for the new American magazine *American Affairs*, argues that populism is likely to be absorbed into a new party system *but in a negative and even destructive way.*

He sees this new system emerging ultimately from the conversion of both major traditional parties of Left and Right (in France especially but elsewhere too) to the 'European idea' from the 1970s onwards. In becoming "European" and "modern," the Left abandoned its original constituency of class—notably the working class; in making the same transition, the Right abandoned its constituency of nation. Those of their respective voters who continued to feel loyal to these particularisms and the loyalties arising from them became an embarrassment to the new model parties and an obstacle to the policies that the European idea demanded.

These policies were a set of rules for harmonizing the EU's economic arrangements, its political commitments, and even its national-cum-democratic character. They were determined by small and often secret committees of bureaucrats in Brussels and, once determined, were not really subject to amendment or repeal by "national" parties responding to the democratic objections of electorates.

If all this sounds a little abstract, the brutal treatment of Greece by the EU troika, overriding its democratic choices by fiat, will make the point: the future of Europe is determined in a political stratosphere and handed down to nations and classes which are required to endorse it as it comes. Those who object, clinging to class or nation, have therefore to be seen and slandered by their own traditional parties as various kinds of "deplorables"—"extremists," "populists," "unrespectables," as bad as "terrorists."

Some of these deplorables break away and found new parties representing their old loyalties; others cross the political spectrum to join parties that now seem more sympathetic to them; and when these defections occur, the leaderships of the mainstream, now the Centre, began to see their common interests more clearly.

Manent's essay is a rich and complex one. If these trends continue unabated, Manent thinks they will lead to a competition between an unrespectable national-populism and an arrogant cosmopolitan centrism—or, in his words, between populist demagogy and the fanaticism of the Centre.

We already see the bare bones of this in the European Parliament, where the mainstream parties of Left and Right now form a coalition against the "extremes" (that is, all the other parties). They do so in defence of European integration, globalization, supra-nationalism, overlapping jurisdictions, more or less open borders, extreme individualism, and cosmopolitan values—and *against* xenophobia, national sovereignty, respect for traditional culture, any communitarian sense of belonging, and democratic patriotism.

It is not hard to see in this list of issues an emerging competition of class interests corresponding to Goodhart's two broad new groups of Anywheres and Somewheres. Macron's victory in France, though achieved through populist methods, was a victory for this emerging centrist consensus in which Manent sees great dangers. Let me cite two dangers in particular.

First, the new political system that Manent foresees would replace an earlier system of Left versus Right in which the battle was over how to share the economic spoils. That system would be replaced by one in which the battle is over such questions as immigration control, gay marriage and the civil rights of religion, multiculturalism and the dilution of citizenship, the transfer of sovereignty to authorities outside the nation, and the loss of any sense of democratic ownership of political decisions. Battles over how to share wealth and income streams are much easier to settle than disputes over morality, ethnicity, citizenship and allegiance which, as we see in the US, can be toxic.

Second, in the old Left versus Right world, both sides essentially accepted the legitimacy of the other. They did so not by saying *Vive la différence!*, but as Manent points out, by acknowledging that the other side would win elections occasionally and when they did, they had the right to govern the country for a specified period.

He observes—I think rightly—that the centrist establishment consensus in Europe does not really accept the right of the "extremes" to come to power. When they do, it thinks it is legitimate to use supranational legal and political powers to constrain and even oust them. See the cases of Hungary, Poland, and Austria, and the imposition of refugee quotas on reluctant member-states. See also some of the reasoning behind the self-dramatizing "Resistance" to Donald Trump.

What Manent's new party system offers, therefore, is a much more partisan and bitter battle over questions that are more difficult to solve and more resistant to compromise than the world in which we grew up. And contrary to *bien pensant* progressive opinion, populist demagogy is much less to blame for the bitterness and intractability of the political battleground than is 'the fanaticism of the centre.'

Nevertheless it is important to realize, as Manent does, that these new political loyalties will not simply replace the older ones wholesale as if a new page in history has been turned. In some cases, where the national political tradition is a revolutionary one, such a complete transformation of the parties might occur. In the main, however, this new political division will infiltrate the existing parties gradually and change their characters slowly, leaving them considerably but not completely changed.

Populism and the Australian Parties

The Right versus Left battle between Capital and Labour was the dominant theme in the politics and in the political parties of all European countries for almost two centuries, but how it played out differed dramatically in Germany, France, and Britain, not to mention Russia. The same will be true of the struggle between national populists and progressive centrists. And here these changes will take place through the refracting medium of Australian political parties.

Like other political parties in the Anglosphere, Australia's parties tend to be flexible, responsive to public opinion, and skilled at adapting political ideas to national conditions. They adapt or reinvent themselves, stick around, and remake new or "foreign" ideas in Australian form.

That is why—unlike the recent changes in France—the Coalition and Labor are highly unlikely to be replaced by two parties representing a progressive elite versus national populists in pure form. If that were to happen, Labor would be the first party and the Coalition the second because that is where most of their respective voters live. But the mainstream Australian parties will want to keep centrists and populists within their own ranks. That will not be too difficult, let alone impossible; there are Left and Right populists and Left and Right progressives in Australia. Each party, realizing this, will mix a cocktail of different policies to appeal to both constituencies in the light of its own traditions.

What will those policy mixes be? I can only hazard a few rough guesses on how each of the parties will shape its policies on what look like the key issues of globalization and moral reform. I realize I am opening myself to mockery.

My guess is that the two parties will divide globalization between them. Liberals will continue to advance economic globalization (and market economics in general—on which Mr Shorten has already declared a populist war) and Labor will champion the globalization of culture and institutions. Liberals will be for free trade, Labor for open immigration. Labor will be readier to sign up to global economic regulations such as Kyoto, while the Coalition will see regulation as a national responsibility shared with others through bilateral free-trade agreements. Labor will support supra-national institutions rooted in "pooled sovereignty" and global governance; Liberals will defend an internationalism rooted in cooperation between sovereign nation states. Labor will be for a multicultural Australia that fosters multiple ethnic identities, the Liberals for policies that stress a unifying Australian one. Labor's foreign policy will rest on the UN, Liberal foreign policy on the US alliance and, perhaps increasingly, on other Anglosphere relationships. The resulting battles will be real and important but in the main not life-or-death quarrels.

There is likely to be a far sharper division between the two mainstream parties, however, on moral-cum-cultural reforms on everything from same-sex marriage to immigration control to Aboriginal history and rights to Captain Cook's "discovery" of Australia. Almost all of these issues arouse strong passions, divide both parties in ways similar to the Remain–Leave divisions in the UK, and resist compromise. Their resolution, moreover, often creates a further set of problems which means they are not settled when they are settled.

Though both parties have divisions on these issues, the signs are that Labor has decided to side with the "progressive" consensus on most of them, and where it still resists doing so (as on 'stopping the boats') it is being pushed strongly in that direction by its new progressive middle-class base in NGOs, the radical churches, the Greens, and the academic-cum-media complex.

The debate over same-sex marriage is the best current example, but it is likely to be followed by major disputes on such issues as immigration, national cohesion, language, Australian history, the nature of citizenship, the character of democracy, and even the nature of Australia itself, that reflect the 'Anywheres' side of the new political spectrum and accordingly repel Labor's earlier class constituencies.

Liberalism, Conviction, and Compromise

What does all this mean for the Liberal Party? Let me answer that with a British story. A newly-elected Labour MP was being shown around the House of Commons by an old Westminster hand. He was shown the Speaker's chair, the press gallery, Annie's bar, the smoking room, and at last the facing green leather benches in the Chamber.

"This is where we sit," said the Labour veteran, pointing to the Opposition benches.

"And is that where our enemies sit?" asked the newcomer, pointing to the other side of the House.

"No, lad," replied the older man. "That's where our opponents sit. Our enemies sit on our side of the House."

For some unaccountable reason the phrase 'Black Hand dinner' floats into my mind. Many of the most important battles in politics take place within political parties rather than between them. These are the battles that determine what goes into a party's manifesto, what broad economic strategy a party adopts, how to compensate those who lose those battles internally, how to reconcile the party in parliament with its supporters in the country over internally contentious issues, and so on.

Burke famously described a political party as a body of men formed to argue for some great purpose. That can be true—and is true—for small parties in systems of proportional representation such as the Greens in Europe and Australia. But large parties like the Tories and the Liberal Party are large coalitions of several interests—interests not merely economic but also philosophical as, for instance, social conservatives— and these groups have overlapping rather than identical interests as well as some reasons for disagreeing with other factions.

Over time political parties—rather like armies—become skilled at defusing internal rows and fostering cooperation between all their members. But they do not always succeed. Party management is always a hard task for even the most skilled politicians. And if they are to maintain party unity for most of the time, they must be able to rely on an irreducible minimum of agreement between the different party factions and the large social interests supporting them. Party members, especially MPs, have to feel that they are on the same side of most vital issues— and jointly and firmly opposed to other parties.

If that is true for party management in stable political eras, it is doubly true for times of upheaval when parties are undergoing great changes and wondering about their real character and purposes. Like, for instance, now.

In this week's *Spectator* its political correspondent, Isabel Hardman, reports on the emergence in the UK Parliament of a group of MPs who feel uncomfortable within the parties for which they were elected and are vaguely hopeful of a party alignment that will bring them together in a new centrist party.

Just today the President of the United States has tweeted an appeal to Republican supporters to vote for the GOP primary challenger to Senator Jeff Flake, who opposes the White House on immigration and other key issues. That is not unprecedented, but it ends a long period of Republican self-discipline in which the White House, Congress, and Republican National Committee machines almost always supported existing office-holders. Moreover, Trump's tweet reflects the growing divide—a veritable Grand Canyon of ideology—between himself and the Republican Congress over trade, migration, and industrial policy.

In Australia the Turnbull government has suffered a series of internal rows and political reverses stemming from the fact that Malcolm Turnbull is a socially progressive leader of a divided but largely socially conservative party.

My own view on this is drawn from Loughnane's Law, promulgated by Brian Loughnane, formerly the Liberals' federal organizer: Liberals tend to win when the leader of the Liberal Party is also the leader of the conservative movement. Be that as it may, however, if Labor is committed to one side of the argument on social-cum-cultural issues, as I argued above, then the Liberals must make a virtue of their divisions in order to capture the largest possible number of voters.

Take same-sex marriage, for instance. If Paul Kelly was right in a recent column, as I believe, its passage will not end the controversy but merely extend it to a range of other controversies over whether the equality right of gays trumps or is trumped by the civil rights of religious people and institutions. Unless some provision for protecting the rights of religious people is built into the marriage legislation, therefore, the Liberals will face a potentially endless series of disputes with one of their strongest constituencies.

Labor is likely to resist such safeguards, however, and if it loses the plebiscite, is likely to argue that "populist" democracy is unsuited to a range of "sensitive" issues on which voters are ignorant or bigoted. And that is not a comfortable case to make in a country with such a tradition of vigorous democratic debate as Australia enjoys.

Conviction politics—in this case progressive conviction politics—cannot be pursued to its logical extreme—in this case the subordination of religious rights to equality rights—by either party without serious loss. For Labor in this case it means alienating its traditional voters; for Liberals it would mean major and continuing internal disputes, the likely loss of elections, and the departure of social conservatives to found new populist parties. In the long run that purity—that principled refusal to compromise—would weaken all existing factions within Australian liberalism. And it would postpone the absorption of populism into mainstream politics when the interests of liberalism are that it should be integrated—and, if possible, integrated mainly within the Right.

The Example of Brexit

That brings me to one final point—and, happily, not a pessimistic one. Contrary to most media commentary, the Brexit referendum is almost a parable of the necessary and valuable uses of populism in politics. Opposition to British membership of the European Union never ceased to be a significant strand of political opinion. It remained at the level of about one-third of respondents, sometimes rising, sometimes falling, for the entire period since the 1975 referendum. But since the leaderships of both parties, together with most cultural institutions, strongly supported the EU, it was rarely at the centre of political debate.

The Tory Party in particular was always far more Eurosceptic than its leaders. 'Keeping Europe out of politics' only became unmanageable when Nigel Farage and UKIP fought and won elections on the issue. That compelled David Cameron to promise a referendum on EU membership.

When the referendum was held, it revealed two things: first, that once party discipline was weakened, most Tories were Leavers, and second, that once a genuine public discussion was held under rules of media neutrality, Eurosceptic opinion proved larger than expected and even grew to become a majority. In other words "populism" in the form of UKIP helped to liberate a genuine and rooted democratic sentiment that might otherwise have been suppressed.

Once the result was announced, moreover, the reaction of the Tory government in promising to implement Brexit meant that this pre-eminent "populist" cause was absorbed into the conventional party system. It became clear that the great majority of Tories were relieved that the party had embraced the cause of British sovereign independence.

It is now hard to imagine the Tories becoming a pro-EU party again, whatever the outcome of Brexit. It is gradually becoming clear also that most Labour MPs are natural Remainers—a fact hitherto obscured by the awkward fact that the Labour leader, Jeremy Corbyn, and his immediate circle, are among the minority of Labour Leavers.

As it is gradually working itself out, however, Brexit will be increasingly debated across the floor of the House and, in elections, between the voters as a Left versus Right issue more than as a populist versus centrist one. Indeed, popular support for UKIP has drained away to mainstream parties since the referendum, and Nigel Farage himself has left politics, at least temporarily, for the media. But its cause continues to win.

The lesson is that if a populist party is drawing votes from the mainstream, then the mainstream party that deals seriously with its issue will eventually win its voters even if it has to argue with them. It is a lesson John Howard never forgot and that explains why he is competing with Menzies for the title of Australia's greatest prime minister.

This is an edited version of the 2017 John Howard Lecture, delivered on August 22 in Melbourne by the author for the Menzies Research Centre, to an audience that included the Hon. John Howard. Originally published in Quadrant, *23 November 2017, https://quadrant.org.au/magazine/2017/11/conservatism-populism-conviction-politics/.*

Mistaken Identities
September 1996

Reviewing a biography of Philip Larkin some years ago in *The New Yorker*, Martin Amis gave a strong defence of Larkin against the charges of sexism, racism, moral squalor, and so on, then making the literary rounds. Much of this defence was built around the idea that Larkin had grown up and lived at a time when racism, as now defined, was so common as not to invite censure, and when sexism did not exist as a category of sin into which one could fall. But, perhaps feeling that he needed to guard Larkin against the secondary charge of making no effort at all to move when the times did, indeed of resisting any such movement with determination, Mr Amis embarked on the following philosophical exercise:

> Larkin the man is separated from us, historically, by changes in the self. For his generation, you were what you were, and that was that. It made you unswervable and adamantine. My father has this quality. I don't. None of us do. There are too many forces at work on us. There are too many fronts to cover. In the age of self-improvement, the self is inexorably self-conscious. [Larkin] couldn't change the cards he was dealt.

Amis here was making an important point and two minor mistakes. The first minor mistake was of thinking of his father, Kingsley Amis, as some kind of typical spokesman for his generation. That must be one of the stranger effects bred by familiarity. The second mistake was the familiar one of generational parochialism. We all have the illusion that the world in which we grew up was a much more stable one than that in which we make our adult way. And because life itself is a training in psychology, we naturally see ourselves and our friends as more complex, variable, and interesting than the simple manly men and womanly women whom we met around our parents' dinner table. This illusion led

Amis to get his dates wrong. The concept of the self, or of personal identity, as something changeable, uncertain, and shaped and continually reshaped by external pressures goes back at least to David Hume and, as we shall see, has been a staple of modern literature and psychology for about a century.

Amis's important insight, however, was that this concept of identity has developed so radically—the self being now seen as almost infinitely malleable—and has been so widely popularized, moving from the philosophy lecture room to the cinema, that it is now challenging a much older religious and social concept of identity, built around such ideas as conscience and the soul. This modern theory of identity has broken out of the laboratory and, as in a 1950s science-fiction movie, is stalking through the town, inserting itself into the heads of regular citizens, and transforming them into other-directed aliens. And since how we think of ourselves determines so much, from the upbringing of children to the treatment of criminals, the conflict between these two theories is of literally human proportions.

Of course, both theories start out with a great deal in common, namely, that an individual identity is put together from three elements, or three sets of elements. The first is that set of psychological abilities which seem to be innate to all human beings and which become evident in the early years of childhood. These are consciousness, memory, and the moral sense.

Consciousness makes us aware of our existence separate from others. Memory extends that awareness backward through time. And the moral sense tells us the terms on which we should deal with those others. Consciousness, memory, and the moral sense together generate that aspect of identity we call the conscience. This is more than just a voice telling us not to take wrong actions in the here and now. It forces us to feel moral responsibility for past actions, and so helps to establish identity as something that exists through time.

Let me illustrate the point. It is sometimes said of a vicious criminal who has undergone a moral transformation in prison and performed great charitable or scholarly works, that he should be released because he is clearly 'no longer the man who committed the crimes.' But would the criminal himself agree with this? Ian Brady, the Moors murderer who tortured and killed several children, became a Christian in prison. He is on record as saying that someone who has committed such crimes has indefinitely forfeited any right of release. Another such criminal might, of course, wish to be released, but almost certainly on the grounds that he had purged his offenses. If so, that too would be an admission of a continuing moral responsibility and so, in effect, a claim of identity extending through time. Indeed, the great likelihood is that criminals like the 'Birdman of Alcatraz,' who seemed to experience a moral transformation, performed their good works precisely because they felt they were the same men who had committed the monstrous crimes and they wanted to build up an equally impressive list of services on the opposite side of the moral ledger. They wanted to atone.

Conscience is, of course, common to all human beings except psychopaths and editors. Memory, consciousness, and the moral sense are, however, only the first building blocks of identity. They make us aware of our individuality, but they do not alone constitute it. The second set of qualities making up identity is our genetic inheritance from our particular parents. It is this inheritance that sets us on the road to being individuals by laying down our potential abilities, tastes, and temperaments. Psychologists seem to have established that this inheritance is extraordinarily rich and influential. We are, it seems, predisposed by our individual genes to have a particular level of IQ, to enter particular occupations, to attend particular churches, to marry a particular kind of spouse, to be law-abiding or criminal, sane or mad, healthy or sick, friendly or suspicious, party animal or wallflower, long or short-lived, and even, as W. S. Gilbert foretold, 'either a little Liberal, or else a little Conservative.'

Every school class has a class hero, a class clown, a class swot (or nerd), a class bully, a class victim, and a class athlete. These identities cling. His fellows come to expect certain kinds of behaviour from him; he learns to provide or modify them as popularity dictates.

That brings us to the third element in identity: the influence of environment. In Ira Levin's thriller, *The Boys from Brazil*, Dr Josef Mengele, contrives the birth of several clones of Hitler, genetically identical to the Führer, quite literally 'little Hitlers.' But even a dedicated Nazi like Mengele recognizes that blood is not enough. A genetic clone of Hitler, brought up in different circumstances, might become almost anything and anyone: perhaps a terrorist leader, improbably a charismatic benefactor of humankind, very likely a mediocre architect. So he arranges for the adoption of his charges by families that fit the description of Hitler's parents: a middle-aged civil servant married to a younger woman. And he completes the environmental conditioning by having the husbands murdered at the same age as Hitler's father had died.

We are left in suspense at the end of the novel as to how Mengele's plot will turn out; but it seemed to me to contain one obvious flaw. These infant Hitlers were deposited in several countries: capitalist America, social-democratic Sweden, and pre-Thatcher Britain, as well as modern Germany. There must at least be the possibility, perverse from Mengele's standpoint, of Germany's being conquered and forced to adopt a regime of politically-correct social democracy by a ruthless Swedish dictator suffering from an especially neurotic case of cognitive dissonance.

For many of the most important components of identity arise from our being born in a particular family, in a particular place, at a particular time in history, and therefore into a particular set of traditions and customs. To take the most intimate example, the first language we learn is an accident of birth. Our religious identity is something we embrace long before we can grasp its importance or implications. Our sexuality is probably determined in the main genetically, but how we regard it is at least strongly influenced by upbringing and social custom. We pick up the manners of our social class, assuming them to be universal laws of good behaviour. We have a natural tendency to emulate our parents, whether they are loving, decent, dutiful people, or selfish, neglectful, and drunken layabouts. We obtain automatic and apparently indefeasible membership in our nation or ethnic group, together with a legacy of accompanying songs, myths, and stories. And all of these things, though external and pre-existing, are absorbed by our fledgling identity and become as much a part of us as our temperament, our IQs, or our digestion. Some of the most important elements of our identity are external, accidental, and above all social.

From the point of view of the traditional theory of identity, that poses little or no problem. 'Art is man's nature,' said Burke, and man is a social animal who draws upon social materials in building his identity. Does this constitute an unnatural imposition by society upon the individual identity? Not at all. Without the influence of society, a person's identity would be like Hobbes's description of natural society: solitary, poor, nasty, brutish, and short (and, one might add, speechless.) The social elements in identity are the means whereby someone's natural gifts and disposition are made manifest to the rest of the world.

And as we grow older, we also grow increasingly discriminating in the use we make of the social elements of our identity. We reflect upon our condition and circumstances—which is why, incidentally, we cannot be successfully conditioned. We may quietly reject some of the things our parents hold dear. We may change our religion. Or take a more detached view of our country, even changing our citizenship. Or learn a new set of manners, whether as conscious social climbing or simply through frequent exposure to a different class.

As William Letwin wrote in *Policy Review*, reviewing a book by one Philip Green advocating egalitarian social policies: '"the environment" is not an objective fact which can be assessed accurately by an objective observer. Instead, each individual largely shapes his own environment by emphasizing some of its aspects while ignoring others, by interpreting its manifestations according to his own beliefs, and by directly acting upon it.' Or, as Shirley Letwin wrote in *The Anatomy of Thatcherism*: 'A human being in possession of his faculties is never merely potter's clay. He is himself both potter and clay because he necessarily decides what to make of whatever happens to him.'

What, however, is the 'person' who does this shaping and choosing? What is the entity that draws upon the different materials in 'the environment' and combines them with consciousness, memory, moral sense, and genetic endowment to shape—and perhaps, as time goes by, to reshape—a particular individual identity?

The religious answer to this question is the soul—a soul which is implicated in both the psychological dispositions of identity and the physical movements of the body. Not that the soul controls identity in a manipulative way, as a driver controls a train, but it is at the core of identity. Around it consciousness, memory, genetic endowment, language, nationality, and all the rest form, so to speak, concentric trenches, inhabited by simultaneous translators, theologians, lawyers, strategists, games-players, and, above all, public relations advisers through whom the soul deals with external reality. The result is an identity which, seen from outside, may have many facets, but which is nonetheless built around a central core.

For practical purposes, it makes little difference whether one calls this entity a soul or gives it some secular explanation such as the Freudian trio of id, ego, and superego. What matters is that both describe a central core of identity.

Of course, one cannot demonstrate such an entity, and I am aware that this account contradicts much of the current wisdom of philosophy and psychology. But it is also in accord with a psychological conviction that most people, including even sceptical philosophers, seem to hold intuitively. So, one must ask sceptics some questions: If the psychological reality of identity includes consciousness, memory, moral reasoning, practical and prudential calculation, a feeling of free will and of moral responsibility for the actions of the person (including even those actions which cannot be wholly remembered as, for instance, actions performed when drunk), how does this differ from a soul? And, furthermore, if abandoning the supposed illusion of a soul leads to dangerous practical consequences, as I shall argue, should we not pause to consider those consequences before we throw out the psyche with the psychobabble?

For it is this concept of a natural core of identity that the modern theories of identity reject—and there are a variety of identities nominated to replace the traditional one. They all, however, begin by attempting to discredit the notion of a central core of identity as possessing a reality separate from its experiences. Hume gave classic expression to this sceptical position:

For my part, when I enter most intimately into what I call myself, I always stumble on some particular perception or other, of heat or cold, light or shade, love or hatred, pain or pleasure. I never catch myself at any time without a perception, and never can observe anything but the perception. When my perceptions are removed for any time, as by sound sleep; so long am I insensible of myself, and may truly be said not to exist. [...] I may venture to assert of the rest of mankind that they are nothing but a bundle or collection of different perceptions, which succeed each other with an inconceivable rapidity and are in a perpetual flux and movement. [...] The mind is a kind of theatre, where several perceptions successively make their appearance; pass, re-pass, glide away, and mingle in an infinite variety of postures and situations. There is properly no simplicity in it at one time, nor identity in different; whatever natural propension we may have to imagine that simplicity and identity.

If there is no there there, however, how can we account for the illusion of one? Quite simply. The most common explanation is that the identity is a false one put there by other people: your parents, your neighbours, your countrymen, and, if you are a child of seven or under, the Jesuits. This false identity consists not only of the digested influences of class, nation, locality, sex, and so on, but also of the moral consciousness we feel to exist at the centre of our being. So even if there is some kind of instinctual moral sense, as James Q. Wilson argues, the moral rules through which it expresses itself have been put there by other people—respectable society, your parents, the church. For one school of theorists, notably Marxism, liberation consists precisely of freeing yourself from this kind of false consciousness.

According to philosophies more radical than vulgar Marxism, however, the man who liberates himself from this primitive prison of false identity does not thereby achieve autonomy. No such luck. He stumbles out onto a crowded stage, and he is there handed a variety of masks which he assumes in response to the hints, shouts, murmurs, and prompts from other actors in a play jointly co-authored by Hume and the Italian dramatist Luigi Pirandello. Here is Laudisi, a character in Pirandello's *It Is So If You Think So*, explaining the theory to Signora Sirelli:

Laudisi: Now, you have touched me, have you not? And you see me? And you are absolutely sure about me, are you not? Well now, madam, I beg of you; do not tell your husband, nor my sister, nor my niece, nor Signora Cini here, what you think of me; because, if you were to do that, they would all tell you that you are completely wrong. But, you see, you are completely right: because I am really what you take me to be; though, my dear madam, that does not prevent me also being really what your husband, my sister, my niece, and Signora Cini take me to be—because they too are absolutely right!

Signora Sirelli: In other words you are a different person for each of us.

Here is a world in which identities are created by situations. What holds a personality together really is a set of skills for coping with external reality. Identities are mere roles or masks we use to deal with other people. In which case, of course, our identities are in effect created by others in a much more radical sense than in the theories of Freud or Marx. In the primitive notions of false consciousness, the villains plant their ideas in our heads and then depart, leaving us with our personal neuroses and reactionary social ideas. But in the more radical versions, other people are constantly rewiring the insides of our heads.

These ideas have spread widely in philosophy, sociology, psychology, and dinner-table conversation, so that people as different as psychologist Robert J. Lifton, with his notion of the Protean self, or David Riesman, with his idea of the 'other-directed man,' may be thought to be expressing variations on them. It is, however, Woody Allen who has produced the *reductio ad absurdum* of this theory in his film *Zelig*—the story of a man so responsive to the expectations of others and the influences of social environment that he becomes in succession a radical Communist, a Hooverite conservative, an orthodox Jew, and a Nazi. And, of course, he is able to assume these various identities convincingly because he is conscious of an inner emptiness—the lack of an authentic identity of his own. Here then is the existential choice offered to us by the modern theories of identity: we can be either the puppets of other people, dummies surrounded by ventriloquists, or we can be the landlords of a vacant lot.

This is, of course, an intolerable choice. But it comes accompanied by an attractive escape hatch: if other people can insert a false identity into the empty space in my head, can I perhaps insert an authentic self there in its place? Authentic because it is rationally chosen and consciously shaped by myself rather than being simply a psychological 'given' that I gradually discover in childhood and adolescence. And the principle upon which this new identity can be selected is the best bonus of all. That principle has been laid down by the greatest living American psychologist, Tom Wolfe, in his essay 'The Me Decade.' It began life as an advertising slogan for a shampoo: 'If I have only one life to live, let me live it as a blonde.'

The charm of this principle for constructing a new identity is that it is almost infinitely accommodating. It enables us to say to ourselves: If I have only one life to live, let me live it as … (fill in the blank)—as a Noble Proletarian, as an Irishman (provided, of course, that I do not start out as Irish), as a woman (if, similarly, I do not happen to be a woman), as a European (from no particular European nation, naturally), or as a proud member of the community of the deaf. (Some of these options will become clearer in due course.)

To the old question, 'Is there a ghost in the machine?,' we can now answer: No, but there is a consumer. The consumer selects his new identity from the vast range of moral possibilities that the modern world throws up. In its simplest form, the new identity is constructed by selecting one facet of one's actual given identity, and elevating it to the whole, or at least to a dominant part, of the personality. George Orwell forecast this process of reification in a 1948 review of Sartre's *Portrait of an Anti-Semite*:

> 'The' anti-Semite, he seems to imply all through the book, is always the same kind of a person, recognizable at a glance and, so to speak, in action the whole time. Actually one has only to use a little observation to see that anti-Semitism […] in any but the worst cases, is intermittent. But [this] would not square with Monsieur Sartre's atomized view of society. There is, he comes near to saying, no such thing as a human being, there are only different categories of men, such as 'the' worker, and 'the' bourgeois, all classifiable in much the same way as insects.

A recent example of this kind of identity building is the gay identity. For a gay is not simply a homosexual; he is someone who has made homosexuality the basis of an entire personality and outlook—morals, politics, and social relations. This will tend to make him, or her, hostile to societies traditionally organized to favour heterosexuality and the family, and persuade him to advocate policies that seek not tolerance but the transformation of popular or traditional attitudes toward homosexuality.

Needless to say, this kind of response is by no means universal among homosexuals. Even today when pressures such as 'outing' seek to enforce a gay identity on all homosexuals, many of them take the view that homosexuality is just one facet of their identity—whether an advantage, or a curse, or simply a slightly awkward fact about themselves—which has little bearing on the rest of their lives outside the bedroom. Their support for sexual reform will tend to go no further than social tolerance and the repeal of punitive laws. They may find the gay identity mysterious, alien, too narrow to express their entire personality, and even repellent.

Here, in a passage from Noel Coward's diary, is the response of one such homosexual (by no means a repressed one) to the gay milieu of Fire Island in New York:

> I came back last night having spent Saturday and yesterday on Fire Island. I don't think I shall ever go again. It is lovely from the point of view of beach and sun and wearing no clothes, but the atmosphere is sick-sick-sick. Never in my life have I seen such concentrated abandoned homosexuality. It is fantastic and difficult to believe. I wished really that I hadn't gone. Thousands of queer young men of all shapes and sizes camping about blatantly and carrying on—in my opinion—appallingly. Then there were all the lesbians glowering at each other. Among this welter of brazen perversion wander a few 'straights,' with children and dogs. I have always been of the opinion that a large group of queer men was unattractive. On Fire Island it is more than unattractive, it's macabre, sinister, irritating, and somehow tragic.

Self-conscious identity building is very different from the earlier argument of Bill and Shirley Letwin that traditional identity can be modified by the reason when it decides to emphasize some aspects of one's environment at the expense of others. The difference is subtle but important and it has immense consequences. It is the difference between piecemeal self-improvement and the wholesale reconstruction of the personality. Someone attempting piecemeal reform will usually refer to what he is doing in modest terms—'I'm trying to be more punctual.' Someone engaged in ideological reconstruction of himself will, appropriately enough, see it in dramatic, even religious terms, as becoming a different sort of human being. He will be re-making himself in accordance with some revelation, either some new principle of reason outside himself, or some inner prompting of the personality, or even both—some impulse extracted from inside himself and expanded into a universal truth about human nature. Thus a lesbian, uncomfortable with femininity, will eventually be struck by the blinding revelation that all gender roles are socially constructed.

Such illumination is not confined to the Left. An example of this kind of self-conscious identity politics on the political Right is the ideological definition of American nationality—the claim that America is unlike other nations in that its nationality is neither ethnic nor cultural, but consists of embracing the principles of liberty and equality set out in the Declaration of Independence and embodied in the Constitution. To be sure, there *is* an ideological component in American nationality which the Declaration in particular dramatizes. (That is not, of course, unique to America; all nations which have played a part in world history as well as their own, notably the French, have furnished such ideological explanations of themselves.) But that ideology, important though it is, is merely the conscious political expression—the distillation—of a much more extensive national culture which is the result of a common language, history, institutions, and, overall, the shared experience of living together in the same territory.

An episode in the Second World War is instructive here. During the Battle of the Bulge, German commandos were roaming around in American uniforms, and GIs seeking to establish the true identity of other soldiers asked questions to test their Americanism. Did they ask their view of equality or rights of popular government? Of course not;

mere ideas of that kind could be parroted—indeed, genuinely believed—by non-Americans. No, they asked them details of American life in the broadest cultural context—the winner of the previous World Series, radio advertising jingles, the capital of their home state, Mae West's bust measurement. In short, the kinds of things that every American would know—but that a foreigner could not easily study. In his book *The Blood-Dimmed Tide*, Gerald Astor describes how two Allied generals coped:

> General Omar Bradley said: 'Three times I was ordered to prove my identity by cautious GIs. The first time by identifying Springfield as the capital of Illinois (my questioner held out for Chicago); the second time by locating the guard between the center and tackle on a line of scrimmage; the third time by naming the then-current spouse of a blonde called Betty Grable. Grable stopped me (the correct answer was bandleader Harry James) but the sentry did not. Pleased at having stopped me he [...] passed me on.'
>
> General Montgomery [...] imperiously directed his driver to ignore the sentry. The guard shot out the tires of his car and held the British commander for several hours. When he heard of the incident, Eisenhower enjoyed one of his few laughs during the Bulge.

In short, what shapes Americans and American national identity is the richness of the entire culture, not merely its conscious political expression.

But cannot someone become an American? And if so, does that not establish the validity of the idea of American national identity as something to be chosen rather than merely accepted? That is certainly the view inherent in America's civic religion of itself and regularly intoned by judges who, when swearing in new US citizens, assure them that they are every bit as American as the descendants of the Pilgrim Fathers. It is, however, a pious fallacy. A new US citizen may have as many legal rights as a native-born American, but he has not been as shaped by the American experience. And if he has really become an American out of sympathy for liberal principles, then his American identity ought to wax and wane in response to the course both of American history and of his own convictions. Suppose that America fails to live up to his political views? Or that he changes those views? Very likely, a consistent philosopher would be feeling twinges of disloyalty at the end of the first week.

A truer version of becoming an American would be that it is a process that is only perceived in retrospect. A foreign resident who has married an American, brought up American children, lived an American life in all the everyday respects from school to supermarket, and worried through the nation's crises, will one day wake up to find that he has become an American. He will find himself unselfconsciously using the pronoun 'we' when referring to Americans. No decision was necessary; no decision could have worked this transformation. Becoming an American is the same process for an immigrant as for a native-born child: living in America. US citizenship is merely a legal ratification of this psychological evolution.

Once identity becomes a matter of choice or conscious decision, however, a Rubicon has been crossed. For there are more radical ways of creating a new identity, whether sexual or national, than by overemphasizing a facet of one's given identity or by accommodating oneself to some external vision. One can adopt another's identity entirely. Thus transvestism is a half-way house of sexual identity politics; but transsexualism is the more radical assertion that one can choose not merely to ape another sexual identity, but even to embrace it in the fullest sense. This is a delusion, of course, since men who have transformed themselves into make-believe women are not genetically female and cannot perform central female roles such as, for instance, giving birth. Nonetheless, taking this delusion to its logical extent, Shulamith Firestone, a radical feminist, has advocated genetic engineering to allow men and women to choose which sexual role—impregnation or child-bearing—they wish to undertake. In reality, this would amount to the deliberate creation of freaks. But it signifies that even nature is no longer seen as a constraint upon identity because literally nothing is impossible for someone determined to become his own creator.

Given the spirit of the age, we could hardly expect such metaphysical ventures to be left to individual enterprise. And indeed

American bureaucrats and the Ford Foundation have created an entire *ethnic* identity by a stroke of the pen. In 1973, in order to establish a rational structure for affirmative action quotas, the Office of Management and Budget (OMB) promulgated Statistical Directive Number 13, as Michael Lind describes in *The Next American Nation*, dividing Americans into five ethnic groups, of which the most creative concoction is Hispanic. Now, Hispanics are not a national group; they include Cubans, Mexicans, Columbians, Chileans, even Spaniards. Nor are they a racial category—since they cover whites, blacks, and Amerindians. Nor—and this is a surprise—are they even a linguistic category, because they include people with Spanish surnames from families which have not spoken Spanish for generations, or as in the case of some Mexican Amerindians, from families which have never spoken Spanish at any time in history.

But since being Hispanic has certain practical advantages—for instance, being the beneficiary of the quota spoils system, or receiving money from the Ford Foundation to advance Hispanic interests—there are now a considerable number of Americans, generally in academia but not exclusively so, who think of themselves as possessing this Hispanic identity. Indeed, as Linda Chavez pointed out, it is quite difficult for anyone with a Spanish surname to escape being educated in Spanish in the public schools, even if they cannot speak the language. The bureaucrats insist that they must be brought up, for the sake of their authentic identity, in their own culture—even though it is *not* their culture and, indeed, insofar as it is a hybrid-Hispanic culture, may not be anyone's culture, except possibility that of an Obama cabinet appointee.

Can we see any common elements uniting these proliferating invented identities? Let me suggest three: first, they are stark and impoverished compared to 'given' identities; second, they are self-conscious and precarious; and third as Kenneth Minogue has pointed out, they are the adversaries of traditional identities.

It goes almost without saying that an identity built upon one facet of a personality will be impoverished alongside the richness of an identity that reflects the full range of influences upon a life. The Marxist categories of proletarian and bourgeois are useless except as economic categories. An identity based upon the fact that you work for wages and are alienated from the product of your labour is no identity at all. If a young Marxist intellectual were to ask for advice on how to live a good proletarian life, what advice would we give him? It would almost certainly not include, say, the breeding of racing pigeons, or buying a garden allotment, though both are important components of a genuine working-class life in Northern England.

Compare, on the other hand, the richness of traditional social identities like that, for instance, of 'the gentleman.' As Shirley Letwin demonstrates in her book *The Gentlemen in Trollope*, this is a subject yielding not only sharp and subtle social observations (and satires), but also a rich vein of moral criticism. One might say, in relation to our topic, that the gentleman in Letwin is the highest example of moral reason operating piecemeal to improve the personality from the material within it. False social identities, which tend to reconstruct the personality in accord with some ideal, inevitably produce a one-dimensional man— the Soviet proletarian, for instance, an examination of whose moral character can sustain nothing more complex than a cartoon or a socialist-realist painting (which may be hard to distinguish from a cartoon).

Second, in addition to being thin, invented identities are also extremely precarious. The more natural our identity is, the more we take it for granted. Self-consciousness is the constant companion of uncertainty. We are self-conscious on entering the room at someone else's party, conscious of other people's needs and enjoyment when we give a party at home. A good example of self-consciousness as the attribute of an uncertain identity occurs in Thomas Mann's *Felix Krull*. Krull, the hero, is travelling in a comfortable first-class train compartment, for all intents and purposes a young aristocrat. As a train attendant is leaving his compartment, Krull smiles at him—a smile, he says, 'that assuredly confirmed him in his conservative principles to the point where he would gladly have fought and died for them.' Or as another translation says: 'It was a smile that did more for the stability of the social order than a thousand conservative pamphlets.'

The point, however is that Krull is not a young aristocrat; he is a confidence trickster. It is extremely doubtful that a real aristocrat would react in this way. He would simply be less conscious of his impact—flaunting his identity only when expected marks of deference were not paid to him. But the confidence man has to calculate such effects with precision because his hold on an aristocratic identity is extremely precarious.

Hence the phenomenon of the marginal patriot—the outsider who seeks to demonstrate his commitment to, say, a national identity by being more nationalistic than thou. John Stephenson, a Paddington-born man of uncertain ancestry, thus became Sean MacStiofain, the chief of staff of the IRA in the 1970s. MacStiofain succeeded heroically, or rather anti-heroically, in his identity as an Irish patriot, going so far as to launch a hunger strike. Near death, however, he gave up the strike, at which point his IRA colleagues suddenly realized he had been an Englishman all along. His Irish identity had always been precarious; it depended ultimately upon his performing heroic feats.

Another instance is the eagerness with which many homosexuals greet any scientific work that suggests that homosexuality may be rooted in the genes. In theory, they need not worry about the tyranny of nature in relation to sexual identity. 'Queer theory,' like feminist theory, is supposed to have established that gender is socially constructed. Yet they give an almost desperate endorsement to the authority of science and nature when that seems likely to support the naturalness and thus inevitability of the identity that appeals to them.

Third—and most significant—the invented identity is both parasitic and adversarial with respect to the real thing. An invented identity, as we saw above, will model itself on an existing one. Homosexual families mimic traditional families by copying the parental role and demanding such perquisites as pension rights for domestic partners. But they are unable to perform important aspects of the role, such as childbearing, and they are often unwilling to accept its disciplines, such as sexual fidelity. Invented national identities similarly copy the outward shell of real nations. For instance, the European Union is gradually acquiring a flag, an anthem, citizenship, and even an army without the prior substance of a single European people with a sense of community and allegiance.

But although they may be fraudulent, these imitations of identity naturally weaken the real identities, whether of family or of nation, by sucking the significance out of the customs and practices that traditionally bolster them. If, for instance, unofficial and transient relationships have their financial arrangements underpinned by the state, then the family derives no special significance from the fact that its own arrangements are similarly protected.

But the hostility of the invented identity goes beyond this parasitism. As Kenneth Minogue has pointed out in *Alien Powers*, the first impulse of someone who has thrown off his old identity and embraced a new one is an evangelical impulse. He wants to tell everyone that once he was blind, that now he sees, but that they are still blind. And what he sees is that his old identity was a fraud and an imposition, and that their current identity still is. Hence, new identities tend to attack and seek to replace their counterparts among existing identities. The gay or feminist identity will define itself by opposition to the traditional sexual identities of male and female. These it will decry as socially constructed and consequently false and oppressive—'Heterosexism' in the approved jargon.

In the case of national identities, the rivalry between ideological nationalisms—analysed with such devastating irony by Elie Kedourie in his classic book *Nationalism*—and taken-for-granted, hand-me-down ethnocultural nationalisms can be especially vicious. For pre-existing loyalties are generally an obstacle to the new national identity that is striving to be born. And since ideological nationalists act upon Charles Stewart Parnell's principle that 'no man has the right to fix the boundary of the march of a nation,' the opposition may legitimately face extirpation. Sometimes, literally so—real people and real peoples were murdered in the campaign to create a new Soviet man.

At other times, ideological nationalism leads to polemics and the slow erosion of former loyalties rather than to Golgotha. Thus the Canadian nationalist identity—the officially fostered bilingual one, manufactured in Ottawa—defines itself by a hostility to the actual nationalisms of Quebec and English Canada, particularly the latter since it is the nationalism of the majority. It is also markedly hostile to the seductive English-speaking American identity next door; the first claim of a Canadian nationalist is that he is 'not American.' Similarly, the Euro-nationalism of Brussels is constantly engaged in polemics against its rivals, the traditional patriotisms of France, Britain, and other European countries which it blames for past wars, racism, and all the fashionable vices.

And in the United States, the theory that America is a nation of immigrants held together only by allegiance to liberal political ideas is in a state of constant tension with the actual American historical identity. For it implies that America is the whole world in microcosm, that everyone is in principle an American, and that therefore America's actual English-speaking culture is merely the property of an ethnic group or a temporary majority and does not deserve to be 'privileged' as the culture of the whole society. (That America's liberal constitutionalism has grown in this soil and might wither in any other is a problem that is only now forcing itself on our attention.) Hence, this deracinated philosophical Americanism is now the carrier of multiculturalism, which holds that America is indeed a constitutional umbrella of liberal political ideas, but one sheltering not individuals but the ethnocultural identities of Anglos, Hispanics, blacks, etc. Ideological Americanism thereby helps to deconstruct America in the most literal sense by making it a loose federation of cultural identities. The parable of the Tower of Babel might have been invented to describe this progress from hubris to incoherence.

What does all this matter? One might suppose that a theory holding that identity is infinitely plastic—a succession of masks chosen in response to the applause of others as much as for the satisfaction of one's (hypothetical) self—would tend to social peace. After all, have not conflicts until now been clashes between the hard and supposedly unyielding identities of nation, class, and ethnicity? Surely a widespread acceptance of the malleability of identity would lead to a tolerance of other identities as equally valid (or bogus) as one's own. Perhaps it would even lead to the construction of a supra-identity of tolerance within which all these identity sub-cultures could comfortably co-exist— a kind of Austria-Hungary of moral visions in which the ruling power demands only the mildest of allegiances, one easily compatible with the identity's integrity.

Alas, it does not seem to be working out that way. Social conflict between different groups seems to be multiplying in lockstep with the increased popularity of the theory of malleable identity.

We can imagine why. There are more identities around, to begin with. A plastic identity is, in principle, arbitrary and limitless. There is literally no group, however arbitrarily selected, which cannot conceive of itself as possessing one and thus forming a particular 'community.' Indeed, the number of groups which claim such basis for affiliation are multiplying rapidly. The late Aaron Wildavsky once calculated, tongue in cheek, that groups of this kind (including women, blacks, Eskimos, Hispanics and the disabled) added up to more than three-hundred per cent of the American people.

Even the process of expansion can sometimes provoke conflict when some members of the group have no wish to share in the proffered identity, and the group as a whole seeks to bring them into line. The outing of private homosexuals by gay activists is just such a conflict which arises when identity is as much a cause as a given fact. Still more extravagant, some ideologues have argued that the deaf are a self-conscious community with their own language, culture, and identity. Spokesmen for their organization—the National Association for the Deaf—have at times denounced attempts to enable the deaf to hear as cultural genocide. They have even lobbied the Federal government to prevent parents of deaf children from relieving their deafness through an operation that surgically installs a hearing device in a child's head and allows him to develop normal hearing and speech skills. (I should, in all honesty, add that the chairman of the study group that made this recommendation is not himself deaf.)

More significantly, identity is not just how we feel about ourselves; to be truly satisfying, our identity needs to be recognized by others. Yet imagine how difficult it must be for some of the groups now in existence to be treated as possessing true identities by the rest of society. For instance, there is the S&M community, which meets in various clubs with names such as The Dungeon. This is a group of sadists and masochists who, according to a 1994 article in *New York Magazine*, formed the Eulenspiegel Society, a 'masochists' rights' group in 1971.

Sadists were admitted later—doubtless the first expression of the masochists' rights the organization exists to protect. In an absolutely wonderful paradox, they complain that they are oppressed by society because they are forced to conceal their lifestyles.

Such forms of identity politics promise long-running cultural wars. There is little prospect that most people, even those privately attracted to these sexual practices, will ever be prepared to grant any sort of respectable social status, let alone official standing, to the Eulenspiegel Society and similar groups. But these groups will continue to push for recognition, legal and otherwise. An organization of pedophiles did manage to get itself recognized, first, as a non-governmental organization by the United Nations through its membership in a larger gay coalition, and subsequently as a tax-exempt educational group in its own right. These caused political rows, and its UN accreditation was later withdrawn. But we may expect the demand for recognition by this and similar groups to be renewed.

And when the demand is resisted, or even when it is conceded without enthusiasm, the disappointed group will seek to force a deeper acceptance from others. As the philosopher John Gray has pointed out, tolerance is no longer enough for such groups because it implies that the thing tolerated merits disapproval. And disapproval will seem especially insulting when a question of identity is at stake. If a practice someone performs or a belief he holds excites disapproval, he may be wounded or privately bitter. If his very identity excites disapproval, then he will become outraged and demand a more substantive surrender by his critics, perhaps even the repression of their objections ('hate speech'). In this context, you might say that the pedophiles want to make us cry uncle. They are a long way from success as yet. But the larger gay community has been quite successful in transforming the moral disapproval of its critics into a medical-cum-psychological disorder called 'homophobia,' the main symptom of which is being accused of it.

What maximizes the likelihood of conflict is that this very refusal to extend approval may be implicit in some other identity. For instance, not even the most multicultural feminist can extend tolerance, let alone approval, to an Islamic identity because of its narrow concept of women's education. Similarly, the Afrocentrist or Hispanic activist is likely to reject the political arrangements and electoral boundaries based upon a non-racial or monocultural concept of American identity and demand forms of political representation which treat ethnic groups as the building blocks of political society. Hence, the emergence of legal theories, in the writings of Lani Guinier and others, that would revive 'fancy franchises' and 'concurrent majorities' on the underlying assumption that minorities and majorities are not continually forming and reforming on different issues, but permanently frozen along ethnic and racial lines. Hence, in numberless ways, the multiplication of chosen identities leads to endless social conflict.

When modern psychologists and modernist writers began deconstructing what they thought was the prison of a rigid and unreflecting identity, they doubtless thought they were liberating the citizens to stroll about in free and equal relationships without bumping into the barriers of race, gender, ethnicity, and class. What they were in fact doing was laying the epistemological ground for a low-intensity civil war.

Originally published in The New Criterion *(September 1996),* *https://newcriterion.com/issues/1996/9/mistaken-identities.*

Two Visions of a Europe Invaded by the Third World: Did Either Get It Right?

30 April 2001

In February 2001, a rusty, decrepit freighter named the *East Sea* ran aground on the Cote d'Azur near Saint-Tropez. Its captain and crew fled, and when police and medical teams arrived on the vessel, they found 900 people—250 men, 180 women, and 480 children—cooped up in the hold. Mainly Iraqi Kurds, they had paid gangs approximately $4,500 per adult and $2,000 per child to be smuggled into Western Europe. In return for this money, they had squatted in a hot, filthy, pitch-black hold, with no ventilation and almost no food or water, for a voyage of eight days. About a dozen swam ashore and disappeared. The rest were abandoned to the attentions of French immigration authorities, most asserting that they were political refugees seeking asylum, many that they were heading for Britain, which has (by European standards) relatively liberal asylum laws.

If these details sound dramatic, the event itself was no more than an everyday occurrence on the borders of Western Europe from the Baltic to Sicily. The Mediterranean trade in refugees has already produced far worse tragedies than that of the *East Sea*: smugglers in fast boats have thrown babies overboard in the Adriatic to divert their pursuers; and a Dutch truck driver has just been sentenced to 14 years in prison for murdering 58 Chinese illegal immigrants, found dead—of suffocation—in a container in Dover last June.

Robert Fox of London's liberal *Evening Standard* estimates that there are between 10 million and 20 million illegal immigrants in Western Europe—the large discrepancy depends on whether you calculate that one known illegal immigrant equals three or five unknown ones—and the number of new arrivals is increasing as the smugglers hone their skills.

Western Europe is not, of course, exceptional in this regard. The recent Census suggests that the illegal immigrant population in the US is 11 million people—almost double the previous official estimate. The borders with Canada and Mexico are notoriously porous; a combination of smuggling rings, liberal asylum laws, cheap air travel, and sympathetic ethnic diasporas ensures that the trade is hard to stop, both practically and politically.

Most of the time, therefore, it is ignored. It takes the beaching of an *East Sea*, or of the ships carrying Chinese migrants to Vancouver in the summer of 1999, or of the *Golden Venture* off Queens in New York in 1993, to shake us out of our complacency; and even then, the effect is transitory. The *Golden Venture* held 300 Chinese migrants who had paid $20,000–$35,000 to criminals for their passage; it was the twenty-fourth such ship known to have reached America this way (many more make it without being discovered by the Immigration and Naturalization Service). Most of the illegal arrivals sought asylum, and—because their plight is truly a tragic one—we do not have the heart to deport them. None of those on the *Golden Venture* has returned home; none of those on the *East Sea* will do so; all will reach some haven in the First World. And because their friends and relatives back home know this, a slow, gradual, peaceful invasion of a wealthy First World by an impoverished Third World will proceed essentially unhampered—exactly as Jean Raspail predicted in 1973, though not exactly in the manner he predicted.

Raspail is a distinguished French author whose novel, *The Camp of the Saints*, was published in 1973. (The English translation has been recently republished by the Social Contract Press of Petoskey, Michigan.) Set at some point in 1973's future (about now, in fact), it tells how the impoverished Calcutta masses spontaneously board rusty old freighters and sail off to find the earthly paradise of Western Europe—more precisely, the Cote d'Azur. As their long voyage drags out, the Western powers, in particular the French government, anxiously debate how to keep them at bay—in vain, because the huddled masses on the leaky tubs are wielding the one weapon against which the West is

Two Visions of a Europe Invaded by the
Third World: Did Either Get It Right?

105

defenceless: its own sense of common humanity. Only a handful of Frenchmen (including a naturalized Indian from the former French colony of Pondicherry) have the ruthlessness to defend France and Western civilization by firing on the unarmed Indians and their local hippie fellow travellers. The political, cultural, religious, and media elites comfort themselves with universalistic slogans ('We're all from the Ganges now'). Ordinary Frenchmen swallow these placebos complacently until the truth dawns; and when it is too late to halt the inflow, they flee inland. The Calcutta masses arrive, sweep all before them, and eradicate the 'Camp of the Saints' where a few armed resisters have gathered. These perish, gaily singing 'Je ne regrette rien' as they are bombed by the new collaborationist government's planes as well as overwhelmed by the alien horde. At the end of the novel, France and the West have succumbed to a kind of ethnic Marxism in which "anti-racism" is the governing ideology and a multicultural society wallows in a combination of Soviet inefficiency and Eastern fatalism.

Raspail's novel got what are politely described as mixed reviews. *The New York Times* gave it two dissections, the first comparing it to a 'perfervid racist diatribe' and dismissing it as 'bilge,' the second giving a slightly more measured verdict ('preposterous,' 'banal,' etc.). Other hostile notices were 'a fascist fantasy … a disgusting book' (*Newsday*) and 'a psychotic fantasy' and 'a dull and stupid book' (*Providence Journal*). The friendlier reviews generally saw it not as a realistic novel, but as a nightmare of symbolism and a novel of ideas: e.g. 'a terrifying nightmare and a sedulous polemic' (*Louisville Courier-Journal*). But even many of the friendly reviewers were troubled by the thought that Raspail's vision, however profound, was tainted by racism.

No such hostility greeted the almost identical thesis, 17 years later, of a BBC film, *The March*, in which the Third World's invasion of Europe was seen in a broadly favourable light. *The March* depicted the impoverished inhabitants of a Sudanese village and refugee camp suddenly deciding to march to the earthly paradise of the European Community. The task of formulating a response falls to a compassionate European Commissioner who is a lookalike for former Irish president (now UN human rights commissioner) Mary Robinson.

As the poor Sudanese marchers make their slow way to the Straits of Gibraltar, the European Commission fruitlessly debates what to do. The Mary Robinson character wants to admit some of the marchers in orderly stages while increasing aid to Sudan; others argue that this will merely encourage a mass Third World exodus; most simply want to get the discussion over with. Europe accordingly does too little, too late: the marchers cross the straits in commandeered boats, are met by armed soldiers, and stand facing them in their quest for justice. The film ends with this stalemate.

Of the many differences between these two fascinating and prophetic works, three stand out.

One: Cultural Identity. While *The March* is a secular political drama about the distribution of economic resources, *The Camp* is a mystical and symbolic nightmare about what is now called the clash of civilizations. In the BBC film, the marchers are inspired by a simple vision of a better life in Europe: they want McDonalds. In Raspail, the stakes are higher— as hints are scattered of an assault by the Eastern gods on the dying God of the Christian West. The illiterate Ganges peasant who leads the Calcutta masses quotes from the *Book of Revelation*; the "Saints" who resist to the end have the same names as heroes who fought the Turks at Lepanto; the deformed monster-child of the Ganges peasant suffers a violent spasm at exactly 3 p.m. on Good Friday; the end of the West takes place at Easter. Even the physical descriptions of the 'Last Chance Armada' as a stinking, formless humanity with a single instinctual drive—descriptions that have given most justification to the charge of racism—constitute a metaphor for Raspail's view of Asian civilizations as torpid, fatalistic, and anti-individualist.

Not that the Saints are saintly, or even Christian. They are prepared to fire on the unarmed invaders (unlike Raspail himself, who—in a 1982 afterword—confessed that he himself 'would not have had the courage to fire one shot when brought face to face with those hordes of living breathing misery'). Insofar as they are faithful to Christian tradition, it is more because it is their tradition than because they are Christians. Even some of the orthodox clergy among them are privately sceptics, defending the faith for the sake of the faithful. These last defenders of

Christian Europe may die like Chestertonians, with a merry smile on their lips; but they justify their actions like Straussians guarding the sacred lie, and they kill with the ruthless despair of Nietzscheans. Christian Europe loses in the end because no European truly believes in it.

Two: Economic Justice. In *The March*, the justification of the Third World invasion is 'We are poor because you are rich.' The best response that the faux Mary Robinson can muster to this—'It's more complicated than that'—is virtually an admission of her opponent's charge. We are given here a debate between the radical left-winger and the agonized liberal, with no recognition that a more sceptical conservative position is possible. In fact, the reason that the West has a greater share of the world's resources is that it created those resources in the first place. Oil in the ground is not a resource until it is extracted, transported, and used in new inventions like automobiles and airplanes at prices that compete with whale oil and other substitutes. Malayan rubber trees were not a native resource until the British imported rubber trees from Brazil. And so on, ad infinitum.

In other words, we are rich because we are productive. If no such thought disturbs *The March*, it is a theme threaded throughout *The Camp*. Raspail sees the West as an economically productive civilization, but one that is psychologically weak. Not only has it lost belief in itself, but it has done its sums and calculated that 700 million white Westerners cannot permanently withstand 7 billion 'Others.' Seen in this light, justice is much more a matter of numbers than of desert.

Three: Geopolitical Power. Each work is a product of its time. *The March*, produced in 1990 only months after the end of the Cold War, shows the West as ineffective, ambivalent, bureaucratic, and hypocritical—but not as a complete pushover. Although the film ends with a standoff, we know from previous scenes that a British officer—unsympathetic—has orders to resist the Sudanese incursion with force. We will have to deal with the just demands of the Third World one day, argues Mary Robinson; for the moment, however, we may be able to maintain our privileged position. We had, after all, just seen off the Soviet Union.

In *The Camp*, by contrast, France simply collapses, the Asiatic masses engulf the West, and a new world comes into being—"anti-racist," anti-Western, anti-individualist, anti-capitalist, and collectivist both materially and spiritually. From the perspective of 2001, this looks less like a vision of the future than an extrapolation of the 1970s—when OPEC's quadrupling of oil prices and America's defeat in Vietnam, inter alia, led to a widespread sense on the Left that it was only a matter of a few years before Communist Third World guerrillas turned up to announce closing time in the gardens of the West. In those days, a Third World invasion of the West was not a right-wing nightmare but a left-wing daydream. Raspail merely turned the dream upside down and described its course with a bitter aristocratic irony.

The future, of course, turned out very differently—thanks, in particular, to Ronald Reagan, Margaret Thatcher, and the peoples of the then-captive nations. As a result, though the Third World is actually thronging westwards—as predicted by *The Camp* and *The March*—the nature of its incursion is very different from those fictional accounts.

Who would have foreseen, for instance, that this 'brown invasion' would include a regiment of blondes? Yet the economic and spiritual collapse of the Soviet world, making prostitution the most attractive career path for Eastern-bloc schoolgirls (according to a Russian opinion poll in the early 1990s), has sent hordes of nubile young Russians, Ukrainians, Latvians, Lithuanians, Estonians, Poles, Hungarians, Czechs, and Albanians into the bordellos of the West. A Raspail writing today might take savage pleasure in describing how the experience of Marxist feminism reinvigorated the white-slave trade.

Similarly, Raspail did not foresee (and *The March* did not acknowledge) the economic resurgence of Asia. Far from being uniformly sunk in economic torpor, some Asian countries have shown dramatic rates of economic growth, outpacing Europe. What seems to have happened since the 1970s is that some Eastern cultures have absorbed and applied Western concepts of economic theory and even individual enterprise.

Above all, the Third World invasions in *The March* and *The Camp* were supposed to threaten the privileges and comforts of the rich. The

Two Visions of a Europe Invaded by the
Third World: Did Either Get It Right?

109

poor might suffer incidentally, but it would be the rich who would be satisfactorily humbled and cast down. Yet exactly the opposite has happened: the rich are the principal, maybe the only, Western beneficiaries of Third World migration—both practically and psychologically. They get amenable Third World maids, gardeners, and nannies for their homes; hardworking agricultural workers, computer programmers, and factory hands for their industries; and attractively exotic escorts for their leisure hours—all far more cheaply than the often tiresome and difficult domestic versions.

Psychologically, Western elites have more or less emancipated themselves from nationalist or cultural concepts such as American patriotism or Western identity. Today, corporate multiculturalism is the philosophy that unites liberal and conservative elites-and, no less important, separates them from the hard-hat patriotism of the people. Indeed, the elites increasingly find the expression of such traditional loyalties embarrassing, alien (paradoxically), irrational, economically misleading, and even symptomatic of bigotry, xenophobia, and nativism. As citizens of an increasingly borderless world, they have outgrown such concepts as nationhood and national sovereignty, and they worry about the threat to liberty posed by those who still embrace these concepts.

The arrival of ever more migrants thus serves several purposes: it reduces the weight and influence of the middle-American masses in politics and culture; it makes multiculturalism seem less a matter of choice than of inevitable adaptation; and it fosters a society that, because it is divided ethnically and culturally, requires a political elite to manage it. And here *The Camp* was extremely prophetic, because the real villain in Raspail's book is not the 'Last Chance Armada' of the Calcutta poor, but rather what Raspail calls 'The Beast'—what Tom Bethell and Joseph Sobran call 'The Hive'—namely, the vast retinue of progressive opinion-mongers in politics, journalism, religion, and other institutions, who, without being organized in any way, invariably come up with the same slogans, analyses, condemnations, and programmes to advance the suicide of the West. This Beast/Hive seeks, first, to explain away any apparently threatening aspect of the coming invasion; for instance, it suppresses the news that the refugees might themselves be motivated by racism or xenophobia. Second, it instinctively loosens any bonds of social solidarity that might strengthen France and enable it to resist; thus, all expressions of doubt about the advantages of the invasion are ascribed to racism, xenophobia, and so on. The French are essentially made ashamed of their Frenchness, as a prelude to imposing on them a new identity. If this sounds grim, it is not. What makes *The Camp* such a funny book is the sardonic portrayal of progressive priests, bien-pensant liberal journalists, fatuous "peace" campaigners, and pious frauds of every kind as they fall over themselves to welcome the invasion.

Raspail himself points out that *The Camp* was intended not as a realistic picture but as a nightmare vision. Yet its portrayal of 'The Beast' is uncannily accurate: post-national elites in Europe and America tell us that we have no alternative to accepting continuing high levels of immigration, because we need immigrants to pay for our retirement and other entitlements. As Oxford demographer David Coleman has pointed out in *The London Times*: 'To keep the support ratio constant at today's level the UK is told it would "need" 1.25 million immigrants per year (or 58 million by 2050, taking the total to 136 million), by which time *well over half the UK population would be of post-1995 immigrant descent.*' (Emphasis added.)

Having thus elected a new people, the elites also propose to turn the traditional concept of assimilation on its head. America demonstrated in the past that immigrants could be successfully assimilated to an existing American cultural and political identity. What is now being attempted, however, is an assimilation of America (and other Western nations) into new cultural and political identities devised ad hoc to make the new arrivals feel at home. After all, we have to live with these people, don't we? So we have to make room for their languages, cultures, beliefs, and social practices; in order to do that effectively, we have to amend many of our own that they might find insensitive—hence multiculturalism, etc.

Nor, finally, do these amendments stop at the trivial. They go to the heart of what constitutes a nation—its historical memory, its institutions and traditions, and its sense of identity. US history is rewritten to play up the contribution of victim groups—and thus to reduce the role of those individuals and groups that most shaped the nation. The concept of individual rights, which was the justification for the American Revolution, is increasingly replaced by that of group rights based on cultural identities. And, just recently, an official British commission concluded that the British identity itself is inherently racist and should be replaced by one that would better reflect the multicultural character of 'Cool Britannia.'

This last is especially significant, because the British identity began as a multi-ethnic one, yet succeeded in establishing a new sense of common loyalty. Like the American identity, it excites the particular dislike of managerial elites because it formed the basis for a self-managing society based on voluntary cooperation. All of the above changes, by contrast, represent moves from a self-managing society to one directed by bureaucratic elites.

These processes are slower than an invasion, but they are perhaps more certain. Although imposed politically, they mimic the organic change that transforms all societies over time. And accordingly, we adapt to them—until we almost forget the world we have lost.

Originally published in National Review, *30 April 2001.*

Clare Hollingsworth, Kim Philby, and Enver Hoxha: Two Degrees of Separation

19 September 2017

In the 1970s, I was fortunate enough to share an office in the London *Daily Telegraph* with the veteran war correspondent, Clare Hollingworth, who died in January this year in Hong Kong at the age of 105. Clare was a wonderful office partner, kind, helpful, generous with advice, and full of good stories.

One was the story of her most famous scoop, achieved when she was just two weeks into a foreign correspondent's job in Poland for the DT. It was the start of the Second World War. She had borrowed a boyfriend's impressive car festooned with an official flag, crossed into Germany, bought some delicacies unavailable in Poland, and drove back to the border: 'And then I was driving back along a valley and there was a hessian screen up so you couldn't look down into the valley. Suddenly, there was a great gust of wind which blew the sacking from its moorings, and I looked into the valley and saw scores, if not hundreds, of tanks.'

She phoned the story to her paper as the British consul was simultaneously phoning the Foreign Office. The Germans invaded days later, giving her a second scoop and the start of a brilliant career in the most dangerous sort of reporting.

Photographs show the young Clare was a beauty, and not all of her stories were of war and revolution. She had been escorted to her first ball at the age of sixteen by a neighbour's son, then at Cambridge, named Kim Philby, who had been as elegant and charming an escort as any girl could hope for.

Later, however, she was among those who came to suspect that Philby had become a clandestine Soviet agent. When he failed to turn up to a diplomat's dinner party in Beirut in 1963, she did the detective work that showed he had defected to Moscow— probably on a Soviet freighter that had departed Beirut so hurriedly that half its cargo was left on the dockside. It was another world scoop, soon confirmed by Moscow itself.

Clare's scoops never really stopped coming, and she was still ringing London editors with story suggestions into her second century. But one story she told me stuck in my mind for what it revealed of the human reality *and* unreality of communism.

For almost all of the Cold War the communist country least open to Western reporters, or Western visitors of any kind, was Albania, a small nation of two million people on the Adriatic, next to Greece and Yugoslavia. Given the extraordinary beauty of its coastline, Albania should have become a prosperous tourist paradise as its neighbours at different times had done. But under its unusually dogmatic dictator, Enver Hoxha, communist Albania had decided on a policy of pure Marxist autarky, shunning such capitalist temptations as foreign investment and tourism. Tirana was probably the least visited capital city in the world.

Hoxha took his Stalinist purity to the extent of shunning even other communist states that had flirted with revisionism, quarrelling first with Tito's Yugoslavia on behalf of Stalin's Soviet Union, and then with the post-Stalin Soviet Union on behalf of Mao's China. Albania's ideological self-identification with China was so extreme that when the Sino-Indian conflict broke out in 1961, wits claimed to have heard Radio Tirana announcing: 'Albania Invades India.'

Clare naturally treated Albania's self-isolation as a challenge. She found a tourist company called Progressive Tours (it still exists, I believe, under a different name) that offered trips to Tirana for true believers in Stalin-Mao politics, put on her drabbest clothes, and signed on. She skipped out of the opening dinner in a Tirana grand hotel and disappeared into the ladies' loo. While she was washing her hands, a woman scrubbing the floor suddenly addressed her in perfect French: 'Never did I expect to spend every night of my life praying on my knees for the Russians to invade.'

She was a woman of good family, thus a class enemy, forced by the regime's theories to carry out this work as a form of humiliation. But she had also been trained in the West as a nurse. So whenever a senior figure in the regime was ill, she was always sent for to provide privileged care. (That kind of hypocrisy was almost universal in the communist world.)

It was a grim introduction to a grim country. Albania had the lowest living standards in Europe, a brutally repressive intelligence police that intruded into ordinary lives, long prison sentences for religious worship, and all the usual shortages and privations of the communist system everywhere. It also had one unique feature, born of Hoxha's paranoia: thousands of concrete bunkers dotted around the country, including Tirana, that were a combination of home and defence fort for Albanians against a Western invasion.

That never happened, of course. And though Albania's communist system started toppling with the death of Hoxha in 1985, it did not actually fall until 1992 when free elections with only modest irregularities replaced the governing Socialists (i.e., the Communists after a light rinse) with the opposition Democrats and set Albania on the road to NATO membership (2009) and EU membership (promised by Brussels on condition of further election reforms in 2018).

It has been a rocky road. That is presumably why ACRE – an acronym for Alliance of Conservatives and Reformists in Europe which is the third largest party alliance in the European Parliament – held its Liberty Summit of member parties in Tirana in early April on the topic of "The Damaging Legacy of Communism." (More here: www.thelibertysummit.org/). Few post-communist countries have had such a poisoned inheritance of repression, backwardness and instability. How would Albania recover from it?

'Slowly' must be the honest answer – at least when it comes to politics. The last 25 years have been marked by political instability, election fraud, riots, attempted coups, extreme partisanship, judicial favouritism, intervention by an Italian-led UN military force to restore order, diplomatic head-banging of local party leaders by the EU, and much else. These things still continue: a demonstration by the opposition outside Parliament was continuing after January for months, almost a tourist attraction. The society is also divided by clans, including their extensive criminal offshoots, which run massive smuggling operations, especially drug-smuggling, and which corrupt police and politicians turn a blind eye to.

Not entirely due to these activities, however, the Albanian economy has grown very dramatically since the early 1990s. The most visible impact of this growth is in the centre of Tirana which now boasts an upsurge of genuinely luxurious "luxury hotels," night clubs and high-end consumer shops with all the usual brand-names alongside museums and official buildings. Outside the centre small-scale bazaars proliferate. There is a modern airport (with polite immigration officers) just out of town. Twice a day Tirana enjoys that rich cultural experience: the Mediterranean traffic jam. And though much of the country outside Tirana remains poor and relatively backward, the southern coast now boasts some of the least spoilt and most beautiful tourist resorts in the Adriatic. So get there early.

Jan Zahradil, ACRE's president, and Dan Hannan, its secretary-general, were right to choose Tirana, on this 100th Anniversary of the October Revolution, as a positively dramatic example of what a country can achieve when once released from the chains of communism. Though Albania's democracy may still be a little, well, unorthodox, shaky perhaps, its freedoms and their results are undoubted. There is a positive fiesta of political debate and argument in the streets and newspapers. And if any doubts about this persist, a visit to one of Hoxha's bunkers – some of which in Tirana have been turned into little museums of communism – should remove them very quickly.

One descends from the bustling chaos of a modern Mediterranean city into a cold concrete hell. Its dank corridors open onto rooms showing how Hoxha's repression worked in practice. There is the machinery for listening into everyday innocent conversations, the methods and machinery of torturing suspected dissidents, the photographs of priests arrested and marched through jeering crowds (themselves victims of intimidation) to prison and death for praying, the long lists of those caught (and shot) for attempting to leave, the contrasting films of the smiling dictator accepting bouquets of flowers from pretty young Pioneer girls ... and then suddenly an oddly familiar name pops up.

On a wall listing the names of those Albanian patriots who were parachuted into the country to support the resistance to Hoxha's regime by Western intelligence agencies between about 1947 and 1953 is a much smaller list of those who caught and killed them. Among the latter is the name *Kim Filbi*. His role was especially important to Hoxha. 'Kim Filbi,' then in MI6, recruited and trained these men, and he knew them as friends, before he sent them off on missions about which he had already tipped off the Albanian secret police through the KGB. They were arrested as they landed and marched off to torture and death.

It is a relief to get out into the open air again, and to realize that in the end the martyred Albanian patriots were on the winning side after all.

Originally published under the title 'Full Marx for Albania' in The Australian, *and republished under the present title in the* Hungarian Review, *19 September 2017,* www.hungarianreview.com/article/ *20170919_tales_of_communist_albania.*

Why Totalitarians Have
a Soft Spot for Cranks
19 January 2020

Recently I have been searching for a word that describes our present system of government. *Liberal democracy* is not quite right (though it has features of both) because the phrase omits too many of its other features: notably, the rise and dominance of cranks, the casual overriding of well-established professional rules, and the imposition of formal and informal censorship on matters of controversy.

All three hang together, and all are dealt with below, but the key one seems to me to be the rise and dominance of cranks. Several people have suggested that the word *idiocracy* is the one for which I have been looking. It is also the title of a clever comedy of a few years back which some commentators predictably argue predicted the presidency of Donald Trump. Its producers have recently coined the witty advert: 'The film that started as a comedy … but became a documentary.' Fair play to them. It is a funny movie, now on video. Watch it!

However, it is not about Trump who, though an infuriating mix of cleverness, boldness, impulsiveness, touchiness, and at times mean-spiritedness, is not an idiot, still less a crank. They are not the same thing, anyway. An idiot is simply a stupid person. A crank may actually be quite clever, but he is in possession of One Big Idea (or maybe two) that drives him to promote it interminably and with no sense of proportion or practicality.

Cranks have been around in politics a long time, probably always—Swift lampoons them as 'projectors' in *Gulliver's Travels*—but there seem to be more of them around lately since the rise of ideological politics in the French Revolution and, still more significantly, with the later rise of socialism. Ideological politics are the attempt to use government to implement some ambitious project of human betterment that will avert a vast catastrophe and bring about a new ideal society without greed, inequality, division and other human vices. Both the end of the world and utopia usually figure in ideology, and it is sometimes hard to tell them apart.

Crankery figures too. The nineteenth-century socialist theoretician Saint-Simon believed that under socialism the oceans would turn into lemonade. That did not happen because it was fanciful nonsense and, besides, there were not any socialist governments around to give it a try. Stalin was around in Russia by the 1930s, however, and as part of the campaign to improve grain production, he supported applying the cranky anti-scientific theories of the geneticist, Trofim Lysenko, to agriculture (largely because they fitted in with Marxist ideology). Grain production and Soviet agriculture suffered, but Lysenko's theories remained Soviet orthodoxy until after Stalin's death. Scientists who criticized them were dismissed in large numbers and some very distinguished geneticists were imprisoned and executed.

There is an almost logical progression here. A political authority claims intellectual sovereignty in some non-political field, genetics, say, or music. Some of its pronouncements are crankish, but they are backed by strong pressures, and the usual professional rules and safeguards are ignored from a prudent cowardice. And when the crankish policy begins to fail, censorship is imposed and its critics are dismissed, silenced, or worse. Crankery = the overthrow of known rules + repression.

We might think that with Saint-Simon and Lysenko in our history, we would be alert in future to such dangers. Not so.

Marxist socialism is itself one vast exercise in crankery applied to politics, philosophy, and economics, and it seems to have a family affection for lesser fallacies. But only thirty years since the collapse of Soviet communism revealed the economic wastelands and the mass graves of its political victims across the USSR, there is now a growing revival of support for socialism/communism/Marxism on the Left and among young people in the Western world.

Any large movement of perverse decadence, which this surely is, will be unlikely to leave other aspects of life alone. As Auden writes in 'The Fall of Rome':

Fantastic grow the evening gowns;
Agents of the Fisc pursue
Absconding tax defaulters through
The sewers of provincial towns.

Let me suggest two areas where crankery has already won significant victories. The first is gender and transgender theory. This holds that someone's identity is not determined by his/her biological sex but by his/her gender identity, which may be malleable and is anyway a matter of individual conviction. As one slogan has it: If your boy says she is a girl, then she is a girl.

That seems false to me, but even if it were true, its effects should be limited at least by its own founding theory. Our social interactions with others, whatever their theoretical identities, should always be shaped by courtesy and good will, including treating them as they wish within reason. But we would surely not base a transwoman's medical treatment on the assumption that her gender identity is a better guide than his biological sex to what they need.

Yet hospitals, schools, colleges and Woke corporations do exactly that when they make available tampons to transwomen. Athletic bodies do likewise when they decree that transwomen with male bodies are eligible to play in women's sports with the predictable result that many able women players who might win in a fair contest are defeated. If this goes uncorrected, it will simply end in the abolition of women's sports.

Admitting transwomen into women's-only 'safe spaces' will similarly end a civilized protection for women in a world that certainly does not seem to be becoming less dangerous for them. Above all, as John Whitehall has documented in *Quadrant*, needless human tragedies and massive lawsuits are hurtling towards us when young people persuaded to undergo transitioning surgery and drug treatments that are life-changing and unalterable at an age when they cannot possibly understand the consequences believe in adulthood they have made a terrible mistake.

Yet in all these cases the major institutions of society have capitulated to aggressive pressure groups pushing a theory that is highly dubious, unsupported by the great majority of clinical researches, regarded by many gays and feminists as a threat to their identities, and above all damaging to its supposed beneficiaries. Not enough attention has been devoted to examining the science behind the activism. An NIH research project on gender transitioning did not include the control group required by the rules. And as Madeleine Kearns has detailed, when sceptics seek to raise these questions in public meetings, they are shouted down and threatened. Crankery—or should it be quackery?—is followed by ignoring the rules and enforced by repression.

It is a similar story in the academy's history wars—reliant as they are on student "rebellions" (which in reality are highly conformist) and enforced by riots and iconoclasm. These too are a consequence of abolishing the border between truth and falsehood in postmodern scholarship. Of course, truth is sometimes hard to discover and to distinguish from persuasively false interpretations. The answer to that is more work in the archives. For postmodern historical interpretation was refuted in the 1920s by Georges Clemenceau, who had led France in the Great War. A young historian kindly explained to him that future historians would re-examine the war from different perspectives and reach conclusions different from his own. 'Yes,' replied Clemenceau, 'future historians will say many things I might dispute. But one thing they will not say. They will not say that Belgium invaded Germany.'

He may have been too optimistic. Relieved of the obligations of truth and accuracy, students all too often replace research with the pre-cooked conclusions of Marxist Critical Theory, as illustrated by *The New York Times* 1619 Project, which starts from the conclusion that slavery is the true essence of American history. As historian Richard Brookhiser said when asked about this recently: 'Two weeks before those first slaves landed, the colony adopted a democratic constitution. No one owns slaves in America today. But we're still voting.' But how often will such rebuttals be heard in colleges in which the administrators as well as the students are striving to "decolonize" the curriculum—and when in effect both cooperate to close down debates and shut out speakers who might enlighten them. Once again, academic (and media) crankery is followed by, first, throwing overboard the rules of scholarship and, next, by the banishment of heretics.

It might reasonably be objected that not all of these are examples of rule by cranks. In part, that is a fair criticism. The cranks are in the streets; the corridors of power contain the cowards who yield to them. But I am not sure that is much of a comfort. I am getting the queasy feeling that in about five years anyone who has criticized Greta Thunberg's absurd views on the demise of the Planet Earth by next Thursday will be up before the magistrates. It seems agreed by all well-meaning people that it is a coarse and brutal insensitivity to express any scepticism about Armageddon from a little child.

All of which is a little odd, not least because the feisty Ms Thunberg is not a child. She is a young woman of some sixteen years, able to vote in progressive jurisdictions, and a rather typical self-righteous adolescent too. Now, it used to be a breach of feminist etiquette to refer to young women as if they were just starting high school. Yet we have not had any feminist complaints that Greta's honorary girlhood is an offensive slight even in these much "Woker" days.

But could you have a better illustration of the coming crankocracy than the assembled leaders of the world nodding solemnly and applauding timidly as a sixteen-year-old adolescent condemns them angrily for not halting the medieval plague about to descend on them unless they replace their business suits with sackcloth and ashes?

They know their place.

Originally published in Quadrant, *19 January 2020, https://quadrant.org.au/magazine/2020/01/the-rise-of-crankocracy/.*

How 1956 Saved Me from All That
19 September 2016

October–November 1956 occurred at the exact moment that I was entering both actual and political adolescence. Boys of my age—I became fourteen in April of that year—were fighting and ferrying the wounded in Budapest that autumn. It was a crash course in political maturity. I was studying for my English GCEs, which included Latin, Greek, and Ancient History but not more "relevant" subjects. In retrospect that did not matter. Watching and hearing the news bulletins that season was a crash course in modern European history.

Not that I was unaware of Hungary and its achievements. No English schoolboy was. When the Hungarian soccer team thrashed us at Wembley in 1953, their game was the admiring talk of the playground next day. I have to boast about our English 'fair play.' We acknowledged their superiority fair and square, and relished the new and more rapid soccer they had introduced to its original birthplace. Puskás was a hero even if we could not pronounce his name. If we had known nothing else, we would have recognised the right side when the news from Budapest came that he refused to return to Hungary after the putting down of the Revolution.

Three years later we did know more, of course. And if I knew somewhat more than most, it was probably because I was a Catholic—and one with burgeoning literary and theatrical tastes. Though the British media reported the communist takeover of Central and Eastern Europe pretty well, the Catholic press (such as the intellectual weekly *The Tablet* and the tabloid *Universe*) gave us a far more thorough and regular account of how religious and other freedoms were systemically suppressed and replaced by an ideological monotone. The show trial of Cardinal Mindszenty, which distilled this repression into a single vivid and photogenic example, was given full coverage in Catholic newspapers. We prayed for the Cardinal and the Church of Silence on Sundays. Young Catholics were therefore slightly more aware of Central European realities than their non-Catholic fellows—and those who went to serious plays and films still more so. Bridget Boland, a talented Anglo-Irish Catholic playwright and screen-writer, wrote a fictionalised version of the Mindszenty case, *The Prisoner*, that became first a play and then a film starring Alec Guinness as Mindszenty and Jack Hawkins as his interrogator. It is intellectualized, perhaps over-intellectualized, as well as fictionalized, but it leaves no doubt as to which was the right side and who was the hero. When the Cardinal was released from his grim prison by the 1956 revolutionaries, he was another confirmation of the truth that a great struggle, one otherworldly as well as of world historical importance, was being waged in Hungary.

That is not to say that Hungary's revolution was not my sole preoccupation as it inevitably was for my Hungarian contemporaries such as the young Géza Jeszenszky, then ferrying supplies and helping the wounded behind the barricades. How could it be? But it happened at just the right moment to strike my imagination. I had only recently discovered politics as a result of reading a good popular biography of Disraeli by Hesketh Pearson and, like so many others, being entranced by his dizzying romantic career—for instance, stating 'the British Empire' as his collateral when he borrowed money from Lionel de Rothschild to finance his purchase of Suez Canal shares to ensure control of that imperial lifeline. I had decided that I was a Conservative, and had gone to the extreme extent of applying to join the Conservative Party, adding one year to my age to do so. The local Tory Party agent, whose job it was to recruit members, smiled sceptically at me and said: 'Even if you are fifteen, which I doubt, you shouldn't get involved in politics for years yet. It's not a nice business. Don't squander your youth on it. Play cricket, chase girls, and if you still have the political bug in ten years, come back then.'

In retrospect again, I rather like that old-fashioned English spirit. I wish it were universal. But it is not. And 1956 was a particularly bad year for it—the year not only of the Soviet suppression of Hungary but also of Nasser's seizure of the Suez Canal. Suez was a crisis that ran throughout that entire summer—as the prime minister's wife, Clarissa Eden said, it ran through her dining room in Downing Street—and as a newly-minted unofficial Tory, I burned with indignation at the failure of the international community to unite against another dictator and defend Disraeli's legacy. I was a fierce supporter of Anthony Eden and his decision to "intervene."

I still do support the Suez intervention, though less fiercely, but my reasons today are very different from the self-righteous jingoism I then felt. Nor did my reasons of that time atrophy. Quite dramatically, they were swept away by my response to what was happening in Budapest. It was a simple reaction, but then it was a reaction to a simple situation. Good people were resisting bad people; Hungarians were rejecting their oppressors; free people were overthrowing communist tyranny; young people were fighting tanks. All those agonizing dilemmas that dominate the minds of modern progressive people—which of two evils to choose, how to navigate through different shades of grey—simply did not apply. Justice and liberty were on the one side; tyranny, murder, and bad faith were on the other. Some ÁVH (State Protection Authority) men were lynched; that was deplorable and deserving punishment; but it did not affect the overall moral calculus of the Revolution more than an iota.

These truths were made flesh in the young people in belted macs, holding stolen guns, and carrying Molotov cocktails, who ran across squares under fire and built flimsy barriers against tanks. They were then transmitted to the world in grainy photographs and black-and-white newsreels that seem today both authentic and a metaphor for authenticity in a deceptively colourful world.

Were there moral complications in the revolution that make my own uncritical and open-hearted support for the revolutionaries look naive today? I did not think so then, and I do not think so now. Moral complications intruded very quickly in the absolute determination of the West to discourage any thought of practical sympathy for the Imre Nagy regime and in the decision of the international community to "prioritize" Suez. I still remember clinging in my indignant heart to all the bitter jokes about a United Nations intervention being a more "miraculous" possibility than that of the Archangel Michael. Much later János Kádár invested massively in moral ambiguity (and derived good returns from it) to sustain his cunning and corrupting regime under Russian protection. At the time, however, the most morally ambiguous aspect of the revolution was that a few of the young revolutionaries still called themselves Communists. The best answer to that, however, was an adaptation of an old Jewish Mother joke: 'To me you're a Communist; to your father you're a Communist; but to a Communist are you a Communist?' When the real Communists returned in the Red Army's baggage train, the pretend Communists showed their true democratic colours by fighting to the end or crossing to the West or being transported to prison camps or suffering some combination of these fates. A cold peace in the Cold War was gradually restored.

But we in the West had changed. The Budapest correspondent of Britain's communist newspaper, *The Daily Worker*, wrote the most eloquent despatch possible in their praise: a letter of resignation. In general, the Western media proved better than their governments by telling the truth of the revolution passionately. Even the West's governments proved generous in offering sanctuary to Hungarian exiles. The exiles themselves both gave the Hungarian people a good name and provided a standing rebuke to any Western sympathizers with 'really existing socialism' in the Soviet Bloc. For a decade or more, it was impossible for any intelligent person to see Soviet Russia as anything other than a monstrous tyrannical Leviathan with Hungary as its most courageous victim.

Although I did not realize it at the time, I had changed more than most. Listening to Imre Nagy's broadcast via the BBC, knowing it would not elicit any help and that the Hungarian people were doomed to many decades of Soviet rule, I wept with frustration. I felt a strong sense of loyalty to Hungarians on both sides of the Iron Curtain. For me 1956 was like the Spanish Civil War to a young socialist in the 1930s. It awoke my serious political imagination. Thereafter Hungary was a great power in my mental map of the world. There was not a great deal I could do about it. For many years after 1956, as my Tory friend advised, I mainly played cricket (actually tennis) and chased girls, pretty ineffectually most of the time. But there was one thing I could do. As a journalist, I could tell the truth about Hungary in1956 and what followed. And that is what I have always tried to do.

Originally published in Hungarian Review, *Vol. VII, No. 5, September 2016, www.hungarianreview.com/article/20160919_hungary_1956_the_ awakening_of_my_political_imagination.*

Game, Set, but Not Match? Reagan, Obama and the Trajectory of US Politics

A Review of *The Age of Reagan: The Conservative Counterrevolution, 1980–1989* by Steven F. Hayward
Winter 2009

On the penultimate page of *The Age of Reagan. The Fall of the Old Liberal Order, 1964–1980*, the first volume of his magisterial political history, Steven Hayward drew this momentous but tentative conclusion:

> In smashing the monopoly of liberalism in 1980, Reagan exposed the fractured and increasingly hollow character of what passes for liberalism in the late twentieth century, and prepared the ground of political debate on which American politics is still being conducted today. That is what makes the closing decades of the twentieth century the "Age of Reagan." Like the post-New Deal era—the "Age of Roosevelt"—the Age of Reagan may prove equally durable.

This possibility looks more likely, though still uncertain, 21 years after Reagan left office than at almost any time during his presidency. One of the many merits of Hayward's second volume, covering Reagan's years in the White House, is that it reminds the reader firmly just how embattled and frustrated he seemed for much of the period. Simply to list some of the main episodes of those years—the attempted assassination and its aftermath, the resignation of Office of Management and Budget director David Stockman, two mid-term electoral reverses, the retreat from Lebanon under fire, the nuclear freeze movement, the 1987 stock market crash, the Iran–Contra hearings, the Savings and Loan crisis, the "Borking" of Robert Bork—is to depict a presidency mired in difficulties and apparently heading for oblivion. All of these setbacks were magnified by an almost comically biased media. And though Reagan enjoyed successes from Grenada to Reykjavik, they seemed brief and atypical interludes in a general story of amiable confusion. About the most flattering impression at the time was of Reagan as Laocoön waging a magnificent but doomed struggle to free himself and America from the coils of Liberaldom at home and abroad.

We have to remind ourselves—or have Hayward remind us—of this contemporary impression because recent Reagan scholarship has presented a far more favourable view of the man and his presidency. Books by liberal historians such as John Patrick Diggins and Richard Reeves have conceded that Reagan was a formidable statesman with great historical achievements to his credit. Reagan himself contributed to this revisionism when his columns, broadcasts, and diaries, published over the past ten years, revealed him not as an "amiable dunce" but as a well-informed, serious man with a strong grasp of major political issues. Events in the real world—which sometimes conquer even the defence mechanisms of intellectuals—came to his aid as well. His economic policies were followed by America's economic recovery, the modernization of US capitalism, and a boom that lasted 26 years with only two brief and modest interruptions. His foreign policy led to the first US–Soviet arms reduction agreement, victory in the Cold War, and the peaceful collapse of communism.

If anything, Reagan's new admirers compensate for their heresy on the central issues of Reaganomics and the Cold War by repeating the standard liberal critiques of his policies on homelessness, budget "cuts," the environment, AIDS, labour unions, affirmative action, and almost everything else. Indeed, these critiques often have a curious taken-for-granted quality as if it is unnecessary to argue such things since everyone knows them to be true.

* * *

By contrast, Hayward, who is the F. K. Weyerhaeuser Fellow at the American Enterprise Institute and a senior fellow at the Pacific Research Institute, sets out to look in detail at almost all the important controversies of the Reagan era (the S&L crisis is a rare exception). In doing so, he examines critically not only what Reagan said and what his administration did but also how the Democrats responded and what the media reported. He discovers, unsurprisingly, that sometimes the Reagan Administration was either seriously mistaken (the Iran–Contra affair) or blunderingly inept (the Bob Jones University tax flap). More often than not, however, he finds that the administration was correct or at least reasonable, the media partisan, and the Democrats alarmist.

The fabled "cuts" in Reagan's landmark 1981–82 budget are a good example of all three. What the administration initially proposed (before congressional haggling added various pork-barrel items) involved no actual reductions in welfare spending at all. Almost all the supposed "cuts" were reductions in a previously planned rate of growth (i.e., budget hikes). As Hayward points out, "overall spending for all social programs in 1982 was still $53 billion *higher* than in 1980." But this modest fiscal restraint was depicted by the media as the imposition of a brutal austerity.

'Hunger in America is back,' intoned Bill Moyers in a CBS special before Reagan's "cuts" had even taken effect. Charles Kuralt similarly reported that food stamp cuts were 'putting people into a 1981 version of the bread line.' (When they eventually came, the 4 per cent "cuts"—$100 million out of $11.4 billion—tightened eligibility, but 22 million recipients remained on food stamps.) 'The impact of the Reagan cuts on minority groups is likely to be severe,' ran a front-page *The Washington Post* news report. Several urban Democrats predicted a long hot summer of riots as a result of the "cuts." (The riots never occurred.) Tip O'Neill, Speaker of the House and their de facto leader, said in a spontaneous television interview that the president 'has no concern, no regard, no care for the little man in America.' Later, in a speech, he accused Reagan of being 'a tightwad, a real Ebenezer Scrooge.'

In the course of his narrative Hayward subjects one after another of these anti-Reagan critiques to a well-researched, critical examination. Almost always they turn out to be either grossly exaggerated or outright untruths. (Perhaps it would be kinder to describe them as metropolitan myths or superstitions of the sophisticated.) This painstaking process sometimes slows down Hayward's otherwise well-paced and highly readable account. But that is a price worth paying for a comprehensive analysis that will serve as a treasure trove for future historians.

It also helps answer another question. How did Reagan's popularity withstand this avalanche of difficulties and bad publicity? His critics have argued over the years that the president's amiability and communication skills persuaded the voters to overlook or forgive the 'cruelty,' 'harshness,' or 'callousness' of his policies. But if his policies were none of those things, as Hayward establishes very clearly, maybe the explanation is that the voters realized that Reagan was closer to reality than his critics in the media and the opposition. This sympathy for the president on matters voters grasped, such as food stamps, would then bolster his credibility on more arcane questions, such as monetarism and missile defence.

* * *

When Hayward moves onto the larger picture of the Cold War, he tackles material on which established opinion is already favourable to Reagan—far more so than when the author began his gargantuan two-volume task. Yet he tells a gripping story vividly—especially the Geneva and Reykjavik summits—with balanced judgments and new material. And as in other recent accounts, Reagan emerges as a statesman significantly different from the portrait of him both admirers and critics have carried in their minds. The simplest description is to say that he saw all the great issues of politics, including peace and war, through a serious (Christian) moral perspective.

Although the SDI turned out to have all sorts of political advantages for America, the overriding appeal of missile defence for the president was the argument that it was more moral to defend the American people than to avenge them with a nuclear strike. This commitment, which was close to nuclear pacifism, won over Pope John Paul II when they met in 1982 in Rome. Meanwhile, the US Catholic bishops defended the "stability" of Mutual Assured Destruction over and against this explicitly moral calculation, even though they had long been uneasy (at best) about MAD.

Reagan's nuclear views reflected a subtle, prudent view of military power in general. He was more than happy to employ a *show* of force as a strategic tactic. He did so on entering office when he signed off on the proposal of US Navy Secretary John Lehman for a massive Anglo-American naval exercise in the North Atlantic to challenge Soviet domination in that region. On the other hand, he was very reluctant actually to use force—according to his Secretary of State, George Shultz, he did so on only three occasions in eight years. When American medical students were threatened by a Marxist coup on the Island of Grenada, he doubled the number of troops requested by the Joint Chiefs (whom he infuriated by falling asleep during their briefing) because he thought more lives would be saved on all sides if the US had an overwhelming predominance. He pointed out, too, that if Jimmy Carter had doubled the number of troops and helicopters in his attempt to rescue American hostages in Iran, he might still have been giving the orders in 1983.

In short there was no discontinuity between the Reagan who denounced the Soviet Union as an 'evil empire' and helped the Contras in Central America, and the Reagan who worked with Mikhail Gorbachev to sign arms reduction agreements. In each case the president was pursuing a tough-minded moral strategy to resist and defeat communism without risking a nuclear war. And as it turned out, that is exactly what happened.

* * *

Even so, Hayward ends his study on an elegiac, questioning note. Did Ronald Reagan create a Reagan era? Or did he merely slow the drift of America towards a somnolent statist future? These questions redirect our attention to American domestic politics. For, as the opening quote makes clear, a Reagan era would be one in which Reagan, like Roosevelt before him, set the terms of American political debate for the foreseeable future. But Reagan is accused, somewhat less by Hayward than by some disillusioned conservative reviewers, of failing in that task in various ways. How valid are such charges?

Reagan certainly failed to turn the culture back to the simpler, more patriotic world of the 1930s that he idealized and even embodied. Gay rights, abortion rights, and other moral novelties continued their remorseless advance through the culture. But he had other things to do—winning the Cold War, reviving the American economy—that seemed more important at the time. Besides, the wholesale transformation of a culture is not something that a president is expected—at least by conservatives—to attempt. It is remarkable enough that he should have restored the standing of the presidency and the belief that America is governable.

Reagan equally failed to reverse welfare-state liberalism. Hayward posits that this is because persuading voters to give up benefits they already enjoy is beyond the power of political man—or at least harder than defeating communism. Maybe so. But Reagan halted the advance of such liberalism. When he left office, he bequeathed to his successors a set of penalties and incentives that for two decades or so made any further flirtation with that liberalism costly and controversial.

Reagan did fail, however—and fail significantly—where Margaret Thatcher succeeded. He failed to convert the opposition party. For a while he seemed to have done so; President Bill Clinton balanced the budget, declared that the era of big government was over, embraced NATO and NAFTA expansion, backed a Republican plan for welfare reform, and sought safety in triangulation. But a series of factors—the Iraq War, George W. Bush's domestic drift leftwards, the political possibilities of the internet, boredom with centrism—pushed the Democrats back towards their statist and wobbly foreign-policy attitudes of 20 years ago. And Barack Obama was elected president on policies that reflected these attitudes.

Obama has praised Reagan, as Hayward notes sympathetically, for changing the 'trajectory' of American politics. But the current administration's policies are a thorough reversal of that trajectory on the economy, taxes, the budget, health care, climate change, and much else. Hence we cannot be sure if the 'Age of Reagan' will prove a durable era or merely a conservative interlude between the "ages" of Roosevelt and Obama.

What is clear is that if the Reagan era is to be durable, then President Obama must not succeed—either politically because he cannot pass his programmes, or substantively because his programmes pass but then produce some blend of higher inflation and lower growth, and are subsequently abandoned. Reaganomics succeeded politically in 1981, but its more lasting success was the long boom in the years after Reagan left office. What matters ultimately is not the popularity of a policy but the popularity (and soundness) of its results. Steven Hayward deserves our gratitude for establishing this vital but unfashionable truth over the full range of policy and the eight years of the Reagan presidency, even if a final judgment on the durability of the Reagan era remains tantalizingly open.

This review of Steven F. Hayward's The Age of Reagan: The Conservative Counterrevolution, 1980–1989 *(New York: Crown Forum, 2009), 753 pp., was originally published in the* Claremont Review of Books, *Vol. X, Number 1, Winter 2009/10, https://claremontreview ofbooks.com/game-setbut-not-match/.*

Reagan Democrat:
The Unsatisfied Life of Jeane Kirkpatrick

A Review of *Political Woman: The Big Little Life of Jeane Kirkpatrick* by Peter Collier
Fall 2012

Peter Collier, founding editor of and consultant to Encounter Books, wrote this surrogate autobiography of Jeane Kirkpatrick as an act of loyalty and friendship because she either would not or could not write her own. Kirkpatrick had a fierce aversion to invading her own privacy. Twenty years before her death, she had been compelled to return a large advance for a memoir of her time in government. She was unable to make much headway on it despite writing reams of material. Somehow they never cohered into a lively finished account.

In the late 1990s, knowing little or nothing of this episode, Collier sought to persuade her to write a conventional autobiography. He thought he had her consent. Over the next few years, they had about ten pleasant discussions over dinner about the shape and direction of the work. But she was continually distracted by another project, a 'big policy' book (published posthumously in a heavily-edited form as *Making War to Keep Peace,* 2007) and by the spiralling tragedies of her family life. Besides, her enthusiasm for it was never keen. And as she saw death approaching, she confessed to Collier that the book about her life would remain unfinished.

Collier lightly replied that then maybe he should write it. 'Well, maybe you should,' she replied. This throwaway remark gradually acquired the force of an obligation for Collier, and drawing on conversations with her friends and relatives, and her private papers, he put together *Political Woman: The Big Little Life of Jeane Kirkpatrick*.

This brief history of the book's origins points us towards an apparent mystery. Why should a woman with such sterling achievements—who had many Republicans urging her to run for the presidency—be so nervous of revealing more of herself and of her struggles in a forum that, after all, she ultimately controlled? Why did she not relish the chance to pay off old scores from her bureaucratic battles in the Reagan presidency? Why did she not want to retaliate against the angry feminists such as Naomi Wolf who had scorned her achievements and questioned her very status as a woman? The answer may be that she herself had doubts, not about her femininity to be sure, but about her achievements and her status in other respects.

George Orwell famously remarked that 'An autobiography is only to be trusted when it reveals something disgraceful. A man who gives a good account of himself is probably lying, since any life when viewed from the inside is simply a series of defeats.' This insight is not peculiar to Orwell. A psychologist told me some years ago that many of the most successful people feel themselves to be frauds, and the more they are praised and rewarded, the more fraudulent they feel. Some feel this more strongly and consistently than others, but most feel it from time to time. And if we actually have experienced defeats, our anxieties will be reinforced and we will likely have qualms about revisiting them in public—especially if we have underlying doubts about our worth in the first place. Does *Political Woman* suggest that this could be true about Jeane Kirkpatrick?

* * *

Her childhood days in Oklahoma and Illinois, as she remembered them later, were idyllic in much the same small-town way as Ronald Reagan's, if slightly more prosperous. Her parents were loving, her home modestly comfortable, her life organized around lessons, tomboy antics after school, recitations, leading parts in plays, deep schoolgirl friendships, and lighter high school romances, all against a hopeful background of America at peace. Jeane Jordan was more serious than most girls; she refused one date in order to stay home reading *The Federalist*. She was more interested in politics too. She was a yellow dog

Democrat—her family's choice—and her best friend was a Republican. (They put the friendship on hold during elections.) In most respects though, she was a popular girl living the good small-town life. She was present in the local cinema when its manager halted the movie and brought this paradise to an end by announcing that Japan had attacked Pearl Harbor. But later in life, she kept a small statue of Will Rogers on her coffee table at the American Enterprise Institute.

There is no reason to doubt the sincerity of Kirkpatrick's nostalgia and her affection for the American Midwest and its provincial Protestant values. But they were not the focus of her worldview and loyalty, as they were for Ronald Reagan and, in a different context, for Margaret Thatcher. As the story about *The Federalist* suggests, she had a precocious interest in "big ideas." As soon as she could, she pursued big ideas in big places by heading to Chicago (briefly), New York, and Paris. Her choice of discipline was political science, and her particular interest was the totalitarianism that had recently wrecked and still threatened the world. She studied with Marxist academics such as Franz Neumann and Herbert Marcuse. She met Hannah Arendt. She spent her weekends in Greenwich Village where she knew James Baldwin well enough to call him 'Jimmy.' In short, she moved in radical circles and, like many an unformed young girl from the provinces, she might have gone to the bad and become a socialist herself. But three events, plus a pragmatic tough-mindedness evident even in her early ideological exploring, saved her from that fate.

* * *

The first was the Alger Hiss case. She took the trouble to read daily reports of the congressional hearings and decided that Hiss had lied and so might well be guilty of greater lies. She became irritated with her radical friends who were caught up in the myth of his innocence and victimhood. The second was the 1948 election. Barnard College was divided between 'country-club Republicans for Thomas Dewey and romantic leftists for Henry Wallace.' Jeane went to a Wallace rally, heard the candidate warn that the FBI would soon be rounding up dissidents if he were not elected, realized that his campaign was effectively a communist front, and voted for Truman. She later believed that casting this vote had been a key moment in her life. Not as key, however, as the third event: her job interview with Evron Kirkpatrick, who headed the Office of Intelligence Research in the State Department.

Evron 'Kirk' Kirkpatrick lived, prospered, and exerted great influence in three overlapping worlds—the academic discipline of political science, the liberal anti-communist wing of the Democratic Party, and the intelligence agencies of the United States. He was close to Hubert Humphrey in the 'Minnesota Mafia,' and at a time when the Democrats were signed up to fighting the Cold War aggressively, he was what Collier calls an 'action intellectual.' He was charming and cultivated but, like Jeane, somewhat self-contained and even Delphic. He was also unhappily married for the second time. Shortly after hiring Jeane, he began to pay her marked attentions, dropping by her office for long chats, taking her out to lunch, and introducing her to such impressive friends as Humphrey and Max Kampelman. He was plainly smitten. She in turn fell in love, began with him what Collier describes as an impulsive 'intimate relationship,' and obviously feeling conflicted, first retreated to a hospital and home, and then fled to Paris.

'Fled' is perhaps the wrong word. Her anguish over Kirk gave her the immediate incentive, but no Julian Sorel has ever been keener to get to Paris than the young Jeane Kirkpatrick has. One of her lifelong friends was a wealthy Frenchwoman whom she had met at Barnard, and her intellectual interest in totalitarianism made her want to immerse herself in the Parisian disputes between Albert Camus and Jean-Paul Sartre. She did so. She met Camus and was his passionate supporter in debates with Sartre. She regretted bitterly that he was eclipsed by the toad-faced anti-American until the Berlin Wall fell. Although sick for much of her ten months there, she discovered a love of France and a taste for French cuisine that never left her. But this was still a sort of convalescence. She was not really healed (or decided on what to do). Kirk decided the matter. He turned up in Paris. They returned to America, overcame the doubts of Jeane's family, and got married in 1955.

* * *

For the next 20 years, with Kirk's help and guidance, Jeane settled into a new life and identity. She had three children, a moderately successful academic career, and wrote a book, *Political Woman* (1974) that ticked all the right academic boxes but, as Collier notes with mordant amusement, concluded that successful political women were much more like Jeane herself than like the strident feminist leaders of the 1960s and 70s. She had found her métier and her milieu. She was a political scientist and an anti-communist liberal Democrat and her circle of friends included the most distinguished members of both groups. This identity fitted in with both her family loyalties and the drift of her scholarly interest in totalitarianism. It reflected her husband's life and opinions too. It was the safest, most respectable thing to be in the ages of Eisenhower and Kennedy. It was an identity in which she felt perfectly comfortable. And it helps to explain her initial doubts about joining the Reagan administration and the fierceness of her reluctance to change her registration and become a Republican later. In the 1950s, she would have thought such an outcome impossible—a sort of treason.

That is not to say her life was untroubled. She had to overcome the distrust of some of Kirk's friends who saw her as a 'home-wrecker,' which was extremely painful for Jeane. She was probably the beneficiary of the break-up of Kirk's marriage rather than its cause, but she felt some guilt, and was often vague about Kirk's marital status when they had met. In addition, as her three boys grew up, they gradually disappointed the high expectations of their parents, one boy disastrously so when he became an irrecoverable alcoholic. A friend remembers Jeane breaking down years later and sobbing that she would happily trade all her celebrity and distinctions for her son's recovery. And as the 1950s wore on into the 60s and 70s, the ideological climate changed. Her secure identity became an embattled one as the radicals she rejected in her youth began their takeover of the Democratic Party and most of the better political science departments. She was one of the small group of academic liberals who resisted the revolution and became known as 'neoconservatives.' Kirkpatrick probably deserved this title more than many others because of the practical tough-mindedness that she brought to her thinking on ideology and foreign policy.

Neoconservatism was a cul-de-sac for young academics. But Kirkpatrick leapt into a new life on the trampoline of an article for *Commentary* magazine, 'Dictatorships and Double Standards' (1979), arguing that authoritarian regimes, being less complete in their repression of civil society, were more likely than totalitarian regimes to evolve into democracies. This article made her famous outside the distinguished circle of her and Kirk's friends. It came to the attention of Ronald Reagan who recruited her into his campaign, appointed her US Ambassador to the United Nations, and gave her a Cabinet position. Her serious public life had begun.

* * *

Kirkpatrick was a successful ambassador to the UN in the fighting tradition of Daniel Patrick Moynihan. She waged what became called 'diplomacy without apologies.' She took on those UN member states— the great majority—that believed they could oppose the US on important UN votes without imperilling their access to American aid and benefits. She challenged the anti-American statements of other diplomats and countered them by reciting the records of their governments on human rights. She revived the spirits of US diplomats and of their colleagues from friendly UN delegations. And she managed to turn around some votes—notably, a Cuban resolution criticizing the US on Puerto Rico— on which previous US ambassadors would have surrendered in advance. As a result, she became popular with the general public and exercised greater influence in the cabinet.

Allied to Secretary of Defense Casper Weinberger and CIA director Bill Casey and enjoying the benevolent approval of the president, she was a formidable force within the administration on a range of issues redolent of 'Dictatorships and Double Standards,' notably the Reagan Doctrine and funding the Nicaraguan Contras. She was right on these issues and Reagan appreciated her stance. On one occasion, to signify his support for her following criticism from Secretary of State Al Haig, Reagan walked the long way out of the cabinet room in order to kiss her en route. Such favours encouraged her to believe she might become the national security adviser when the post became vacant. But when Bill

Clark resigned in late 1983, she lost the internal bureaucratic battle, refused the secondary post of counsellor to the president, and after a fairly long diplomatic interval left the administration to campaign for the Reagan Doctrine as a private citizen and academic expert.

Jeane was realistic enough to accept that her career in government had ended in defeat. That defeat was unfair but also unsurprising. She was simply no good at bureaucratic infighting and no match for such professionals as George Shultz, Mike Deaver, and James Baker. She had not cultivated them; they were hostile to her ambitions; and when the crunch came, they united against her. They also had ammunition. She was probably over-invested in her thesis in 'Dictatorships and Double Standards.' It was of only moderate application to the main Cold War dispute with the Soviet Union and issues such as arms control. Also, as Collier points out, she was too rigid in her scepticism about the positive use of democracy promotion and human rights diplomacy to the point of being uninterested in the work of the National Endowment for Democracy (NED). Reagan himself had embraced the NED and this approach, which was being conducted by her own disciples such as Carl Gershman and Joshua Muravchik.

* * *

Above all, Kirkpatrick had one or two serious lapses of prudential judgment that allowed her opponents to present her as too risky to head the National Security Council (NSC). The single most damning example of her bad judgment was her resistance to siding with Britain in the Falklands War. She defended this on the grounds that Britain had not always supported US interests and that Washington's obligation to support Britain as a NATO ally did not apply to issues outside NATO. She did not see that winning the Falklands War was not merely a British interest but a vital British interest and that Britain was not merely a NATO ally but a US ally on a worldwide range of interests. Everyone else in the NSC—Reagan, Bush, Casey, Weinberger, even Haig—saw these realities. She did not. And it damaged her.

Not enough, however, to prevent her being considered as a presidential candidate five years later. Was she ever serious about the

Republican nomination in 1988? She took the proper soundings, rounded up potential donors, hired campaign consultants, and recruited a possibly key supporter in the governor of New Hampshire. She even became a Republican. Having marched her troops to the top of the hill, however, she promptly marched them down again. After agreeing to walk onto the stage with the other Republican hopefuls for a 1987 debate moderated by Bill Buckley—unannounced for maximum theatrical effect—she decided it was not for her and pulled out of the debate and the race. It is very likely that she flirted with running just as she flirted with writing an autobiography. But she drew back when the moment came.

She could not avoid controversies, however; they attached themselves to her with superglue. Two in particular arose following the end of the Cold War. The transformation of Poland into a democracy and the collapse of the Soviet Union led her old adversaries on the Left to question her argument that totalitarian states were less likely than authoritarian ones to become democracies. The Kirkpatrick Doctrine had therefore been disproved. Then her argument—rooted in conservative realism—that the US could now afford to be a "normal" nation pursuing its national interests prudently aroused opposition from the second generation of neoconservatives who favoured a more interventionist policy of democracy promotion. Between 1989 and Kirkpatrick's death in 2006 neither dispute was settled, but the balance of the debate shifted back in her favour—in the first case, decisively. Shortly before her death, Aviezer Tucker, a young scholar whose specialisms include a study of post-totalitarianism, pointed out that post-authoritarian societies were plainly superior to post-totalitarian societies in their ability to adjust to democracy. The reason was straight out of Jeane's essay: authoritarian governments do not decapitate all the non-political elites in society; totalitarian governments do just that. So a post-totalitarian society is one in which the only surviving expert elites are the national security and intelligence ones—and what we get is Putin's government by *siloviki*.

* * *

Looking back on Kirkpatrick's life, a dispassionate observer sees a happy, fruitful, and successful one marred by some private unhappiness, mainly over her children, and a very forgivable failure to get to the very top of the political tree. She had a 40-year marriage with her soul mate, a successful academic career, a dramatic leap into the Cabinet, a UN ambassadorship (the first woman to obtain that bauble) in an administration that won the Cold War, the respect of colleagues and opponents, and the affection of many friends. But did she see it that way? Or did she, like Churchill, feel that her achievements, though widely admired, were below what she expected of herself? Did she even look at her life and feel, like Orwell, that it was little more than a series of defeats?

Who knows? All we can say is that she was very reluctant to write about her life and even to discuss large areas of it with friends. She is extremely fortunate, therefore, that a light remark to Peter Collier triggered a biography that is truthful, sympathetic, highly readable—and supportive of the dispassionate observer's view that Jeane Kirkpatrick's was a life well lived.

This review of Peter Collier's Political Woman: The Big Little Life of Jeane Kirkpatrick *(New York: Encounter Books, 2012), 241 pp.,* was *originally published in the* Claremont Review of Books, *Vol. XII, Number 4, Fall 2012, https://claremontreviewofbooks.com/reagan-democrat/.*

Farewell to an Iron Lady
15 May 2013

If you want to understand the essential nature of Thatcherism and of Mrs Thatcher—their beating heart, so to speak—it is to be found in some words that she addressed to a television interviewer, Michael Brunson of Independent Television News, towards the close of the 1979 election campaign. Mrs Thatcher liked Brunson whom she knew to be fair and whom she suspected of being favourably inclined to her. Because of that friendly suspicion, she let down her pre-election guard somewhat and exclaimed with unrestrained passion: 'I can't bear Britain in decline. I just can't bear it.'

Gallons of ink have since been spilled on treatises about what Thatcherism is and about the ideological tendencies on which it draws. More such ink will be spilled below. But this outburst catches the central idea and emotional impulse of Mrs Thatcher's philosophy when it has been stripped of the particular policies and conservative and classical liberal ideas in which it gradually became clothed over time. A decade and a half later, when she returned to the theme in writing the introduction to her memoirs, she confessed a little more cautiously that while she thought it would be presumptuous to compare herself with Pitt the Elder, the eighteenth-century statesman who defeated France in the Seven Years War and laid the foundations of the Second British Empire, she nonetheless had to admit that if she was honest, she felt as he did: 'I am sure that I can save this country and that no one else can.'

Human beings are complicated animals, however, and the more intelligent they are, the more complicated they become because they have to reconcile their various impulses both with each other and with the awkward facts of life. In addition to being a passionate patriot, Mrs Thatcher was also an instinctive economist, a devout Methodist, a committed anti-totalitarian, a lifelong student, a highly practical politician, and a deeply un-frivolous woman. All of those aspects of her personality found expression in her public policies over time.

Given that the post-war decline of Britain had been principally an economic one, especially in the 1960s and 1970s when she became active in high politics, she gradually developed a critique that explained that decline as a failure of state control and socialist ideas. Her remedies for this failure, while cautious and flexible in dealing with problems as they arose, were drawn almost entirely from the tradition of classical liberal economics. (It helped that this tradition was largely an Anglo-Scottish one.) Yet when British interests were challenged from another direction or on different grounds, as in the Falklands War and the Cold War, she drew both on a tough-minded realistic tradition of national interest and on a more moralistic one of liberal internationalism to justify her patriotic purposes.

If a fierce patriotism drove her, it was governed by a highly practical prudence. Her two central victories in the Falklands War and the miners' strike illustrated this. She did not expect or plan for the Argentinean seizure of the islands, but a politics of national regeneration could hardly refuse such a challenge. Her conduct of the war thereafter alternated cautious diplomacy with bold military action. She took calculated risks on both halves of the policy but only after she had digested the best expert advice. Once victory was sure, she was adamant in refusing the pleas of her great ally, Ronald Reagan, that its fruits be compromised away. Similarly, she surrendered to the miners' union demands in 1981 when she was informed that the nation had insufficient coal stocks to resist a strike. But she at once began preparations, including a build-up of coal stocks at power stations, to resist any strike later. When it came three years later, she defeated it hands down.

These two outright victories ran completely counter to the usual post-war British politics of fudge, compromise, and splitting the difference. They were a declaration that a new kind of self-confident and determined conservatism was in the driving seat. Together with her prominence in Cold War diplomacy, and her successful economic policy, they established her domestic dominance, entrenched her economic and labour union reforms as the new consensus of British politics, elevated her international profile, and enabled her to influence events from Poland to Namibia that would usually have been outside London's ambit.

That suited Mrs Thatcher very well since she believed that British influence in world affairs had been exercised mainly for the good of mankind, and in particular for the benefit of liberal civilization. She was very happy to maximize it for that reason among others. But she was realistic about the limits of British power even if she disliked conceding these limits openly. As Robin Harris points out in his impressive biographical study, *Not for Turning: The Life of Margaret Thatcher*, she resisted admitting that the local facts of power in Asia had compelled her to yield Hong Kong to China even though that was clearly the case. There may have been method even in this myopia since the outcome of her negotiations with Deng Xiaoping, namely 'One China, Two Systems,' has worked to the benefit of China, Hong Kong, and Britain itself. But it obscured her fundamental realism of outlook even as it encouraged her to push for more than she could reasonably expect. What helped her actually to get more than she could reasonably expect was the improvement in Britain's economic and financial circumstances. When the British economy began its spectacular rise in the 1980s, she found Britain revalued upwards and herself hailed as the pioneer of a new worldwide free-market revolution.

In brief, Mrs Thatcher set out to save Britain but she ended up helping to save the world too—or at least helping to make it a freer and more prosperous place.

None of this would have seemed remotely possible in 1975 when she was elected Tory leader. All but a handful of her colleagues in the 'Shadow Cabinet' were either Tory grandees or Heathite managerialists who regarded her as a narrow, bigoted, suburban woman of primitive views—'*Daily Telegraph* woman' in a phrase minted by the High Tory writer and politician, Ian Gilmour. She earned this contempt honestly because she was the first major party leader to stand against the social democratic consensus—broadly speaking, a comprehensive welfare state resting on a state-run 'mixed economy'—forged by the Labour government of 1945–51, then entrenched by the Tory Party's practical endorsement. Even in the final stages of its decomposition in the 1979

'Winter of Discontent,' this consensus could count on the practical support of most members of the Tory establishment even if the party's grass roots were always hostile to it. Thatcher stood with the Tory rank-and-file on the common-sense grounds that without such firm opposition, Britain would drift deeper and deeper into an enervating statism.

As she says in the introduction to her memoirs about her colleagues in the post-war Tory establishment:

> What they said and what they did seemed to exist in two separate compartments. It was not that they consciously deceived anyone; they were in fact conspicuously honourable. But the language of free enterprise, anti-socialism and the national interest sprang readily to their lips, while they conducted government business on very different assumptions about the role of the state at home and of the nation state abroad. Their rhetoric was prompted by general ideas they thought desirable, such as freedom; their actions were confined by general ideas they thought inevitable, such as equality.

Thatcher was in small but good company against this social democratic consensus. In 1975 when she stood for the Tory leadership against the former Prime Minister, Edward Heath, she was backed by only one other member of the Shadow Cabinet, the noble Sir Keith Joseph. In her four years as Opposition Leader, she was in a Shadow Cabinet dominated by rivals and opponents. Even so, she gradually edged them towards a more robust election manifesto than most wanted. And when the election came, she had the spirit for it.

'Maggie Thatcher? Reactionary?,' she asked in a 1979 speech; 'Well, there's a lot to react against.' But she did more than simply react. She won three elections against the social democratic consensus. She defeated it 'in the fine print of policy, especially in government,' and on key issues: the abolition of exchange control, labour union reform, the defeat of inflation, the "Big Bang" that made the City of London the main financial centre for Europe, the sale of one million council houses to sitting tenants, the privatization of twenty-six major state-owned industries ... the list goes on and on. But her domestic achievements can be summarized in a single statistic: one decade after she took office, ten years after Britain's Winter of Discontent, the British economy had become the fourth largest economy in the world.

Her domestic success was not total. It did not include the welfare state, where she left reform too late, or Europe, where she was brought down in part because she was beginning to oppose the same leftwards drift she had fought in her own country. Still, in the end she created a new consensus—not quite what she wanted, but better than what she had fought in 1979, and far better than if the Tories had continued drifting thoughtlessly left under an uninterrupted succession of Heaths, Majors, and Camerons.

Maybe the most persuasive judgement comes from one of her opponents in the 1987 election. Writing in the *London Review of Books*, he said: 'Mrs Thatcher clearly regards herself as a dea ex machina, sent down from on high to "knock Britain into shape." She will wield her powers over the next few years dictatorially and without compunction. On the other hand, there is a tremendous danger—to which Dr [David] Owen has succumbed—in believing that "Thatcherism" is somehow now invincible, that it has established a new consensus and that all the rest of us can do is debate alternatives within its framework. It is essential to demythologize "Thatcherism."' What makes this persuasive, in a way contrary to its argument, is that its author is Tony Blair who ten years later had persuaded Labour that Thatcherism had established a new consensus and that the party could win power only by debating alternatives within its framework. Her final achievement was to convert the opposition.

Those achievements explain why Mrs Thatcher was generally described in media reports as 'the most important peacetime British Prime Minister' of the twentieth century and perhaps of all time. But that description, though flattering, risks being misleading and even inadequate. It implies that she was an Attlee rather than a Churchill and that her achievements were confined to domestic policy. In reality, she had a strong impact abroad as well. This is not merely a reference to the Falklands. Her success in that war does not make her a great wartime leader on the scale of Churchill or Lloyd George because it was on too small a scale. But wars are far from being the sole test of international power and influence. Preventing wars and winning decisive conflicts without them are even better indicators.

Indeed, Mrs Thatcher's record here was stellar. Unlike Churchill who sorrowfully conceded late in life that Britain was weaker following his stewardship than beforehand, she left her country stronger than she found it on entering office. How so?

She was President Reagan's most reliable ally in the last stage of the Cold War. She played a decisive role in helping other West European governments to resist the powerful peace movement—it could put millions of protesters onto the streets of their countries—and thereby getting US missiles stationed in Western Europe. When that was achieved in 1984–85, it produced an almost instant if disguised change in Soviet policy. It persuaded the Soviets that they could no longer win the Cold War by military intimidation. At the very least, therefore, she was an active force in ensuring that the West did not lose the Cold War.

She then played her second important role in the Cold War, acting as a go-between for Reagan and Mikhail Gorbachev in their crabwise dance towards its peaceful solution. Her search for a new type of Soviet leader settled on Mikhail Gorbachev in 1984 when he visited Chequers on a stop-off air-flight. She debated him over the lunch table—Mrs Thatcher famously enjoyed arguing with people and generally liked them the better for it—pronounced him 'a man we can do business with,' and recommended him warmly to the President both publicly and privately. Reagan reached the same conclusion and acted accordingly. For the next three years, he worked with Gorbachev to end the Cold War peacefully in a series of Soviet–American summits. Though absent from these events (somewhat to her frustration), Thatcher had helped set the stage for the gradual Soviet surrender on arms control at the Geneva, Reykjavik, and Washington summits. She therefore helped win the Cold War—and to do so peacefully.

But these summits, though they ratified the West's peaceful victory, did not bring an end to communism. Indeed, from the Soviet standpoint, they were part of Gorbachev's strategy to rescue communism from its internal stresses and strains by freeing up resources locked inside his military budget, attracting aid and investment from the West, and thus stimulating and reforming the civilian economy. This was a sensible strategy, yet as we know, perestroika failed and communism collapsed. What brought about the end of reform communism was competition from the revived capitalism in the West—and that was at least as much the work of Thatcher as of Reagan.

Thatcher had been the subordinate partner in the Reagan–Thatcher relationship on military and diplomatic policy. She fought and even won some battles with Reagan—for instance, on the Soviet gas pipeline—but in general, he laid down the broad lines of policy to which she largely conformed. Given the relative size of their two economies, that should also have been true of economic policy. Yet it was not so. Owen Harries, the distinguished Australian editor of *The National Interest* magazine, once argued that where Thatcher and Reagan differed on economic policy, she would probably be regarded by history as the more important and influential economic reformer. That looks increasingly likely. Again, how so?

In the first place, the recovery of the British economy in the 1980s was more impressive because it started from a lower economic point and occurred in a more left-wing country. Then, Thatcher had harder opposition to overcome—her labour market deregulation, for instance, had to overcome resistance from timid Tory 'Wets' as well as from Labour MPs. Next, as we have seen, the reforms had to defeat major non-parliamentary challenges from the labour unions, above all, the 1984–85 miners' strike. Once the miners were defeated, the British economy began its long boom combining economic growth with price stability.

That transformation did not stop at the Atlantic's edge. Both the British and US economies became demonstration effects of what free market reforms could accomplish in a remarkably short time. The birth of the information economy was one among these accomplishments. But even though very similar ideologically, these two demonstration effects were not identical in terms of policy: tax cuts were America's principal intellectual export; privatization was Britain's. Of the two, privatization turned out to be the more important globally since both Third World and post-communist economies were burdened by large inefficient state industries. Once embarked upon, privatization succeeded with surprising speed. The Soviets, and still more remarkably, West European Communists and Social Democrats were forced to change course by increasing evidence that it promoted greater efficiency, a wider spread of capital ownership, and a cultural spirit of enterprise. The most unlikely converts were forced to take note.

While researching my book on Reagan, Thatcher, and the Pope, I found this unwitting tribute to the Iron Lady in the Soviet Politburo archives: a 1986 conversation between Gorbachev and Alexander Natta, the General Secretary of the Italian Communist Party:

> Natta: At the same time we, the communists, having either overestimated or underestimated the functions of the "welfare state," kept defending situations which, as it became clear only now, we should not have defended. As a result, a bureaucratic apparatus, which serves itself, has swelled. It is interesting that a certain similarity with your situation, which you call stagnation, can be seen here.

> Gorbachev: 'Parkinson's law' works everywhere ...

> Natta: Any bureaucratization encourages the apparatus to protect its own interests and to forget about the citizens' interests. I suppose, that is exactly why the Right's demands of re-privatization are falling on a fertile ground in Western public opinion.

For that reason Thatcher, even more than Reagan, posed an economic challenge to the Soviet Union. The challenge was: either reform or fall ever further behind the capitalist West. The comparison between the British recovery after a decade of free market economics and the continuing stagnation of the Soviet economy after seventy years of statist communism was simply too embarrassing to ignore. When Gorbachev's perestroika was introduced, however, it destroyed the communist system it was designed to save. Gorbachev therefore, while he deserves credit for not employing brute force to sustain Soviet power, was not really an active mover and shaker in the transition to post-communism. He was essentially an effect rather than a cause, a response to Thatcher, Reagan, and the policies of strategic and economic competition that they promoted. Without Reagan and Thatcher, there would have been no Gorbachev.

Once the command economies of the Soviet bloc collapsed in 1989, revealing the extraordinary wasteland of state planning, moreover, it was the Thatcher model that the new democracies mainly sought to emulate. She, Reagan, and John Paul II were all heroes in post-communist Europe, but it was Thatcher to whom the new economy ministers such as Poland's Leszek Balcerowicz, Czechoslovakia's Václav Klaus, and Estonia's Mart Laar looked as their model of how to reform a bankrupt socialist economy. And the more that they followed the Thatcher model, the more quickly their economies rose from the dead.

Yet it was not only in the post-communist world that Thatcher was seen as an inspiration. Thatcherism had an important impact both in the lagging Third World economies and in the rising NICS (or newly industrializing countries) in Africa and Asia. Privatization, the better control of public debt, lower taxes, and the reduction of barriers to trade and capital movements—these became the new conventional wisdom in Ministries of Finance around the globe. Their result—'globalization'— became the watchword of World Bank and IMF reports. Mrs Thatcher herself emerged in retirement as a kind of economic heroine of Asian capitalism, invited regularly to Asian countries and frequently consulted by their governments. Her death was treated there as a significant event as analyst Martin J. Sieff pointed out in his column for the *Asia-Pacific Defense Forum*:

> Thatcher's passing … was widely and sympathetically reported throughout the official media in China. Most major newspapers carried long features praising her achievements on their front page. The English-language *China Daily* turned over the entirety of its back page to her—an unprecedented honour for any foreign leader in modern times.

The reason is that her reform programme was seen as an important test by Asian economic reformers. Deng Xiaoping had embarked on his free market 'Four Modernizations' programme in the same year that Mrs Thatcher was elected. She was not a main inspiration for them in the first instance. His models were probably Lee Kuan Yew in Singapore and the

Taiwanese (though Deng could hardly admit that). But these models were flawed insofar as they were experiments, however successful, in a city-state and a small economy respectively. What Thatcher demonstrated was that free market reforms could transform a large advanced economy that was sclerotic and a polity that was allegedly ungovernable even under democratic constraints. That encouraged Deng's reformers to persist with their policies. As the Thatcherite reform programme expanded further in the 1980s, they took note of such deregulatory changes as the financial "Big Bang" in their design of Shanghai as a financial centre. With successful results as Sieff again demonstrates:

> Chinese economists and bankers watched closely as the deregulated City of London and its banks utterly outstripped Paris and Frankfurt, despite Germany's far larger economy at the time and France's central power role in the European Community to become the dominant financial centre of Europe and once again one of the three largest, wealthiest, and most important in the world.

> Thatcher's free market example therefore helped explain why the unregulated 'anything goes' Chinese economy and financial system continued to roar in a continuing bull market boom through the last decade of the 20th century and the first decade of the 21st century, while Japan's far more cautious, integrated, and consensual banking and financial system went into a tailspin in the early 1990s followed by a generation-long stagnation from which it has yet to fully recover.

China's success, which continues, compelled other Asian governments (notably India) to go down similar reform paths. These economic transformations brought literally billions of Asian workers out of subsistence economies (and worse) into the global labour market. They have created new middle classes across Asia. And, not irrelevantly, they have reduced the cost of living for poor people in Western countries even as they lifted the standard of living for poor people in Europe and North America. As Mrs Thatcher would be the first to point out, these results are the latest success for the traditional British (or Whig) economic policy: sound money, property rights, and free trade and capital movement. And they occurred in part because Mrs Thatcher both implemented them and argued for them.

If the world can see that Margaret Thatcher was a great world historical figure, why was her reputation at home more controversial? The short answer is that Mrs Thatcher, like Franklin Roosevelt, was a great reforming politician whose reforms had to overcome bitter opponents and vested interests from the striking miners to the 'Wets' in her own party to the liberal intelligentsia that controlled most of Britain's cultural institutions—including Oxford that refused its most famous graduate an honorary degree and the BBC that treated the street parties celebrating her death as serious indicators of public opinion. Such struggles leave deep wounds especially on the losing side. The continuing hostility of her various opponents was a reflection of the completeness of her victory over them. At the time of her death, they still nursed grievances and revenge fantasies.

The extreme Left's bitterness fuelled the more repulsive responses to her death: the street parties and the chanting of the 'Ding Dong, the Witch is Dead.' These usually turned out to be led or inspired by middle-class public sector people in non-jobs. They are a symptom of the cultural decline of Britain which she did not manage to stem (thinking it necessary to defeat the labour unions and the Soviets first). She herself would have seen the street parties as comforting evidence that she had deeply wounded the Caliban Left. Ten years after losing office, she had responded to a mob chanting 'Thatcher, Thatcher, Thatcher, Fascist, Fascist, Fascist, Out, Out, Out' by turning to her speechwriter, Robin Harris, and saying 'Oh, Robin, doesn't it make you feel nostalgic?' But as the respectful and affectionate reaction of the crowds to her funeral showed, these extreme hostilities are ludicrously out of step with public opinion.

The 'Wets' in the Tory establishment whom she outmanoeuvred have mainly conceded that she got the big things right. They still nurse a wounded vanity because in winning the battle with the labour unions, she also demonstrated that their entire political strategy was rooted in a defeatism that proved mistaken. Managing an inevitable decline looks very foolish when the decline is reversed. Their modern equivalents—the

Cameron "modernizers"—began by distancing themselves from her on a similar calculation. They have now reversed themselves and argue that Mrs Thatcher was 'a modernizer' herself. This argument is essentially a semantic game: modernization is an empty concept that needs filling with content before it can be assessed. Thatcher's modernization consisted of sound money, ending exchange rate control, cutting taxes, building up defence, privatization, etc. Cameron's modernization consists of same-sex marriage, "ring-fencing" foreign aid, sharply cutting defence, allowing the UK financial sector to be regulated by Brussels, etc., etc. They are not quite the same thing. Still, the semantic game is nonetheless an admission by the Tory establishment that her body is now well worth snatching.

The critics of her opposition to Britain's joining the Exchange Rate Mechanism and the euro itself have, for understandable reasons, have fallen silent. She now looks as prescient on euro-federalism as she had previously been on market economics and the Cold War.

Her liberal opponents in the intelligentsia—moderate Labour, the cultural establishment, the BBC, the universities, etc. etc.—have retreated from their earlier criticisms which were too embarrassingly snobbish ('suburban,' 'odiously vulgar,' etc.). They now suggest in a world-weary way that she was not that important really, a conventional Tory politician until 1975, when she saw an opportunity to rise and adopted an economic liberalism then in the air. She was more a symptom of global changes than their inspirer. She did not really make much of a difference, etc., etc.

Well, maybe it is more comforting to be defeated by a trend than by a person. But this is an argument that could be employed to demonstrate that no statesman is ever more than an innocent bystander since, almost by definition, a successful statesman has historical trends on his side. None of these critics argued *at the time* that Mrs Thatcher was the beneficiary of favourable historical trends; indeed, they very often argued the precise opposite—that she was defying such trends. This dismissive claim is also false biographically. As Charles Moore's new biography makes clear, she gradually developed a political position that was subtly different from the Tory establishment's policies in both government and opposition. In the early 1960s, she told a meeting of despairing Tory MPs brought together by the Institute of Economic Affairs that they should go into a different business if they could not persuade the voters that Marks and Spencer gave them a better deal than the Post Office. In 1968, when she was the leading woman frontbencher in the Tory opposition, she gave a major lecture to the annual party conference in which almost all the ideas that later became known as Thatcherism were clearly laid out. (I attended the lecture and well recall the excitement of the younger Conservatives afterwards. Someone high in the party was finally speaking their language.)

Above all, her convictions (and the global achievements to which they led) were rooted originally in the values of provincial England in the 1930s–patriotism, hard work, diligence, prudence, the Methodist faith and a moral earnestness that metropolitan liberals liked to mock. These were what Shirley Robin Letwin called the 'vigorous virtues' in her study, *The Anatomy of Thatcherism*, and which she saw as the essence of Thatcherism. They are the virtues that enable people to be self-reliant and to live in a free society. And they are the essential foundation of the softer virtues such as compassion since only self-reliant people are in a position to help others. Mrs Thatcher did not merely approve of these virtues in a theoretical way. She lived them. She was a grocer's daughter who saw in simple practical terms how the free market brought goods from all over the world to a small town in Lincolnshire. She was a hard-working scholarship girl who knew that knowledge is both hard-won and precious, and who never stopped learning. And she was a well-brought-up Methodist girl whose favourite religious quotation was John Wesley's 'Earn all you can; save all you can; give all you can.' Her revolution was provincial before it conquered the world, a moral revolution before it was an economic one. Margaret Thatcher was a Goddess of the Copybook Headings.

In a way, that was why she was hated and despised. She reminded people of obligations they had forgotten and of shortcomings they wished to forget. She was a walking reproach to a certain kind of cynical worldview.

In the face of death, however, these passions dissolve, or should do so, and in most cases they did. As the funeral approached, a general sentiment seemed to coalesce in all but the hardest critics that she was one of the great figures of British history. As with Ronald Reagan's funeral, the event itself seemed to settle the question.

Yet the funeral, which she herself had largely planned, was by no means a celebration of her worldly achievements. It was the traditional Christian farewell to a humble soul seeking the mercy of God. She took the need for such mercy as seriously as she took more strenuous Christian truths. On the last pages of her memoirs, she tells of attending a Catholic mass in a Warsaw church where the congregation had welcomed her warmly as someone whose messages to them during the Cold War had shown an understanding sympathy for their lives under communism. She then reflected that '… the full accounting of how my political work affected the lives of others is something we will only know on Judgment Day. It is an awesome and unsettling thought. But it comforts me to think that when I stand up to hear the verdict, I will at least have the people of the Church of the Holy Cross in court as character witnesses.'

Rest in Peace.

Originally published in Hungarian Review, *Vol. IV, No. 3, May 2013,* *www.hungarianreview.com/article/farewell_to_an_iron_lady.*

After She Lost, Did Margaret Thatcher Win?
21 September 2020

By most historical standards 1989 should have been a year of triumph for Margaret Thatcher—and judged in a historical perspective, it was exactly that. It was the year that saw the fulfilment of her main political and personal hopes with the fall of the Berlin Wall, the collapse of the Soviet Empire in Europe, and unmistakable signs that the USSR itself was fatally struck. Paradoxically, it was also the year in which she herself was beset by increasing difficulties in both foreign and domestic affairs, quarrels with her closest allies and colleagues, avoidable major errors, and the first intimations of her own political mortality.

But Thatcher's long march to 1989 began in 1984 with her visit to Hungary. It was written up at the time as evidence of the 'softening' of Thatcher. She had visited a street market in Budapest and received a 'warm, indeed passionate,' welcome from the crowds of shoppers. The British press reported that she had discovered Communists were human beings like herself. In fact, Thatcher had always known that. What she discovered—or, rather, confirmed for herself—was that the shoppers were not Communists. Wherever she went in Eastern Europe before the fall of communism, she received a warm, indeed passionate, welcome because she was regarded by ordinary Eastern Europeans as a symbol of opposition to communism.

Her visit to Budapest had been conceived as a roundabout method of reopening contacts with the Soviet Union. János Kádár, who had ruled communist Hungary since the Soviet suppression of the 1956 Hungarian Revolution, was close to the Soviets and especially to Andropov, who as Soviet Ambassador to Budapest in 1956 had masterminded that suppression. Kádár was a cynical but faithful old Communist who made plain the rules of Hungary's Cold War game: the Soviets would allow him considerable freedom to experiment with a quasi-capitalist economy provided that the country's membership of the Warsaw Pact was never questioned.

That did not surprise Thatcher, who was hoping to send Kádár as a messenger boy to the Kremlin. She and Reagan had been sending out messages of interest in better East–West relations for a year in their speeches. But these had either been ignored or not understood as such by a paranoid Andropov. Thatcher reiterated these messages to Kádár, telling him that Reagan had been disappointed at the summary dismissal of his personal appeal to Brezhnev. Andropov should know that Reagan was still interested in better relations. In turn Kádár told Thatcher that Andropov was a hard, calculating man but one who listened and could be dealt with. Was not he ill? Yes, but he was improving.

All this information about Andropov proved useless as well as misleading six days later, when he died. Thatcher reported back to Reagan that establishing better relations would be a 'long and slow process.' But Gorbachev had already been identified by the British as a better prospect—and five months later, during the short rule of the sickly Chernenko, she met him at Chequers and the process of establishing better relations began in earnest. There was, however, a subtext to Thatcher's visit that was to prove highly significant.

One motive for the Hungarians in inviting her was to demonstrate the relative success of the "liberalized" Hungarian economy. Communists all over the Eastern Bloc were increasingly aware that the legitimacy of their regimes was quietly collapsing. They were looking for a substitute legitimacy as Marxism became more and more of a laughingstock. Some opted for extreme nationalism—notably, Slobodan Milošević in Yugoslavia. Others saw that democracy was the only real modern legitimacy. They were calculating that they should reinvent themselves as social democrats, lose the first multi-party elections, and return to power when the chaos they had left behind doomed the first democratic government. (Hungarian, Czech, Slovak, and Polish Communists all managed this trick in the next decade.) The Hungarian Communists would have liked Thatcher's *imprimatur* on their reforms. She was quite open to persuasion on their value. In the event, she was extremely disappointed.

Even so, the Communists' desire for capitalist approval, in particular for Thatcher's approval, gave rise to a distinctive British diplomacy over the next few years. It had three stages: first, to establish better trade and commercial relations with Eastern Europe in order to lessen its reliance on the COMECON Bloc; second, to make an improvement in human rights a condition of improving these economic ties; and third, to insist on internal political reforms in return for greater investment.

This economic diplomacy was supplemented with gestures of political support for democratic and religious dissidents: for instance, the British foreign minister was the first Western diplomat to place a wreath on the grave of Father Popiełuszko in Poland. In other words, as the communist political structures of Eastern Europe began to crack under such pressures as John Paul's campaign for religious liberty and the growing resistance of dissident movements, Thatcher stepped forward to offer economic inducements for communist governments to do the right thing and open up avenues to liberty. And as time went on, her conditions for help became tougher.

Her next visit was to the Soviet Union in 1987. This was one trip from which she had something personal to gain—an election was coming up and she would benefit from the sheer glamour of the Iron Lady conquering Moscow, if only by agreement. From that standpoint, the visit was an unqualified success: she enjoyed enormous and almost entirely favourable publicity. International press reports gave out that her debate with Gorbachev over the relative merits of communism and capitalism had gone well over schedule because both sides had enjoyed it. She debated three Soviet political commentators on Moscow television and, as even Gorbachev privately admitted to the Politburo, made mincemeat of them with her experience in parliamentary repartee. As in Hungary, she was mobbed by friendly crowds at a Moscow housing estate and on a trip to Georgia. All of this—against exotic Russian and Georgian backgrounds—greatly boosted her election prospects at home. She went home to win a landslide election victory.

By the time Thatcher left Moscow, she had concluded that the ground was cracking under the Soviet system—even if, as she noted, the regime still had enough residual power to stage a delegation of 'impeccably distinguished Soviet stooges' who hymned the achievements of socialism in advance of her meeting with the great dissident Andrei Sakharov and his wife, Yelena Bonner. But *perestroika* and *glasnost* were generating more hopes than they could fulfil. And as she observed, quoting de Tocqueville, the moment a despotism begins to reform is the moment of its greatest danger.

Her visit to Poland in November 1988 was more consequential because Poland's communist system had advanced further toward disintegration. The 'artificial peace of totalitarianism,' imposed by the declaration of martial law seven years earlier, had failed to "normalize" the country. Pope John Paul II's third pilgrimage to Poland in June of the previous year had cracked the ice and revived *Solidarność* or the Solidarity Movement. And the shoots of free politics were now beginning to grow again.

Thatcher had consulted the Pope before setting out. It was plain to both of them that Eastern European communism, especially in Poland, was at the point of collapse. The regimes were so discredited that they had to rely on the moral authority of their opponents for their continued power—first the Pope, then Wałęsa, now Thatcher. General Jaruzelski's main motive for inviting the British Prime Minister was the hope she might argue that economic rationality required support for his economic reforms. On the eve of her visit, the regime announced that it was closing the Lenin Shipyard on the 'Thatcherite' grounds that it was unprofitable, indeed sustaining heavy losses.

A trap was being sprung for her: she was supposed to endorse treating Lech Wałęsa as if he were the leader of the UK miners' strike, Arthur Scargill. If that was what the regime expected, what it got was a lecture in the true nature of free market economics. Thatcher pointed out that profits and losses were concepts that made sense only if there was a market. Since the Lenin Shipyard was selling to only one customer, namely the Soviet authorities, its viability depended almost entirely on changes in the rouble–zloty exchange rate. Even so the shipyard was making smaller 'losses' than its 'competitors.' It was being proposed for closure because the regime felt political resentment towards it.

Throughout the official portions of her visit—including the state dinner where she was alongside Jaruzelski—she made these and similar points about Poland's economic troubles. She also repeated the Pope's moral arguments for Solidarity: if the communist government wanted the Polish people to show economic responsibility, it should grant them the freedoms that go with it. And she gave these arguments a sharp personal edge. When it came to applying tough economic reforms to deep-seated problems, she told Poland's Communist leaders, the difference between them was that she had been elected three times to carry the reforms out.

More important than her official engagements, however, was her demonstration of sympathy with Solidarity. She did not only lay a wreath on the grave of Father Popiełuszko but also visited his parents and his church. Next day she flew to Gdańsk where, accompanied by Wałęsa, she laid another wreath on the shipyard memorial to the workers who had been shot down in 1970. She had a meeting over lunch (cooked by Wałęsa's confessor, Father Jankowski) with the Solidarity committee in Gdańsk. She then visited the Solidarity church, where a packed congregation of families rose at her entrance and sang 'God Give Us Back Our Free Poland.'

Everywhere in the city, she was cheered by huge crowds—from the moment she arrived, when hundreds of workers threw their caps into the air in unison, to the moment of her departure in a small boat, when the huge shipyard cranes were dipped seawards in her honour. It was, she writes in her memoirs, one of the most moving days of her life. She was unable to hold back her tears. But she also drew a very practical lesson from it. Before leaving Warsaw, she saw Jaruzelski a final time and told him, as one hardheaded politician to another, that Solidarity looked to her like an unstoppable political force. He made no comment.

Two months later—on 19 January 1989—Solidarity was recognized as an independent labour union. Three weeks after that, the round-table negotiations on new political structures began. An agreement on new elections was signed in April, and the elections themselves were scheduled for June. The method of voting was an unusual one: the voters crossed out the names of those candidates they wanted to reject. Voters joyfully crossed out the names of the Communists who had oppressed them for forty years. Solidarity won every contested seat but one. In July, the new parliament dominated by Solidarity kept its word given in the round-table negotiations and elected Jaruzelski president—by one vote. One month after that, Jaruzelski, whose own candidate for Prime Minister had failed to form a government, asked Tadeusz Mazowiecki (whom he had jailed eight years before) to be the next prime minister.

Mazowiecki took office at the head of Poland's first post-Second World War democratic government on 12 September 1989—exactly ten years and three months after John Paul II had landed in Poland and appealed to God, 'Let Your Spirit come down and renew the face of the land—this land.'

On the day before that, the Hungarian government had opened its border with Austria to allow East Germans vacationing in the country to escape to the West. Two months later the Berlin Wall was opened up. By spring 1990, the Soviet Empire had shrunk down almost to the territory of the USSR itself.

Yet that triumphant year also marked in January the end of her historic partnership with Ronald Reagan who left the presidency that month, and except for a handful of modest interventions, left politics too. She was the recipient of his last message as President, as she had been his last official visitor in November 1988, when the three-day event had been a nostalgic celebration of their joint stewardship of the Anglo-American special relationship. She was the guest of honour at dinners given by Reagan and his successor George H. W. Bush and at a farewell lunch given by Secretary of State George Shultz. As a former Thatcher aide, I was invited to the last of those occasions which was bathed in an atmosphere of warm affection—she and Shultz had generally been on the same side in diplomatic and even internal administration rows—and he gave her a large expensive handbag as a parting gift to amused applause. In retrospect, these farewell courtesies benefited greatly from the fact that Reagan had one of the very few political careers that ended in unqualified success in which she rightly shared.

Most observers assumed that the British Prime Minister would continue to enjoy the same warm personal and political alliance with the first President Bush since they had been friends during the previous eight years, liked each other, and seemed to be on the same broad ideological wavelength. All those reasons were valid enough, but the expectation of another Anglo-American partnership unravelled quite quickly. It did so on the issue of nuclear weapons in Germany.

Thatcher's own successful Cold War diplomacy, amplified by together with Western Europe's 'Gorbymania,' meant that German opinion was moving in an almost pacifist direction. It was particularly (and reasonably) concerned about the likelihood that in any conflict the short-range nuclear missiles would fall on Germans on both sides of the rusting Iron Curtain. With an election coming up, Kohl had to reflect those fears. Thatcher, on the other hand, was legitimately concerned that the more the West reduced its nuclear missiles, the more it would be compelled to increase defence spending to counter the USSR's massive superiority in conventional forces. A year later, this dispute would look archaic. But both sides had a reasonable case, and both looked to Bush to decide the matter at the NATO summit.

In the run-up to the summit, Bush began by sympathizing with Thatcher. He was still conducting his own review of foreign policy prior to jumping into NATO politics. The first smoke signals that emerged from it suggested that the Bush administration would be tougher than Reagan which might have helped Thatcher who since Reykjavik had worried that US policy was dangerously flexible on nuclear weapons. Soon, however, a different narrative began to be heard: the Brits were too obstructive not only on NATO but also on European integration; Germany was the leading economic power in Europe which would have to be reflected in US policy; and Thatcher, though admirably brave and principled, was rigid, and preachy, and isolated within the alliance; and Kohl, a loyal ally, needed NATO's help to stay in office. It also became clear that even though Bush genuinely liked Thatcher, he was not comfortable or easy with her, and still more significant, that his aides would not be averse to taking her down a peg.

In the usual crabwise diplomatic dance, the Bush administration gradually swerved to support Kohl over Thatcher. At the NATO summit, it was decided that nuclear negotiations would cover medium-range missiles and not completely rule out covering short-range ones in time.

Bush had made a clear choice. It was seen in the media and elsewhere as a clear defeat for Thatcher. That judgement is confirmed in the third volume of Charles Moore's official biography in which he cites Thatcher's diplomatic alter ego (and effectively her unofficial Foreign Secretary) Charles Powell, as saying: 'Once Bush turned to Germany, that was the end of it all.' To that, Moore adds, 'He meant it was the end of the Anglo-American dominance in international affairs which she and Reagan had achieved and which, she believed, had brought victory in the Cold War.'

It was not, though, the end of her premiership which had two years to run. But as Hamlet remarked, when troubles come, they come not in single spies but in battalions. And in 1989, Thatcher had to confront large problems, rebellious senior colleagues, and a restive public opinion that weakened and hampered her conduct of policy. The two main problems were 'Europe' and the UK economy. In the next two years, they would bring about the resignations of her Foreign Secretary, her Chancellor of the Exchequer, and in due course herself.

'Europe' as an issue had seemingly been put into political cold storage by the Single European Act in 1986, which Thatcher hoped would shape a freer and more competitive European economy. But the EU Commission President, Jacques Delors, reversed the impact of the Act by making it a vehicle for extending regulation through regulatory 'harmonization.' In September 1988, he then urged the British trade union movement to take advantage of it to challenge her economic and social reforms. She responded twelve days later in the Bruges Speech by declaring that she had not reformed Britain in order to see Brussels reversing her reforms. That speech is sometime seen as the first step to Brexit. It certainly ignited a long debate within her party that won her strong support from ordinary party members but also pitted many of her most senior colleagues against her on maybe the single biggest issue in UK politics.

'Europe' was implicated too in her troubles over the economy. In 1988 and 1989, the UK economy suffered from a return of inflation that Chancellor Lawson sought to restrain by getting the pound to join the EU's Exchange Realignment Mechanism (ERM, a sort of ante-room to the euro). He was joined in his campaign by Foreign Secretary Geoffrey Howe, and for two years they pressed hard on Thatcher to do so. She lost both of them—Lawson resigned in late 1989—through her sceptical resistance to joining the ERM, which continued until a few weeks before she lost office in 1990. But the difficulties caused by the inflation, the measures to restrain it, and the ERM dispute all weakened the government and made every other domestic difficulty (for instance, the unpopular poll tax in local government) that much more damaging. By late 1989, the seeds had been sown that would gradually lead to Geoffrey Howe's resignation, a challenge to her leadership by former Defence Minister Michael Heseltine, her failure to win in the first ballot and her withdrawal from the second, her replacement by John Major—his first major statement as prime minister that Britain was at the heart of Europe, and a little later Britain's forced withdrawal from the ERM.

All these events seemed to confirm the wisdom of a personal letter that Charles Powell—who was both a great public servant and, together with his wife Carla, a devoted and attentive friend to Lady Thatcher to the day of her death—had written to the prime minister on the morrow of her 1987 election triumph. It suggested that she should retire while she was at the height of her success. The letter became public only years later. But it has shaped the conventional wisdom about her career, namely that she stayed on too long and that her reputation had suffered as a result. It is certainly an arguable view. But is it a view that does justice to the achievements of her final two years (in which Powell himself played a distinguished part) and of events beyond that?

We know from declassified papers that Thatcher's departure was regarded with incomprehension in Washington, Moscow, and around the world. That was because despite her internal battles, Thatcher had remained a major figure in settling international disputes and maintaining progress in liberating and democratizing Europe despite her weakened position right through 1989 and later.

Her almost unknown achievement in this was her shepherding South Africa out of Apartheid and into democracy without the bloodbath that many thought would inevitably accompany that transition. It is unknown because most people do not want to know it. They interpreted her opposition to sanctions as support for white South Africa when it was in fact a necessary adjunct to a vigorous diplomatic engagement with the South African government to persuade it to accept the necessity of democracy and black majority rule, win an election on that basis, negotiate with the African National Congress, free Nelson Mandela and move to regime change. Indeed, in the mid-1980s she had waged a vigorous and very tough diplomatic engagement with the South African government. But she lacked a South African Gorbachev until February 1989 when F. W. de Klerk became State President. She helped him persuade the white electorate to accept freedom for Mandela and a multi-racial democracy. We now have all the details of that diplomacy thanks to Moore's comprehensive biography, the book describing how that diplomacy was conducted by her ambassador to Pretoria, Robin Renwick, and not least the testimony of both Mandela and de Klerk. That success alone justified her staying on beyond 1987—not to mention a Nobel Peace Prize.

Her second and far greater achievement was the fall of the Berlin Wall. That was the achievement of many hands, but she and Reagan played the main Western roles (along with Pope John Paul II) in the First Act of the play, and she played a vital subordinate role in the Second Act. When the Wall fell, she had two immediate reactions and shortly afterwards a third. Her first response was a simple unadorned delight that people across Central and Eastern Europe had recovered their freedom. Her second was a nervous anxiety that the reunification of Germany (which she saw was a logical consequence of giving Germans their democratic liberties) risked destabilizing the balance of power in Europe by making Germany too powerful and in particular might undermine Gorbachev's position in Moscow and even reverse his *perestroika* and *glasnost* reforms there. And her third response was to reject the argument that the reunification of Germany should be accompanied by a rapid progress towards the political unity of Europe since—she argued—that would strengthen rather than restrain German power. In addition, there was a contradiction in the idea that restoring national independence to the new democracies should be remedied by the surrender of sovereignty to Brussels by all of Europe's democracies.

Thatcher's anxieties over German reunification were driven by her visceral dislike of Germany, but her arguments were both reasonable and prescient, and initially they were shared by Mitterrand, Bush, and Gorbachev. As with the NATO decision on nuclear weapons earlier in the year, however, Bush gradually moved to support Kohl (who emerges from those days as one of his country's greatest statesmen) in his shrewd drive towards German unity. And when Bush moved, Thatcher's allies in high places left her side one by one.

As she admits in her memoirs, her German policy met with unambiguous defeat. Probably too she was fighting an inevitability—as among others her good friend, Hungarian Prime Minister József Antall, recognized clearly. Again, however, she was amply justified in trying to ensure that the democratization of Central and Eastern Europe did not proceed in a way that threatened Gorbachev's position since if he went, the whole process of Soviet reform might be halted or even reversed. That was a real possibility as the 1991 Soviet counter-coup showed. It is significant, however, that the counter-coup occurred so late as to make its failure almost inevitable and to guarantee the survival of post-Soviet democracy. At least for a time. As Moore notes in his biography, one of those who thought that Gorbachev's surrender to the West over reunification was a humiliating defeat for his country was the KGB Resident in Dresden, one Vladimir Putin.

And as for her struggle to defend national sovereignties against Brussels, when Cabinet colleagues rebelled against her over her resistance to the accelerating surrender of national powers to Brussels in late 1990, Thatcher lost that battle too. At least for a time.

Epilogue

When Thatcher lost office in the dying days of 1990, having received the decisive blow to her hopes of remaining prime minister at the Paris Conference that ratified the liberation of Central and Eastern Europe, the end of the Cold War, and her own world-historical status, she went into a deep depression. Friends and colleagues rallied round to help her, most from admiration and affection, a few from the desire to ensure she would cause the Tory Party and its new leader as little trouble as possible. They arranged a private office, a business manager and team of talented advisers, accommodation in Westminster, and a crowded social diary. But no one could really provide her with what she really needed: the challenge of serious political activity that counted for something. And given that she was now a private citizen, how could she possibly get that?

In August 1991 she got it. Soviet hardliners imprisoned Gorbachev in his Crimean villa, announced a state of emergency on television, sent tanks and troops into Moscow, made some arrests, and planned to attack the Russian Parliament (the White House where Boris Yeltsin had repaired to lead the resistance). Western governments initially dithered, some assuming the coup would succeed. President Mitterrand referred to Yanayev as the 'new leader' of the Soviet Union on television; Helmut Kohl said merely that he hoped the Soviet Union would respect the agreements made by Gorbachev; others disappeared into meetings. (Thatcher happened to be meeting with Galina Starovoitova, a former spokesperson for Yeltsin, and learning she had his mobile number, rang him up on the barricades. He answered the call, and asked her to help. She immediately stepped onto the street outside her office and told the world via television that 'we shouldn't necessarily assume the coup would succeed' because the 'young people were no longer servile' and 'people power could prevail.'

That prediction was immediately confirmed by events. In short order the coup collapsed, Gorbachev returned to Moscow, Yeltsin took charge, the Soviet Union was constitutionally buried, and it was replaced by independent republics including a sovereign Russia governed by Yeltsin.

Bush and John Major had been irritated by Thatcher's intervention, but Yeltsin was 'thrilled' by it; József Antall, not coincidentally, had also rallied Central Europe against the coup; and Thatcher was reinvigorated, going on to write her memoirs and to remain a powerful presence in British politics for another decade.

One year later, Britain crashed out of the ERM, effectively dooming any chance of Britain joining the euro, and justifying her earlier resistance to it. From the grave, she won the internal British debate over EU membership when the country voted for Brexit in one referendum and two elections. And it is becoming clearer daily—see the decision of the German constitutional court that challenges the EU's legal supremacy—that euro-integration is not solving the problem of German power but making it more problematic for both Germany and the EU.

Would those things have happened as they did if Thatcher had retired in 1987? Or would they rather have been tackled earlier if she had remained in office after November 1990? Over to the counter-factual historians.

Originally published in Hungarian Review, *Vol. XI, No. 5, September 2020, www.hungarianreview.com/article/20200921_after_she_lost_did_ margaret_thatcher_win_.*

Did William F. Buckley's Conservative Project End in Failure?

20 July 2017

There may not be many positions in American journalism reserved for recognizable conservatives, but there is at least one that guarantees the standard 15 minutes of celebrity. It is that of the conservative critic of conservatism who laments that conservatism is not what it used to be and probably never was. Some distinguished writers have occupied this position—Garry Wills, Andrew Sullivan—generally on the way to something better; and some duds have too, generally on the way to various types of literary obscurity. The latest occupant is Julius Krein, editor of the new journal *American Affairs*, who used the opportunity of a review in *The Washington Post* of Alvin S. Felzenberg's new biography of William F. Buckley to seize the post.

And 'seize' is the word. His first sentence declares that the biography arrives 'just after the political and intellectual collapse of Buckley's conservative project.' Now, that is telling it straight. All the same, it contains too much prediction for my taste.

American conservatism is undoubtedly in flux and arguably in decline, but the cycle of political events which drives us to that judgment is far from complete. Without going to the lengths of Chou En-lai, we should wait a few years to see how fortune and philosophy favour the Trumpettes, the Never Trumpers, and everyone in between, including the latest 'new nationalist' intellectuals grouped around *American Affairs*.

I should also enter a second qualification: Mr Felzenberg's biography has not yet reached Budapest where I am now ensconced. All that I have learnt about it, as Bill himself would have guessed, is that I am mentioned once, on page 298, quite neutrally, as having taken over *National Review*'s editorship a little before the magazine's 35th anniversary. So, I shall be a disinterested but vigilant critic when I get the book. Until then, I cannot comment on Mr Krein's criticisms of the book's merits or otherwise.

Buckleyite conservatism itself is another matter. On that I have opinions, which are provoked by this early passage in the review: 'Buckley exerted a significant degree of influence on only one president, Ronald Reagan. He loathed Dwight Eisenhower; was considered a nuisance by Richard Nixon, Gerald Ford, and both George Bushes; and was shut out of Barry Goldwater's campaign.'

Let us examine this passage from back to front. Was WFB shut out of Goldwater's campaign? Not at all. He was sceptical of its chances and gave its handling to William Rusher, *NR*'s long-standing publisher, to whom Bill deferred on a number of major questions. Rusher was one of a small coterie of Republican activists who pushed Goldwater into running and shaped the early campaign. It fell apart after the convention. But *NR* was key to its rise through Rusher. And Buckley demonstrated that the ideas fuelling Goldwater's rise had a potential national appeal when he ran on them for the New York mayoralty.

Was he considered a 'nuisance' by Nixon, Ford, and the Bushes? At times certainly; that is an occupational hazard, and not the worst one, for scribblers advising the Prince. Machiavelli was sent to the torture chamber; Buckley was bought off with a post at the UN that he turned into a book. Game, Set, and Match to Buckley on that one. Though Buckley lost most of his battles with moderate Republican presidents, he did so on a rising tide of influence as Nixon's GOP led to successively more conservative ones and for most of Buckley's life America became an increasingly conservative country.

Did he loathe Eisenhower? For most of Eisenhower's time in office, yes. In fact, he defined the new conservatism largely in opposition to the policies of Eisenhower whose conservatism deserves more criticism than it receives today. It was a largely inert one in domestic politics; social problems grew while the economy boomed; in foreign policy, it encouraged an illusion of 'rollback' while privately embracing the 'containment' it had denounced in the 1952 election. When Hungarians rose in 1956, the Eisenhower administration cold-bloodedly turned its back on them. Buckley was not alone in thinking this a shameful betrayal and organized protests against it. But he was persuaded not to pursue this to the point of third-party politics.

But it is the line 'Buckley exerted a significant degree of influence on only one president, Ronald Reagan' that most startled me, reminding me of an old Soviet-era joke. At a Moscow meeting of the Union of Socialist Writers, one regional representative gives a buoyant report: 'In our region, Soviet literature has made astounding progress. Today, we have no fewer than 277 writers producing literature full-time, whereas in backward Czarist times the region could claim only one: Leo Tolstoy.'

To exert a significant influence on the president who won the Cold War, revived the American economy, created the conditions for the information revolution, helped to shape a new kind of open-world capitalism, and handed his successor a strong partisan lock on the presidency is no mean claim (or in Mr Krein's case, no mean admission). To be sure, Buckley had important disagreements with Reagan in office—Bill was by nature too restive to be a loyalist for long—and Reagan had important failures of policy. That said, there is a clear overall link between the major policies advocated by Buckley and NR (and adopted more generally over the years by the conservative movement he helped to create) and the principal successes of the Reagan administration, which, as it happens, were world-historical successes.

Mr Krein might agree with much of this, and maybe I should end there. But he goes on to make a larger argument that tempts me: 'that 20th-century American conservatism simply never made any sense. Far from a coherent program of high principle, it was always a largely accidental combination of inherited reflexes and political opportunism.' He thinks there was no central core—'no there there'—in conservatism. And he asserts that this incoherence reflects the trajectory of WFB's own career, which began with defending segregation and ranting against Eisenhower and ended with counselling against deficits and the Iraq War while in the meantime protecting conservatism against crackpots and bigots only at the cost of staffing it mainly by 'talk show hosts, sycophants and second-rate economists.' And more in like vein.

That strikes me as something of a caricature—Mr Krein's more than mine. Were Wilmore Kendall, Russell Kirk, Richard Neuhaus, and Milton Friedman among the talk-show hosts, sycophants, and second-rate economists cited above—or in more recent times Rick Brookhiser, Jonah Goldberg, Michael Novak, Ramesh Ponnuru, etc., etc.? I doubt it.

And has Buckleyite conservatism—which is undoubtedly in a crisis as evidenced by the shouting, curses, and stormings-out—really and finally cracked up? Or run out of steam philosophically? Or has it instead encountered new and massive challenges, which in turn have provoked disagreements and quarrels among people who had previously agreed with each other on most matters—as the French Revolution destroyed the long friendship of Burke and Fox?

Of course, public philosophies change over time, sometimes markedly so, because the problems that history throws at them change too. If they do not change in line with history, what you get is a politics of frozen and irrelevant gestures—something like today's leading Democrats playing members of the French Resistance about as convincingly as the cast of the British sitcom '*Allo, 'Allo*. Today's politics continue to revolve around some of the conservative themes that *NR*'s conservatism pioneered even after the Cold War had removed anti-communism from our quiver. Tax-and-spending proposals do not count here because they are always at the core of political debate (though conservatives ensure that there is a debate if they achieve nothing else). But immigration, which powered the rise of Trump in the primaries, was launched into post-Cold War politics by *NR*'s 1992 cover story 'Time to Rethink Immigration' and was then kept alive through dry climes by the magazine among others. The very fact that there are serious, even quite bitter, philosophical disputes taking place both within *National Review* and between *NR* and its conservative critics on this and other issues is a tribute to the continuing energy and fertility of conservatism. If Mr Krein wants another example, what about nationalism?

But I am forgetting; nationalism is one of the main issues that *American Affairs* exists to explore and explain. It does so very well, incidentally, in both of its first two issues. I congratulate Mr Krein on a lively and serious magazine, and I wish it well. I could not help noticing something else: the influence that the late James Burnham plainly exercises over the magazine. He is the subject of a major article in the first issue, one by Mr Krein himself, and he crops up on several occasions in issue number two. His theory of the managerial revolution is one of the two main sets of theory explaining the current upheavals of the Western world, according to Michael Lind in an article on 'The New Class War.' (The other theorist is J. K. Galbraith who, as Mr Lind notes, was linked with Burnham by their joint friendship with WFB.) Mr Lind is always worth reading, not least here where he develops a grand social theory on the largest scale, taking Burnham's theory of managerialism and updating it to the post-industrial and financial global economy. But Burnham also crops up, less expectedly but in context quite naturally, in an article on whether Confucianism will become the next state religion of China. (Probably not, is the answer, but his thought will be incorporated in whatever does.) Indeed, a kind of self-conscious Burnhamite realism pervades the magazine in which a fragment of conventional wisdom, generally a conservative one, is looked grimly in the face, knocked down, and then reshaped into a dourly determined theory of not wearing ideological blinkers while pursuing the national interest. It is all very exhilarating.

Reminiscent too. For James Burnham was, according to Bill Buckley, 'the dominant intellectual influence in the development of this journal [i.e., *National Review*]. … His commentary, during such crises as are merely suggested by mentioning Budapest, Suez, Berlin, the Bay of Pigs, Vietnam, was sustained by the workings of a great mind.' That influence went beyond geopolitics, however. Burnham was also the main influence keeping Bill and *NR* from advocating either political abstention or third-party votes in the 1950s and later when he was clearly playing with such ideas in his visceral opposition to Eisenhower. He persuaded Bill that the way to long-term influence in politics was to establish and promote a conservative movement within the GOP rather than outside it. In that spirit, whoever coined the term, he argued that *NR* should always support 'the most viable conservative candidate' in any race rather than the purest. And that course, pursued by Buckleyite conservatives, led to Reagan in 1980.

Why is Mr Krein so dismissive of Bill Buckley and the conservatism he fostered when both men are pupils of the same master? One reason, always lurking in such judgments, is that he may know but does not yet feel the truth of Enoch Powell's judgment that 'all political lives ... end in failure.' Buckley did know that and he spent the last decade of his life turning more and more to considerations of the next world. But a more likely and fruitful reason is that he misunderstands the real Bill Buckley.

He treats him in this review as a failed political philosopher who tried to keep too many balls in the air, with the result that most of them spilled off the stage into the wings or the orchestra stalls. Hence the seeming disintegration of a body that was never fully integrated. But Bill was not a Michael Oakeshott working out a new basis for conservatism or a Kenneth Minogue delving into the deepest errors of liberalism—though he liked to present such people, explore their ideas, and argue with them. He was several other things. In this context, there were really two Buckleys with two different roles on the world stage—one who was an irrepressible rebel constantly intrigued by amusing people and arresting ideas; the other who was (or was persuaded by Burnham to be) a serious man who over time disciplined his philosophical arguments and exploited his cultural prestige to bring about real political change in his time.

It sounds extravagant to say so, but this second Buckley was an Antonio Gramsci for the television age who transformed the fool's gold of celebrity into the real gold of conservative votes. The first Buckley, no less extravagantly, was a Diaghilev of opinion journalism, determined to shock and entertain, turning to a succession of editorial Cocteaus and demanding: 'Astonish me, Jean!'

That is why I know how he would have responded to Mr Krein's review. He would have sent him a note congratulating him on the piece. Then he would have invited him out for a drink. Then he would have offered him a job at *National Review*.

Just ask ... oh, any number of people in *NR*'s Index of Authors.

Originally published in National Review, *20 July 2017, www.nationalreview.com/2017/07/julius-krein-william-f-buckley-analysis-conservatism-success-failure/.*

Athwart History

A Review of *The Right: The Hundred-Year War for American Conservatism* by Matthew Continetti
Summer 2022

'The Right' is a term that, as we are currently reminded by the travails of Republicans in the US and Tories in Britain, covers a multitude of sinners. And the longer the period under inspection, the bigger the multitude grows. Consider the United States from 1921 to the present—the period covered by Matthew Continetti's important new book, *The Right*, which analyses how American conservatives saw and reacted to political currents in the United States during those years. It is a period that divides neatly into two halves: the years 1921–1989 were essentially the years of America's rise and dominance; those between 1989 and 2022 have been a time of disappointment, crises, and growing internal conflict. A nadir seems to have been reached today when the ruling national party and most of the nation's cultural institutions all insist that America is a racist, sexist, and white supremacist country from bottom to top—and when the principal conservative response is a confused and indignant stupefaction rather than a credible refutation and a confident prescription for recovery.

A fellow of the American Enterprise Institute and the founding editor of *The Washington Free Beacon*, Continetti begins his survey in a thriving 1920s America governed by Republicans faithful to a classical liberal view of limited government who had recently repelled postwar progressive interventionism under Woodrow Wilson. America roared for a decade, but it then foundered on the rocks of the Great Depression. Franklin D. Roosevelt's New Deal introduced a very significant, if initially modest, innovation by making government itself the provider of economic security of last resort. Whatever its later economic failures, the New Deal succeeded politically and—along with immigration

restrictions (from 1921 on) and the attack on Pearl Harbor (1941)—
ensured that a united country entered World War II. Victory in war
completed the transformation in what most Americans saw as the
legitimate role of government: an activist liberalism responding to
essentially conservative social and moral impulses. Overwhelming public
support for the G.I. Bill following the war is a perfect example.

Because the United States emerged after 1945 providing the world
with 50 per cent of its GDP, it had the power to apply its new activist
liberalism to international affairs, which it did with great success,
strengthening European economies with the Marshall Plan, establishing
global financial and trading institutions that revived the world economy,
and forming a powerful anti-Soviet alliance in NATO that shaped a
mainly stable peace for the duration of the Cold War. By and large these
new rules and institutions were good for America and for General
Motors. In the 1950s, the country enjoyed rising living standards, wider
educational opportunities, the worldwide spread of a healthy American
popular culture, a marriage and baby boom, a strong (albeit complacent)
national religious culture, diplomatic dominance in international
institutions, and a sense of national well-being under a respected war
hero's presidency.

It was into this world that American conservatism was born, with—
to select one significant moment—the founding of *National Review*. The
infant movement immediately looked around itself ... and did not like
what it saw in the least.

As William F. Buckley, Jr's founding statement—famously
announcing that the magazine would 'stand athwart history, yelling
Stop'—went on to say, its form of conservatism intended to roll back not
only international communism but also the 'effronteries' of the twentieth
century because 'in its late maturity America [has] rejected conservatism
in favor of radical social experimentation.' It seems an odd response to
the sober conformity of the Eisenhower years, but as it turned out, not an
absurd one. America's repressed discontents would break out a decade
later in the 1960s. Besides, argues Continetti, how Buckley judged
Eisenhower's America was determined, in part, by his comparison of it
with the Harding and Coolidge administrations that boasted of their

'normalcy.' At least, that comparison becomes the author's justification for starting his study of conservatism thirty years before the movement actually announced itself. When Buckley brought together the scattered, independent, and mutually incompatible social critics who were the core of his early venture—Whittaker Chambers, Russell Kirk, James Burnham, Frank Meyer among them—he was in effect recruiting them for a crusade to return America to the Golden Age of Normalcy.

Normalcy, however, was a divided kingdom. Though Republicans dominated the politics of the 1920s and early 1930s, they were themselves divided between the bankers and politicians of Wall Steet and Washington who ran a respectable regime *and* a tight fiscal ship, and (very much on the other hand) voting blocs, Continetti wants us to know, that included anti-Semitic college professors, primitive anti-Darwinian fundamentalists, and, above all, the nativist, anti-Catholic, and racist yahoos of the Ku Klux Klan. And yet it is worth recalling that the infamous 1925 Scopes Trial was prosecuted by a former Democratic presidential nominee, and the Klan, born from the ashes of the defeated Confederacy, was a part of the Democratic, not the Republican, coalition. Here Continetti finds his theme:

[T]he endless competition and occasional collaboration between populism and elitism. Is the American Right the party of insiders or outsiders? Is the Right the elites—the men and women in charge of America's political, social, economic, and cultural institutions—or is it the people?

These questions were briefly made irrelevant by the Right's collapse in the face of the Depression, a unifying war effort, and twelve years of Franklin D. Roosevelt. But Continetti's narrative resurrects this divided Right with the arrival of Buckley and *NR*, traces its turbulent zig-zag way through the Nixon, Reagan, and both Bush presidencies, and leaves it defeated, discredited, and in his view terminally shamed in the wake of Donald Trump's 'insurrection.'

As the 1950s move into the 60s, 'the Right' applies to more and more, sometimes overlapping, factions. Most of the time the term describes 'movement conservatives,' or the groups brought together by Buckley under the umbrella of 'fusionism.' Harvard political scientist

Samuel Huntington in a 1957 essay in the *American Political Science Review* criticized this 'New Conservatism' as detached from real political struggles and predicted that a more rooted, realistic conservatism would emerge when America's liberal institutions came under fundamental attack.

His prediction was confirmed in two instalments following the revolutions of the 1960s. Liberal Supreme Court decisions restricting school prayer and liberalizing pornography prompted Christian evangelicals and other social conservatives to found what was called the New Right. This was absorbed into the broader movement of conservatism relatively easily. At almost the same time, however, a radical revolution inside the pre-eminent liberal institution, the university, drove tough-minded social scientists and moderate liberals rightward into the conservative camp, which they greatly strengthened on such issues as education, affirmative action, the treatment of riots, anti-Soviet politics, and anti-anti-communism.

These scholars were the first generation of neoconservatives, and their arrival on the Right, though welcomed by Buckley and the fusionists, gradually alienated a harder-edged coalition of libertarians, culture warriors, and evangelicals on issues like trade, immigration, school prayer, and (after the defeat of communism) foreign policy. This loose coalition of dissenters, which began as a reaction to neoconservatism, got the confusing name of 'paleo-conservatism,' as if its adherents had come over on the *Mayflower*. As politics changed, the different articulate, argumentative factions within the Right would fall to disagreeing.

Whatever American conservatism's internal differences at the time, it was united against the dominant liberalism, which became more overreaching under Lyndon Johnson and more anti-American after George McGovern. The calculations of Richard Nixon and the large general appeal of Ronald Reagan, meanwhile, gradually welcomed these different conservatives into the GOP's large canopy alongside longstanding institutional allies such as corporations, the military, Wall Street banks, and churches, while Ripon Society liberals drifted out of the big tent. Since the 1980s, Republicans as a whole have been synonymous with the Right.

Continetti weaves together the many threads of a complicated history both of philosophical ideas and of political struggles without losing any of them. His analysis of serious intellectual disputes— for example, the early battles between Frank Meyer, Russell Kirk, and Brent Bozell over whether the 'fusionism' of virtue and liberty could provide a generally agreed-upon philosophical foundation for conservatism—are both accurate and easy to follow. He summarizes major historical controversies such as McCarthyism and the second Gulf War crisply and well. His portraits of the scholars and politicians from Nixon and Buckley to Patrick J. Buchanan and Trump who cooperate, plan, and argue through these debates are largely fair—though it is plain that Continetti is more sympathetic to the elitists than to the populists. And although almost everyone active in the conservative movement in those years gets the amount of attention he deserves—a steep challenge, to be sure—one exception is M. Stanton Evans, a journalist and editor, as well as a historian with a comprehensive biography of Senator Joe McCarthy to his credit, and an extraordinarily popular figure at almost every gathering from the Sharon Statement onward who more than once united a fractious conference by his wit. (Readers can seek out Steven F. Hayward's superb new biography, *M. Stanton Evans: Conservative Wit, Apostle of Freedom*, for more.)

Though the Republican Party is inevitably the main vehicle for centre-right politics in America, it is not a fixed entity. Its character at any one time will be sharply defined by its current leader, qualified to a greater or lesser extent by the character of a successful recent leader. That is probably a general truth about either party in a two-party system. Robin Harris recognized its importance when he gave his brilliant history of the United Kingdom's Conservative Party the title of *The Conservatives*, referring less to its mass membership than to its leaders from Robert Peel to Margaret Thatcher. And once the conservative movement got up and running, the various strains on the Right (libertarians, traditionalists, neoconservatives, nationalists, etc.) have tried to engage in a constant dialogue with whoever happened to be president or party leader—more constant than the latter often wished.

That dialogue never included Dwight Eisenhower—a conservative by temperament whose cold, skilful, non-ideological management of the rising American empire in good times initially appalled Buckley because it appeased the Soviet Union, especially over Hungary in 1956, and prudently accommodated modest advances for domestic liberalism. However, James Burnham persuaded Buckley, and through him the conservative movement, to adopt a strategy of generally supporting the most rightward viable candidate in the Republican field. With that, the interests and destiny of movement conservatives became intertwined with those of corporate America, regional and national elites, the US military, conservative Christian and Jewish denominations, and all the other established economic and cultural interests assembled on the right side of American politics.

Omitting those who failed to win elections or to make much impact when they did, I would nominate Nixon, Reagan, Newt Gingrich, and Trump as leaders who significantly shaped the GOP for good or ill, the two Bushes as leaders who led it down dead ends, and Pat Buchanan as a brilliant, wayward outsider who (almost as significantly) failed to lead it in other directions. Continetti is excellent in charting the ways in which all these leaders wooed, won, bedazzled, pleased, and betrayed conservatives over the years. It is the real—or a better—story of his book.

Stan Evans quipped that he had never really liked Nixon until Watergate, and as president Nixon had certainly given conservatives reasons to be disappointed: his quiet extension of affirmative action, his rapprochement with the Soviet Union, his opening to China, his betrayal of Taiwan, and (Evans notwithstanding) Watergate itself, which gravely weakened the Right until Jimmy Carter rescued it by his milquetoast incompetence. As Continetti rightly argues, however, Nixon's reputation has still not caught up with his achievements, even or especially among conservatives. He contrived a responsible American exit from Vietnam on the basis of continuing US military aid to Saigon (which the Democratic Congress gutted in 1975, dooming America's ally). He began the long defection of blue-collar workers to the GOP (until lately the unnoticed counterpart to the Left's authoritarian long march through the institutions). His opening to China divided the two communist superpowers, laying one foundation for the West's victory in the Cold War.

Following the successes of the Reagan Revolution (about which, more below), George H. W. Bush a year into his presidency broke the dramatic promise he made on the campaign trail, 'Read my lips: no new taxes,' in order to seal a budget deal with the Democrats. Continetti downplays the significance of this decision, even excuses it, judging that 'within months of assuming the presidency, Bush *knew that he would have to*' raise taxes (emphasis added). In fact, the broken pledge had catastrophic effects, splintering the Reagan coalition by abandoning the one broad policy that united all factions, and making some conservatives all but enemies of the president, despite Bush's effective diplomacy that ensured peaceful and stable ends to the Cold War and the Kuwait one. And once Democrats had secured the president's betrayal, they lost all interest in providing the lopsided budget cuts they had promised. Bush duly lost the 1992 election to Bill Clinton.

When Clinton embarked on a financial and ideological spending spree, the Republican who stepped into the role of leader of the opposition was Congressman Newt Gingrich of Georgia. An oddly futuristic conservative fascinated by new technologies and space travel who had shaped the House Republicans into an aggressive coalition with a positive 'national' program of reform, summed up in the 'Contract with America,' Gingrich won a historic landslide in the 1994 midterms and as House Speaker set about trying to govern the country alongside the White House. The conventional wisdom is that he failed in an impossible task—an unwelcome message for Republicans hoping for a 2022 midterm victory—and Continetti seems to share that view. To be sure, Gingrich was outmanoeuvred politically by Clinton on occasion, wasted some of his opportunities on secondary issues, and eventually lost the speakership. But he also transformed the House Republicans— previously a lacklustre crew of tourists to Washington—into a strong congressional party that wins more elections than it loses. And Gingrich was also more than half of the reason why Congress and the president brought spending under control in the 1990s and passed a strong, beneficial welfare reform bill that the Left has been trying to undo ever since. Continetti acknowledges some of this, but most conservatives either do not know the story or prefer to let Clinton take the credit.

President George W. Bush was blown off his intended political course and 'humble' foreign policy by the 9/11 terrorist attacks, to which he responded with the War on Terror and, more significantly, the kind of liberal internationalism conservatives endorse only nervously and reject if it is pushed too far and too fast. The Iraq War went badly, exaggerating the fear of unwinnable wars, and poisoned Bush's other key policies. Democracy promotion is something that most Americans approve of in the abstract, but for which they do not wish to make serious sacrifices. Mass immigration was a step beyond that failure because, according to all the polls, most Americans did not want more immigration and conservatives wanted less while their party leader in the White House was fighting hard for considerably more of it. It says a great deal for the firmness of the conservative coalition's conviction that it blocked two 'comprehensive immigration reform' bills even though they were supported by the president, the congressional leadership of both parties, the media, the universities, and almost every cultural institution in America. The failure of the war, democracy promotion, and immigration reform—much aggravated by the 2008 financial crash—meant that Bush's presidency ended on a note of bitter regret. Conservatives entered 2009 in an unsettled mood of distress and anxiety while America celebrated its first black president.

And that is where they stayed for the next few years until Donald Trump came down the escalator and into the Republican primaries. Trump's immediate impact was due not only to his own extraordinary personality but as much or more to the large gap between the opinions and mood of the conservative half of the country and the official Republican leadership. As interviews at the time showed, many voters intended to support Trump despite their disapproval of his profanity, personal behaviour, and moral character. They felt culturally dispossessed, economically left behind, trapped in an increasingly alien land, patronized, despised, ignored, and completely without hope that the Republican Party they usually backed would rescue them. Trump might not be able to either, but he was a fighter, and he would at least represent their point of view.

Immigration was only one issue on their grievance list, but it was a 'gateway' issue to the entire 'populist' worldview (a term the book overuses). It gave Trump his early boost and captured his audience. Which made the defiant, rock-solid refusal of all the other Republican primary candidates to pledge to limit or reduce immigration all the more shocking. It was as if I had wandered into some Off-Off-Broadway production of a Bertolt Brecht play which showed the capitalist class so imprisoned within its orthodoxy that it literally could not hear the human cries for help across the footlights.

That obdurate, albeit embarrassed resistance was directed to almost all the other populist issues—some of them more intellectual, such as the growth of judicial power that overrides popular majorities and executive authority, but also including de-industrialization, the plight of the underclass, wage stagnation, trade protectionism, illegal and runaway immigration, failure to enforce border controls, contempt for the United States and its symbols, multiculturalism as an alternative to a common culture, racist expressions of contempt for 'whiteness,' discriminatory racial quotas and 'goals,' globalist betrayal of American interests, the spread of effectively independent administrative bureaucracies with legal powers, restrictions on free speech and academic freedom in universities, the expansion of the concept of 'hate speech,' and—most sinister of all— the selective enforcement of the criminal law, even its weaponization, to reward friends, punish enemies, and even to ignore serious crimes. Many of these innovations were either causes or consequences of a legal revolution that, as Christopher Caldwell has shown in his book *The Age of Entitlement: America since the Sixties* (2020), replaced the official US Constitution with a de facto constitution built on the metastasizing of anti-discrimination law into an all-encompassing structure of bureaucratic power to regulate the minutiae of work and social life.

Obviously, more conservative Americans were aware of all these controversies, especially those involving legal reforms, in a sense since they had either debated them or even participated in their passage into law. But that participation was not always wise or helpful. Thus, the first President Bush vetoed the 1990 Civil Rights Bill that the Democrats had urgently pushed through to circumvent a rare Supreme Court decision (*Wards Cove Packing Company, Inc. v. Atonio*) limiting the impact of quotas. Although his veto was welcomed by conservatives, when the bill was presented a second time slightly amended the president signed it because he was worried that support for his earlier veto might have been inspired by racist motives. As it happens, that bill was the first time that 'disparate impact' was entrenched by legislation rather than by a court decision. It was a major advance in transforming civil rights law into the bureaucratic tyranny Caldwell describes.

It is not that such matters were not discussed in the intellectual journals and magazines among which Continetti has lived his adult life and upon which he rightly places such importance as the heralds of democratic debate. But they were somehow unable to come to terms with these issues' real significance. Recognizing the need to defend the United States and American patriotism against hostile disillusionment with both, David Brooks in *The Weekly Standard* proposed to make the case for 'national greatness' conservatism. The effort was well meant, but when he set about doing it, Brooks found that either he would have to move into 'populist' territory such as multiculturalism, history standards, defence of sovereignty, and immigration, or stick to somewhat anodyne topics such as museums, statues, and appropriate public architecture. Brooks's campaign dribbled into the sands after a promising start—perhaps sensibly, since he would have run into trouble in the past two years even sticking to statues and museums.

A central explanation of Trump's appeal, as *Commentary*'s former longtime editor Norman Podhoretz has pointed out, is that he is quite untroubled by the kind of doubts and hesitations that restrained Bush, Brooks, and most of us in politics and journalism. He is the id of conservatism or, just perhaps, a brilliant imitation of it (since there seems to be craft as well as instinct in his politics)—and that explains why his impact on US politics has been, despite even Reagan's unparalleled success, greater than any Republican leader since the 1920s. Both in

2016 and 2020, and indeed between both elections, Trump charged into the china shop. Yet important distinctions must be made about that garish picture. Even if his words were often brutal, fiery, and irresponsible, all of his actions as president seem to have been constitutional and legal—which cannot be said of the so-called 'Resistance,' including judges and national security officials who conspired to obstruct the workings of government and to pervert the course of justice. And it was not until he lost the second election, after four years of frustrated compliance with the rules of a rigged game (no, not the election itself), that Trump broke his bonds, cast off all mental restraints, lived down to his words, and embarked on the self-destructive course of urging that the transfer of power be blocked.

Continetti is not the first person to cry, 'Gotcha.' But his 'gotcha' is addressed to the conservative movement as a whole, not just to Trump personally. He springs the trap concealed in his 100-year framework by linking the events of January 6 all the way back to the 1920s, the anti-Darwinian bigots, the Ku Klux Klan, and the ever-lurking ogre of populism. In the book's final chapters, he lays out the argument that the permanent battle is between the prudent 'elites' of the mainstream Right running the show and the wild-eyed 'populists' from William Jennings Bryan to Pat Buchanan to Donald Trump waiting to jump from the shadows and urge protectionism, immigration control, isolationism, and—in moments of candor—rioting upon the unwary voter.

To be sure, battles between elites and populists (or, more precisely, their respective political representatives), both between and within political parties, are plainly important skirmishes in the endless battle of politics. But to see the relationship between them as the permanent central reality of the right side of the spectrum, however, goes too far, ignores too many other factors, and is vulnerable to confusion.

To begin with, it loads the dice. Other things being equal, we are reasonably inclined to think that the elites are likely to be better than the sweaty working man at dealing with complicated issues. But that is not always true. Academic social research suggests that well-educated people may not be more dispassionate judges of public events, merely better at defending their prejudices. The test of what works is better than a well-constructed fallacy.

As a test of political success between Left and Right elites, there is no contest. Most of the entire period covered by Continetti, though it begins with the eclipse of the Progressive movement, has been a long march through the institutions of political and social power in America by progressives under various labels. As the Eisenhower–Nixon era with its stabilizing comforts and challenges wound down, starting in the late 1960s, conservatives had to contend with a new range of social, economic, racial, and even *national* discontents (listed above) on which their touch was less sure. What is more, the collapse of communism replaced one foreign enemy with a dozen domestic ones, liberated and energized by their loss of a disreputable patron. Radical leftism went native, and in doing so, it became more successful. If you wish to see a monument to the legacy of progressive activism in Washington, look around. Half of the official buildings in the city house agencies that combine a highly dubious constitutional foundation with unlimited lawmaking powers. Indeed, if you want a counter-example to the monumental success of progressivism, consider the Religious Right's campaign for school prayer, on which it enjoyed overwhelming popular support but after fifty years has won nothing more than the right of a football coach to say a private prayer on the field—and for which it is depicted by major cultural institutions as a sinister threat to liberty.

That contrast is a bitter rebuke to the elites who controlled the GOP for most of that time—and more than a rebuke to the GOP's populist allies within the conservative movement. It was worse than a betrayal; it was an oversight. The party did not treat populist issues as priorities.

How did that happen?

Conservatives never really came to terms with the fact that, by the turn of the twentieth century, the populists and the elites in the United States had changed places—ordinary Americans were commonsensical and pragmatic, rooted in everyday reality, while the elites were driven by unruly passions that were justified by arcane academic jargon on everything from open borders to cultural appropriation. An anti-American *intelligentsia* (or perhaps *lumpenintelligentsia*), miseducated in the very best schools, rose slowly through the major public and private institutions of American life and gradually altered the rules governing that life without gaining meaningful democratic consent to their own new rules, or much caring about it. Their dominance, denied until recently, has now expanded grotesquely into the movement of radical Wokeness that threatens the country.

Conservative elites should surely have noticed this earlier and taken stronger political actions to restrain and remedy it. After all, they had been educated in the same institutions and by the same teachers as their liberal and increasingly radical colleagues. Maybe they saw their differences with old classmates across the partisan divide as less serious and more tolerable than did those who obeyed more rules and regulations than they made. Or if not more tolerable, then perhaps more transient. A common reply from conservatives to parents who complain that college has made their children hate them has been: 'They'll change when they enter the real world.' Instead, their children have changed the real world, and they have done so for everybody, including other people's children in suburbs, slums, and small towns.

Politicians and intellectuals in the 'populist' camp, like Pat Buchanan, saw Wokeness in embryo because they listened to what ordinary people were saying and did not treat their grievances as material for 'wedge issues.' As a journalist, Buchanan had to take their complaints seriously because they were the audience for his columns. That is why his writings in the 1980s and 90s proved a better guide to the politics of the future than most of those who dismissed him.

In short, if we are to take this elite-populist relationship as the key to understanding the Right, then we must conclude that each side let the other down: the elites did so over a period of more than thirty years, the populists from between the 2016 primaries and a January afternoon in 2021. Continetti remains worried by populism and tries to exorcise it by discussing why two conservatives he deeply admires, Irving Kristol and Ronald Reagan, took a different view of populism.

Irving Kristol presents Continetti with the greater problem because he had made an unusual principled case for conservative populism against the elites. Admittedly, Kristol had gone back and forth on the matter:

> In the 1970s he fretted over populism's tendency to devolve into lawless revolt, conspiracy theory, and scapegoating of vulnerable minorities. By the mid-1980s, however, he saw the activism of the populist New Right as 'an effort to bring our governing elites to their senses.' The events of January 6, 2021 took place more than a decade after Kristol's death but confirmed his initial reservations.

I agree that Kristol would certainly have condemned the events of 6 January as a lawless revolt inspired by conspiracy theory (though it does not seem to have been directed against any minorities). But would not Kristol also have condemned the events of 2020 across America that destroyed property and lives on a much larger scale, which were encouraged by America's progressive political, academic, and media elites as justified responses to a supposedly white supremacist America? These went largely uncontrolled, misreported, and unpunished then and later by the police, the mainstream media, and the courts; and were financially supported by leading public and political figures. Surely, those events would have confirmed Kristol in his later view of populism as a necessary 'effort to bring our governing elites to their senses'? It is, at the very least, a plausible conclusion.

Now, we come to Continetti's view of Ronald Reagan, which is in many respects the most interesting and novel passage in the book. Reagan is the single most successful conservative of *The Right*'s 100 years. He restored America's pre-eminence in world politics, revived its failing economy, won the Cold War, united the various conservative factions into a harmonious coalition, and passed on a Republican dominance in US politics that his successors promptly squandered. What is more, he did so while working within the laws, regulations, principles, and customs of the United States, which indeed he venerated. So why is Continetti uneasy about him?

Although an early subscriber to *National Review* who devoured the arguments of the conservative intellectual movement, Reagan was really at heart a populist, Continetti laments, and therefore a dubious or misleading guide to the future of conservatism. Now, I am not at all sure that Reagan was a populist unless populism means something anodyne like 'responsive to the opinions of the voters' (which is something all democratic politicians have to be). I am even less sure that populism is a useful concept as the word is employed by most political pundits today: namely, as the manifestly bad alternative to 'liberal democracy.' This usage has been devised mainly to wrong-foot democratic opponents of liberal parties by writing them out of respectable politics. Fortunately, Continetti offers a better definition in his own discussion of populism when he declares that it had become one element of a Right that was 'unabashedly opposed to liberal elites, sceptical of credentialed experts, and hostile to the established voices of print and cable media.' Reagan made this populism more respectable by injecting 'the populist rebellion of the late 1970s with his peculiar qualities of optimism, sunniness, humor, and unflappability.' For Continetti, his example had subsequently warped our understanding of its dangers.

Is this fair or reasonable? Surely, Reagan's supposed populism had two features. The first was his unembarrassed celebration of America and American institutions that went deeper than statecraft. The second was that Reagan—while being more than a populist himself—recognized the legitimacy of populist grievances and treated populism's political leaders respectfully. He fought for their causes with a cheerful bravery, and even when he lost (as over the nomination of Robert Bork to the Supreme Court), he conveyed the comforting democratic truth that no cause is ever lost permanently in a free society. In doing so, he reconciled populist (and other) constituencies to political realities. His amiable rhetoric treated all fellow-Americans—and notably, opponents—as people of goodwill who could be trusted with freedom. In all these ways, he strengthened the American regime. On the day he left the White House the United States was unusually stable and at peace with itself, as much as in the Eisenhower years, and far more so than eight years previously. Reagan's reputation rose steadily between then and his death in 2004, which led to some very rare soul-searching among journalists as to whether they had covered his administration fairly. In short, Reagan's success was an astonishing achievement—in part, a populist one—

because it consisted of governing *with* the grain of the American character, especially its conservative side, while offering all Americans the reassurance of a unifying patriotic rhetoric and symbolism.

The riot on 6 January occurred thirty-three years after Reagan left office. In the few years on either side of that day, American politics has developed an atmosphere worse perhaps than the 1950s atmosphere surrounding McCarthyism and its opponents, of which conservative poet Peter Viereck wrote, 'I am against hysteria, but I am also against hysteria about hysteria.' With *The Right*, Matthew Continetti has written a fine, comprehensive, and readable narrative of the rip-roaring history of American conservatism with its amazing repertory company of statesmen, philosophers, and eccentrics. It is a remarkable achievement and a great read but one over-influenced by the 'insurrection' and the blowback to it that took place when its final pages were being written. Readers like me will look forward to the second edition with an Afterword on populism in the Age of Woke.

This review of Matthew Continetti's The Right: The Hundred-Year War for American Conservatism *(Basic Books, 2022), 496 pp, was originally published by the* Claremont Review of Books, *Vol. XXII, No. 3, Summer 2022, 33-38, https://claremontreviewofbooks.com/athwart-history/.*

The Death of Hugh Hefner, the Shaming of Harvey Weinstein, and the End of the Playboy Philosophy
14 October 2017

It is less than three weeks since the "American icon," Hugh Hefner, breathed his last in the Playboy mansion and was transported to California to be interred in a mausoleum next door to the body of Marilyn Monroe. He and Monroe never met, but she was the first of the naked celebrities who became the hallmark of *Playboy*, appearing both on the cover of its first 1953 issue and as its first centrefold and apparently ensuring that the magazine sold out. Ever the sentimentalist, Hefner spent a full $75,000 on a grave in this desirable location. He liked the idea, he said, of spending eternity next to the famous and fragile movie-star.

Marilyn was not available for comment, but she might have been annoyed that none of the $75,000 went to her, just as she never received any payment from *Playboy* for the photographs that began the making of its fortune. Four years earlier, badly needing the cash, she had received $50 for the photographs which, in the manner of these things, passed through several hands until they reached Hefner's and those of his customers.

If Hefner and Monroe end up in the same part of the Next World, which is questionable, she might have something to say about this pay differential. But then so might a large number of other "playmates."

These and other details of 'Hef's' iconic life were revealed with a sympathy at times amounting to reverence in most of the media obituaries that followed his death. Their theme was that he was the man who brought the sexual revolution to America, advanced the civil rights revolution alongside it, and combined these two revolutions in a sophisticated liberal lifestyle package that appealed to an American middle class then emerging from a restrictive puritan ideal.

There were, of course, qualifications. Hefner had some help in spreading the Playboy philosophy from the Pill, the Kinsey Report, and the growing liberalism of American law. The philosophy itself, together with the consumer lifestyle it promoted, were obviously directed more to the tastes and interests of men, in particular bachelors, than to those of women. (Indeed, Hefner was quick to identify the feminists of the sixties and seventies as enemies of the entire Playboy phenomenon.) As a result of such changing tastes, Playboyism, like its leading exponent, looked increasingly dated and 'unsophisticated.' And, finally, it was impossible to ignore that the high-minded philosophizing and consumer empire both rested on naked female flesh.

The New York Times got the balance right. Its obituary leaned to the favourable:

> Hefner the man and Playboy the brand ... both advertised themselves as emblems of the sexual revolution, an escape from American priggishness and wider social intolerance. Both were derided over the years—as vulgar, as adolescent, as exploitative and finally as anachronistic. But Mr. Hefner was a stunning success from the moment he emerged in the early 1950s.

And an assessment by the paper's leading conservative columnist, Ross Douthat, was close to an exorcism:

> Hugh Hefner, gone to his reward at the age of 91, was a pornographer and chauvinist who got rich on masturbation, consumerism and the exploitation of women, aged into a leering grotesque in a captain's hat, and died a pack rat in a decaying manse where porn blared during his pathetic orgies.

> Hef was the grinning pimp of the sexual revolution, with Quaaludes for the ladies and Viagra for himself—a father of smut addictions and eating disorders, abortions and divorce and syphilis, a pretentious huckster who published Updike stories no one read while doing flesh *procurement* for celebrities, a revolutionary whose revolution chiefly benefited men much like himself.

When I read Mr Douthat's words of brimstone, I thought he might be stoned by righteously indignant libertines. He did attract some abuse, but also a surprising number of sympathizers who began along such lines as: 'I never thought I would agree with Mr Douthat, but …' That becomes more understandable when you read both Douthat and the anonymous editorialist carefully and realize that they contain more overlap and less contradiction than a hasty reading might suggest.

Their rhetoric is sharply different; the facts they describe are much the same. What makes the difference is the attitude each writer takes to Hefner's life. Planting himself firmly on traditional Christian ground, Mr Douthat, a believing Catholic, thinks he opened a gateway to the moral squalor of today's American popular culture; the *NYT* scribe, standing on a surfboard as it hurtles down the stream of that culture, treats Hefner as, on balance, a pioneer who (doubtless reacting to an oppressive Puritanism) went too far in the right direction and so into seedy, exploitative, and vulgar territory.

Mr Douthat is confident; his colleague uneasy. It is almost as if they both sensed that a social change was on the way—or even that one had occurred but not yet been fully sensed by the cultural arbiters of the modern world.

Two weeks later *The New York Times* published the story that one of those cultural arbiters, Harvey Weinstein, the Hollywood producer, had sexually harassed at least a baker's dozen (and apparently many more than that) of young actresses in ways both bizarre and disgusting, managed to keep this news out of the media by bribery or legally silencing his victims, been protected by an *omerta* permeating the film industry and subscribed to by both sexes, constructed a protective image of contemporary virtue by loudly allying himself with liberal political causes and politicians, and in general created an image that he was both formidable and untouchable.

That he was neither became clearer as every passing day revealed more actresses he had allegedly harassed (or in three cases raped—according to *The New Yorker*), some of them famous names, some who had appeared in his movies, some who had won awards doing so. Within a week he had been dismissed summarily by the company he created, been abandoned by his friends, threatened with losing the Oscars he had won, lost his wife, and was facing the prospect of criminal charges and a prison sentence.

It is always unpleasant to watch a pack of hounds turn on and rend a fugitive even when the fugitive has it coming. All his old associates run for cover; no chits for past favours can be redeemed; his accusers grow in number and vehemence (though not necessarily in credibility).

We never knew!

Yet it was apparently common knowledge in the movie business, whispered about by the Weinstein staffers, gossiped about by waiters at his favourite restaurants (who knew his *modus operandi* when it came to seducing starlets), and even joked about at Oscar performances and on the sitcom *30 Rock*. It is the old, old story: everyone knew and no one knew until it was in their interest to know it—as it had previously been in their interest to be ignorant about it. Now the difference is that they are volubly ignorant.

It was a different time.

But what time was that and who made it different? Modern social etiquette, even in Hollywood, was not always either brutally transactional or coercive. Ray Milland, learning that Audrey Totter (one of *film noir*'s bad girls who was actually a good girl) was about to have dinner with a notorious seducer, insisted on going along to help her escape. It was Hefner-ing of sexual revolution that put a stop to that kind of chivalry, making it seem a different kind of coercion and delegitimizing it to the point where people looked away from harassment as well as from flirting.

Sexual harassment is what powerful men do.

Really, all of them? That is the feminist interpretation of Weinstein's M.O., and we'll be hearing a lot more of it. Even in this case, however, the hypocrisy and lies are not all on the one side. If the silence of the stars was transactional, as it plainly was, maybe some of the sex of the starlets was transactional too. But the coming new sexual etiquette is likely to insist that we must believe the victims at all times, even when that same rule in the child-sex abuse panic of a generation ago led to innocent teachers of both sexes spending years in prison before the lies of their accusers and prosecutors were exposed.

And this is not just another tale from Hollywood. Weinstein was an influential donor in the liberal politics and the Democratic Party. He was a friend of Hillary Clinton. He bankrolled Tina Brown's magazine, *Talk*, to enable Hollywood to influence Washington and vice versa. He had talked his way into national prominence by proclaiming that Hollywood was the compassionate conscience of America. And as his world was collapsing, his first response was to offer to redeem himself by destroying the National Rifle Association. You could not make it up.

So more hangs alongside Harvey than some Hollywood reputations, as his former friends realize. When Tina Brown gave a qualified defence of her old boss, some instinct prompted her to mount a pre-emptive attack on the vast right-wing conspiracy that might profit from the scandal: 'Harvey is an intimidating and ferocious man,' she wrote. 'Crossing him, even now, is scary. But it's a different era now. Cosby. Ailes. O'Reilly, Weinstein. It's over, except for one—the serial sexual harasser in the White House.'

But that only drew attention to an obvious name missing from her list: a serial sexual harasser who used to be in the White House and whose enabling wife she championed passionately until recently: the Big He, Bill Clinton. To be sure, there are risks to Donald Trump in this scandal. But the Clinton machine and its cash nexus with Hollywood is definitely finished. Hugh Hefner doubly so. He died at just the right time. His obituaries today would all be written as if by Ross Douthat.

And Marilyn Monroe must be turning away in her grave.

Originally published in Quadrant Online, *14 October 2017, https://quadrant.org.au/opinion/qed/2017/10/tale-two-tossers/.*

Conduct Unbecoming:
Me-Too and Sex in the Public Space
30 November 2017

It took less than two weeks before the Harvey Weinstein sex scandal and its impact on cultural politics spread from Hollywood and Broadway to the Westminster Parliament in London. 'Sexminster' and 'Kneegate' are the names of the scandal locally. It is being treated by the media as an outbreak of sexual harassment among MPs so shocking that it may bring down Theresa May's Tory government.

Yet one cannot help noticing that so far the total of all reported "offenses"—which range widely from one rape to two reports of Ministers touching knees surreptitiously over dinner—is only a small fraction of the rapes and serious assaults alleged against Weinstein alone. Whatever pretensions the House of Commons may still cherish, it is very far from being Hollywood-on-the-Thames.

Though we are still in mid-scandal, several careers have already been destroyed. One of the more able Ministers in the government, defence secretary Michael Fallon, resigned after admitting that he was guilty of falling below the high standards required by the armed forces (he had stroked a woman reporter's knee and kissed another woman reporter without adequate warning.) There has been a slight pause in the Westminster sex allegations in the last few days. But sex never sleeps; nor does tabloid inquisitiveness. There has been a further cascade of revelations in recent days about sexual harassment in the US entertainment industry. And, finally, in the most significant sign that the times, they are a-changin,' leading Democrats and media liberals are saying that they were wrong to dismiss the accusations by several women of sex harassment and (in one case) rape against former President Bill Clinton. He should now be shunned by decent society, said one. We seem to have reached a general social conclusion after a remarkably brief and one-sided debate: sexual exploitation of vulnerable women by powerful men has been a vast hidden epidemic in our society and must now be halted once and for all. But how?

That is not difficult to answer. George Macdonald, the Scottish religious novelist (who inspired C. S. Lewis), once wrote that it was the duty of a man to protect women against all men, starting with himself. If all men were to act consistently on that principle, there would be no little or no problem of sexual harassment to solve. But as every man must concede (including the author of this column), only a small minority of men (generally with names prefixed by "Saint"), consistently live up to this standard. We should be encouraged to do so by our moral upbringing and by the general messages of our culture. But since both sexes are composed of fallen creatures, we will always fall well below one hundred per cent success in this endeavour even in a high-minded society.

An additional problem is that we do not live in a high-minded society but in a liberated one. And the liberation of manners, in alliance with the law of unintended consequences, has had effects the reformers did not expect. One woman writer on the website conservativehome.com demanded a new set of rules that included forbidding the naming of women's body parts as swear words in order to create an atmosphere of greater respect for women. I understand that plea and feel a wistful hope it might be answered at some times and places such as mixed company. But it seems to me completely utopian as a universal rule. Almost the entire armed forces would let down Michael Fallon by falling below it minute by minute.

It might just about be possible to revive the custom that men do not swear in the company of women that actually prevailed until fifty or so years ago. But that reform would have to surmount the obstacles that women themselves use the 'C' and other words, as marks of liberation, and that their usage has been introduced and approved not by the submerged tenth of society but by its cultural leaders in literature, academia, and the media as litmus tests of honesty, authenticity, and frankness.

The most serious result of this "liberation" is really not widespread sex harassment of the weirdly promiscuous kind employed by Harvey

Weinstein. That is an exotic sin of exotic places. Most men do not have the power to get away with such behaviour; it is largely illegal anyway which deters most of the few tempted by it—Weinstein will go to prison; and above all it is weird. How many men dream of masturbating naked in front of attractive women? It is the *absence* of women that gives masturbation its niche appeal. Being caught at it by a hot date would fill most men with acute embarrassment.

For the majority of people, both men and women, what liberation has wrought is two problems. The lesser one, as chivalry has evaporated, is genuine sexual harassment by (usually) men with a little brief authority over someone they desire—the 'groping' charges of the last month. Laws already deal with that, and the lesson of the last month is that social willingness to invoke those laws is now catching up with them. The greater problem is that when the old informal restraints have atrophied, we do not live in a world without rules but in one where the rules are unknown until one of them is broken. For many people the attempt to initiate a sexual and/or romantic encounter in one of the most daring things they will ever do. Many, especially beginners, will get it wrong, either misunderstanding or being misunderstood. They will blunder across an invisible line. And then all hell breaks loose.

We are not likely to restore the old standards of modesty, restraint, and discretion, at least not any time soon. That would mean repealing not only the sexual revolution of the 1960s, but also the associated revolution of manners. Instead, we facean acceleration of a more recent development: the spread of formal or even legal rules of sexual engagement to replace the Christian moral etiquette of two generations ago. That replacement may be better than nothing, but it is certain to be both less effective than a broad morality (sensitively) enforced by an overwhelming consensus; and less fair to both men and women in a battle of the sexes waged by both sides. The latter drawback is already clear from how the scandal is rushing along—and the kind of implicit rules that are emerging in its wake.

To begin with, there has been the erasing of common sense distinctions in the term sexual harassment. It is as elastic as an old-fashioned suspender belt since it seems to mean everything from a flirty drink invitation to an actual rape. Mr Fallon was finally felled by the claim of a woman political correspondent that he had tried to kiss her as they walked back from a (mildly alcoholic) lunch twenty years ago. Maybe he should not have kissed her. His wife probably thinks so. Doubtless she was right to resist. But when she rebuffed him, he did not persist. And they seem to have been on civil terms since then. Does a simple "pass" in error—a *faux pass*, so to speak—amount to sexual harassment? And if the lady had responded enthusiastically, would the kiss still be harassment? After all, though bad things like divorce sometimes start with a kiss, so do good things like romance, marriage, a family, and someone at your bedside in your last moments.

Some stern sociologists insist that the most tentative advances are wrong if the protagonist is in a position of power over her prey—yes, there was at least one such gender-bending allegation at Westminster. One can see the rough-and-ready calculation behind that rule. There should be a presumption that an MP's junior staff is out of bounds sexually. Anyone who proposes to cross that line must clearly and explicitly discard authority when doing so.

That said, the argument rests upon a very formal and unreal notion of power. A political reporter is not less powerful than a minister; in many respects the reporter is more powerful, able to do real damage to a ministerial reputation if offended or rejected. Similarly a male boss in love with a secretary may well be inferior in power to her for that very reason. Power in these circumstances does not flow along the lines of a bureaucratic chart. And who has power to start with? The patriarchy? Or an organized sexual minority with good PR which demands sex-change operations for minors against medical opposition?

Power is not always easy to define when love or sexual obsession enter the room—which is why consent is a vital if partial part of any new rulebook. Yet consent is being abolished in the name of consent. Much feminist argument insists that the only legitimate sexual consent is that of equal sexual enthusiasm (and that, of course, is almost never present in their theories). Consent under the influence of alcohol or sympathy or "pressure" is really rape. That too is completely unrealistic. People inside and outside of marriage consent to a sexual encounter for all sorts of reasons good and bad: a transactional performance on the casting couch; a celebration of genuine love; farewell sympathy for someone being rejected or at least not embraced permanently. That last kind of yielding occurs more often as a motive for women than for men, I think. But it's not unknown in reverse: hence the upper-class English term, a *boff de politesse.*

Such reluctant couplings may not be wise or moral, but they do not amount to harassment, let alone rape, and only a narrow-inverted Puritanism would suggest they do.

In particular the idea that if two people have sex after drinking, then the man is a rapist, is a discriminatory application of this consent rule. It also rests on the assumption that women are nicer and more moral than men. While I am prepared to concede that in a small way—see above—I have to add the qualification: they are not really *that* much nicer than us.

Heather Macdonald of the Manhattan Institute points out that if women spend large amounts of money on transforming themselves into sex objects, they cannot revert to the status of outraged Victorian maidens at the first gauche kiss or vulgar innuendo (though that is what is currently happening in both Hollywood and Sexminster). By the same token she also warns men not to move too easily from defending college males from false charges of rape in kangaroo courts to approval of the promiscuity that landed them there.

Rules do not work unless supported by a common moral understanding of what is decent and indecent. Without that, men will be too afraid of offending to risk the most honourable pass; women will feel insulted by conventional courtship; each sex will fear, resent, and eventually avoid the other. And that will end a great deal. But not well.

Originally published in Quadrant Online, *30 November 2017, https://quadrant.org.au/magazine/2017/12/conduct-unbecoming/. (A shorter version of this column appeared in* The Australian.

Churchill and Dunkirk:
Can Poetic Licence Tell Historical Truths?
13 March 2018

London in 1940 under the Blitz had its grim moments, but in the main, it kept its sense of humour. One joke that ran around the capital told of an officer in a smart Guards regiment, recently returned from Dunkirk, who was asked at a cocktail party what the experience had been, well, *like*?

'My dear,' he said, raising his hands to indicate distress. 'The noise! And the *people*!'

Those who have seen recently the Hollywood movie *Dunkirk*, from the director Christopher Nolan, can confirm the officer's complaint about the noise (as, indeed, several of the few remaining veterans have done). But the film has a higher view than the Guards officer of the people there.

Dunkirk belongs to that category of story that has not one hero but several heroes who represent in different ways the heroism of the British people as they queue up on the beaches (as they were to do for many years of rationing at home) to be rescued by the Royal Navy and a flotilla of small boats manned by the weekend sailors among their neighbours.

One hero is a RAF pilot who after bringing down an enemy plane strafing the rescue, runs out of petrol, lands his own plane on the now empty beach, methodically burns it, and stoically surrenders into five years of captivity. Another is a weekend sailor who dutifully obeys the Admiralty's call, sailing across the Channel, picking people up from the sea, restraining one shell-shocked soldier who struggles against going back to the beach to rescue others, dispensing common sense decency as a sort of balm.

Not everyone is heroic or uncomplicatedly patriotic. Some are afraid, the shell-shocked soldier for one, some are angry at official delays, some panicky, some hostile or suspicious, thus unjust, to those they do not know. And how could it be otherwise? Not only is defeat in a world war (or what was soon to become a world war) a risk facing them, but so is the imminent prospect of their own deaths or imprisonment.

Yet the evacuation proceeds (more quickly in the movie than in real life), hundreds of thousands of soldiers are saved (for future deployment), the Navy rescues most of those on the beach (including many French soldiers guarding the retreat), the 'miracle' of Dunkirk happens, and the British people start on the long march to victory. *Dunkirk* the movie does not acknowledge this. It abjures our knowledge of this future to end on notes of realism and defiance.

'Wars are not won by evacuations,' says a soldier as he reads Churchill's famous speech from a newspaper to his mates, going on to describe the 'miracle' as a 'colossal military defeat.' Through the soldier's pedestrian reading, however, we hear the statesman's firm promise that the fight will continue until, with the help of the Empire and the New World, victory will be achieved 'in God's good time.' As we hear the words, we see the civilians welcoming the dejected soldiers home and literally cheering them up.

Dunkirk is a film about a people's war, not in the socialist sense of a war for equality, but depicting a mixed bag of ordinary decent people fighting for themselves and their undramatic virtues and now ready to make heavy sacrifices for them. Churchill remains in the prompter's box.

He does a great deal better in *Darkest Hour*, which depicts his arrival in Downing Street from the resignation of Neville Chamberlain to the Commons triumph of the speech read by the soldier in Dunkirk after the colossal military defeat. Dunkirk is as off-stage in this film, however, as Churchill is in *Dunkirk*. And even then the people edge their way into the action in Whitehall.

Both films have received strongly favourable reviews, but the reviews of *Darkest Hour* are tributes more to the film's quality as a brilliant (and brilliantly acted) political drama than to its historical accuracy. Gary Oldman is Churchill to the life and screenwriter Anthony McCarten has given him some splendidly Churchillian lines.

Told at one point that the Lord Privy Seal wants to talk to him, Churchill replies: 'Tell him that I am sealed in the privy and can only deal with one shit at a time.' Too salty for the great statesman? Churchill once responded in the Commons to a Labour MP, William Paling, who had called him a dirty dog: 'Yes, and you know what dirty dogs do to palings.'

The plot is a simple one: Churchill has become Prime Minister without the support of his own Tory Party, which still admires Chamberlain and Foreign Secretary Lord Halifax, who still plot to restore the appeasement policy by responding to a peace initiative from Mussolini. I despair of historical justice ever being given to Chamberlain, but in fact he recommended to the King that Churchill be appointed prime minister because he was the only Tory who could lead a national government, and once Churchill entered Number Ten, Chamberlain gave him consistent support in the War Cabinet until he died from cancer in late 1940. Churchill's eulogy of his old rival to the Commons is one of his greatest and most moving speeches.

And there are other historical inaccuracies. For instance, Labour leader Clement Attlee was a quiet pedestrian speaker, not the passionate ranter shown in the Norway debate that brought down Chamberlain. Attlee did not take part in the debate anyway; the Labour speaker on that occasion was Arthur Greenwood, to whom the frustrated Churchill supporter, Leo Amery, fearing Chamberlain would survive, shouted 'Speak for England, Arthur!' in a moment of genuine parliamentary drama. That is not in the movie, presumably because it would require too much explanation.

Do these minor inventions really matter? I am inclined to think they do because many people will get their only knowledge of these events from what is a wonderfully exciting movie. And not all the inventions are minor. Though it is true, for instance, that Churchill had to win over an initially sceptical Tory Party in the few crucial days between acceding to power and the Dunkirk debate, he did not do so in anything like the manner depicted here. Though Gary Oldman's (or Anthony McCarten's)

Churchill is a dynamo of energy and passion, he is also shown as curiously self-doubting and introspective. Again, Churchill did suffer from the 'black dog' of depression, but that was largely when he was becalmed out of power and unable to make an impact on great events that were going disastrously wrong for England. Power acted as a tonic on him. As he himself wrote later, he felt upon receiving the commission to form a government that his whole life had been 'a preparation for this hour and this trial.' And so did those around him. General Lord Ismay, who was Churchill's chief military assistant at the time, once said that he knew Britain would win the war when he saw a senior civil servant *running* to carry out a prime ministerial order.

In the movie, however, when Churchill is wondering what to do in response to the plotting of the appeasers, he abandons his car and takes to the London Underground where he seeks counsel from a cross-section of ordinary Londoners who include a West Indian who quotes Macaulay's *Lays of Ancient Rome* to encourage him. It is an affecting scene, but it is not a true portrait of Churchill (who routed the Mussolini plan very easily and went on to dominate the Cabinet and the Commons) nor perhaps of the opinions of Londoners before Dunkirk had made a major impact on them. These are serious criticisms, but they do not contradict the essential truth of the view that Churchill and the British people strengthened each other at a moment of acute national crisis—Churchill by his eloquent and confident leadership, the people by their stoic willingness to fight on against great odds in the belief, perhaps an atavistic belief, that victory would eventually be theirs. Nor do they mean you should not see the picture. Even if it takes poetic licence a little too far for intellectual comfort, it is in the service of a thrilling movie—and one, moreover, with a solid political moral.

No, it is not that Brexit is a good thing and the way to go. Both movies have that subliminal impact, in my view, and since that is plainly right (the behaviour of the European Union negotiators confirms the fact), I am happy with it. But the film's political moral is a more subtle one that may not have been intended by its progressive screenwriter: all of the arguments that Lord Halifax advances in the movie for working for peace with Hitler through Mussolini are the same arguments that the

Left advances on every other occasion to weaken the West's defences and to make risky concessions to the hostile power *du jour*. In *Darkest Hour*, those arguments are comprehensively and persuasively rubbished, and the audiences join in the satisfaction that Churchill defeats their advocates. One leaves the cinema feeling this history lesson is well worth the cost of a little sacrifice of historical accuracy to the god of poetic licence.

Originally published in Quadrant, *13 March 2018, https://quadrant.org.au/magazine/2018/03/truth-fiction/.*

They Strolled down the Shamrock Path to Murder—And Then?

23 June 2018

In a recent issue of *The New Yorker* there was a review by Patrick Radden Keefe of a documentary film, *I, Dolours*, composed largely of extracts from an interview with Dolours Price, a former Provisional IRA terrorist (she preferred the term *volunteer*), which describes in detail how she helped in the kidnapping, murder, and burial of Jean McConville, a widow and mother of ten children, in Belfast in the 1970s. More than 3,000 people were murdered in the Troubles, but the circumstances of Mrs McConville's murder were particularly horrifying. Her children clung crying to her skirts in a vain attempt to prevent her abduction, and the Provos made them wait almost thirty years before confirming her death. As a result, her murder has become notorious beyond the norm of terrorist horrors on both sides of the Irish border.

After the Good Friday Agreement, the IRA admitted the kidnapping and murder of McConville, and Price broke the Provo code of *omerta* further by acknowledging that she had taken part in these actions on the instructions of Gerry Adams. He denies this, of course, but he also denies that he was in the IRA. In the film, however, Price gives more details of what happened and of the much more central role she played than anyone had revealed before.

She was a member of a group within the Provos called 'The Unknowns' who took on tasks requiring an especially strong stomach—among which was transporting their victims, usually informers, across the border to the Republic where they could be killed and buried. Some of those being transported were unaware that they were 'marked for death' and given various soothing explanations for the journey. Their murderers were often only slightly better informed. Price learned that

McConville was a mother with a large family from her victim during the ride. She went ahead anyway.

Indeed, she did rather more. She and her two companions were supposed to hand McConville to local Provos for the actual murder. But: 'They didn't want to do it,' she says, of the local IRA men. 'They couldn't bring themselves to execute her. Probably because she was a woman.'

'So you guys had to do it?' Ed Moloney, the American journalist who carried out the interview, asks. 'There had been a grave dug by the Dundalk unit,' Price says. So the three Unknowns took McConville to the edge of the grave and shot her in the back of the head.

Price paid no legal price for her role in this murder, but she may have suffered a worse penalty. Keefe tells us that she 'had struggled with alcohol and prescription pills, and been diagnosed with PTSD [and] she was being treated at a local psychiatric hospital.' She died in 2013, not long after the interview, of an overdose of pills. Though Keefe tells us that she was composed and coherent in the interview, he also observes that in describing the murder she slips into the third person—and what Anthony Daniels has explained as the excusative version of the passive voice: 'It is clear in the film that she is acknowledging her own responsibility, yet she recounts the act as though it was carried out by someone else.' McConville 'was taken by the three volunteers to the grave, and shot in the back of the head by one of the volunteers,' Price tells Moloney.

In the end, however, she faces up both to what she has done and to the limited benefits of a purely psychological confession. Some consequences she cannot escape: 'Do the disappeared haunt you?' Moloney asks Price. 'Yes,' she replies. 'I think back on those who I had responsibility for driving away. I'm not a deeply religious person, but I would say a prayer for them.' Moloney asks if she regards such forced disappearances as a war crime, and Price responds, 'I think it's a war crime. Yes.'

One cannot help being reminded of Act V, Scene i, of *Macbeth*:

Lady Macbeth: Here's the smell of the blood still: all the perfumes of Arabia will not sweeten this little hand. Oh, oh, oh!

Doctor: What a sigh is there! The heart is sorely charged.

Gentlewoman: I would not have such a heart in my bosom for the dignity of the whole body.

The film *I, Dolours* is, among other things, an opportunity for the rest of us to reflect on the truths of Jean McConville's murder and of the wider massacre that was the Troubles. Keefe's book on the case, *Say Nothing*, which is to be published next year, is likely to be another one. But we have missed other such opportunities, and we should not miss this one. *I, Dolours* should be shown at peak viewing hours on the major establishment media in Ireland and Britain, including both the BBC and RTE, and made the subject of their principal discussion programmes. American media too should treat it as an important event. For it demonstrates the harsh and terrible consequences of terrorism, for the terrorists as well as for their innocent victims—and Jean McConville *was* innocent, whatever comforting myths about her being an informer that Gerry Adams and the Provos still tell themselves to keep the ghosts of the disappeared at bay.

It is vital those consequences be known because many of the young people who became Provo terrorists did so from motives and ideals that were essentially frivolous. They had posters on their university walls of Che Guevara, of whose mass judicial executions they knew little and cared less. They had seen French students hurling stones at policemen in Paris during the 1968 *manifestations* but they somehow did not notice that these riots provoked an election landslide for de Gaulle. They failed to apply any critical faculty to the Irish Republican myths that brushed a million Protestants out of history and out of their minds, but not out of Ireland. They ignored the clear signs that Unionist leaders in the North and Irish prime ministers in the South were moving progressively to remove the discrimination and abuses that still afflicted both sides of Ireland, albeit the North disproportionately. Details, details. For they felt revolution was in the air and they did not want to miss the party.

As a result, they shot policemen and blew up innocent bystanders in a terrorist campaign that made most Ulster Protestants their determined enemies, retarded the necessary civil rights reforms that were eventually achieved by democratic politicians, and succeeded not in achieving a united Ireland but in making Ian Paisley First Minister at Stormont. Some who joined the party realized this malign drift of events in time and got out of the struggle before they had committed themselves too deeply to murder and worse. But others had pulled a trigger or planted a bomb that left a man maimed, or a woman dead, or a child orphaned. And they now faced a future of bleak choices.

To deliberately kill another human being is to cross a Rubicon, and the Rubicon is an oddly deceptive river. It is moderately difficult to cross but quite impossible to re-cross. So the temptation is to continue on the same course. After all, as the theologians will tell you, any sin is easier to commit the second time, even murder. And if one can justify a first murder, does not that justification point to the necessity of a second murder, and a third, until eventually you find yourself at a freshly-dug grave behind a frightened mother of ten with a gun in your hand. You never expected to go that far, but after the first murder, what choice did you have?

You had another choice, of course, but initially at least it is a painful, bitter, and lonely one requiring repentance and restitution. Sean O'Callaghan took that second course in 1976 when he resigned from the IRA in which he had been an active "volunteer" for a decade, contacted the Irish authorities, and for two long periods worked inside the IRA as an informer for the Dublin and London governments, betraying several major terrorist plans and saving countless lives. That did not calm his guilt sufficiently for the two murders—of Eva Martin, a teacher and part-time volunteer soldier, and Peter Flanagan, a Catholic senior officer in the RUC Special Branch—he had committed while in the Provos. He went into a police station in Tunbridge Wells and confessed to their murders, was convicted on his own evidence, and sentenced to jail. After his release and the gradual end of the Troubles, he became an adviser to governments on terrorism, the author of an autobiography, *The Informer*, and a journalist. One of his last articles appeared in *Quadrant* in April last year.

Sean died of a heart attack in October last year while visiting his daughter in the West Indies. In March this year he was the subject of a remarkable service of celebration and thanksgiving at St Martin in the

Fields—a festival of reconciliation that brought together people from both sides of politics and both sides of the Irish Sea. Familiar hymns were sung. Prayers were said for Sean—and also for Eva Martin and Peter Flanagan. There were readings by Sean's family, by young prison offenders whom the later Sean had mentored, and by friends like historian Ruth Dudley Edwards and writer Douglas Murray. Lord Salisbury, a cabinet minister at the time when Sean was in prison, revealed that—strictly against the rules—they used to have regular telephone calls to discuss how to handle the IRA in negotiations. On one occasion, Sean had asked if British intelligence listened in.

'I certainly hope so,' replied Lord Salisbury, 'because they'll get a far higher quality of strategic advice than they usually do.'

Let Sean have the last word. His son, Rory Hanrahan, read a poem written by his father about an IRA arms smuggling operation that he had helped to foil:

I see seven tons of American
Guns and bullets
Towed into Queenstown or Cobh,
As we call it now.

My Guinness and my secrets satisfy.
Seventy-six thousand bullets
Will not shatter one limb,
Or spatter brain on a pub floor.

I finish my pint and walk
The forty yards home.

The Furies had gone elsewhere.

Originally   published   in   Quadrant,   *23   June   2018,*
https://quadrant.org.au/magazine/2018/06/lethal-ignorance-anointed/.

Abortion and the
End of Irish Exceptionalism
7 June 2018

In Bernard Shaw's great play *John Bull's Other Island*, an English liberal character who at first seems a silly-ass Englishman but who later emerges as a more Machiavellian one, exclaims enthusiastically at one point: 'Home Rule will work wonders under English guidance.' This is a sure fire laugh line in the theatre. It is also a prediction of something that finally happened on Friday, 25 May, with the landslide passage of the referendum to liberalize Ireland's abortion law more or less in line with English precedents. And it symbolizes the end of a 100-year diversion in Irish history from West Britain to a prickly independent Catholic Republic back to West Britain again.

That something this important was at stake was realized very early by William Butler Yeats, who had commissioned the play from George Bernard Shaw to open Dublin's Abbey Theatre. Yeats rejected the play and gave several reasons for doing so, but his main motive was almost certainly that it was alien, both politically and in literary form, to the kind of Irish national theatre that Yeats was trying to establish. Shaw thought so and many years later described the incident as follows: 'Like most people who have asked me to write plays, Mr Yeats got rather more than he bargained for. It was uncongenial to the whole spirit of the neo-Gaelic movement, which is bent on creating a new Ireland after its own ideal, whereas my play is a very uncompromising presentment of the real old Ireland.'

So the play was presented in London's Royal Court Theatre in 1904 and published with a new introduction in 1912. These were the years, especially after 1910, when the Irish Party held the balance of power in the House of Commons, when the demand for Irish Home Rule became a (perhaps the) major issue in British politics.

Home Rule meant that Ireland would be governed by an elected Irish Parliament exercising sovereignty over most matters except defence and foreign policy, which would remain with the 'Imperial Parliament' in London. Ulster Unionists, overwhelmingly Protestant, objected to Home Rule, and prepared to fight it, on the grounds that it would prove to be 'Rome Rule.' That dispute has rightly dominated the accounts of most historians of the period.

But there were other disputes occurring at the same time—one between literary nationalists and Catholic nationalists (who were famously shocked by a frank discussion of underwear in J. M. Synge's play *The Playboy of the Western World*, on its first night at the Abbey Theatre), for instance, and another between Home Rulers who were content with the devolved Irish Parliament and those who wanted a more decisive break with Britain and its liberal commercial civilization.

West Britain was the name given to an Ireland that, whether ruled from Dublin or Westminster, was part of a larger political and civic culture shared with England and the rest of Britain. It was the Ireland we encounter in James Joyce's short stories, the plays of Sean O'Casey, and the comic songs of Percy French. While Ireland was culturally as well as politically united with Britain, its great figures included people such as Parnell, Wilde, Yeats, Shaw, and, earlier, Burke, Sheridan, and Thomas Moore, who moved easily between Dublin and London, and who shaped the politics and culture of both. If Home Rule had been achieved before 1914, that shared culture would presumably have continued against a slightly different political background of UK federalism.

That was not what some wings of Irish nationalism wanted. In addition to seeking a more fundamental political break with Britain, they wanted an Ireland that would differ from Britain in a range of cultural matters: in language, in sports, in literature, and above all in religion—in short, the ideal of a Catholic and Gaelic Ireland evolving away from Britain in every respect possible. To accomplish such a revolutionary change in manners and mores, however, they needed a revolution. Simply establishing a devolved parliament would not have done such a colossal trick. They thought that they needed a revolution on more-immediate grounds too, namely, because Britain would never concede Home Rule.

My own view is that they were wrong on that. If the Great War had not intervened, Ireland would have had Home Rule in 1914, and if the revolutionaries' Easter Rising had not occurred in 1916, thereby precipitating an Anglo–Irish War and later an Irish Civil War, Ireland would have had Home Rule in 1919, not least because Irishmen had joined the colours in large numbers to fight for King and Empire. But the Easter Rising and, no less important, the execution of its leaders in 1916 by the British destroyed the Home Rule cause, made a complete political break with Britain inevitable, and provided Ireland with the 'blood sacrifice' that the more mystical revolutionaries such as Patrick Pearse always believed essential to a break with English civilization.

That is what Ireland got by degrees after the civil war ended and a stable democracy was established. Éamon de Valera was the dominant political leader of the years, broadly from 1930 to 1965, when Ireland was reshaped as a distinctively Catholic state and society. It was he who introduced the 1937 Constitution, which gave the Catholic Church a special place in the society, declared that women should not be forced out of the home 'through economic necessity,' prohibited divorce, and claimed sovereignty over Northern Ireland (aggravating the already bad relations with both London and the Ulster Prods). That constitution, with its flaws and merits, reflected a wider social reality, in particular the overwhelming social influence of the Catholic Church.

This was so massive that bishops were able to order without legal authority the cancellation of Saturday-night dances, on the grounds that they might deter attendance at Sunday Mass. Other expressions of this social power included the excommunication of Catholic students who went to Burke's Trinity College without Episcopal permission, a stipulation that persisted well into post-war Ireland (in earlier times Trinity had itself banned Catholic students); the decision of the cabinet not to attend the funeral service for Ireland's first president, a Protestant, in Dublin's Anglican cathedral but instead to wait outside in carriages; a long-lived and embarrassingly crude literary censorship; the semi-religious celebration, on holidays and official occasions, of the 1916 Easter Rising as the foundation of the state; official sympathy for the Church's rules on Catholic–Protestant marriages ('Ne temere') that disadvantaged Protestants who feared losing their children; and the widespread effective incarceration of girls and young women in laundries run by religious institutions (but often supplying services to the state) for breaking the period's outwardly austere moral code. This last was the 'Magdalene Laundries' scandal, which continued to the 1990s. Since then it has been thoroughly exposed and perhaps exaggerated.

Many of the new rules were felt by citizens of all denominations to be burdensome: for instance, making the Irish language compulsory both for passing examinations across all subjects and for entry into the civil service. Even the bishops thought that de Valera was too rigid in insisting on it, and its impact was to make the Irish language widely unpopular. Taken together, however, the rules also amounted to a soft but persistent discrimination against Protestants, especially poorer ones, that made them feel they were only half-members of the society. Accordingly, there was a steady exodus of them from the Republic to Northern Ireland and Britain.

Now, one should not exaggerate the oddity or scandals of those times. The 1937 Constitution had some distinctively liberal clauses protecting the rights of Jews and Protestants—not trivial considerations in 1937—and was passed in a referendum by quite a modest majority. It was also the first written constitution to include the word 'dignity.' And it puts parents rather than the state in charge of education. Though there were some very real cases of oppression in those years—the Magdalene inmates and some displaced Protestants, for instance—the atmosphere of Irish society was often more relaxed than its formal rules and regulations.

An idealized portrait of that Ireland can be seen in *The Quiet Man*. It is not the whole truth, but it is not a total fiction either. After all, de Valera's Ireland was a society made in the image of most of its citizens, who therefore felt comfortable within it. It was also popular with socially conservative foreigners, English as well as American, who liked the calmer social atmosphere reminiscent of their own countries in earlier days. And de Valera's Ireland turned many a blind eye to those who quietly non-conformed, and when blind eyes are exercised in this way, they will often improve their vision. Mark Steyn tells the story of the director Hilton Edwards and the actor Micheál MacLiammóir, who were for many years the most famously gay couple in Dublin, and who together ran the Gate Theatre (leading local wits to name their Gate and Yeats's Abbey theatre as 'Sodom and Begorrah').

At MacLiammóir's funeral in 1978, the Taoiseach and half the Irish Cabinet attended, and at the end they went up to Edwards, shook hands, and expressed their condolences—in other words, publicly acknowledging him as "the widow." It happened in a state where homosexuality was illegal and where few people suggested that it should be otherwise. The Irish officials at the funeral treated MacLiammóir's relict humanely and decently, not because they had to but because they wished to. I miss that kind of civilized tolerance.

If your discomfort with de Valera's Ireland went too deep to be assuaged by this tolerant hypocrisy, however, there was always the Dublin–Liverpool boat to take you to the actual Sodom and Gomorrah over the Irish Sea, for a modest fee. (My father was the purser on it; I do not think he felt particularly wicked.)

It was the nearness of Britain, however, that weakened an already shaky social experiment. What de Valera, universally known as Dev, wanted was to impose on the Irish people a cultural transformation that neither the Soviets nor Kemal Ataturk, with far more effective instruments of persuasion to hand, succeeded in imposing on their own populations. The great majority of Irish people no longer spoke Gaelic, and they resented being forced to do so in school and elsewhere. Marriages broke down in Ireland as elsewhere, but the only recourse for unhappy Irish couples wanting legal separations was to catch the Liverpool boat. Literary censorship was very easily evaded by the same method. British newspapers with any mention of contraception were removed from newsstands by the censors, but their more indirect influence on morals and politics was harder to recognize and prevent.

Since the Irish at home were notably reluctant to marry (the average age of marriage in rural Ireland for a man was as late as the mid-30s), a lot of young Irish people married their historic enemies, the English, as my father did. Those marriages meant that large numbers of Irish and British people had cousins across a very small pond whom they visited regularly through childhood and later. My sister and I spent every day of our school summer holidays in Dalkey, eight miles south of Dublin, rushing to greet the same friends on the same day year after year. Our Irish cousins returned these visits from time to time, and many stayed on in Britain. At least half of them have spent their adult lives living and working in the UK. In retrospect, it is surprising that de Valera's Ireland, sapped by so many English temptations as it was, lasted as long as it did.

Seeing its fall was like watching an impressive sandcastle, replete with towers and battlements, gradually yielding to the incoming tide until it suddenly collapses entirely and leaves only memories of its impressiveness behind. One can easily enough list the separate influences that undermined it. The economic prosperity that began under Dev's successor, the practical-minded Seán Lemass, and accelerated later in Celtic Tiger days enabled Irish people to vacation abroad more easily and Irish emigrants to return to good jobs at home, bringing more-liberal attitudes with them in both cases. As the 'Troubles' in the North revived and wore grimly on, the 'physical force' tradition of Irish republicanism seemed less and less heroic, more and more vicious, not what a modern and progressive society should celebrate. Entry into the European Union meant surrendering Irish sovereignty to a political entity that wanted more control over Irish life than London had enjoyed since the 1910 election had put Home Rule into play.

And the social power of the bishops took a series of massive hits, one after another. The first was from television: a popular broadcaster, Gay Byrne of RTÉ's *Late Late Show*, had asked a newly married woman what she wore on her wedding night. 'Nothing,' she replied, to the consternation of the Bishop of Limerick, who phoned in to complain. Parishioners were told not to watch the show the next week. Then a thunderbolt struck: its ratings went up. Indeed, it is still on air.

That was the beginning of the end. What little social power the bishops still retained was thoroughly destroyed a few years later when a series of grave sex-abuse scandals, both heterosexual and homosexual, hit the Church. And then the Magdalene Laundries scandal added another torch to an auto-da-fé run by a hostile secular establishment, as did scandals involving other institutions, left over from Victorian times, that had lasted longer in Ireland than in Britain. In a very short time, the Church in Ireland, as elsewhere, went from a dominant and revered institution to one distrusted by its lay members and despised by politicians and journalists who had previously feared it.

I remember my surprise when I realized this was happening in 1996. At the first night of Riverdance in Manhattan, I was invited to the backstage party (by, interestingly, an old friend from UK politics, the former Tory Party chairman, Cecil Parkinson, who had invested in the show). Talking to one of the dancers, I wondered why the Church had played so little part in the show's history of Celtic and immigrant America. 'Oh,' she replied. 'We think that Ireland is about much more than the Catholic Church, and the country is moving out of that kind of repressed world.' (Not an exact quote—I was not taking notes—but a fair summary of a longer conversation.)

In short, an Irish identity built on the Catholic Church had collapsed, and the nation—or, rather, its cultural elite—was looking for a new identity in which Catholicism was treated as something between an embarrassment and a threat. That process has continued ever since, accelerating recently, until Ireland voted by a margin of two to one to liberalize abortion law on lines similar to those of UK law and, still more significantly, celebrated that result in wild public rejoicing. Three years before, Ireland had voted in favour of same-sex marriage by a margin of 62 per cent to 38 per cent, becoming the first country anywhere to introduce gay marriage in this way. Ireland's 100-year experiment in self-conscious cultural transformation had proved to be a mere detour: from Britannia West to *Cathleen ni Houlihan* to Britannia West again.

It is hard even for a natural West Briton like me to be happy about this. If Home Rule had not been derailed by the First World War—with a whole series of historical "what ifs" following on from that—I think I would have found that era's West Britain a very tolerable place. There would have been no Easter Rising, no partition, no Irish Civil War, no cultural-cum-political break with Britain, and therefore no building of a fortress Catholic Republic by Dev. Of course, the Catholic Church would still have been a highly influential force within the somewhat more liberal environment of a Home Rule Ireland constitutionally linked to Britain. Catholicism might also have been more influential throughout Britain as a result. But the Church would not have been able to exercise the kind of unaccountable authority that it had enjoyed and misused for the better part of a century.

Accordingly, it would not now be suffering the malign consequences of that abuse in unpopularity, rejection, contempt, and a law that will provide abortion on demand in practice. Since I share the distress of my *National Review* colleagues including Michael Brendan Dougherty (and of Ireland's own doughty No campaigners such as Declan Ganley and David Quinn) at the enthusiasm for the legal change, I can hardly welcome Ireland's cultural embrace of West Britain that is a much less congenial place morally and politically to conservatives than it was in 1912. But there is one consolation for us. In the coming battle to preserve the right for doctors and nurses of conscientious objection to abortion—and similar protections for the rights of yesterday's religious majority—the more robust and diverse liberal tradition that West Britain implies should come to our assistance. Ireland is unlikely to go back to being a one-ideology society any time soon.

The Irish nation is able to accept this reversion without much, if any, loss of face because Britannia West comes in the fashionable guise of Europa. Dublin is not rejoining Britain, goes the official mantra, it is enjoying the fruits of its commitment to the EU and its corporate liberalism. This is not entirely self-deception. True, most Irish people look to London rather than Brussels for their careers, markets, and social models—the patron saints of West Britain are Sir Terry Wogan, the Irish broadcaster who became the most popular man in Britain (and a British citizen), and Conor Cruise O'Brien, the biographer of Burke and the Burke of his own day, who became editor-in-chief of Britain's leading liberal newspaper, the *Observer*. But the minority that looks to Brussels for its politics and morals is disproportionately influential and politically powerful. It has embarked on another cultural transformation of Ireland, both for its own class interests and in order to maintain a sense of separateness from Britain: Ireland is to be a new model European republic inside a federal EU. Whether Brexit occurs or not, that identity would continue to distinguish Ireland from a Britain that will always be a reluctant European. It is a dream, of course, and a different one from Dev's dream. But as the heavy bill paid by Ireland to remain in the euro zone (and to save German banks) demonstrated after 2008, it is likely to prove an equally demanding dream.

Originally published in the National Review, *7 June 2018, https://www.nationalreview.com/2018/06/ireland-abortion-referendum-irish-exceptionalism-ending-european-identity/.*

Cardinal Mindszenty:
The Power of the Prisoner
4 December 2012

Cardinal József Mindszenty was almost the first post-war European figure to become a symbolic victim of totalitarianism. His arrest and trial were almost simultaneous with the Greek crisis, the declaration of the Truman Doctrine and the Czech communist coup that between them marked the start of the Cold War. He was selected by the Hungarian Communists under Mátyás Rákosi to be an example of the allegedly criminal past and to establish the permanence of their new order. They succeeded instead in erecting a vast international question mark against their rule.

It is right that the House of Terror Museum should devote a conference to the Cardinal's significance. He is only now being given the significance in Hungarian history that his courage and steadfastness deserve. But it gave me a macabre feeling to realize that the conference proceedings took place in the very building in which the Cardinal had been beaten and brutalized. I am never quite sure of the status of exorcism in current Catholic thinking, but I am fairly sure that the distinguished prelates at the conference would agree that Dr Mária Schmidt's establishment of the Museum in that building has exorcised some very unpleasant ghosts.

It may seem odd that I took such an interest in Cardinal Mindszenty since I was only six when he was arrested. The explanation is simple. I was brought up in a Catholic home in Liverpool, where we took the Catholic weekly newspaper, *The Universe*, which covered the communist takeover of Central Europe in general and the communist attack on religion in particular. So I was well aware of the Cardinal's fate and of the injustice done to him. Indeed, because this attack was directed against a Cardinal, the entire Catholic world was gripped by a drama that might otherwise have been of interest only to a small number of politically sophisticated people. And what a drama it was!

A single, slim, ascetic priest against the might of an empire—but he has God on his side. For a moment the Devil wins; the Cardinal confesses. But he has forecast his own weakness in the face of torture, confessed his sin in advance so to speak, and his sentence is quickly followed by a Papal ruling of excommunication against all connected with his trial. One might suppose that an officially atheist regime would be indifferent to excommunication; they might even scoff at its medieval flavour. Not at all. The Papal bull of excommunication becomes something that the Hungarian Communists want withdrawn (for whatever odd reason of their own). Even as the Cardinal heads for prison, they agitate against it. That is only the first act of a three-act play. There are still two more thrilling acts to come—in which we shall encounter cowardice, betrayal, and the end of noble work.

In a sense that drama is not over; it continues posthumously. There are many people who would be happy to see the Cardinal forgotten, and not all of them are on the Left. He was not always a comfortable companion for his allies and co-religionists. He insisted on truths and prerogatives that many anti-communists and many Catholics would like to have relegated to the attic along with old toys and broken doctrines. He believed he had been given the responsibility for eternal truths, and he was never prepared to dilute those truths, let alone to exchange them for fashionable opinions or to subject them to Machiavellian calculations. He was given strength of character but also the understanding to realize that the strongest can be broken. In the more subtle tests to which he was later exposed, he did not break. Indeed, he scarcely bent when he might reasonably have done so. Let us see why, and what the results were.

The Four Lives of Cardinal Mindszenty

The life of József Mindszenty as a historical public figure—his earlier biography was covered by others at the conference—falls somewhat neatly into four segments. The first is his time as Bishop of Veszprém in the Second World War when, among other things, he opposed the deportations of Jews from Hungary, gave shelter to Jewish refugees, and was imprisoned by the fascist Arrow Cross government for refusing the entry of their troops into the Episcopal home. When he was appointed Bishop of Esztergom and thus Primate of Hungary, he already enjoyed national stature and had demonstrated firm authority. He promptly used this authority to defend the Church, in particular Church schools, against the post-war communist-dominated governments.

The second period was, of course, from 1948 to 1956 when he was arrested, tortured, tried, convicted of various trumped-up charges, and imprisoned by the Rákosi government. János Kádár was the apparatchik most responsible for the judicial process (if judicial is the right word) that persecuted the Cardinal. This period of eight years was in my view the most significant and influential period of the Cardinal's life. I shall return to it later to argue why.

The third period was his second imprisonment from 1956 to 1971 when he took refuge in the US Embassy in Budapest following the Soviet invasion and re-imposition of communist rule, this time under Kádár's ruthless but shrewd leadership. For the embassy, the Cardinal was a minor nuisance. He took up a lot of room in what was then quite a small embassy building, and a junior embassy official had the task of rounding up American Catholics visiting Budapest to attend his Sunday mass. But he was an excellent symbol of America's protection of religious liberty. His imprisonment was the work of Kádár who was hostile to the idea that his captive should be allowed out of the embassy to any destination other than a prison—unless he and the Vatican effectively agreed that his original conviction had been fair and just. This no one was prepared to do at first.

Indeed, this stand-off was initially quite acceptable to the Church and to the US government. From both their standpoints, it served to remind the world of the true nature of the Soviet Union and its satellite regimes. It gave America the kudos of providing sanctuary to a Cardinal. And it gave the Church a living martyr. Martyrdom is not a pleasant experience for the martyr, of course; Mindszenty was still in a prison—a comfortable prison, to be sure, but one in which he was still deprived of liberty. Kádár and the Hungarian Communists, on the other hand, were trapped by their own ruthlessness. They could not release him without loss of face; and if they kept him in the embassy, they inadvertently glorified him up as the world's foremost prisoner of conscience. All that they could hope was that, given the passage of time, the Cardinal would become a burden to the Americans and an obstacle to the Vatican—and so be quietly eased off the world stage.

In the fourth period of his life, 1971 to 1975, that is more or less what happened. In a series of manoeuvres, the Cardinal was pushed semi-voluntarily into exile. The price for his release was his description by the Vatican as 'a victim of history' which is either a weasel phrase or a capitulation to Marxist theories of history. He was allowed to write his memoirs but deprived of his ecclesiastical title. The government of the Church of Hungary was turned over to other and more flexible hands. These steps did not turn out exactly as intended. Mindszenty turned this exile to good account by touring Hungarian communities throughout the world, telling them of the current state of Hungary and the continued, if milder, persecution of the Church and the faithful. He therefore continued to be an obstacle to Kádár's government, then attempting to establish its respectability with Western governments and investors—and to a lesser extent an obstacle to the Vatican attempting to mend relations with Kádár. After a short period, he died in exile, this time unbroken, but also unhappy because the Church had taken a wrong turning in its dealings with the Hungarian government, with the Soviet Union, and with the armed doctrine of Marxism.

Mindszenty and the 1960s

In his history of the idea of the West, *From Plato to NATO*, David Gress, the Danish historian, sees Western intellectual and progressive opinion in the period from the early 1930s up to the recent present as swinging between two poles—anti-fascism on the Left and anti-totalitarianism on the Right—in reaction to world events. Most of the 1930s was marked by a strong current of anti-fascism with the Popular Front being its main expression. The Nazi–Soviet pact brought in two years of anti-totalitarianism in response to the open alliance of the twin totalitarian powers. Operation Barbarossa ended that with a bang, but it also produced 6–7 years of anti-fascism in the official form of the wartime alliance. The onset of the Cold War brought that too to an end. We then had an extended period of anti-totalitarianism from 1947 until the 1960s when a modern variant of anti-fascism appeared under the name of anti-imperialism. In the United States, that period began with opposition to the Vietnam War. It began somewhat earlier in Europe with a series of events: de Gaulle's distancing from the United States, the rise of Italian and German terrorism, the spread of revolutionary movements across Western Europe, the gradual drift of social democratic parties to the Left and towards a more fraternal relationship with the communist and neo-communist Left, and eventually with Europe's own opposition to America's war in Vietnam. This produced the phenomenon of moral equivalence on the European Left: if the Soviet Union was illegitimate because it was totalitarian, the United States was illegitimate because it was imperialist. From a post-1989 perspective, such a comparison is transparently fraudulent and even dishonest; at the time, it was the height of West European sophistication.

Mindszenty's prestige rose and fell in line with these movements of political, usually progressive, opinion. In that sense he *was* a victim of history. When anti-totalitarianism was in vogue, he was generally seen in the West as a hero; when anti-fascism or anti-imperialism became the fashionable ideology, he was at best an irrelevance, at worst an embarrassment. Though these swings of opinion took place in the world of the progressive intelligentsia, they influenced both governments and the Church. Their influence on governments could be seen in the higher priority that all Western governments placed on détente or rapprochement with the USSR during periods of anti-fascism, such as the 1970s.

This influence on Western governments turned out to be temporary, if not superficial, as Reagan and Thatcher later demonstrated when they rejected it and embarked on a stronger anti-Soviet policy. In the case of the Catholic Church, however, the influence was deeper and it took two forms.

Intellectually, the 1960s saw the growth of several movements seeking to reconcile Catholic teaching with Marxism. The most extreme of them was liberation theology which sought to interpret Christianity as a kind of metaphor for Marxism with the proletariat as the Church, *Das Kapital* as the gospels, and revolution as salvation. But there were also more moderate Christian–Marxist dialogues scattered through Western Europe. And these ideas became fashionable at all levels. The Church became far more critical of capitalism than of socialism, far more protective towards the Third World than towards the West. Social encyclicals during this period, such as *Populorum Progressio*, had a definite left-wing flavour to them even if it was sometimes qualified in the footnotes. Like the drift leftwards of social democratic parties, the atmosphere of Catholic thought became less harsh towards communism and the communist world, and less friendly to the United States and to the concept of the West. That ideological drift removed or at least softened one obstacle to a new Vatican diplomacy towards the communist world.

However this new Vatican Ostpolitik also seemed desirable on other and very different grounds—namely, the grounds of realpolitik. The Vatican wanted to improve the position of the Church in communist countries in all sorts of practical ways. It wanted to open seminaries, to reduce official discrimination against Catholics, to have the communist authorities recognize Catholic bishops, and in general, to work within the laws and practices of communist states that it had shunned in the 1950s. It embarked on its own version of Willy Brandt's Ostpolitik because, like other currents of opinion in the West, notably social democratic opinion, it believed that the communist governments had strong roots and even legitimacy in popular support. The Church began to accept therefore that Soviet domination and communist rule were permanent facts of life. It would have to live with them.

Those arguing for this policy did not lack plausible justifications. One, as we have seen, was a wish to improve the conditions in which the Church lived under communism in order to preach the gospel more effectively. A second was the desire for peace which in a world of nuclear weapons was readily understandable. Even if communist governments were repressive, risking nuclear war to overthrow them seemed to be a much worse evil. Finally, the growing intellectual prestige of Marxism inside and outside the Church—described above—made this new Vatican diplomacy intellectually simpatico.

'We will never know,' wrote Georges Bernanos, 'how many acts of cowardice have been committed out of the fear of being thought insufficiently progressive.' It is at least possible that the Vatican's Ostpolitik was one such act of cowardice.

Whatever the force of that critique, Ostpolitik was not a policy to the taste of Cardinal Mindszenty. He did not believe that the communist governments in Central Europe had strong roots in popular support. Nor did he think that they were a permanent fact of life that could force the Church to make political concessions to them in order to carry out its pastoral duties. If he had been released into Hungary, he would have sabotaged this new policy even if he had tried loyally to carry it out. From the US Embassy—and later from exile—he was an obstacle to the policy simply by virtue of his status as Primate of Hungary. That explains the slightly shabby manoeuvres that exiled him to Vienna until his death in 1975.

In retrospect, Mindszenty was posthumously vindicated within a decade of his death by John Paul II who, both before and during his papacy, carried out a strategy of cultural resistance towards communism that undermined and eventually overthrew it. The Church of Poland had always been more resistant to Soviet communism than other Central European Churches because of its immense social power inside Poland. Neither Karol Wojtyla nor the great Primate of Poland, Cardinal Wyszyński, believed that Poland's communist government was a permanent and unavoidable reality. Neither of them believed in the permanence of the Yalta division of Europe. And when Wojtyla became Pope John Paul II, he embarked upon a radically subversive diplomacy at variance with the cautious acceptance of the European status quo that had marked the policy of his recent predecessors.

This contrast between the visionary Polish Pope and his more cautious diplomatic advisers is shown in miniature in his 1983 visit to Poland when the country was suffering the worst of the regime's repression. Here is a brief excerpt from my own account in *The President, the Pope, and the Prime Minister*:

John Paul's pilgrimage to Poland in June 1983, which was allowed by the regime to demonstrate that normalisation was working, had exactly the opposite effect. On arrival his grim demeanour and condemnation of the 'humiliation' and 'suffering' of martial law told Poles that he shared their agonies. 'He is sad. You see, he understands,' a woman told a reporter. In the days that followed, however, he began to change the national atmosphere. His sermons argued that to tell the truth was the first step to liberation. This was a moral rather than a political point. But it undermined the regime's official myths that communist power was permanent and there could be no return to pre-martial law days. He insisted over official objections on meeting Lech Wałęsa. He told Jaruzelski that any 'renewal' (the regime's word) of Polish society had to begin with his acceptance of the Gdańsk accords. He repeatedly used what Weigel calls the 'unsayable' word, solidarity, in sermons. He engaged in public dialogues with large crowds in which he urged them with fruitful ambiguity to 'persevere in Hope.'

Not all churchmen liked this dissidence in clerical garb. Cardinal Casaroli, the practitioner of realpolitik, asked at one point: 'Does he want bloodshed? Does he want war? Does he want to overthrow the government? Every day I have to explain to the authorities that there is nothing to this?' But there *was* something to it. By the time the pilgrimage was over, the Pope had cracked the regime's facade of unshakable power. He had aligned the Church with Solidarity, dispersing the regime's hope of a separate peace with religion. He had restored the people's hope and trust in each other that his election had originally stimulated. In short he had created the social conditions for underground Solidarity to survive and challenge the regime. Cardinal Mindszenty was not there to see this—nor the gradual surrender of communism in the Hungary of 1988–89. But these events vindicated his years in the US Embassy and the power he had then exercised from his apparent impotence as a prisoner.

Yet when a final judgment of the Cardinal's historical significance is made, it will surely conclude that his time as a prisoner of the Communists was the greatest period of his life. It was certainly the most influential since it informed the world of the nature of Stalinist communism in the most dramatic forms. His trial contained many elements that subsequently became familiar as the Cold War continued. There was, for instance, its revelation of the character of the Stalinist show trial and thus of Stalinism—something the Western allies had forgotten about or repressed in the wartime years when "Uncle Joe" was our principal ally. There was the phenomenon of "brain washing" about which we talked about a great deal at the time: getting someone to believe in his own guilt by a combination of brutality, deprivation of sleep, and constant argument from skilled interrogators. It seemed almost a form of witchcraft and it was certainly a technique admirably suited to witch-hunting. There was the absurdity of the charges—they included the allegation that he was plotting to steal the crown jewels and hand them over to Otto von Habsburg in an effort to restore the Monarchy and give himself political power as the leading cleric in a Catholic state. Such absurdities were a common feature of Stalinist show trials in which communist foreign ministers would admit to having been recruited to the British secret service by such figures as the playwright Noel Coward, author of the song *Mad Dogs and Englishmen.*

So the Cardinal's trial was, among other things, an introduction to the nightmare world of totalitarian politics where nothing was substantial, real, trustworthy, or reliable—except apparently the brutal power that sustained the whole mad and lying enterprise.

It inspired in particular what is today a rare understanding and sympathy for the Church in the artistic community. Hollywood made a very competent, largely accurate, and somewhat sentimental film starring Charles Bickford, then an established Hollywood star, as the Cardinal. The film had flaws but it spread the basic truth of his trial to a vast audience.

Bridget Boland's play, *The Prisoner*, later filmed with Sir Alec Guinness in the leading role, was a more serious artistic and intellectual enterprise. It was built around the moral and intellectual duel between the Mindszenty figure (not named as such) and a principled communist interrogator who admires him but is determined to break him for the cause of preserving people's faith in the regime. Thus, it had the usual feature of such films identified by George Jonas (in his review of a later film *Sunshine*) as follows: 'In such films the fascist thugs are simply thugs, but the communist thugs are figures of intriguing moral complexity.' Still, the device is a legitimate one dramatically, and it enables the playwright to deal with one central and powerful theory about totalitarianism: namely, that it rests even more upon assent to the Lie than it does upon Terror. As Václav Havel later argued, a communist regime was often relatively content to leave someone alone provided that he would publicly assent to the regime's truth *du jour*. It might be a grocer putting in his front window a sign that read 'Workers of the World Unite' or a Cardinal confessing to a plot to steal the crown jewels. What matters is submission to the Lie since that deprives the dissident of his main strength and weapon: fidelity to the truth. As long as the dissident keeps that faith, the totalitarian regime is unsafe. His submission to the Lie thus strengthens the totalitarian structure—in principle, maybe forever.

On this theory, when Mindszenty was beaten into giving the Rákosi regime's version of events, he should logically have strengthened the regime. Instead, it weakened the regime. Not merely was his confession greeted with general scepticism (where opinion could be freely expressed), it was also greeted with disgust. He had warned in advance that he would be broken; it had clearly taken some time for the torturers to break him; in the end he, not the Communists, wrote the narrative. Among scores of trials where the prisoner confessed to lies, Mindszenty's alone is the one that long remained in the mind of the international public. It therefore showed the limits of totalitarianism: submission to the Lie depends on Terror and cannot be procured or sustained without it.

That outcome had (and has) two consequences. The first is that totalitarian governments rely ultimately on brutes. Once the ideology begins to crumble, as it invariably does, totalitarianism gradually loses its intellectual and principled supporters. Its survival then rests upon brutes—including brutes in high positions such as those who tried to engineer the Soviet counter-coup in 1991. Second, it established that Orwell's worst nightmare—the permanent triumph of the Lie—is ultimately a false fear. Mindszenty's forced submission to the Lie actually weakened totalitarianism. And his continued visible presence in Hungary, even imprisoned in a foreign embassy, was a permanent threat to the regime's standing.

That was also Bridget Boland's conclusion in her play: the communist interrogator in *The Prisoner*, though he has broken the Cardinal, admits that he is in the end the defeated one. The Mindszenty figure goes back into the world to face people he fears will believe he has betrayed them. We know, of course, that the outside world understands his decision and fate, and sees him in a heroic light. It is the communist interrogator who is shown in the final scene as being behind bars. He is in a political situation not unlike that of Kádár after 1956—unable to release Mindszenty without loss of face, but also unable to keep him imprisoned without bearing international shame for doing so.

One mystery remains. Mindszenty was able to bear all his travails, including shame at his own weakness, because he was ultimately sustained by the biblical passage: 'And I say also unto thee, That thou art Peter, and upon this rock I will build my church; and the gates of hell shall not prevail against it.'

If the Cardinal had lacked religious faith, however, he might have been sustained by a somewhat lesser authority, that of the historian, Thomas Babington Macaulay, a liberal Protestant historian hostile to Catholicism, who, in a famous passage from his review of Ranke's *History of the Popes* delivered this prediction about the Catholic Church:

> She saw the commencement of all the governments and of all the ecclesiastical establishments that now exist in the world; and we feel no assurance that she is not destined to see the end of them all. She was great and respected before the Saxon had set foot on Britain, before the Frank had passed the Rhine, when Grecian eloquence still flourished at Antioch, when idols were still worshipped in the temple of Mecca. And she may still exist in undiminished vigour when some traveller from New Zealand shall, in the midst of a vast solitude, take his stand on a broken arch of London Bridge to sketch the ruins of St Paul's.

So the mystery is not why Cardinal Mindszenty and John Paul II foresaw the outcome of the struggle between communism and the

Church. Macaulay had done so one hundred and fifty years before them. The mystery is why so many leading figures in the Church did not foresee the same outcome. And why some of them today are still puzzled about what happened.

The article is the revised version of a lecture given in the House of Terror Museum, Budapest, 21 September 2012. Originally published in Hungarian Review, *Vol. III, No. 6, December 2012, www.hungarianreview.com/article/cardinal_mindszenty_the_power_of_t he_prisoner.*

What Every Young Tory Should Know: A History of the Party without Veils or Code

A Review of *The Conservatives: A History* by Robin Harris
22 November 2011

'Read biography,' said Disraeli, 'for that is life without theory.' Robin Harris is very far from being a devotee of the Disraeli cult. Modern conservatives, he believes, misinterpret both Disraeli and Gladstone by exaggerating those of their ideas that still have purchase today and by ignoring those things they cared most about at the time. But he has taken Disraeli's advice on biography further than the Master in two senses.

The first sense is that he has written a biography of the Conservative Party in all its twists, turns, efforts, failures, achievements, and—not least—occasional nervous breakdowns since its early beginnings in the rhetoric of Burke and the statecraft of Pitt the Younger. I write 'biography' rather than history because this book traces the ways in which the Tory Party, much like a human being, has changed in response to the large social changes of two hundred years while retaining more or less the same identity throughout.

Describing this essential identity is not a simple matter since its constituent elements emerge, merge, diverge, and merge again in different ways at different times over the period. But these main elements are clear enough and, though any list will be debatable, they include:

- The Conservative Party has traditionally sought to ally Britain's ruling class of the day—initially the 'landed interest'—with rising social classes upon the common principle of defending property. Where social classes without property either were or included potential recruits, it has supported and facilitated their aspirations to property.

- Tories have generally been seen by themselves and others as the patriotic party both because they have encouraged and profited from occasional jingoism and, more seriously, because they have sought to root major policies in the long-term interests of the British state. Broadly speaking, from the 1688 'Glorious Revolution' until very recently, this has meant a grand strategy built on the worldwide promotion of sound finance, property rights, free trade, and free capital movements. Andrew Gamble, a sympathetic critic of Toryism from its Left, calls this combination 'Anglo-America' because the United States inherited the task of defending this liberal world order after 1945.

- Because the Conservative Party emerged gradually into history out of the factional political disputes of the Napoleonic period and later, pure ideology plays a lesser role in its life than in that of the Labour and Liberal parties. That is not to say ideology plays no part at all—merely that Tories hold all political ideas to account in the light of their performance more sceptically and thus sooner than others. In the Burkean tradition of ordered liberty, liberalism was made for man, not man for liberalism.

- The Tory Party, finally, represents strategic and economic realism in domestic political debate against the utopian idealism of its various opponents. This willingness to deal with unpalatable facts is why it has earned the honourable name of the 'Nasty' Party. It is the party that cleans up the mess that spendthrifts, pacifists, and utopians invariably leave behind.

These different elements combine, dissolve, and re-combine to produce policies that even when they alter over time, are nonetheless supported by a consistent tough-mindedness. Thus, although the Conservative Party has mostly supported free trade, it spent the first thirty-five years of the twentieth century divided over—and eventually advocating—imperial protectionism. This departure from the economic orthodoxy of 'Anglo-America' was justified by distinctly hard-nosed calculations: first, that Britain would need a larger economic base in order to remain the equal of rising world powers such as Germany and the United States; second, that tariff revenue could finance higher defence expenditure without the need for higher income taxes.

Those calculations were not wrong, but the policy failed—and in retrospect it looks doomed to fail. Appeasement too, in the hands of the Tory-dominated National Government, was a hard-nosed policy designed to rescue a worldwide empire from the consequences of imperial overstretch. As Dr Harris mordantly notes, however, this policy failed as well. One is now surely justified in adding 'Europe' as a third example of a tough-minded strategy for national revival that has failed. Realism is no guarantee of success; it merely offers better odds than unrealism.

As these examples also show, this tough-minded Tory tradition allows for a wide variety of political responses to national problems. Tories have been on both sides of innumerable major issues ranging from the extension of the suffrage to 'Europe' over time. Some even make a fetish of this flexibility: 'catching the Whigs bathing and running off with their clothes' is their sole concept of political imagination. Granted this wide latitude, however, what determines the actual policies Conservatives have adopted?

Here comes in the second sense in which Dr Harris has followed Disraeli's injunction to biography. He explains the broad and changing directions of Tory policy as the result of the different preferences of its more dominant leaders. At the Carlton Club meeting that led to the break-up of the Lloyd George coalition (and, later, to the formation of the 1922 Committee of Tory backbenchers), Bonar Law had declared: 'The Party elects a Leader, and that Leader chooses the policy, and if the Party does not like it, they have to get another Leader.' Dr Harris interprets this remark less as a successful bid for power (though it was certainly that) than as a sociological description of how the Tory Party works.

Accordingly, he sees the Tory Party almost as nine different parties shaped by the personalities of nine leaders—Peel, Derby, Disraeli, Salisbury, Baldwin, Churchill, Macmillan, Heath, and Thatcher. Each leader contributed some element to the Tory identity; that element often persists today. Disraeli transferred to his party his own 'zeal for the greatness of England,' and partly for that reason he made the party more popular nationally than it had been ever before. Salisbury, a pessimistic aristocrat sceptical of democracy, made the Tory Party both a political home for the middle class and a well-organized electoral machine, thus becoming against all the odds his party's most successful democratic leader until Margaret Thatcher. Stanley Baldwin made his inter-war party 'the natural party of government' with his emollient soothing of popular fears. (But this judgment is not necessarily a compliment—see below.)

Heath made the Conservatives the 'party of Europe,' but since he exaggerated its benefits and glossed over its drawbacks, he left the country (still) unresolved problems and the Tory Party material for seemingly endless splits. Margaret Thatcher was the first leader 'since Peel to devote pride of place to economic policy over other aspects of government' and her 'unevenly virtuoso' performance revived the self-confidence of a Conservative Party that was floundering and uncertain under her predecessor. Etc., etc.

These nine leaders are not the sole recipients of Dr Harris's critical gaze. He sees other leaders playing important roles: Bonar Law saving the party from ruin twice; Neville Chamberlain undermining the Tory reputation for strategic realism; John Major undermining its reputation for economic competence. But for various reasons (usually brevity in office), leaders such as Balfour, Chamberlain, Eden, Douglas-Home, and Major did not impress a distinctive identity on their followers. Most were caretakers of the parties bequeathed by their predecessors. As to 'Cameron's Party,' Dr Harris attaches a discreet question mark to it reflecting the unfinished nature of the modernization project. In general, however, the message of this book is that any accurate biography of the Tory Party will mainly reflect the influence of its most significant leaders.

This is a bold and original approach—and Robin Harris would seem to be its ideal practitioner. He is a former Director of the Conservative Research Department who in the Thatcher years hired David Cameron. He is an established historian and the author of an elegant biography of Talleyrand. He knows the Conservative Party in both theory and practice. And—full disclosure—he and I have been friends for almost thirty years, and we both assisted Lady Thatcher in the writing of her memoirs. My expectations for this book were therefore high; but Dr Harris has exceeded them.

In the first place, this book is genuine history written with real authority. It describes persuasively how people at the time felt, spoke, and acted about the political controversies in which they were engaged. It does not impose our parochial concerns or our opportunistic interpretations on them. Quite the reverse. It demolishes a number of cherished Conservative myths, notably the idea that the main object of Disraeli's political life was to promote social reform rather than (a) the political interests of the landed gentry and (b) himself. What it principally achieves, however, is to bring dead controversies to life in the course of showing how they contributed to the birth and rise of the Conservative Party.

Nor—and this suspicion might perhaps have been provoked by Dr Harris's Thatcherite career—is the book an example of teleological history. His list of significant Tory leaders is definitely not a kind of apostolic succession that reaches its destined high point in the elevation of the Blessed Margaret. Mrs Thatcher is given her impressive due in the chapter on 'her' party. But high marks for Thatcher are more or less inevitable in any history of the Tory Party that is not avowedly anti-Conservative. Dr Harris's critique, though favourable overall, contains sharp criticisms of her governance and ideological legacy. Indeed, the very structure of a book that treats Conservative history as a succession of political biographies militates very effectively against any kind of teleology.

Also, this history is finely written and highly readable with an undercurrent of dry wit running through its narrative ('When Balfour, or any other Conservative leader, lost the bores, he lost the party.') Its pen pictures of leading Tories are models of economic description. And its final judgments on them—and on the Tory parties they led—are balanced but unsparing.

Given that Dr Harris is writing about electoral reform and church politics in the nineteenth century, economic decline, social reform, and war in the twentieth century, and environmentalism, and cultural politics in the current century, he cannot judge his chosen leaders by any single criterion. As his narrative moves into and through the last century, however, one standard emerges against which most of them have to be measured (if only because they hoped to measure themselves favourably against it). It is their success or otherwise in halting and reversing the decline of Britain since its late Victorian hey-day.

This is a tricky standard because in retrospect Britain's relative decline was inescapable in a world of rising nationalisms and continental superpowers. Also, at least one of the leaders examined here—namely, Churchill—is unique in having overcome a supreme national challenge by virtue of extraordinary leadership. But Churchill himself lamented in later years that Britain had lost its status as a front-rank power despite this last glorious achievement. That was largely because of an underlying economic and industrial decline to which his and other post-war Tory administrations contributed through their political and economic timidity. (Dr Harris focuses in particular on the failure to adopt ROBOT—a 'road not taken' which I leave his readers to discover for themselves.) And if the test is responding to that decline, then the spotlight must turn on five Tory leaders: Balfour, Baldwin, Macmillan, Heath, and Thatcher.

My one serious quarrel with Dr Harris is his almost contemptuous dismissal of Balfour. Although Balfour failed miserably as a party leader, presiding over a prolonged internal civil war, and though his droll witticisms in coping with major crises irritate Dr Harris, he both diagnosed the 'national efficiency' deficit of Britain after the Boer War more seriously than any other political leader and proposed more realistic remedies to it than Joseph Chamberlain and the protectionists—namely, much greater national emphasis on education, apprenticeships, science, technology, and management. He fell from power before being able to carry through many of his reforms. Though he may not deserve inclusion in the pantheon of Tory leaders who shaped the party, he nonetheless has an honourable place as a Prime Minister who at least began to tackle national decline intelligently.

Macmillan and Heath between them represent a very different strategy to break the cycle of decline. It was a vigorous policy sustained over several years in each case. And it was an innovative one. Except for the brief 'Selsdon' free-market interlude that began the Heath government, the strategy introduced two ideological novelties into the Tory tradition. The first was a massive degree of centralized statist intervention—indicative planning and incomes control in Macmillan's case; prices and incomes control, industrial subsidies, and corporate economic planning in Heath's. Tories had flirted with corporatism before, notably in the 1930s, but never on this scale. The second innovation was a reckless degree of fiscal and monetary expansion disguised rhetorically as 'a dash for growth.' This combination was supposed to ensure that the ensuing boom would produce economic expansion and industrial innovation rather than inflation, overheating, and a balance of payments crisis. In fact, it produced a succession of different crises: the long sterling crisis inherited by Harold Wilson in Macmillan's case; stagflation, the 1974 miners' strike, the three-day week, and the defeat of his government in Heath's case. In retrospect, the differences on economic policy between the Heath and Macmillan administrations and Harold Wilson's intervening government look minor but, where they exist, they are to the credit of Wilson who maintained a somewhat more responsible monetary policy. (His 1974–76 government is a different matter.)

Macmillan and Heath tested the limits of Tory flexibility almost to destruction—but not beyond that point. The former was a sentimental neo-socialist, the latter a desiccated technocrat. Each took his party deeply into dogmatic statism under the misleading banner of pragmatism. Yet both exercised rigid discipline over their parties until the final smash-up and both retain influential Tory admirers today. There seems to be a confused logic underlying such support: When Tories pursue conservative and/or free market policies, they are acting ideologically; when they pursue socialist or statist policies, they are acting pragmatically. The practical effect of such logic (seen in such writers as the late Ian Gilmour) is that conservatism becomes the only ideology to which anti-ideological Tories object. This warped logic still influences Tory debate.

Baldwin's case is more complicated. He was a semi-mystical political dreamer who saw his role as being to create the national solidarity needed for class cooperation in industrial reform and economic revival. Against that soothing background his Chancellor, Neville Chamberlain, pursued a tough, orthodox fiscal policy, and other Ministers arranged for British industry to set up cartels in return for limited protection. This combination would have faltered in the long run; it reinforced the defensive mentalities and restrictive practices of British industry. But in the peculiar circumstances of the Slump—and here my view is slightly more favourable than Dr Harris's—it did pretty well. Britain recovered more quickly than any other advanced nation, and modern industry began to spread across southern England.

This achievement was real, but it fostered the national complacency that Baldwin embodied. It was also set at naught by the rise of the dictators and the onset of the Second World War. For these challenges, Baldwin's talents were quite unsuited. He was baffled by Hitler—Dr Harris describes his response as a 'mental shrug'—and he intuited that the national mood would permit only gradual and pacific responses to German threat. It was under Baldwin that Appeasement became the settled national policy (though it would become a more active one under the energetic Chamberlain). Britain thus drifted into war. His admirers claim, with some justice, that war found the British people united by Baldwin's social emollience. But war also found British industry and industrial relations insufficiently modernized and efficient and—under a wartime national government that included Labour and then a post-war Labour government—made them less so. Dr Harris's verdict is damning:

> Baldwin won huge majorities. He just did not know what to do with them. At a deeper level, undoubtedly he reflected the mood of the times. This, in fact, was the problem. He reflected it too well. In Baldwin the country got what it wanted and, arguably, and to stray into more disputable territory, it got what it deserved. But it did not get what it needed.

There are, of course, echoes here of a more recent prime minister. Not Mrs Thatcher, it need hardly be said. She probably hated Britain's decline with more real passion than any political leader since the First World War. Her 'project' was the revival of Britain in all important respects; but she expected to root this in a recovery of the British economy. (The Falklands War was an unexpected challenge turned to good effect.) Her methods were more or less the opposite of the Macmillan–Heath recipe: she favoured macro-economic fiscal and monetary restraint and a micro-economic policy of removing obstacles to enterprise (including subsidies). Not everything went as intended by a long chalk. But she drove through necessary reforms against strong opposition by virtue of brave political leadership and sustained administrative stamina. The broad economic and foreign policy successes that followed are so well known as to make repetition of them needless here. It is simply silly to argue, however, that changes of this magnitude and controversy could have been achieved either by emollient Tory leadership or by social democratic negotiations between 'stakeholders.' Dr Harris is entirely right to conclude that 'it is difficult to argue that these achievements, taken as a whole, were anything other than startling, when compared with the record of other modern British governments— not least modern Conservative governments.' For a generation Britain's long decline was finally halted and reversed.

Owing to the extraordinary fiscal ingenuity of Gordon Brown and Tony Blair, however, normal service has been resumed. Britain is faced yet again with economic slowdown and financial crisis, and it falls to a largely Conservative government to deal with these familiar hobgoblins. This task would be hard even for a well-integrated government, but it has fallen by chance into the hands of a Tory Party undergoing a combination of identity crisis and nervous breakdown. Dr Harris refrains from any final historical judgment on the Cameron Tory Party in a short last chapter. (In a slightly failed attempt at discretion, he exiles his more pungent comments, including a crisp demolition of 'Red Toryism,' to the footnotes where journalists in search of headlines should repair.) Even so, he raises some questions—the most troubling of which concerns the philosophical nature of the modernizing project of which Cameron conservatism is the most mature expression. What does it stand for? In Walter Mondale's scathing question to an earlier candidate bearing 'new ideas': 'Where's the Beef?'

As others have noted, the more Cameron modernization is explained, the less anyone understands it. There is something elusive and will o' the wisp about it. Initially, it defined itself negatively as a movement opposed to the unreconstructed Thatcherite Tories. It proudly announced that there was such a thing as society. It renounced any foolish intention of 'banging on' about crime, immigration, Europe, or other supposed obsessions of more traditional Tories. Its adherents were constantly looking for a 'Clause Four moment' when they could demonstrate their distance from the 'Nasty' past by dissing a prominent Die-Hard. But there is a strictly limited appeal in not being Norman Tebbit. Only those who follow politics closely would even realize that a dramatic gesture of ideological revolution was being bravely made. (Sorry, Norman.) Something more positive was required.

What followed was a series of photo-ops and exercises in gesture politics—the windmill on the roof, the bicycle to work, the dash to the Pole. This development of the Cameron project was a sort of cultural make-over—'the Dianification of Toryism' as I have argued elsewhere—to render the Tories an entirely different party, one of socially liberal herbivores, acceptable to its critics in Metroland. Cultural makeovers are notoriously hard to pull-off, however, since those being culturally transformed notice the process more quickly than anyone else. And they do not always like it. The main result of this makeover, visible in the 2010 election results, was to strengthen UKIP by driving dissed-off Tories towards it. It made only modest inroads in the voting bloc of Liberal centrists who had many other suitors.

The 2008 financial crisis made these cultural gestures look frivolous—as well as shocking the Tory leadership, which had rooted the Cameron project in the assumption that economic growth would continue smooth and uninterrupted under New Labour. That was a curious assumption to start with: every previous Labour government had ended in economic crisis—why should this one be different? If the crisis embarrassed Cameron and Osborne, however, it also rescued them by imposing a more realistic economic policy upon the party—and by giving them a serious purpose in office. They have to save the British economy by public spending cuts that eventually reduce the deficit. That political commitment is now fully half of the Cameron project.

Not going bankrupt is, however, a very inadequate political philosophy. It is an aim shared by all parties (even if their methods for achieving solvency differ) and it does little more than lay the groundwork for positive policies. Such policies exist—Michael Gove's education reforms, Iain Duncan-Smith's welfare changes—but there is little about them that is distinctly Cameronian. Much the same could be said about the flagship idea of the Big Society, which amounts to a re-working of the traditional conservative celebration of mediating institutions but one without a manual of instructions. Other signature Cameron issues, such as his ultra-Green commitment to carbon reduction, look both doomed and embarrassing as their costs become apparent. Yet those issues on which the Cameron modernizers had imposed a vow of silence on the party—immigration, Europe, and crime—now constitute the main topics of public debate as they spiral downwards in a series of crises. Those crises—especially the crisis over the euro—would represent welcome political opportunities for almost any imaginable Conservative Party. But these opportunities drive the Cameron Tories into silence and paralysis—and not simply because they are in a coalition with Lib-Dems. Cameron modernization, as originally conceived, has run into a dead end.

That is not really surprising if, as Dr Harris mordantly and (in my view) correctly remarks, there is no such thing as a new political idea. The best we can do is to mine our political tradition for old ideas whose time has come round again (as Thatcher did). Neophiliac Tories determined on new ideas will therefore find themselves either borrowing ideas from other political traditions (as Heath and Macmillan did) or indulging in empty gestures that disintegrate on coming into contact with harsh political reality.

Dr Harris hints at guidance—no more—in suggesting that the three most successful and significant Tory leaders are Disraeli, Salisbury, and Thatcher. Here, for the last time, I differ slightly with him. I would first add Churchill to the list and then separate out Churchill and Disraeli from Salisbury and Thatcher. All four are distinguished by what Salisbury called, in paying tribute to Disraeli, 'zeal for the greatness of England.' That is one indispensable element of English Conservatism. Disraeli and Churchill, however, were romantic buccaneers whose brilliant imaginations and passionate loyalties sometimes overwhelmed the cool practical realism that is the other necessary counterpoint in the great Tory melody. Salisbury and Thatcher both possessed that realism in unusual measure. It explains their harmonious and sympathetic relationship with their own parties—one not shared by most Tory leaders—and their long political success. Realism is no guarantee of success; but it does offer better odds than unrealism.

What the modernizers and other conservatives now need to do is to delve into the Tory tradition for directions out of their present world of shades and illusions. They could do no better than to start with Dr Harris's book.

This review of Robin Harris's The Conservatives: A History *(London: Bantam, 2011), 640 pp., was originally published in* Conservative Home, *22 November 2011, www.conservativehome.com/platform/2011/11/read-biography-said-disraeli-for-that-is-life-without-theory-robin-harris-is-very-far-from-being-a-devotee-of.html.*

Trade, Culture, and Saint Andrew's Cross: Reflections on the Scottish Referendum

21 November 2014

In his fine and important book *Who Are We? The Challenges to America's National Identity*, the late Samuel Huntington, a US political scientist of great rigour and high reputation, recalled the changing fortunes of patriotism in the second decade of the twenty-first century from the evidence of Charles Street in Boston. Prior to the 9/11 attack on the World Trade Center building in New York, one American flag flew in the street. It was in front of a liquor store. Within two weeks, of the 9/11 attack, seventeen American flags had been raised there. 'With their country under attack,' Huntington commented, 'Charles Street denizens rediscovered their nation and identified themselves with it.' This sentiment did not last, however. Within a few months, the flags on Charles Street were being hauled down. One year later, only four were still flying.[1]

The rise and fall of the Stars and Stripes on a Boston street was an accurate reflection of the rise and fall of strong patriotic sentiment in the American people following 9/11. As he implied, 'flag-waving' was an activity that had fallen out of fashion among many Americans, especially in liberal Boston. Indeed, the very term 'flag-waving' had become a dismissive one, indicating that the speaker preferred a more modest love of country and was critical of those whose patriotic expression was jauntier and jingoistic. But an outright attack on America revived a passionate patriotism for most Americans, symbolized by the widespread wearing of flag-pins in the lapel. That bolder patriotism gradually cooled

---

[1] I am indebted to Roger Kimball for reminding me of this passage from the Huntington book, which is full of profound reflections on the nature of both political sovereignty and national identity. My review of it is here: www.theamericanconservative.com/articles/who-are-we/.

in turn. Most of the post-9/11 flags were hauled down; news anchors gradually put aside their flag-pins (attacked by some as 'fascist'); and the de-constructionist elements (multiculturalism, bilingualism, etc.), identified by Huntington as 'challenges' to America's national identity resumed their rise. Nonetheless, three more flags that had been present on 9/10 still fluttered on their flagpoles, and the latent power of patriotism had been demonstrated.

The flag is a symbol of sovereignty and allegiance—the sovereignty of the ruler and the allegiance of the citizen—but also a symbol of love of country. In democracies the ruler is the people under the law; citizens express allegiance to themselves and their own collective sovereignty when they salute the flag. That changes hardly at all when the ruler is a constitutional monarch since, as H. G. Wells among others pointed out, such polities might better be described as 'crowned republics.' It becomes a little more complicated when the ruler is a legitimate but non-democratic one, a king, or a foreign imperial power. If such a ruler provides good government, protecting liberties and rights, providing impartial justice, offering channels of influence and change to the people, citizens seeking a different ruler or system of rule are probably obliged to do so through peaceful methods such as civil disobedience. If he is an oppressive despot, they may enjoy a right of rebellion but they must exercise it prudently. In all cases citizens may well love their country and revere its flag even while despising its government. Indeed, that is a common combination of emotions in democracies. And even under cruel despotisms, the citizenry may well shrink from actions that would damage the despot because the same actions would damage the country as well.

Finally, states and political systems are all in process of constant flux even when they seem to be stable and eternal. In the last 100 years we have seen the collapse of European dynasties, the retreat of European world empires, the eruption of revolutionary states, the occupation of historical nation states following wars, the creation of new nation states on an unprecedented scale, the peaceful emergence of multinational states, and the establishment of global institutions with some features traditionally associated with statehood. All these changes have been accompanied by changes in flags. New flags have been designed, old

Trade, Culture, and Saint Andrew's Cross:
Reflections on the Scottish Referendum
259

ones discarded, shameful ones desecrated—red stars being torn from their ragged centre. These changes continue. Scotland almost became an independent state recently and will shortly be a statelet within a fresh federal British constitution. Croatia entered the European Community. Catalonia threatens to hold its own referendum on independence against the wishes of Spain. Hungary resists initiatives from Brussels and the IMF in pursuit of its economic freedom of action.

So what explains these changes in rules and flags—whether they are imperial, national, federal, or local? Sentiment is, of course, the underlying reality. Allegiances, loyalties, and ideologies change in response to great events and to large social movements. War is one such event; 1914–18 destroyed the Hohenzollern, Habsburg, and Romanov dynasties, ushering in new nations and new political concepts. Among the large social movements with an equal or great impact, however, are trade and culture—which, when you add technology to them, become communications. To see how they operate, take first the changes in the imperial and post-imperial loyalties of the British Empire.

One common explanation of the expansion of the British Empire is 'trade follows the flag.' This expression seems to have been kicking around since the mid-nineteenth century as a justification for colonial expansion. The earliest actual quote I came across was from the historian J. A. Froude in 1870: 'The removal of a million poor creatures to Canada and the establishment of them there would probably have turned out a profitable investment. Trade follows the flag.'

Almost all other citations of it, however, turned out to reject the argument. Here, for instance, is R. Hargreaves in 1945: 'There is a glib saying that "trade follows the flag;" an apophthegm that succeeds in putting the cart before the horse with greater aplomb than almost any other cant phrase in common use.' Today the general view of imperial historians is that the flag follows trade.

Lord Palmerston got there before them, however, when he described the policy of the British government as 'Trade without the flag where possible; trade with the flag where necessary.' That is also an accurate definition of liberal imperialism, Anglo-Saxon style. It describes a system with two large advantages: first, it keeps the administrative and military costs of governing colonies to a minimum; second, it is able to survive (and even prosper) when those colonies have gained independence. Contrary to the forecasts of Marxist and Left historians generally, the prosperity of Britain grew faster after the "loss" of its empire. It was those colonies that cut themselves off from trade with Britain (and other advanced countries) for political reasons that then fell behind economically.

However—and here is the nub—if the flag follows trade, so does culture. Trade is an exchange of goods, and as Matt Ridley has documented very persuasively in his book, *The Rational Optimist*, this exchange introduces new ideas, new possibilities, new opportunities, and new conceptions of the good life to previously somnolent societies along with the goods that are traded. Trade therefore has disruptive consequences for traditional societies. It undermines traditional hierarchies; it introduces new ambitions; it casts doubt on the customs and standards that have heretofore been unthinkingly accepted.

These are revolutionary cultural changes. They are resisted. Traditional leaderships frown on the trader—in complex societies such as India they frown on entire trading classes—and try to keep its influence to a minimum. If their opposition to the disruptive influence of the trader reaches the point of excluding him and his goods altogether—well, that is when Palmerston concludes that the flag is necessary. It was Palmerston who as foreign secretary initiated the Opium War to prevent the Chinese Emperor from removing the right of his subjects to smoke good British opium.

Opium aside, most Victorians regarded trade in goods and ideas with or without the flag as the march of progress. They recognized that it had some ill-effects, but they thought that its overall impact—notably, ending evils such as slavery and piracy—was beneficial. We are less certain because of the moral catastrophes that shamed Europe in the twentieth century. We are more concerned with protecting indigenous peoples and preserving wild environments. But aside from a few extreme environmentalists, we do not really feel that we can actually halt or reverse progress because we would have a guilty conscience if we were to deny the world its practical advantages from spectacles to artificial hearts, from low infant mortality to IPods and laptops.

So both the flag and culture continue to follow in trade's wake.

As the heirs of Palmerston found, the flag and culture are trade's quarrelsome siblings. A liberal empire eventually runs up against the fact that its subjects take these new ideas of liberalism and democracy, imported along with cheap cotton goods, so seriously that they want them for themselves. Macaulay famously gave India a modern education; the British appointed Indian judges and senior bureaucrats in the nineteenth century. At first, the ambition of these gifted native students was to be English gentlemen of Indian background. To a remarkable degree, those ambitions have been realized (with the curious twist that the Indians are today far more gentlemanly than the British). If the empire had become permanent in the early twentieth century, as Joseph Chamberlain proposed, however, the logical end result would have been India governing Britain. Numbers count.

That seems quite an attractive prospect today. In that age, it was simply not considered. Hence the more that the educated Indians became English gentlemen—and Nehru who shaped India far more than Gandhi was indisputably an English gentleman—the more they drifted inevitably into nationalism. The culture that the flag had planted turned against the flag. And culture won. The flag was eventually lowered on many a flagpole in capitals with Anglican cathedrals, English public schools, British road signs, gentlemen's clubs with mixed racial membership but no ladies, and the Queen's portrait still on the local currency.

After an interval of about two generations, needed to let post-imperial resentments cool, some remarkable things happened. One was that, as I have already mentioned, Britain's economic ties with most of its colonies grew stronger after decolonization. What was more remarkable, however, was that Britain's cultural ties with its former colonies grew stronger too. As a result Britain, though greatly diminished in power terms, is a cultural superpower. That was so even before the internet. But the invention of the internet—because it increases the importance of culture in comparison to other factors in a nation's life such as geographical proximity—has intensified the relationship between

Britain, its former colonies, and other nations where the English language is a national one or one used by the nation's political and cultural elites.

In short, ties of language and liberal culture have proved durable even when these nations have been divided by religion, politics, and national independence. Where once the flag has liberated culture, culture today unites peoples now living under different flags.

A powerful example of this cultural influence is the Anglo-Irish relationship. If the First World War had not intervened, Ireland would have been granted Home Rule within the United Kingdom in 1914. But the withdrawal of Home Rule for the duration, the 1916 Easter rebellion, the execution of its leaders, the Troubles, the division of Ireland into two sectarian states—all these events ensured that the relationship between Britain and the Irish Republic was either hostile or painful for almost ninety years following the separation. That political awkwardness was aggravated by the fact that some of the 1916 leaders wanted to break with Britain not only politically but also socially, morally, and culturally. In the language of the time, they wanted to destroy the 'West British' aspects of Irish identity and social life.

To a great if temporary extent that was politically achieved by Éamon de Valera's 1937 Constitution which shared state power with the Catholic Church—to the eventual disadvantage and discredit of both. Both then and after, however, southern Ireland became less diverse, more economically stagnant, and more repressive culturally than its next-door neighbour. The IRA drove out many Protestants by intimidation in the years immediately after independence. Until the early 1960s, poorer Protestants faced discrimination in official jobs. The Catholic clergy had enormous social power even beyond their legally privileged position— bishops, for instance, banned Saturday night dances by fiat to ensure a healthy Mass attendance the next day. Irishmen who fought for Britain in the Second World War were subject to punishment and discrimination. And there was a heavy-handed moral censorship of books, plays, and films. Although the scale of this cultural repression has been exaggerated—it was a relatively gentle repression by European standards and reflected rather than opposed the values of most Irish people—it was real enough; and it was intended to divide the Irish people from the British in moral and cultural matters in order to exaggerate their differences.

Yet the deep social and familial ties between Britain and Ireland, the common language (English),[2] the common marketing of goods, including cultural goods such as magazines and newspapers, to both Irish and British markets, all prevented this essentially ideological project from succeeding. All through the years since 1922 there has been mass movement—for the purposes of emigration, education, tourism, and above all marriage—between England and Ireland. Irish workers of all classes, Irish doctors in particular, were found throughout England. Thousands of Irishmen left neutral Ireland in the Second World War to join the British Army or Merchant Marine—my father among them. Intermarriage between the English and the Irish is more common, I believe, than intermarriage between any other two of the four nations of Britain—again, my parents among them. Legally the Irish were able to come and go to Britain as if the Free State and later Republic still had been constitutionally part of the United Kingdom—and vice versa.

The eruption of terrorism from the late 1960s to the Good Friday Agreement in 1998 strained the political relationship between London and Dublin, sometimes severely, but it had only small impact on the friendships of ordinary people or within 'mixed' families. Sir Terry Wogan, a genial Irish broadcaster, remained the most popular man in England throughout this period. And as the late Conor Cruise O'Brien— who was a passionate opponent of the IRA—liked to observe, opinion polls showed that if you asked Irish people which nationality they would like their daughters to marry, a large plurality chose an English husband.

This extensive and continuing set of social relationships undermined the de Valera project of a culturally distinct Ireland. It was further

---

[2] Successive governments in Ireland sought to replace English by Gaelic as the national language through education and official bilingualism in the public sector. This intended imposition had the predictable effect of making Gaelic unpopular. It is still protected officially but no longer enforced on reluctant people. It has therefore recovered in popularity among middle class Irish people with cultural interests and historical loyalties. At no point was the status of English as Ireland's real national language seriously threatened.

damaged by the scandals in the Catholic Church, by the Celtic Tiger prosperity that brought Irish people home from liberal environments in Europe and America, by the Good Friday Agreement that removed its political justification, and by the Anglophone liberalism that people imbibed from the internet. For better or worse—and in fact for both— Britain and Ireland are now as culturally close as they were in 1914, maybe closer. That closeness was symbolized by the huge popular success of the Queen's visit to Ireland in 2012. No one now uses the phrase 'West Britain1, but it is the social reality of Anglo-Irish relations today.

Just recently, I found a modest confirmation of this truth in the most famous song of one of the most famous West Britons, Percy French, whose light verse and music were popular throughout the Victorian and Edwardian worlds. His most famous song was 'The Mountains of Mourne,' which has a melancholy melody of great beauty but semi-comic lyrics. It is supposedly a letter from an Irish workman in London to his sweetheart at home in which he describes what he sees there but misunderstands what he sees: he thinks the traffic policeman is a man of great power, for instance. When I looked up the lyrics recently, I found a verse that I had never heard sung before. Irish friends, including writers, had never heard it sung either. That seems to be more than chance— maybe a sense that this particular verse was politically uncomfortable until 2012. But here it is:

I've seen England's King from the top of a bus
I never knew him, though he means to know us
And tho' by the Saxon we once were oppressed
Still I cheered, God forgive me, I cheered with the rest
And now that he's visited Erin's green shore
We'll be much better friends than we've been heretofore
When we've got all we want we're as quiet as can be
Where the Mountains of Mourne sweep down to the sea

In other words, the promise of Edward VII's visit in 1903 was finally redeemed in 2012 by Elizabeth II. It is now permissible for Irish people to speak kindly of the English monarchy of which the symbol is the flag. With the removal of that final taboo, the two islands now enjoy a relationship that is quite different from that between two countries foreign to each other. They live under two flags but are united by a common culture.

If Scotland had chosen political independence in the September vote, the same paradox of political separation alongside social unity would probably have been achieved more quickly and more easily (since independence would have been realized by a free vote rather than through insurrection and civil war). As with Ireland, the Scots would probably have continued to enjoy free movement and residence in England (and vice versa). Maybe Scottish residents in England would have continued to enjoy voting rights in England too, as do the Irish.

At the same time, Scottish politics would have evolved away from English politics to reflect different national circumstances—as also happened between Ireland and Britain. Today's friendly Anglo-Irish relations have not revived any projects of constitutional unity with Britain.

Has the referendum vote in Scotland settled its future as part of the United Kingdom with equal permanence? It probably has not. Indeed, the fact that a referendum on withdrawing Scotland from a stable and prosperous UK was held at all—let alone that the status quo got only 55 per cent of the vote—is an unacknowledged tribute to the continuing power of nationalism. Nonetheless, it failed—and for two reasons.

First, the economic case for independence was incoherent and thus ultimately unpersuasive. If Scotland were to survive and prosper as an independent state without England's subsidy to its public finances, it would need to turn itself into a low-tax, low-regulation, workfare economy on the free market model of, say, Singapore. But Alex Salmond, the leader of the independence cause, promised that an independent Scotland would be an even more egalitarian and generous welfare and regulatory state than the UK. If so, who would pay for it? The European Union, even if it were to admit Scotland, would not play the role of Sugar Daddy to Scottish socialism. So Salmond could never explain how he would pay the bills for a Scottish utopia. That failure ran up against the lingering thrift mentality of Scottish voters—and the No campaign hit hard, repeatedly, and successfully at this weakness.

Second, an opinion poll ten days before the vote suggested that the Scots would narrowly vote for independence and Scotland would depart the UK. That concentrated minds wonderfully. A competing nationalism suddenly emerged. A slumbering British nationalism awoke in the souls of ordinary Scots. Unionists of the street suddenly appeared and started talking the language of patriotism, history, fellowship in war and hard times, matching the SNP's optimistic and idealist language with one of their own. It was that upsurge of British identity patriotism that turned the final tide.

All in all, a negative campaign on the practical difficulties of independence and a positive campaign on the historic achievements of Britain together defeated Scottish independence. But the defeat was not a decisive one. The referendum vote was a narrow victory; the turnout was much higher than that in recent general elections; many in the (growing) ranks of Scottish nationalism feel cheated and want revenge; and the main cultural currents in Scotland favour the lost cause. Almost all commentators noticed that the artists, bohemians and activists were on the side of independence. Though England and Scotland remain under one flag, they are moving towards a cultural separatism.

That is highly significant. National identity, loyalty to the Crown or a Republic, patriotism, national feeling, all that we mean by the flag— these are not solid unchanging properties like a rock. They are matters of the heart and the imagination. They can and do change. As we have already noticed, one hundred years ago ancient dynasties and long-established empires were swept away by a political cataclysm. They were replaced by new states and new loyalties, new anthems, and new flags. That can happen—and it almost happened in Britain this year. An overarching British identity was seriously challenged because it had been devalued over such a long period that for many British people it ceased to have a strong appeal to the heart.

This overarching British identity did not die of old age or some sociological sickness. Indeed, as we saw in the final days of the campaign, it is not actually dead among ordinary British people. But among the country's political elites patriotism had long become something to be ashamed of and avoided. In Scotland, the establishment instinctively avoided a patriotic appeal until the very end of the campaign when it faced possible defeat. For several decades, European elites have argued that the nation state is dead, losing power upwards to supranational institutions and downwards to organized ethnic, gender, and other minorities. They believe that nation states are a declining factor in a world of international law and global organization. Even conservatives in Europe seem to accept the argument that patriotism is a dark emotion too likely to shade into authoritarian and jingoistic doctrines to be respectable or accepted. In the mind of 'Davos Man,' nationalism is an emotional dogma quite contrary to the economic rationalism of globalization.

In fact, the two go hand in hand; each reinforces the other. Globalization actually makes nationalism more possible by making smaller political units more viable. The earliest modern discoverer of this truth was C. Northcote Parkinson of Parkinson's Law in the 1950s. In fact, Parkinson discovered several useful laws—his third law runs as follows: 'Expansion means complexity, and complexity means decay.' Small countries are likely to be richer, easier to manage, endowed with governments closer to the people, and thus likely to better governed than larger states.

Thus, as *The Economist* pointed out a few years ago:

Of the ten countries with populations of over 100m, only the United States and Japan are prosperous. Of the rest, India's economy is dwarfed by that of the Netherlands (15.5m people); the economies of Nigeria and Bangladesh are much the same size as that of Puerto Rico (3.7m) ... [O]f the ten countries whose GDP per head is highest when measured in terms of purchasing power, the most populous apart from the United States and Japan is Belgium.

How do we account for this? The answer is simple: if there ever was a link between prosperity and bigness, it was dissolved by globalization (which is shorthand for the reduction of barriers to trade and capital movements). Globalization ensures that the size of the nation need no longer coincide with the size of the market. An industry can expand to the size appropriate to its market in a world with declining barriers to trade. At the same time, a government can shrink to the size that its citizens find most convenient to control.

America is the exception to that rule—it is both large and prosperous—because its federalism distributes power outwards and downwards to levels where it can be better controlled. Switzerland is another example. Europe might imitate America's success if it were to model itself on Switzerland and adopt the principle of subsidiarity in distributing power downwards to regions and localities. In fact, the opposite is happening on both continents.

Think of it this way: federalism in a country is the equivalent of free trade between countries. Each in its context provides what the lawyers call 'jurisdictional competition.' If you do not like the mix of tax and regulation in Alabama, you can move to Texas; and if you do not like the mix of tax and regulation in France—and why would you?—you can move to Britain, as hundreds of thousands of French people have done in recent decades. Federalism and free trade both promote the freedom of businesses and citizens who can vote with their feet.

Not surprisingly, that does not suit governments and the political classes when they want—as they all eventually do want—to tax and spend more than their subjects. So under federalism the central government continually seeks to expand its powers. The more successfully it does so, the more it spends, and the more political constituencies it recruits for its power games.

Governments have a similar incentive under free trade rules. They try to turn free trade treaties into vehicles of regulation so that they are able to prevent citizens from escaping somewhere else with lower taxes. The EU began as a market of governments—citizens and businesses and trade can move anywhere in it. But later treaties have transformed it into a cartel of governments which—by harmonizing regulations and taxes—makes it easier for high-tax governments to remove competition from their smaller neighbours—smaller usually both geographically and in size of government too. The result is a gradual transfer of power over the lives of citizens from national parliaments accountable to the voters to remote bureaucracies. The further result is the growth of a transnational political class that seeks to increase the power of international bodies over governments in order to increase its own power over their citizens. They believe that they can create a new flag either on the basis of trade alone or on creating new official cultures through political power.

As a result, ordinary existing nationalisms—whether large or small, new or long-standing—have rival patriotisms in the hearts of European, global, and American elites. The main rivals are Europeanism in Europe and multiculturalism in the United States. Both these ideologies seek to weaken national patriotism in order to change the character of their societies. Multiculturalism is an ideology that seeks to deconstruct the national identity of an existing nation under the same flag; Europeanism is an ideology that seeks to create a new nation by uniting many existing ones under a new flag. They have their adherents. But neither has yet become more than a niche loyalty even though they enjoy lavish official support and the sympathy of those government officials, international agency bureaucrats, NGO executives, "denationalized" corporate managers, and academics ambitious to be the vanguard of the new or transformed nation. Those failures—the failure of "diversity" to become the patriotism of most Americans, the failure of Europeanism to generate a European "demos" loyal to the EU ahead of particular member states—are reflected in flags. The Stars and Stripes still stands for traditional American ideals; the blue flag with its circle of stars still has a corporate rather than a patriotic meaning.

Old-fashioned patriotism therefore survives in humble hearts, perhaps weakened and lurking in the shadows, until it is tempted in to the open by a 9/11, or a threat to the nation such as that mounted in Scotland, or the anniversary of a D-Day, or in Hungary a remembrance of the Revolution of 1956. It then emerges, speaks, and changes things.

But it cannot safely be taken for granted. If a nation is a daily plebiscite, an imagined community, then patriotic nationalism needs to be respected and valued. Once it no longer appeals to the hearts of the people, it ceases to be a vital political support for the institutions and coherence of the state. When culture decays, the flag is eventually hauled down—in the metropolis as once in the imperial possessions. When God, King, and Country no longer possess the heart, other beliefs and loyalties rush in to replace them. For like all other loves, love of country can be killed by neglect and indifference.

Originally published in Hungarian Review, *Vol. V, No. 6, November 2014, http://hungarianreview.com/article/20141121_culture_and_the_flag.*

The First Appearance of 'Illiberal Democracy'—An American Debate

22 December 2003

With his two recent speeches advocating a forward strategy to promote democracy in the Greater Middle East, President Bush has placed the concept of democracy at the very centre of American political controversy. It was, of course, already on its fringes. Three debates over democracy at home and abroad have been roiling the intellectual world for several years now. One of those debates—the controversy over the place of democracy in US foreign policy—is being fought out between neoconservatives and conservative 'realists.' The other two debates … well, let me draw a temporary veil over them except to say that they are as much about democracy at home and in Western Europe as about Iraq and the Third World.

A presidential speech trumps any number of books and learned articles because it implies a change of government policy. When a president promises to promote democracy in the Greater Middle East, he is announcing that the US will transform its relations with the local powers there. In this instance, Bush is plainly urging democracy not only on hostile powers such as Syria and Iran but also on traditional 'friends' such as Egypt and Saudi Arabia. How is this to be accomplished? That is less clear. But we will presumably nudge them toward democracy with economic favours; coerce them with sanctions if they resist; and seek to undermine and replace them if they remain obdurate.

To describe this as ambitious is to be guilty of understatement. If such a grand strategy were to be pursued without extreme care and subtlety, it would risk producing regimes hostile to the US and hospitable to terrorism—in between periods of anarchy—in a vital strategic and economic region. Admittedly, such regimes already exist, and periods of anarchy occur there from time to time. But prudence should warn us against adding to the problem. Nor is it sensible to inform such regimes they have nothing to lose by opposing us since we are determined to overthrow them in any event.

Prudence and Other Values

Before embarking on his democratization drive, therefore, Bush might want to examine the debate earlier this year between conservative realist Fareed Zakaria and neoconservative Robert Kagan. "Debate" is perhaps too mild a word to describe Kagan's sulphurous review of Zakaria's book, *The Future of Freedom: Illiberal Democracy at Home and Abroad*, in the pages of *The New Republic* and the subsequent exchange of barbs between the two writers. This exchange was, however, a serious confrontation between the leading proponents of the two schools. Kagan is the leading neoconservative advocate of promoting democracy. He outflanks even Bush on this topic, since he wants to promote democracy worldwide, including in China, rather than merely in the Middle East. Kagan seemed to take Zakaria's scepticism about the wisdom of promoting democracy in all circumstances as a personal affront; he interpreted Zakaria's warning that democracies not securely rooted in well-established liberal traditions and institutions would either develop authoritarian features or collapse altogether as inspired by a personal preference for aristocratic rule. If this made the debate occasionally bitter, it also meant that Kagan's critique was unusually thorough.

Who won? Kagan scored a number of effective points—for instance, that some of the regimes cited by Zakaria to demonstrate the failings of illiberal democracy were not democracies under any definition. On the whole, however, Zakaria won on the main points relevant to the current debate:

One. Democracy needs social, economic, and political underpinnings in order to flourish. These include the rule of law, a tradition of free speech and free inquiry, the concept of a loyal opposition, a private sector, and the development of a middle class used to making independent decisions.

Two. Democratic governments without these underpinnings tend to go off the rails. Zakaria stresses the tendency of such governments to develop illiberal features—as in today's Russia. Sometimes democracy collapses altogether. Latin America and the Middle East furnish examples—Argentina, Brazil, Lebanon, Iraq—in which elected governments have been overthrown in military coups. Kagan responds by arguing that democracy cannot be blamed for the sins of 'failed democracy.' But what if a democracy fails at regular intervals—as Argentina and Brazil have both done?

Three. Liberal institutions and practices can exist without democracy and elections. Once a country reaches a certain stage—a certain level of prosperity, or the acceptance by the government of legal restraints on itself such as a bill of rights—then pressure builds for democratic as well as liberal rights. Liberalism actually can be promoted from outside more readily than democracy. For instance, the US is more able to persuade an authoritarian regime to release political prisoners or to respect academic freedom than to dissolve itself by holding elections.

So the US government should be ready to offer various types of assistance: diplomatic pressure on a regime to abandon torture, public support for crowds demonstrating against a shaky despotism, mediation to persuade a dictator to go into exile. And that in fact is what the US has traditionally done. One of the main points in Bush's recent speeches was an erroneous admission that the US had put and kept despotic regimes in power because of Cold War priorities. This argument, originally advanced by the Cold War Left but now adopted by younger neoconservatives, greatly exaggerates US responsibility for Third World despotisms and endorses the idea of American omnipotence that is these despotisms' standard excuse for their own failures.

Question: If the US is omnipotent, why is Fidel Castro still in power? The prosaic truth is that, with a handful of exceptions, Third World despotisms were put and kept in power not by the US but by domestic forces such as the army and local elites. (Not a single existing Mideast despotism was installed by a pro-American coup.) If Washington was not prepared to overthrow them in a series of Iraqs—which, reasonably enough, it was unwilling to do—it had to deal with them. Sometimes that meant forging military alliances, sometimes merely recognizing and trading with them, sometimes pressuring them to moderate their human-rights abuses.

There were cases—e.g., Zaire—in which US relationships with odious regimes were too close and too prolonged. Even so there was no guarantee that if the US expressed disapproval of Mobutu, he would fall from power. In the end it took foreign invasions to oust him. And the people of Zaire are no better off for his departure. In the more numerous cases where domestic popular opposition to dictators reached serious levels—in, among other countries, the Philippines, Korea, and Chile—the US supported their overthrow. Sometimes that help was crucial at the margin; but in almost all such cases, the overwhelming impetus toward democracy was domestic. The US merely helped local people.

In short, America is neither so powerful nor so wicked as it is depicted in the Cold War leftist critique that was swallowed by the president and regurgitated at Westminster. So the first lesson for President Bush is to be aware of the limits of American power; the second is to recognize when other societies are ready for democracy and capable of benefiting from our help; the third is to offer the right kind of help rather than suggesting democratic elections as the universal remedy; and the fourth is otherwise to do no harm.

That last lesson is no mere platitude. Some US support for authoritarian regimes is entirely defensible in terms of American interests—including moral interests. For instance, the annual US subsidy to Egypt was incurred, among other reasons, in order to prise Egypt out of the anti-Israel coalition and into a peace treaty. If abolishing that subsidy were to produce a 'rejectionist' Egyptian regime, we would not advance human welfare by doing so. So, in addition to the other qualifications to the policy of promoting democracy, we must add such considerations as peace and, yes, the 'stability' that is essential to prosperity.

Undermining the Ballot Box

If Zakaria is fundamentally correct in the first debate (over democracy abroad), he is more vulnerable to attack in the second debate (over democracy in America). The main paradox of current politics is that we are uncritically promoting democracy in the Middle East without apparently noticing that it is increasingly constrained at home by the transfer of power from elected bodies such as Congress to unaccountable institutions such as the courts, federal agencies, and international organizations. Not only does Zakaria not notice this transfer, but—following the traditional conservative suspicion of unrestrained populism—he calls for even more power to be transferred to institutions run by elites, on the grounds that democracy is in danger of running amok. This invites criticism not only from neoconservatives such as Kagan but also from unmodified conservatives such as the Hudson Institute's John Fonte who argue that traditional understandings of liberal democracy are being subtly transformed into a new hybrid multicultural regime of post-democracy that illegitimizes the concept of majority rule. In other words, Zakaria's diagnosis and prescription for the ills of American democracy is literally perverse: he calls for more power to the elites to cure the problems caused by the elites' exercising too much power. This leads him into a number of questionable stances:

One. Thinking that many problems are too difficult for the voters and their representatives to understand and solve, he proposes they be transferred to specialist agencies like central banks. But the reason that we leave central banks to set interest rates and monetary policy is that we now believe these to be technical questions capable of expert resolution. In the 1970s, when there was a serious dispute between Keynesians and monetarists, there was necessarily a political battle over monetary policy. Only when that expert debate was largely settled were the rest of us content to leave it to central banks. And if ever the experts agree on welfare policy, tax policy, or public spending, we may do the same. But until then, the public will demand to choose among expert solutions through the political process.

Two. Zakaria points out that democratic referenda, such as California's Proposition 13, tend to produce simplistic reforms that generate unexpected problems because they have not undergone the careful compromises of legislative crafting. But the same criticism could be made, at least as strongly, of judge-made 'rights' legislation such as *Roe v. Wade*. From both these cases one might reasonably conclude that representative democracy is generally the best method of solving political problems. Judicial lawmaking should be rare; but as the decision of the Massachusetts supreme court establishing gay marriages illustrates, non-democratic legislation by the courts has changed American life far more thoroughly and controversially than the occasional referendum (which anyway is quite likely to be overturned by the courts). Yet it is referenda and not the courts on which Zakaria trains his fire.

Three. In a powerful and persuasive chapter of his book, Zakaria laments the decline of authority and the falling quality of the elites—their greater selfishness, their lack of public spirit, and their disconnection from most Americans. His criticisms strike home. What he does not seem to realize, however, is that these criticisms are far more disabling to his argument for non-democratic restraints on democracy than to democracy itself. After all, it is the elites who wield the non-democratic restraints. And the more they use their powers to correct democracy rather than merely to restrain or delay it, the more sinister their failings must appear and the more dangerous the weakness of mechanisms to correct them. Democracy generates its own authority in the voting booth, and wields its own correction in the form of throwing the rascals out. But professional standards are weaker than two generations ago, and—as the American Bar Association among other bodies illustrates—they have become much more politicized. Elites were once relied upon by conservatives like Zakaria (and me) to restrain mobs; today they are often distinguishable from mobs only by their credentials.

Nor is the rise of unaccountable elites in nominal democracies a purely American problem. Indeed, in most respects the US is lagging behind Western Europe in the degree of power that it allows elites to exercise undemocratically. Recent elections and referenda in several European countries reveal a growing resistance to remote and unaccountable bureaucracies. This is the theme of the third debate—namely, what is the democratic legitimacy underlying those international structures that increasingly influence our lives? This issue has been misrepresented, in discussions about such questions as the Kyoto Accords and the International Criminal Court, as a conflict between nationalism and internationalism or between European multilateralism and American 'unilateralism.' It is, in fact, a conflict between two opposing kinds of internationalism: the American concept of an internationalism in which power flows upwards from the democratic nation state and the European vision of a trans-nationalism in which power flows downwards from 'the international community.' As Francis Fukuyama pointed out last year, the European vision is another way of transferring power to elites: 'The very idea that this legitimacy is handed downwards from a willowy, disembodied international level rather than handed upwards from concrete, legitimate democratic publics on a nation state level virtually invites abuse on the part of elites who are then free to interpret the will of the international community to suit their own preferences.' Until the US begins to present the choice in this clear-sighted way, however, it will continue to be wrong-footed in these debates.

To sum up, then, we risk promoting democracy in the wrong place at the wrong time. Rather than a wholesale push for democracy in the Third World—where promoting liberal institutions would be a more prudent policy—we should focus our attention on protecting traditional concepts of liberal democracy in the United States and on defending a democratic internationalism in foreign affairs. To do so will mean refining and even abandoning the conservative attachment to elite restraints on democracy that once served us well but that now privilege our enemies and our opponents.

Originally published in National Review, *22 December 2003,* *www.nationalreview.com/2003/12/debating-democracy-john-osullivan/.*

The Unexpected Surge of American Nationalism: Not an Essay Question
16 February 2017

Even those who disagree with the thrust of 'For Love of Country—A Defense of Nationalism' by Rich and Ramesh, notably Jonah Goldberg and Ben Shapiro, think well of some particulars in it, and those who agree with its broad argument, including Yuval Levin and me, give additional reasons for believing it to be a good thing: a perceptive and fresh analysis of a topic, nationalism, newly central to politics in the age of Trump. This is a rich pudding containing a lot of plums. Outdoing little Jack Horner, I will pull out a few and retire to a corner to chew them over.

Almost all of the points I discuss are in response to Jonah, Ben, and Yuval. Rich and Ramesh say kind words about my earlier *National Review* writings on America's identity and culture, and I can happily return the compliment since I am in more or less in complete agreement not only with the broad argument of their piece but also with its side arguments and overall tone. Also, though the election of Donald Trump is one of the two main reasons why we are all debating nationalism, I do not think we should focus excessively on what he says about it. The new president is a force of nature and not to be underestimated but not someone I would select to lead a philosophy seminar or a debating team.

Thus, when he disavows 'American exceptionalism' as a phrase that makes him uncomfortable because he does not want to humiliate the foreigners who will shortly be losing to America, I do not think he is saying the same thing as Obama. Obama was telling Americans that, hey, every people thinks it is special—i.e., nobody is, we are not. Trump was saying: when you intend to shoot a man, it costs nothing to be polite. It was an affirmation of exceptionalism rather than a denial of it.

We are debating nationalism, however, less because Trump says he is for it than because a number of conservative writers, represented here by Jonah and Ben, responded to his support by declaring that they were against it. Nor were they saying so just because it felt good to contradict the then-candidate (though I imagine it did). Quite the contrary. Several conservatives advanced the argument 'If nationalism is Trump's defense against the accusation of not being a conservative, it's no defense at all, since nationalism is incompatible with conservatism rather than a strand in it.' That is a *précis* of several columns by different authors, but it is not too distant from what Ben writes (with *élan*) and what Jonah writes (with cautious *élan*.) To my mind, that is the reason for this debate.

It is a relief to me, however, that we are not debating a concept of nationalism that would pretend to make (ethnic) nationhood the sole legitimate basis for statehood. Elie Kedourie demolished *that* proposition in his book *Nationalism,* and the dire results of Woodrow Wilson's attempt to redraw Europe along lines of national self-determination confirm Kedourie's sceptical conclusion. As Earl Wavell said of Versailles, the war to end all war produced the peace to end all peace. States are the products of history and reflect very different founding principles: dynastic marriages, conquest, revolution, war, 'velvet divorces,' treaties, referenda, constitutional separatism, etc., etc. It is likely that we will have to clear up some messes history leaves behind from time to time, as after Versailles, but no conservative would propose embarking on a wholesale reconstruction of states in accordance with a single theoretical principle that most existing states violated.

When people cite what earlier conservatives have said in condemnation of nationalism, it is often this definition and its utopian implications that they have in mind. I cannot say for certain that is what Bill Buckley had in mind when he said he did not have an ounce of nationalism in him. But if he was using the term in its colloquial sense, then I have to respond either that Bill was fooling himself or that knew himself less well than the English schoolboys whom, according to his own account, he harangued on the vices of George III in his school dormitory.

Nationalism in this debate, however, is about the attitude that conservatives should take toward their nation and state and, by extension, toward the kind of policies, mainly in international relations, that its government should pursue. Jonah's leading argument is that nationalism, except in small doses, is a bad thing, and is to be distinguished from its wiser and more principled brother, patriotism. Both are passions, but patriotism is a passion that has been refined and disciplined by liberal ideas—in the US, the flag, the Constitution, and the liberties for which they stand. Nationalism, however, is the raw spirit, unrefined, and dangerous. Without the right ideas to restrain the passion, nationalism, and nationalists will threaten others, wage wars, and produce carnage from a sort of national egoism.

Much of this I can accept. But what is the 'passion' under discussion? It is the love of country. It is a pre-rational sense of fellowship, common destiny, and loyalty that, because of the spread of communications, has expanded from the inhabitants of a village to the citizens of a nation united by, well, several things—a common language, common institutions, the mystic chords of memory, songs, poems, etc. Might this sense of common-fellowship encompass the globe and produce global citizens in time? Possibly. I cannot forecast the future, but for the moment 'the largest we' is the nation.

All institutions rest in part on such passions—the local mafia as well as the local police. It matters to everyone whether their governing principles are criminal or charitable. But the ur-passion of group solidarity or loyalty that sustains them is essentially the same. Nationalism is the sense of solidarity that unites a nation as opposed to a golf club or an army platoon.

Thinking along the same lines, Jonah compares nationalism to the physical attraction that underpins marriage: it is a start, but if the marriage has to survive, it must be allied to some higher ideal. Okay, but let us look at this further. Physical attraction is indeed the root of many things as well as marriage, including promiscuity, pregnancy, sexually transmitted diseases, jealousy, infidelity, divorce—at one extreme, murder, and at the other, self-sacrifice for home and beauty. Which of these different results flow from physical attraction depends on the ideals that govern it: promiscuity when it is governed by selfishness, self-sacrifice when governed by romantic altruism, and marriage when governed by a deep emotional or sacramental commitment. All these are expressions of physical attraction, however, and the best marriage will struggle to survive if that disappears entirely.

Marriage in this comparison plays the part of patriotism. If Jonah were to say that patriotism is nationalism governed by high ideals, and fascism a form of nationalism corrupted by vicious ones, we would be on the same page. But he wants to draw between nationalism and patriotism a clear, bright line that I do not think can be maintained. What are the marks of distinction between the two apart from the fact that, as we all acknowledge, different nations have different cultures, traditions, and political ideals and therefore different styles of nationalism (some nice, some nasty) as a result?

Would it not make better sense to think of nationalism as a spectrum, with aggressive, exclusivist nationalism at one end and, at the other, the kind of green pacifist nationalism of some Left intellectuals in Orwell's wartime England ('soil and bloodlessness'?), with patriotism being the usage reserved for the nationalism of countries with a constitutional, liberal tradition and outlook? It would reflect the fact that love of country infuses these very different nationalisms just as sexual passion drives both marriage and adultery—and that a constitutional patriotism cannot long survive if it loses touch with its fundamental root in this emotion. Jonah comes close to conceding this when he complains that 'many intellectuals use terms such as "civic nationalism" to describe patriotism and "ethnic nationalism" to describe the blood-and-soil variety.' Like him, I prefer the traditional word, but 'civic nationalism' conveys the idea that patriotism is one variant of nationalism rather than a separate species—and that is, I think, the truer argument.

I doubt that I have convinced Jonah, however, and I will proceed to the next logical point: what principles should infuse America's (or, in my case, Britain's) national identity and culture. If we stand outside any national loyalties and consider this abstractly, we will probably think that nationalism should be inclusive internally—that is, admitting all ethnic groups into full citizenship without discrimination—and non-aggressive externally, forswearing irredentist claims, for instance. Circumstances alter cases, but this kind of civic and pacific bourgeois nationalism seems likely to arouse or invite conflict less than most other kinds.

Both Jonah and Ben want to go much further than this, however. They want not only to bind nationalism within a straitjacket of liberal constitutionalism but to assert that this transforms it into a unique and different passion. Here is Jonah explaining why American patriotism is deeply different from all nationalisms:

> Our statues of soldiers commemorate heroes who died for something very different from what other warriors have fought and died for for millennia. Every one of them—immigrants included—took an oath to defend not just some soil but our Constitution and by extension the ideals of the Founding. Walk around any European hamlet or capital and you will find statues of men who fell in battle to protect their tribe from another tribe.

Now, of course, there is a great deal in what Jonah wrote in this passage. Though GIs in the Second World War were fighting for home and beauty as well as ideals, and though they may not have kept the US Constitution permanently in the forefront of their minds, they had absolutely no doubt that they were on the side of liberty, equality, and decency. They knew what they were fighting for. I happily acknowledge the truth of that claim from outside the American nation; and as a Brit, I make exactly the same claim for British troops in the same war. That is not surprising, since the values and ideals of 1776 are an expansion of the Whiggish ideals of Britain's 1688 Glorious Revolution—the first liberal revolution in history. These ideals are threaded through the national self-understanding of the other great Anglophone settler nations—Australia, Canada, and New Zealand. And they partly explain why these five countries, despite lesser differences of political ideology and real interest, have so often found themselves fighting on the same side in the same wars and believing themselves to be fighting for causes higher than national self-interest.

I am not trying to dilute American exceptionalism here; America is the leading liberal nation state in every regard. In both embodying liberal principles and proclaiming them to the world, moreover, it becomes more missionary in its liberal advocacy than other nations in the liberal family.

And that will raise other questions below. But the family of liberal nations is a family all the same and liberal all the same.

But are we muscular liberals quite as different from European nations as Jonah and especially Ben suggest? It is not the case that all Europe's wars were wars of princely expansion or ethnic rivalry designed to add soil to the national territory. Europe's most devastating and costly wars were wars of principle—the Crusades; the Thirty Years War and other post-Reformation religious armed conflicts; the twenty-year-long war waged by Revolutionary and Napoleonic France under the banner of 'the Rights of Man;' the wars for Greek independence, for Italian unification, and for European liberal constitutionalism against the Habsburgs in 1848; and the First World War, which was essentially waged to defend a settled European order based on law, commerce, and diplomatic restraint from the lawless 'militarism' of the new Germany symbolized by its invasion of Belgium. All these conflicts, including the two world wars of the last century, were tainted by national interest, especially at Versailles. But they were not driven by national interest, and no European statesman would have embarked on them for material or territorial gain, as opposed to profiting from them if fortune happened to smile in the right direction.

In short, it is not only the good guys who are moved by what they suppose to be noble principles—and what sometimes are noble principles. And if these principles differ with each other, and especially over apparent fundamentals (e.g. utopian equality over practical liberty), they will lead to conflict over time. And, sadly, they are far more likely to lead to prolonged bloody conflict than are disagreements over whether a frontier was drawn in the right place or a royal baby should count a disputed province in his future kingdom. Such wars end quickly. But Nazis, Marxists, and democrats were so strongly hostile to each others' ideas that they fought to the finish—and one set of bad guys was among the big winners. Of course, conflict is more embedded in Marxism and Nazism, indeed consciously so, than in liberal democracy. But liberalism has the capacity to become an armed doctrine too. Experience in the wars of the twentieth century suggests that moderation in wars of ideology does not last long even on the liberal side. American patriotism ought not to be intolerant in principle, but it sometimes is in practice.

It even has the potential of becoming an orthodoxy imposed on dissenters in domestic politics as, Jonah demonstrated very persuasively in *Liberal Fascism*. That leads me to be less happy than Jonah is, for instance, with the term 'un-American.' It suggests just that orthodoxy I suspect. And I wonder what the position is of those Americans, born, bred, and educated in the country, who grow up to reject the American idea—for instance, those who go to college and become Marxists. Have they thereby excluded themselves from the national community? In fact, the concept of the 'un-American' strikes me as downright un-American—a half-step toward totalitarian liberalism. Now, there is an answer to this criticism—see below—but it is not an answer that gives aid and comfort to any brand of ideas-based nationalism, a.k.a. 'propositionalism.'

We need other things to restrain our civic nationalism or liberal patriotism from following even good instincts in the wrong direction— and to build a (safely quarrelsome) national community on lasting and secure foundations. What are they?

Ben Shapiro has a very clear answer. He argues that there is a simple, binary choice between propositional patriotism and what he calls the 'blood and soil' variety, or ethnic nationalism. And he chooses the former. Americans are held together, he believes, by the principles stated in the Declaration of Independence, implicit in the US Constitution, reaffirmed in Lincoln's speeches, and summarized as life, liberty, and the pursuit of happiness. Ben does not blink at any of the logical implications of this assertion. It is sometimes alleged by critics of ideological nationalism that it reduces the ties between Americans to mere statements of philosophical sympathy and that these are not enough to unify people spread across a continent or to sustain them through hard times. Rather than expressing indignation at this accusation, he embraces it and argues that it is mere ethnic 'tribalism' that would really divide Americans:

And once nationalism is tribalism, the question becomes why America should remain one nation rather than many. My connection to my local community is stronger than my connection to bureaucrats in Washington, DC. My connection with those who share my faith and my ideas is stronger than my connection with somebody living 2,000 miles away in an area I have never visited. It is not a coincidence that 60 per cent of Trumpian nationalists in Texas were willing to secede from the country if Hillary Clinton became president, and 48 per cent of California Democrats are willing to secede from the country now that Trump is president. Nothing holds us together, once we rule out idea-based nationalism in favour of blood-and-soil-based nationalism. And, make no mistake, it is a choice; the two forms of nationalism cannot be synthesized. One form must have primacy.

Well, Ben and I should perhaps have a drink next time we are both in the same city since I have to say honestly that I disagree with almost everything in that long quotation. I have not heard of any mass exodus of California Democrats since November 8, and I do not think Texan Trumpians would have left home if Hillary had been elected. People say such daft things all the time in political debates without the slightest intention of acting on them. And both sets of partisans living in the same town would be helping each other to put out a forest fire if one threatened their community. Ben himself is connected to other Americans living far away, by many ties beyond political liberalism—most important, that they have lived, died, and sacrificed to give him a country in which he is a free man. Many of those to whom he owes this large debt differ from him on political fundamentals, and yet they consider him a fellow American who has a claim on them ahead of foreigners if he is in need. Most Americans, indeed, would think it odd that they should have to pass a test in political theory to satisfy him on their patriotic credentials. When questioned about such things as the Bill of Rights, moreover, many Americans give the *wrong* answers quite innocently. And on the opposite side of that political divide, I have no doubt that if some crisis arose for his neighbours or the nation, Ben would find himself responding to it like a volunteer fireman in Dixville Notch.

Why is that? It is, I think, because Ben is mistaken on his concluding point, that if we rule out 'propositionalism,' we are inevitably saddled with ethnic nationalism, blood and soil, etc. For a host of reasons, an ethno-nationalism is not a present choice for large multi-ethnic settler nations such as the US. There is a third nationalism, however, that he never discusses—and that is a form of nationalism rooted in America's common culture and in the lived experience of freedom and fellowship in American life. The American idea is powerful and good, but it is the abstract distillation of that experience. The experience itself is richer, constantly influencing us, and it shapes American patriots far more deeply. And it serves to unify Americans without their needing to reflect consciously on it. As Rich and Ramesh argue in their article, it 'attaches to the country's people and culture, not just to its political institutions and laws. Such nationalism includes solidarity with one's countrymen, whose welfare comes before, albeit not to the complete exclusion of, that of foreigners.'

And there is a final paradox: that an American identity rooted in cultural familiarity will be more genuinely liberal than one based on the American idea. It allows someone to reject the dominant ethos of his society—that Marxist professor above—without losing his claim to be an American. Does that mean the death of liberal Americanism? Not at all. As Orwell pointed out in the British context, someone who has spent his life breathing a free atmosphere will find himself talking freedom against all his professed principles. Thus, a Marxist law professor would write to *The Times* to complain that some proposal was contrary to all the traditions of English liberty.

Ideas are less likely to restrain themselves than be restrained by traditions of decent behaviour that become second nature to us. That is why Americans should not be afraid of their own cultural nationalism— whatever they choose to call it.

Originally published in National Review, *16 February 2017,* *www.nationalreview.com/2017/02/nationalism-patriotism-america-* *britain-jonah-goldberg-ben-shapiro/.*

Britain under the Iron High Heel
September 1989

Is liberty in Britain—and especially freedom of speech and of the press—under threat from an authoritarian government and a domineering Prime Minister? This is an allegation made with increasing certitude by British politicians, writers, and journalists of a Left-liberal inclination, and listened to with increasing horror by liberal Anglophiles on this side of the Atlantic. From Mrs Miniver's England to 'Margaret Thatcher's Britain' is, it seems, a journey from the open air of freedom to, if not the prison cell, then at least the interrogation room. And even though British policemen used to be thought wonderful, British thought policemen are not.

Harold Pinter on the subject sounds like a character from one of his own plays: 'The power of the police to do whatever they like is extraordinary. ... The people are bewildered, undermined, fearful, lost. ... Phones are bugged. I know people under surveillance.'

Pinter's fellow-dramatist, John Mortimer, the creator of *Rumpole*, is hardly less apocalyptic: '... censorship has emerged far more blatantly and can be seen as the determination of government to stifle unconventional opinions, criticism which it finds unwelcome, facts which it finds embarrassing or—and this can be seen most clearly in the plans for the future of the BBC and the independent television companies—to dismantle institutions which it feels unable to dominate.'

* * *

Lord (Roy) Jenkins, a leading member of the centrist Democrats (recently formed from a merger of the Liberals and the Social Democrats) and a former Home Secretary in a Labour government, is more moderate in his criticism: 'Freedom to make profit is sacred, but freedom from censorship or for unorthodox views or behaviour is vulnerable.' But Duncan Campbell, the famous investigative journalist, interprets Margaret Thatcher's alleged hostility to press freedom (and himself) more darkly: '... security forces are being given greater license, and the deliberate suppression of investigative journalism plays a major role in facilitating state counterterrorism.'

Such views have found a ready acceptance among London's Left intelligentsia, particularly journalists, who sometimes seem to take a professional pride in being repressed. The magazine *Index on Censorship* devoted a special issue to liberty under Thatcher—the first such issue to be devoted to the affairs of a democratic country. Critics of the government, borrowing from Soviet dissidents, founded a newsletter entitled *Samizdat*. (One is reminded of Kingsley Amis's definition of the underground press—'newspapers sold outside Underground stations.') In a similar spirit, modelled this time on Czech dissidents, the leftist weekly, *The New Statesman*, midwifed Charter 88, 'to demand political, civil, and *human* rights in the United Kingdom'(emphasis added). It was signed by, among others, the novelist Martin Amis, the actress Dame Peggy Ashcroft, and the biographer Lady Antonia Fraser (all of whom are still at liberty and on television).

Soon the bad news crossed the Atlantic. Professor Ronald Dworkin of Oxford, himself an American and well-known in the United States as a legal philosopher, had written in *Index on Censorship*: 'Liberty is ill in Britain. ... The sad truth is that the very *concept* of liberty ... is being challenged and corroded by the Thatcher government.' It was true, Dworkin conceded, that Mrs Thatcher's challenge to freedom 'had nothing to do with totalitarian despotism.' Its character was altogether less impressive—'a more mundane but still corrupting insensitivity to liberty.'

Another American, James Atlas, returned from a flying visit to report in the Sunday *New York Times Magazine* that 'to hear people talk, England in 1988 was Prague in 1977.' Not to be outdone, *The New York Review of Books* invited Peter Jenkins, the distinguished British political correspondent, to consider the question of Britain's disappearing liberty, but he may have disappointed his hosts by the moderation of his criticism and the scepticism he applied to the prevailing alarmism. So the

Columbia Journalism Review took no risks; it invited Duncan Campbell to do his turn. He duly obliged with: ' ... in the Britain of the future, if the government murders environmentalists and destroys their property, ... or bugs and burgles the political opposition, ... or sends poison-pen letters and hate mail to civil-rights activists, no one shall be permitted to know.' Finally, Mrs Thatcher's jackboots made an unfashionable appearance in *Vanity Fair* when Gail Sheehy, in her profile of the Prime Minister, wrote: 'People I interviewed complained of their phones being bugged, their mail being opened, but declined to go on the record for fear they would lose their government funding.' In short, the British people groan under the iron (high) heel.

* * *

Now it is important to note that those of us who reject such charges are not saying that Mrs Thatcher and her Ministers are passionate advocates of a Freedom of Information Act (they plainly are not), or that official secrecy in Britain is not excessive (it plainly is), or that tensions between the government and the broadcasting authorities are not often fierce (they plainly are). Yet all these criticisms could have been levelled with perfect accuracy against previous governments, both Labour and Conservative. A more reasonable critic, the former editor of *The New Statesman*, John Lloyd, has said of the Thatcher government: 'its sporadic but sharp intolerance of press revelation follows no clearly sinister path, but seems to proceed from ... a lack of interest in liberalizing and opening out the mechanisms and decisions of government at least as marked as any of its predecessors.' The point at issue, however, is not whether Mrs Thatcher's government has a record roughly similar to that of its predecessors, but whether it has a much worse one which deserves such extreme descriptions as 'corrupting' and 'corrosive' of liberty.

There are four main counts in the indictment, the first of which involves Peter Wright's book *Spycatcher*. In that book Wright, a disaffected former employee of MI5, the British counterintelligence service, describes his efforts to prove that its former head, Sir Roger Hollis, was a Soviet spy, and also his own participation in a conspiracy of MI5 agents to bring down the Labour government of Harold Wilson whom they suspected of being a Soviet agent of influence. Such a book would be so plainly open to a successful prosecution in Britain under the Official Secrets Act (which dates from 1911, somewhat before Margaret Thatcher came on the scene) that Wright in 1985 gave it to a publishing company in Australia where he now lives.

Over the next three years there was a rash of trials and injunctions as the British government sought both to prevent publication of *Spycatcher* in Australia and the printing of extracts from it in newspapers in Britain. These came to an end when the House of Lords, the highest British court, lifted all restraints on publication on the ground that—*Spycatcher* having already appeared in the United States and also having been passed for publication by the Australian High Court—there was no point in locking the stable door after the horse had manifestly bolted.

* * *

Thus the bare facts. What, however, do they signify for this argument?

The first point to grasp is that, as regards the original decision to suppress *Spycatcher* by legal action, no British government would have acted differently. British governments of every political colour have taken the position that the intelligence agencies should remain secret, even to the somewhat ludicrous extent of not officially admitting the existence of the secret service (MI6). Indeed, earlier governments resorted to the Official Secrets Act to prevent or punish much lesser breaches than were committed by *Spycatcher* in allegedly revealing the inner workings of, and some of the most damaging episodes in, the most secret branches of British officialdom. For example, the Labour government of 1964–70, in which Lord Jenkins was a distinguished Minister, prosecuted a Tory candidate and a newspaper editor for revealing a military assessment of the Nigerian Army!

Wright himself, living in Australia, was beyond the reach of prosecution under the Official Secrets Act. But there was a convenient precedent for acting against his book: the 1976 suit by the then-Labour government to prevent, on the civil grounds of confidentiality, publication of the diaries of a former Labour Cabinet Minister, Richard Cross-man. Armed with that example, the Thatcher government duly took its stand on the principle that employees of MI5 owed the Crown a lifelong duty of confidentiality from which no other consideration could absolve them. And this principle was firmly upheld by Lord Keith in the House of Lords' final judgment:

> The work of a member of MI5 and the information which he acquires in the course of that work must necessarily be secret and confidential and be kept secret and confidential by him. *There is no room for discrimination between secrets of greater or lesser importance, nor any room for close examination of the precise manner in which revelation of any particular matter may prejudice the national interest. Any attempt to do so would lead to further damage.* All this has been accepted from beginning to end by each of the judges in this country who has had occasion to consider the case. (Emphasis added)[1]

But what of the point that Wright had revealed serious misbehaviour by MI5? Would not protection of secrets in such a case amount to a cover-up of wrongdoing? If a high value is placed on protecting official secrets, then allegations of MI5 misbehaviour can be investigated only by internal procedures which must themselves be secret. Yet successive British governments of all political stripes have preferred the risk that such investigations will cover up misbehaviour to the opposite one of allowing the widespread publication of intelligence secrets on the gambler's argument that some of them might halt or prevent a security scandal.[2]

---

[1] Here I differ from Peter Jenkins who, in *The New York Review of Books*, argues that Lord Keith in fact imposed a 'test of harm' with these words: '[A] government is not in a position to win the assistance of the court in restraining the publication of information imparted in confidence by it or its predecessors unless it can show that publication would be harmful to the public interest.' That judgment, however, immediately precedes the sentences quoted in the text in which Lord Keith withdraws any apparent concession in regard to the security service, arguing that revelations by its members or former members are harmful to the public interest by their very nature.

[2] New legislation before Parliament, which for the first time puts the security service on a statutory footing (i.e., admits its existence and lays down the ground rules for its operation), establishes among other safeguards an independent staff counsellor to whom

Even as these questions were being debated, however, the case which had stimulated them became moot when Wright revealed in a television interview that he had grossly exaggerated MI5's conspiracy against Harold Wilson. To quote the report in *The Independent*:

> Mr Wright then said that there had not been 30 conspirators in MI5 as stated in the book. He said: 'I should think the maximum number was eight or nine.' Very often when the dispute was discussed at the end of the day, when MI5 'management' had gone home, there were only three people present. ... When pressed to say how many of the conspirators were really serious about the plot, he responded: 'One, I should say. Really serious.' He conceded that the part of the book which discussed the meat of the conspiracy was 'unreliable.'

Somehow or other, this report, although appearing almost five months before his own article came out in *The New York Times*, escaped James Atlas who wrote of *Spycatcher* that 'it does contain some embarrassing revelations, among them an account of the campaign ... to discredit Prime Minister Harold Wilson as a Soviet agent and drive him from office.'

To sum up, the attempt to suppress *Spycatcher* was standard law and practice in Britain. Mrs Thatcher differed from previous governments only in the persistence with which she defended the principle they have all embraced.

* * *

Mrs Thatcher also differs in having carried into law a reform of the Official Secrets Act which several recent British governments have considered but at which they have balked. (It comes into force later this year.) This reform represents the second of the four main charges in the indictment against Mrs Thatcher. Her critics maintain that the new Official Secrets Act will, as one of them has put it, 'essentially do away with the "harm" or public-interest defence, making the disclosure of

---

service members can take their complaints and who in turn has access to the Home Secretary and the Prime Minister.

government information a crime—no matter what kind or whether disclosing it would pose a danger.'

This turns the facts on their heads. To begin with, the 1911 Official Secrets Act imposed no test of harm in prosecutions for publishing classified information. All that the authorities had to establish was that official information—*any* official information whatever—had been published. As against this, the new law contains three major changes.

First, large areas of government information have been removed from the protection of official-secrets legislation altogether. It will no longer cover most government business, let alone all.

Second, the government will now have to prove that the unauthorized disclosure of information would damage the public interest. Thus the 'test of harm,' far from being removed from official-secrecy law, is in truth introduced into it here for the first time. Only in the narrow and well-defined exceptions of disclosure by members of the intelligence services of information relating to their work, or of disclosure relating to special investigations carried out under a statutory warrant signed by the Home Secretary (i.e., telephone tapping), will the government not need to prove damage to the public interest. But since the government never had to prove damage before, that does not constitute a change for the worse.

Third, the government will now have to prove such harm to the satisfaction of a jury. Ministers will not simply be able to certify that harm had been done, as previous proposals for reform have suggested.

In other words, by any normal standard, the new law represents a liberalization rather than a tightening of official secrecy. The only ground for maintaining otherwise is Peter Jenkins's argument that the narrower and more reasonable the law, the more likely it is to result in successful prosecutions. But this is paradoxically to charge Mrs Thatcher with being *too* liberal, which is not exactly the conclusion to which the logic of her critics normally leads.

* * *

It is broadcasting, however, where the logic of Mrs Thatcher's critics goes most askew. Again, relations between governments and television were scenes of pitched battle long before Mrs Thatcher arrived in Downing Street. Harold Wilson refused to be interviewed by the BBC for a long period, and both Labour and Tory governments in the 1970s applied behind-the-scenes pressure on the BBC not to transmit particular programmes, generally programmes on Northern Ireland. Where Mrs Thatcher has departed from her predecessors is in her willingness to take *public* issue with the broadcasters on these matters.

This, indeed, is what Lord Bonham Carter, a former vice chairman of the BBC, singles out for criticism. In an article in *Index on Censorship*, he discusses the controversy which began when Mrs Thatcher's Home Secretary released to the press a letter to the BBC chairman seeking to cancel a programme in which an advocate of IRA terrorism and an Ulster Loyalist extremist were to be interviewed. Lord Bonham Carter does not object too strongly to the Home Secretary's letter as such. 'It is common practice for Ministers—and indeed members of the opposition,' he tells us, 'to ring up the director general, or the chairman of the board of governors, to protest about programmes which they fear may be objectionable or contrary to the interests of the country or their party.' But on this occasion, by releasing his letter to the press, the Home Secretary (so says Lord Bonham Carter) challenged the independence of the BBC. It is a curious notion, particularly coming from an advocate of openness, that private pressure is preferable to public criticism, and a still more curious one that the independence of the BBC is more subverted by honest debate than by the quiet masonry of establishment contacts.

Be that as it may, neither type of pressure has deterred the BBC from broadcasting interviews with terrorists and, earlier this year, in a real departure from established practice in Britain (and one that has supplied the material for the third of the major counts in the indictment against Mrs Thatcher), the Home Secretary used his powers to prohibit such interviews. But while British practice can supply no precedent, there is a precedent of sorts from the neighbouring Republic of Ireland where interviews with IRA terrorists have been banned since Conor Cruise O'Brien, who was then the Minister of Posts and Telecommunications, imposed the prohibition in the mid-70s.

I should at this point declare an intellectual interest. I have for the past decade been calling for the banning of television interviews with terrorists. A terrorist is an advocate of murder, and as I see it, advocacy of murder is, or should be, beyond the boundaries of acceptable public discussion. O'Brien goes further, arguing persuasively that such interviews constitute an actual incitement to murder: that the terrorist knows he would not receive flattering attention if he were not killing people; that therefore he must continue killing people in order to continue being treated as important; and that others who wish to receive similar flattery are themselves induced to embark upon a career of murder. Strong arguments would be needed on the other side to offset such palpable and serious dangers. What are they?

The justification commonly advanced is that 'we need to know what these people think.' But we invariably do know what they think long before they appear on television to tell us. Is anyone unaware of the aims and beliefs of the PLO, or of the IRA, or of the Red Brigades? Moreover, what they say on television is not necessarily what they think (which is much more accurately conveyed by what they do). It is sugared propaganda. Finally, even if we needed to know what the terrorist thought and could rely on his honesty in telling us, a straightforward report and analysis by the journalist himself would be a more efficient and reliable method of conveying such information. And it would not have the side-effect of conferring respectability upon murderers.

None of this is meant to suggest that a ban on terrorist interviews is not a restriction of free speech and journalistic inquiry. It obviously is. But it is a restraint that is legitimized by more important considerations. And to sacrifice these considerations to an absolutist view of free speech, as Mrs Thatcher's critics do on this issue, is to exhibit what O'Brien has described as 'unilateral liberalism ... the kind of liberalism which is sensitive exclusively to threats to liberty seen as emanating from the democratic state itself, and is curiously phlegmatic about threats to liberty from the enemies of that state.'

In short, in the single case where Mrs Thatcher has imposed or extended a form of censorship, she has acted with considerable

justification and from motives that have nothing to do with restricting
unpopular opinions as commonly understood.

* * *

Liberty of a different kind is at issue in the still sketchy proposals to
reform the broadcasting system (which brings us to the fourth main count
in the indictment). These proposals are designed to widen the freedom of
the consumer to choose from a greater number and variety of television
networks (ground-based, cable, satellite, etc.) while keeping "porno-TV"
at bay. In place of the existing Independent Broadcasting Authority
(IBA), which "awards" franchises to commercial television companies
on arbitrary judgments of quality, there is to be an Independent
Television Corporation (ITC), which will auction franchises to the
highest bidders (with quality safeguards). And to ensure that unregulated
TV does not beam into decent British homes the terrifying spectacle of
Italian housewives taking their clothes off, a Broadcasting Standards
Council (BSC) has been established.

The proposals are certainly open to criticism. The BSC, for instance,
could develop either as a reasonable ombudsman for viewers currently
ignored by the broadcasters, or into a slightly absurd Grundyesque body
straight from one of those old Ealing comedies, with fatuous vicars,
earnest civil servants, and puritanical lady aldermen deprecating vulgar
language and censuring the untoward appearance of a backside on prime
time. Even so, this new system of regulation is, as it happens, lighter and
less intrusive—in a word, more liberal—than the existing IBA, which
enjoys both powers of economic regulation *and* a legal responsibility,
backed up by powers of prior restraint, to ensure that programmes do not
offend standards of taste and decency. The new ITC's oversight will be
confined to broad guidelines covering diversity and quality, and the BSC
will have neither influence over the future disposition of television
franchises nor power to ban particular programmes.

But it is not so much these particular proposals as Mrs Thatcher's
plans for deregulation and wider choice in television which have
attracted the sharpest criticism, generally on the ground that greater
choice will mean fewer people watching the established "duopoly" of

BBC and IBA. Lord Bonham Carter sees this as 'an attempt to erode the authority of these two bodies which have so long been guardians of the independence of broadcasters.' Brian Wenham, a former BBC mandarin, opposes greater choice because, with four television channels already operating, 1the broadcasting market is already well-deployed, if not yet wholly saturated.' And John Mortimer equates greater choice with a vision of 'thirty-seven third-rate channels peddling thirty-seven similar varieties of rubbish'—a destructive reform inspired by a desire 'to dismantle' and 'break up' the BBC because it provides serious controversy and embarrasses the government.

Mortimer's criticism shows his hand. He objects to greater diversity of programming and opinion because it would dilute the influence of a semi-monopoly whose political values and artistic standards he finds congenial. And it is, of course, true that the more channels there are, the less influential any one channel is likely to be. But would a distinguished civil-rights lawyer like John Mortimer really support a policy to close down all newspapers except *The Guardian* and *The Independent* on the ground that the average quality of the press would then rise? And if he did, would he feel entitled to call himself a liberal and denounce those in favour of a multiplicity of newspapers as authoritarians bent on undermining his two favourite newspapers by depriving them of their rightful readers? And if he did that too, would he expect to be taken seriously as a critic of other people's despotic tendencies?

Once again, ironically, if there is a liberal in this particular argument, it is Mrs Thatcher with her deregulatory willingness to trust the viewers to choose wisely.[3]

* * *

---

[3] Two other items are generally added to the charge sheet: Clause 28, which prohibits local governments from spending public money to promote homosexuality, and the proposed removal of the right to silence of the accused in criminal prosecutions. Since neither is directly connected to the central controversy, namely, the tension between official secrecy and the freedom of the media, this is not the place to examine them. But suffice it to say that the former, properly considered, has nothing to do with free speech, but only with the disposition of public funds, and the latter, properly considered, is liberal both in character and effect.

It is, thus, simply false to suggest that the state of British liberty has grown worse under Mrs Thatcher compared to previous governments, or that she is hostile to free speech. Why then do so many writers, academics, journalists, artists, television directors, and portable all-purpose intellectuals denounce her in such strident terms? What makes grown men and women declare that they are living in the darkness of an authoritarian regime that is steadily snuffing out what remains of traditional liberties? Why do people whose experience of life's hardships is confined to a state-subsidized university education and a trainee producership at the BBC compare their plight with that of Soviet and Czech dissidents who have been imprisoned, beaten, subjected to psychiatric torture, worked almost to death in labour camps, dismissed from their professional posts, forced to take demeaning jobs for the express purpose of being humiliated, exiled to remote towns far from their family and friends, deprived of medical care when they were desperately ill, and in general treated worse than even the lowest criminals are treated in a civilized society?

It will not suffice for the signatories of Charter 88 or the editors of *Samizdat* to reply, as they do, that they make no claim of enduring oppression on the scale suffered by Václav Havel or Andrei Sakharov. For that is precisely the claim they made when they gave their organizations those names.

One possible explanation is that these people do not really believe what they say—a hypothesis which gained plausibility when the Ayatollah Khomeini pronounced a sentence of death on Salman Rushdie for his novel *The Satanic Verses*. Rushdie himself had been no slouch in the anti-Thatcher agitation. He was a signatory to Charter 88. And he took a generally dark view of what Britain and the West mean in the world, telling readers of *The Nation* in 1986: 'In my British incarnation, I have America's bombs for neighbours and could find myself in the absurd position of dying for Ronald Reagan.' In the event, of course, the threat came from another source. When it did, there was a rallying of the Left intelligentsia to demand that the British government should protect Rushdie, issue a strong protest to the Iranian government, and defend the continued publication of *The Satanic Verses* against Muslim agitation within Britain.

Thus, Harold Pinter marched to Downing Street at the head of a delegation of writers who called on the government to take action to end the 'intolerable and barbaric' threat from the Ayatollah. That appeal, with its Palmerstonian hint of defending the liberties of British citizens against the jabbering threats of mad mullahs abroad, was echoed elsewhere. Hugo Young, a liberal journalist whose biography of Mrs Thatcher had attacked her 'informal attitude which narrowed the limits of liberty,' declared in response to the threats against Rushdie from followers of the Ayatollah in Britain that if they did not like the tolerant climate in the country, then they should go back to Teheran. (This shocked *The New York Times* correspondent, who observed that Young was 'sounding like somebody more at home in Rupert Murdoch's ultraconservative tabloid *The Sun* than in the liberal *Guardian*.') Similarly, writing in the liberal *Financial Times*, Edward Mortimer voiced his outrage that the actions of a 'faraway foreign despot' might affect 'our own freedom to read and write as we see fit.'

Almost overnight, Britain—even under 'Mrs Torture,' as she appears in *The Satanic Verses*—had ceased to be a nation entering the darkness of authoritarianism and had been restored, at least temporarily, to its former status as the home of liberty and tolerance.

But if the Left intellectuals do not really believe their own anti-Thatcher propaganda, there can be no doubt that their hatred and fear of her are entirely genuine. Last year the London *Sunday Telegraph* interviewed a number of intellectuals for their opinion of her and were rewarded with some of the most snobbish and personally bitchy remarks ever visited upon a public figure. They ranged from the director Jonathan Miller's 'her odious suburban gentility and sentimental saccharine patriotism' to Lady Warnock's dislike of her 'patronizing voice' her looks ('not vulgar, just low'), and her general embodiment of 'the worst of the lower middle class.' The Mistress of Girton College, Cambridge, was particularly incensed by a television programme which showed the Prime Minister buying clothes: 'There was something quite obscene to see her picking out another blouse with a tie at the neck.'

What lies behind these sentiments, surely, is an impotent rage at the lasting defeat Mrs Thatcher has inflicted on socialism. In their less partisan moments, leaders in the other parties will accept that many of the achievements of 'Thatcherism' are permanently entrenched, and that free markets and an individualist social philosophy must be part of any prospective government's thinking. But nobody likes being defeated, and the discrediting of a deeply-held belief is felt more intensely than most setbacks. The patriots of socialism, who make up such a large part of the London intelligentsia, need a 'stab in the back' legend with which to explain their rout. What better excuse than that the game was rigged, the press bought, the television networks intimidated, intelligence scandals suppressed, official secrecy blanketed on the land, and the voters led like lambs to the polling booths? But it all remains an excuse, just as the charges against Mrs Thatcher on which it is based remain a combination of misrepresentations, distortions, and paranoid fantasies.

Originally published in Commentary, *September 1989, www.commentarymagazine.com/articles/john-osullivan-2/britain-under-the-iron-high-heel/.*

Ex-Friends

**A Review of *Twilight of Democracy: The Seductive Lure
of Authoritarianism* by Anne Applebaum
Fall 2020**

In 1960 Jacques Soustelle, a longstanding Gaullist disillusioned by
his hero's crabwise moves toward granting independence to Algeria, told
the general that all of Soustelle's friends were opposed to this policy.
'*Changez vos amis*,' responded de Gaulle briskly. 'Change your friends.'

Soustelle did not follow this advice (and spent years in exile as a
result), but Anne Applebaum does in this readable and passionate
curiosity of a book. A Pulitzer Prize-winning historian and staff writer for
The Atlantic who has written extensively on Soviet communism,
Applebaum invokes the grand abstractions of democracy and
authoritarianism with her title, which suggests an exploration of how
Europe and America have gradually moved from the triumph of democracy
after 1989 to its allegedly weakened and (in some cases) even suicidal
state today. That is indeed the theme of the book. But it is explored in an
oblique way by examining how some of Applebaum's friends have
contributed to this process of democratic change and decay, and how this
process has in turn affected them and their friendships with her.

'Badly' is the simplest answer. Her account opens with a party on the
last day of the twentieth century at the provincial Polish home she shares
with her husband, Radek Sikorski, then a junior minister in the first Law
and Justice coalition government, and ends with a summer party almost
exactly twenty years later in the same house. Much else has changed,
however. Having switched parties in 2007, Sikorski was the senior
foreign affairs minister for seven years in a Civic Platform government.
And that is only one reason why, as Applebaum herself observes, few of
her friends at the first party are guests at the second, and almost none of

those at the second had been present at the first. She has switched milieux.

Telling the story of democracy in the post-Cold War world through the making and breaking of friendships has advantages. It makes for a lively narrative and it allows for amusing anecdotes and clever pen-portraits. There are both here. Its serious disadvantage is that unless your close friends are people like Angela Merkel, Donald Trump, or Boris Johnson (Applebaum scores 33 per cent on that test), there is likely to be a large disproportion between the historical facts being told and your method of telling them. The *reductio ad absurdum* of this approach is the title of comedian Spike Milligan's autobiography—*Adolf Hitler: My Part in His Downfall* (1971).

Contrast this approach with the vastness of the topic—namely, the evolution of democracy, or the large number of parties that have risen, fallen, disappeared, and sometimes reappeared in Western democracies since 1989. To over-simplify, Europe's mainstream social democratic parties have declined precipitously; its mainstream centre-right parties have been weakened; 'populist' and Green parties have risen on Right and Left; and in order to keep power and resist them, centre-left and centre-right have increasingly been forming centrist 'grand coalitions.' Italy, Spain, Germany, France, Denmark, Holland, the Irish Republic, Sweden, and the European Parliament (where last year the centrist grand coalition fell to 43 per cent of memberships, and recruited the liberal bloc in order to retain its governing majority) all represent variations on this theme.

Look at France's Fifth Republic more closely: an original Left–Right division has splintered into a multi-party system that includes Gaullist conservatives, Emmanuel Macron's new centrist liberals, the neo-Jacobins of the Right in Marine Le Pen's *Rassemblement National*, and the radical Left's *La France Insoumise* under Jean-Luc Mélenchon. In the first round of the 2017 presidential elections, these four parties split the vote so evenly that it was almost accidental that Macron and Le Pen went into the final round. Nor should we forget the once-mighty Socialist Party that shrank to 7 per cent in 2017 but will probably recover by 2022 as others fail.

One might reasonably argue that these trends signify the high noon of democracy insofar as older parties that neglected their constituencies lost ground, new parties arose to champion their grievances, and the 'Overton window' of issues it was legitimate to debate expanded. Aren't such things usually seen as the marks of a vibrant democracy? But Applebaum sees these trends as the 'twilight of democracy' in part because she concentrates mainly on countries where right-wing populists have won elections—on Poland, Hungary, and the United Kingdom, which all have stable majorities of the Right—on populism generally, on Brexit, and on Donald Trump. Whatever name we give these changes, however, they are certainly big and significant. What caused them?

Causes and effects are not always easy to identify in politics because some very dramatic effects, including some revolutions, have long-germinating causes. But here some causes push themselves on our attention: the 2008 financial crash and its long recessionary aftermath; the long-running euro crisis that has devastated the economies of Mediterranean Europe and caused a still-recurring series of banking and financial crises; barely controlled mass migration, dramatized by the refugee crisis of 2015, resulting from the failure to control Europe's borders; and the alienation of voters from an opaque governing system that transfers powers from national governments to Brussels and thereafter pursues policies European Union elites favour but electorates detest, and deep-sixes the opposite policies as quietly as it can. Applebaum considers the possibility that these crises had caused the upheavals of European politics above, but rejects it:

> The recession of 2008–2009 was deep, but—at least until the coronavirus pandemic—growth had returned. The refugee crisis of 2015–2016 was a shock, but it has abated. By 2018, refugees from North Africa and the Middle East had mostly stopped coming to Europe, thanks to deals done with Turkey by the EU and its mainstream politicians.

But why were the changes in electoral politics unrelated to the major crises that had occurred in the previous decade? Is Applebaum arguing that they could not have done so because the voters are too short-termist to connect dots separated by a year or two? If so, she is unwisely condescending to them. Or is she reproving the voters for not being short-termist enough and moving on contentedly when their betters have solved the crises? In which case she underrates the good sense and seriousness of ordinary people about public matters that touch their lives deeply.

Whichever it is, the more important point is that the voters have proved wiser than the EU leaders and Ms Applebaum. For the refugees have not stopped coming; there's an Italian political crisis over the latest surge of migrants as I write; European courts are still trying to weaken Hungary's border restrictions; and Turkey's President Recep Erdogan has not only threatened to allow refugees to cross the border into Europe if his wishes are thwarted but has also demonstrated his power to do so by ordering Turkish police to knock down fences at the Greek border. As long as people continue to see these things as threats, they will vote to prevent them.

If Applebaum cannot quite identify the causes of upheaval, she is still more puzzled over why some friends ended up on the wrong side of the barricades. 'What, then, has caused this transformation?' she asks. 'Were some of our friends always closet authoritarians? Or have the people with whom we clinked glasses in the first minutes of the new millennium somehow changed over the subsequent two decades?'

The rest of her book is an attempt to discover the explanation mainly by interrogating the careers and opinions of those of her friends who have transformed so mysteriously. These interrogations are interrupted from time to time with her own reflections on politics and political theory that may throw some light on the problematic biographies. For example, she sees parallels to some of the new 'authoritarians' in the French intellectuals of the interwar years whom Julien Benda criticized in his classic study, 'The Treason of the Intellectuals' (1928), for subordinating the love of truth and beauty to partisan ideologies. These reflections are interesting, and I generally agree with them (though I have always thought Benda could have made a good living using a steamroller to crack Brazil nuts), but they do not seem to fit, let alone explain, the very different personalities who are the mainstays of the narrative.

That is especially true of the chapter describing the writers, columnists, and politicians around the London *Spectator*, where Applebaum was their colleague for some years, many of whom were also active supporters of Brexit. They are an exceptionally distinguished bunch, as it happens, including Boris Johnson, Simon Heffer, Roger Scruton, and, ahem, me. I cannot really complain about the portrait of me which suggests a combination of boulevardier (jovial, witty, fond of champagne) and James Bond villain who emerges from behind the scenes occasionally to cast Scotland aside unsentimentally or to move Viktor Orbán around on the international chessboard. But the glaring difficulty about my assistants, Johnson, Heffer, and Scruton, is that there does not seem to be an iota of evidence that they are in any way 'authoritarian.' Or that Brexit was an essentially authoritarian idea or development in British politics. Quite the reverse. It was plainly a campaign to restore Britain's status as a self-governing democracy.

Applebaum finds it hard to see this, perhaps because she lived in Britain on a small island of Brexiteer opinion set in a silver sea of establishment Europhilia. She points out that she never heard anyone in this wider London who thought that leaving the EU was a political possibility. I do not doubt her. This general Europhilia meant even strong Brexiteers rarely bothered to make the case for Brexit. It seemed futile. We assumed that the best we could hope for was a decentralized 'EU à la carte.' But opinion polls since the 1975 referendum show that in Britain, uniquely among EU member states, there was always a substantial percentage of public opinion—sometimes a majority—that wanted to leave the EU. That percentage grew gradually in the decade running up to the referendum as the EU adopted greater political integration under EU rules of qualified majority voting, and as the euro, refugee, and Greek crises dominated the headlines. So, when the referendum campaign kicked off in February 2016 with its strict rules of media impartiality, these revealed many intelligent people making reasonable arguments in favour of 'Leave.' That percentage soon became a modest majority—and also a self-conscious and more confident one. That helps to explain why it remained stable and determined in the face of powerful media, legal, and parliamentary campaigns to reverse Brexit or at a minimum to dilute it in the three years following the actual referendum.

Because Applebaum does not accept this reality (as I see it), she has to find other reasons why Brexit won and—an even more difficult task— why her friends supported it. Her answers on the first topic are that it was a moment of madness achieved by lies, manipulation, and misuse of campaign funds on the part of unscrupulous demagogues. Lies there undoubtedly were, but they were told by both sides. Those told by official sources in the form of economic predictions (a.k.a., Project Fear) have proved astoundingly wide of the mark; those told (allegedly) by Leave campaigners were standard election exaggerations. (I have to write 'allegedly' because recent court cases have ruled both that Leave campaigners were falsely accused by the official UK elections agency of misusing campaign funds, and that Leave's most famous 'lie'—the cost to Britain of EU funding—would have been completely inoffensive if it had made explicit that a weekly UK loss of £350 million gross translated into one of £250 million net. Case dismissed!) Altogether, the 'Remain' side had the weight of money, international opinion, and establishment authority on its side. If Viktor Orbán were to win an election on the back of such support, Applebaum would declare it rigged. But Remain lost; Leave unexpectedly won.

In dealing with the more intractable problem presented by Scruton, Heffer, and Johnson, Applebaum makes the argument that their desire to leave the EU was really about something else entirely. In Johnson's case, it was personal ambition and the desire to get into 10 Downing Street. Suppose that to be so—which I do not. Such an ambition is the incentive democracy employs to get politicians to offer what voters want. It probably played a part in the calculations of all the leading politicians in the Brexit debate. We cannot know what Johnson would do if he were to follow his secret heart. But we can know what politicians write for the public record in the light of all factors in any case. My guess is that when he wrote two *Telegraph* articles—for and against Brexit—on the eve of his personal decision, Johnson realized that since the curse of political impossibility had been lifted, Leave actually had the better of the argument. He has certainly made good on that decision in the last five years, if not yet on other hopes for his premiership.

Scruton and Heffer are explained in the book as people who supported Brexit from an odd distorted nostalgia. They heartily disliked what Britain had become during their lifetimes, and though they did not believe that the UK's membership in the EU had brought this decline about, they nonetheless voted for Brexit in the hope that Brexit would somehow reverse it. Now, Heffer and Scruton undoubtedly have nostalgia among the other strings on their bows and employed it very effectively in some of their writings. Scruton's *England: An Elegy* (2000) is a moving lament for the lost England of his childhood, as Applebaum happily concedes in what for a moment becomes a tribute. As Roger's friend and exact contemporary, what he wrote spoke powerfully to me. But both men knew that it was we ourselves who allowed this decline to happen, and it is only we who can reverse it—or, more accurately, chart a course to a better country that we cannot fully imagine but that will reflect in part the spirit of what we have lost or, with luck, merely mislaid.

Roger and Simon were both fully aware that Brexit itself cannot do that or anything like that, but that the opposite of Brexit—continued EU membership—would mean that we cannot even attempt such an enterprise because we would then be a subordinate part of another country with its own destiny. That is why Roger, Simon, and many other, less-talented advocates of Brexit stressed the vital importance of democratic sovereignty. Without sovereignty and the democracy it protects, ordinary people cannot shape the future of the country in which they live. If you doubt that, try amending a bad EU law.

Throughout the Brexit campaign, Remainers simply refused to listen to this argument or to give any weight to democratic sovereignty in their cost–benefit analysis of EU membership. That is why they lost both the referendum and the long three-year constitutional struggle about it afterward. My feeling is that Applebaum makes this mistake on the larger canvas of European democracy. She interprets the ideological battle being waged across the continent as one of 'liberal democracy' versus 'populism' or, better, 'authoritarianism.' That is certainly how Europe's political establishments in Brussels, Paris, Berlin, Rome, etc., wish to frame the debate.

But the EU itself has conceded the existence of a 'democratic deficit' since the mid-1970s, and it makes periodic attempts to get around it. The deficit persists because it is the result of institutional arrangements and philosophical beliefs thought essential to 'building Europe' out of a multilingual association of 27 countries with their own histories and identities. For instance, the European Commission, an unelected body, has a near-monopoly on proposing legislation which amounts to an advance veto. Legislation that does not get proposed cannot get passed. The spirit of such EU law- and regulation-making, moreover, is that movement toward ever-closer union is inevitable and irreversible. Or as Jean-Claude Juncker, then president of the Commission, said during the Greek crisis: 'there can be no democratic choice against the European treaties.' And when countries *have* exercised choice against European integration in referendums that *were* allowed under treaty rules, the EU has insisted that second referendums be held to reverse an unwelcome vote, or simply ignored supposedly binding results, or in a few cases allowed opt-outs from the treaties in return for their being passed.

That approach to building Europe has depended on the support of national political parties placing the cause of European integration above the interests and sympathies of their traditional constituencies. Thus, as Pierre Manent has argued in a French context: the Right put 'Europe' ahead of nation, and the Left put it ahead of class. That explains the disaffection of their electorates, the rise of new parties, and the gradual retreat of the mainstream parties into grand coalitions marked by a pro-European 'fanaticism' (Manent's term) that hopes the electorate will eventually consent to what is imposed on it in the form of 'More Europe.' Not only did the political upheavals above emerge in response to this 'authoritarian' form of politics, but the 'populist' form they took was an expression of liberal democracy rather than an attack on it.

In a penultimate chapter Applebaum returns to America to find this same conflict between those with an abiding faith in 'American Exceptionalism'—America as both a shining city on a hill and a militant democratic missionary to the world—and those who cling to darker images of the United States as a corrupt, decadent, brutal, greedy, and hypocritical power—erected on class, race, creed, or some other domination; a fallen nation as unworthy as any other behind a veil of high ideals. The first camp contains Thomas Jefferson, Abraham Lincoln, Martin Luther King, Jr, Ronald Reagan, and Michael Gerson, Bill Kristol, and Mitt Romney; the second, and more heterogeneous, camp includes Emma Goldman, the Weathermen, Howard Zinn, Franklin Graham, Eric Metaxas, Pat Buchanan, Laura Ingraham, Roger Kimball, and of course Donald Trump. Does this seem an unfair summary of her case? Here is her account of how this camp gave succour to Pat Buchanan and birth to Trump:

By 2016, some of the arguments of the old Marxist Left—their hatred of ordinary, bourgeois politics and their longing for revolutionary change—met and mingled with the Christian right's despair about the future of American democracy. Together, they produced the restorative nostalgic campaign rhetoric of Donald Trump.

Now, even if the president's campaign rhetoric is overheated or Buchanan's pessimism extreme, shouldn't we ask other questions of them first? When Trump says that American institutions such as the FBI leadership are corrupt, shouldn't we ask: 'Is that true?' And if the FBI leadership has conspired to spy on his campaign to portray him falsely as a Russian 'asset' would not that excuse some overheated rhetoric from him? And if Buchanan laments the loss of the 'popular culture that undergirded the values of faith, family, and country, the idea that we Americans are a people who sacrifice and suffer together, and go forward together, the mutual respect, the sense of limits, the good manners; *all are gone*' (emphasis added), shouldn't we ask not only 'Is it true?' (it seems to be so) but also 'Why is he saying that?' For there is a difference between criticism, however nostalgic, that is meant to shame, improve, and reform, and criticism intended to defeat or overturn. A little exaggeration in the former might not be a bad thing.

That is an obvious distinction, of course, but suddenly it is also a relevant one for Applebaum as least as much as for Buchanan. For there is now a third team in American politics. Certainly, the current upsurge of Woke antinomianism and anarchy, fuelled by a racist anti-racism, is a sorrowful challenge for Buchanan. But is it any less of one for Applebaum? Reverence for the Constitution of the United States is integral both to his cultural loyalty and to her propositional patriotism. That cannot be said of the Black Lives Matter movement, or of Antifa, or of the Woke Ivy League graduates who now staff the newsrooms, NGOs, law firms, corporate boardrooms, courts, and bureaucratic agencies of the United States. Their vision of America is of one of systemic racism whose institutions of white supremacy must be overthrown and replaced, like the statues of Abraham Lincoln and William Wilberforce who until recently were heroes to all races. And many of them are her friends and professional colleagues.

It is early days but another vista of broken and renewed friendships may be opening up. Will Anne Applebaum be making new ex-friends? Or making up with old ones?

This review of Anne Applebaum's Twilight of Democracy: The Seductive Lure of Authoritarianism *(Doubleday, 2020) 224 pp., was originally published in the* Claremont Review of Books*, Vol XX, No. 4, Fall 2020, 31–34, https://claremontreviewofbooks.com/ex-friends/.*

Goodbye to All That:
An Original Eurosceptic Looks Back
An Overview of the Long History Leading up to Brexit
3 February 2020

As the amiably vulgar crowds of Brexiteers sang in loud celebration under Nigel Farage's beaming approval in Parliament Square (to the puritan disapproval of *The Independent*'s Tom Peck: a 'knuckle-dragging carnival of the irredeemably stupid,' retweeted by historian Simon Schama as 'brilliant'), I was at a small private celebration in a Budapest restaurant with my American wife, Irish writer "cousin," and a Swiss friend raising glasses of delicious Hungarian fizz to the recovery of Britain's democratic sovereignty.

Other Eurosceptics have testified to feeling a slight sense of anti-climax as the moment came. It was indeed a little like New Year's Eve—we had known this night was coming for a long time, we wanted it to happen, but the next morning we would be starting on a different and perhaps tougher work schedule rather than a vacation. That said, we would be independent contractors rather than salaried employees.

My own feeling, however, was not so much that I was embarking on a new task as that I was laying down an old one. I first became a Brexiteer (or, as we were then confusingly known, an 'anti-Marketeer,' because the European Union, then the European Economic Community, or EEC, was known colloquially as the Common Market) in the late 1960s. The Tories were then the pro-Europe party in substance even though all parties were formally undecided. In the course of attending discussions of the Tory leadership on the EEC (as a junior aide, I hasten to add), I reached the heretical conclusion that the economic case for 'joining Europe' was weak and the case against surrendering our sovereignty to do so was therefore strong. In the 1970 election, in which

I stood as a Tory candidate for Gateshead West, I stressed the conditional nature of our manifesto pledge on Europe: 'Our commitment is to negotiate, no more, no less.' My Euroscepticism was firming up.

Not that anyone gives a damn about what a first-time Tory candidate in a safe Labour seat thinks about anything. As the party professionals say in their wisdom, a parliamentary candidate is 'just a bloody legal necessity.' Thus Britain joined the EEC in 1973, despite my opposition, and was then faced with a referendum in 1975 on whether to confirm or reject the (now defeated) Tory government's handiwork. By then I had risen to a far more influential position in the Tory world: I was an editorial and parliamentary correspondent in *The Daily Telegraph*, an independent paper known colloquially as "The Torygraph" since the Tory faithful bought it and the Tory leadership had to take its editorial advice into account.

Also, I was among the relatively few active Tories who had bucked the official party line and campaigned for a No vote in the hapless anti-Market effort. I had spoken to the voters and I knew we were doomed.

On 4 June 1975, therefore, I sat down at my clattering typewriter in the *Telegraph* offices and embarked on a melancholy task. As one of the minority of editorial writers opposed to EEC membership, I had been asked by editor Bill Deedes to write a light account of the referendum campaign that would appear on the morning of the vote. Bill said he wanted my squib to offset the solemnity of the editorial, but my suspicion was that he was a secret No voter who wanted it to offset *The Telegraph*'s stern admonition to vote Yes. And he may have been right. In its small way that squib was the modest beginning of the *Telegraph*'s Euroscepticism, which has since played a big part in achieving Brexit— the full story of which is told in *The Telegraph* itself.[1]

In principle, Bill could have ordered a No editorial, but pressure from the establishment for an endorsement of Britain's EU membership was so overwhelming in 1975 that it would have seemed eccentric,

---

[1] Tim Stanley, 'How *The Telegraph*'s Battle for Brexit Began in the Early 1990s,' *The Telegraph*, 1 February 2020, www.telegraph.co.uk/politics/2020/02/01/telegraphs-battle-brexit-began-early-90s/.

unpatriotic, even treasonable. So I read through "the files" of the previous month's campaigning and started bashing out the piece:

From the Establishment and the respectable anti-Establishment, from *The Economist* and *The New Statesman,* from Lord Feather [of the Trades Union Congress] and Mr Campbell Adamson [of the Confederation of British Industry], from Prime Ministers Wilson (Labour) and Heath (Tory), from the Royal Commission Volunteers to 'Actors and Actresses for Europe,' from the farthest reaches of the civilized West End, the same advice, the same dire predictions of life outside the Market ('God, it was hell out there in 1972'), the same comforting assurances of a bright future inside, less ecstatic admittedly than similar forecasts before we had entered ('Come in, come in, the water's lukewarm' was their newer message) have been proclaimed with an almost religious fervour.

Religion itself had been conscripted for the European cause. The Bishop of London, preaching in St Paul's, had said that those concerned about sovereignty were guilty of the heresy 'My country, right or wrong,' which was 'essentially selfish and inward-looking.' Big Business spoke with one voice: the CBI's Ralph Bateman declared that it would be 'madness' to leave the EEC, and Mr Barrie Heath told the workers at the engineering company, Guest, Keen and Nettlefolds that membership in the EEC was not a political issue at all. It was a simple matter of economic and industrial efficiency.

'Is he Sir Barrie?' asked Enoch Powell, the leading Tory campaigner for a No vote. 'No? Well, he soon will be.' He was, too—given a knighthood three years later 'for services to exporting.'

If the Yes campaigners looked like a group of "suits" who had just emerged from too good a lunch at the Savoy, the Noes seemed to be an odd blend of Left and Right eccentrics in denims and hunting pink, respectively. But the Left—above all, its favourite, Tony Benn—predominated. After he left frontline politics, Benn morphed into a lovable British eccentric, with his mug of tea and his nostalgic lectures on workers' control, but at the time he was seen by Middle England as its main enemy on the Left. Dominic Sandbrook recently cited my old joke in his social history of Britain in the 1970s: 'Mr Benn often complains that the press and television are biased against the anti-Marketeers. And he is absolutely right. They keep on reporting him.'

As a result of this unbalanced campaign, the British people were being pushed to stay in this modernizing New Europe in the resigned spirit of 'If you know of a better airport lounge, go to it.' My article, however, ended with a warning: 'In supporting Europe, the entire British establishment has put all its money on one horse—admittedly the favourite. But what if, like most of the establishment's fancied runners in the last twenty years, it comes in fourth?'

Not that I would ever dream of saying 'I told you so,' but that is exactly what happened. Leaders in all the main political and cultural institutions had told themselves a number of defeatist stories to justify breaking their previous loyalties and surrendering an ever-growing share of their own freedom of action: Suez had demonstrated the shrinkage of Britain's independent role as a world power; the Commonwealth was no help in arresting our own decline; we needed the cold bath of economic competition to wake ourselves up—and that would be provided by unimpeded access to the European market that had enabled EEC members to grow more rapidly than Britain in the previous two decades. Underlying these soliloquies was a feeling that Britain could only overcome this declinism by merging itself into a larger world power. As a critic of that attitude, Enoch Powell, said in the late sixties when Britain was still hesitating: 'Their message is: We were big once. We want to be big again.'

Yet, even at the time, none of these arguments really withstood sceptical examination. Consider each one:

- If the country needed a cold bath of competition, it could have obtained that more thoroughly by adopting free trade with the world rather than by joining a Europe cosseted by a common external tariff.

- No country, even the United States, had untrammelled power, as the Vietnam War had just established. But the British had defeated the Malayan Communists ten years earlier and were about to see off the Indonesians in the largely unreported Borneo

War. They had no real reason to reproach themselves for lacking power and influence internationally.

- Furthermore, the real source of British decline lay in the inefficiency of British industry and the excessive power of the trade unions. Membership in the EEC would do nothing about that. Indeed, for both Labour and pre-Thatcher Tories, 'Europe' was a way of evading that truth rather than tackling it. Europe would do what we feared to do ourselves, they argued, but no one could ever explain how.

- The British Commonwealth had its limitations, but Britain was Australia's largest single trading and investment partner in the early 1960s until EEC membership explicitly set out to reduce that trade through quotas.

- Above all, though full access to a larger European market would indeed be a benefit to Britain, this was overstated as a factor in Europe's post-war growth. At least as important was the move from low-productivity jobs in agriculture to high-productivity jobs in industry on the continent after 1945. But the British economy had made that transition between 1870 and 1945. We could not get the same benefit twice.

All these factors soon became academic, however. No sooner had Britain confirmed its EEC membership in the 1975 referendum than Europe stopped growing. The benefits of an expanded market that were supposed to follow British entry failed to arrive on schedule or at all. Europe itself went into a long sleep of stagflation. And the Brits fell deeper into the Slough of Despond, until four years later they reached its lowest point in the Winter of Discontent, when strikes spread over Britain like the coronavirus these days. It took the arrival of Margaret Thatcher to restore strength and prosperity to Britain by the only method that works—creating the framework of financial and economic stability that enables people and industries to save themselves by their own efforts.

For most of the next decade, therefore, the EEC as a political issue faded into the background as Thatcher's fight to revive Britain through her own efforts ('her' referring here to both Britain and Thatcher) dominated life and politics. Britain's relationship with the EEC was structured mainly around the attempts of the new prime minister to get a large British budgetary rebate from Brussels to compensate for the fact that the EEC budget was structurally biased against the Brits, who paid in a lot but got little back because 40 per cent of EEC spending was on agriculture. 'Europe' came back into the headlines after 1986, however, as a result of three developments: Thatcherite Britain recovered economically to become the world's fourth largest economy; the EEC adopted a single market, in which regulatory 'harmonization' in Brussels replaced the principle that all EEC members would mutually recognize one another's standards; and the Left in Brussels and Britain saw that this harmonization, enforced on the principle of 'a level playing field,' would give Brussels the power to control everything that moved across the continent. And Brussels was not a Tory city.

Jacques Delors, newly chosen as the EU Commission president, told the British labour unions this good news in a famous 1988 speech. Within ten years, he said, 80 per cent of economic and social legislation would be determined by Europe. And within a very short time, the Labour Party and the unions had switched sides to become strongly Europhile. Most Tories took longer to realize that the balance of political advantage of the European issue had changed, but it was always likely that a Tory government presiding over a booming deregulated economy would resist a Brussels takeover run by a socialist. Thatcher responded to Delors only two months later, in what became known as the Bruges Speech (drafted by her close adviser and personal friend Charles Powell, who was a moderate Eurosceptic). Here is its most famous passage: 'We have not successfully rolled back the frontiers of the state in Britain, only to see them re-imposed at a European level with a European super-state exercising a new dominance from Brussels.'

Not all Tories, nor all cabinet ministers, were happy with this open and robust resistance, however, and for the next two years a quiet civil war spread across the party, fought over Europe and issues related to it. They wanted quiet diplomacy and compromise with Berlin, Paris, and Brussels. Having served in Downing Street for two years as a special adviser to the prime minister, I had moved to the US in 1988 to edit

National Review. From there I returned to London, to write speeches for her, most of which had Bruges-type passages, from time to time. I had a ringside seat, therefore, from which to observe the growing divide between Thatcher, supported by the party faithful, and the majority of her Cabinet, supported by what has to be called elite opinion over European policy. That reached a climax when she rejected moves at the EU summit in Rome to move toward far greater Euro-integration, political, and economic, and returned to London to face a crisis. Foreign Secretary Geoffrey Howe resigned; former Defence Secretary (and fierce Europhiliac) Michael Heseltine stood against her in a leadership election; she failed to get the necessary super-majority ... and returned from the Paris conference in celebration of the end of the Cold War to face the second round of the leadership election.

In New York, I had written some passages for the prime minister to deliver the next day in a speech responding to a Labour motion of no confidence and boarded a plane for London. In London, one minister after another was undermining her will to fight on by telling her she was already as good as defeated. When I got off the plane, she had already announced her intention to resign, delivered a humdinger of a speech in Parliament, and sent me an invitation to Downing Street for a drink the day after. That party of old friends and advisers from the early Thatcher years onward was one of those odd occasions in which feelings of tragedy and sadness are dissipated in a catharsis of wit and hilarity. I do not know when I have felt sadder or laughed more.

But I went on from there to address a meeting of the Bruges Group, formed to advance the Tory Eurosceptic cause, that had been arranged months before. To my surprise, I found that although they were saddened by the prime minister's departure, they did not think it would significantly change the drift of government policy toward a looser relationship with Europe. I tried to make their flesh creep by pointing out that she had been ousted because of—in large measure—her militant Euroscepticism and that two of her three potential successors were strong Europhiles. As it turned out, the third was John Major, who turned out to be as Europhiliac as Heseltine. Of the five prime ministers since Thatcher, four have been almost equally so (though sometimes in light disguise). By means of occasional anti-Brussels rhetoric without consequence, successive Tory leaders were able to keep the restive Brexiteer majority of their grassroots supporters under control until Nigel Farage invented two Leave parties in succession in order to give right-wing voters a genuinely Eurosceptic party to vote for.

That was vital. But would it have been enough if the intellectual case had not been made in the years since Thatcher's defenestration? Former chancellor Norman Lamont has said recently that he thought that in 1993 he might have been the first frontline politician to suggest that Britain might actually leave the EU rather than try, always ineffectually, to reform-cum-liberalize it. I think he is right and that his isolation in challenging such an intellectually challengeable institution as the EU is a marker of the astounding groupthink that has gripped cultural, media, and political elites in the West right up to the recent Tory election victory. And though Lamont was the first serving major politician to challenge that groupthink, he was building on the interventions in the European debate that Thatcher continued to make in the two decades after she left office.

Along with Robin Harris, another Thatcher aide and later the author of a biography of the lady that took no equivocating prisoners, I was fortunate enough to work with the former prime minister both when she was writing her memoirs and when she wanted to make speeches on especially important topics. Ever the scholarship girl, she used those occasions to develop a soundly based analysis of subjects as important and as different as the euro and the relationship between Russia and the West. All her speeches are available at margaretthatcher.org, but to see her views on the European issue in the round, look at both the Bruges Speech she gave in government and her speech at The Hague not long after she left it. But the speech that probably best represents her growing influence on the issue is her 1992 speech to the World Economic Development Conference in the US. I recall that speech well. She had invited Robin and me to help with its writing in the British Embassy in Washington. As so often with a Thatcher speech, the writing continued well into the small hours. She retired about 3:30 a.m. We did some editorial cleaning up on the computer, and at about 5:00 a.m. we let ourselves out of the embassy onto Massachusetts Avenue. No taxis were to be had. We schlepped our cases about a mile down to the hotel on Dupont Circle to catch a few hours' sleep.

But we were re-energized by the speech's reception the next day. It was delivered just after Britain had been forced out of the European Exchange Realignment Mechanism, which she had never liked, had been forced by political weakness to join shortly before losing office, and had criticized as trapping the pound at too high a rate and inflicting a recession on the economy. Crashing out of the ERM confirmed these fears, and her speech was interpreted by the media as an 'elegant I told you so.'

As others have pointed out, however, notably Tom McTague at *The Atlantic*, that speech looked forward to future European controversies as well as back to the ERM. In particular, Thatcher warned of the consequences if a single European currency were to be introduced, as it was eight years later: 'Huge sums would have to be transferred from richer to poorer countries and regions to allow them to take the strain. Even then, unemployment and mass migration across now-open frontiers would follow. And a full-fledged single currency would allow no escape hatch.' She then laid out the political consequences, too:

> [T]he growth of extremist parties, battening on fears about mass immigration and unemployment, offering a real—if thoroughly unwelcome—alternative to the Euro-centrist political establishment. If, in addition, you were to create a supranational European federation, and the people could no longer hold their national parliaments to account, extremism could only grow further.

McTague remarks that this was a remarkably prescient speech. It was more than prescient, moreover, because these arguments not only kept alive the Eurosceptic case in the 1990s, they later injected it with performance-enhancing drugs when the euro crisis, the Greek crisis, the migration crisis, the rise of populism, and the collapse of centre-left and centre-right parties altered the political landscape in the twenty-teens. We read the runes of those crises more intelligently because Thatcher had explained them in advance. In her accurate prediction of how the country would respond to escaping from the ERM, did she perhaps also predict the likely response of Britain to Brexit?

The histrionics of this time will soon be forgotten. The benefits will be increasingly appreciated. Dire warnings of what will happen when the economic straitjacket is removed will quickly prove false. The patient may perhaps wave his arms around a bit at first. He may even make a noise. But his odd behaviour reflects the torture of the straitjacket, not an inherent disordered condition. And the long-concealed truth quickly dawns that this patient was perfectly sane all the time.

I think so; we will know in time. For the moment, however, I am inclined to think of Brexit as Mrs Thatcher's last victory and the fulfilment of Thatcherism. In the final stage of her career she reached Eurosceptic conclusions on the euro and more broadly, in her retirement, on Britain's European commitment. She took time to do so. As a practical politician, she was always a work in progress, feeling her way in new policy areas, but as she grew more confident on an issue, making judgments that were generally consistent with all her other political instincts. The more she encountered the EU, the more suspicious of it she became. It seemed to her to concentrate the centralizing and levelling passions in one vast bureaucratic machine insensitive to the sovereignty of nations and to the aspirations of citizens. Above all, she believed it simply did not suit the British who had grown up under different institutions and with a different social outlook.

Some years ago, I was asked by an Italian political conference to assess how history would judge Margaret Thatcher on Europe. I replied that she would prove to be either ahead of her party or behind history. If Brexit occurred successfully, then Thatcherism would be seen as the start of a new phase of British history, leading either to an adventurous independent English nationalism in the style of (though in very different circumstances from) Elizabethan England or perhaps to a renewed closeness to the countries of the Anglosphere straddling the world. If Britain voted to remain in Europe, Thatcher would seem to have been behind history, and Thatcherism would look like a glorious last stand by Old England, the England that more or less invented classical liberalism in 1689, before it was subsumed into a collective European non-identity.

In either event, she deserved well of the people she governed for eleven years. Without her, they would have been given no choice in the matter.

As Brexit turned out, she proved to be ahead both of her party and of history, and can truly now rest in peace.

As for myself, I feel a sense of relief as well as of satisfaction. In much of my writing life, both as a "ghost" and as a commentator in my own voice, I have been devoted to arguing for a self-governing democratic Britain, first as a member of a loose and lightly regulated Europe and, when that possibility was ruled out by a persistent Brussels majority, as an ex-member of the EU. That second possibility has now been achieved, and I think securely so. There will still be alarms and excursions about our future trading relationship with the EU, and the government can be confidently expected to make other blunders along the way. But I really do not see the country being persuaded to rejoin the EU under any dispensation. But reporting and analysing those controversies I can leave with perfect confidence to my colleagues such as Madeleine Kearns and Michael Brendan Dougherty, who have done such a tremendous job of covering the final days of European Britain. That burden has now been lifted from my shoulders. I must turn, quite happily, to other concerns.

But to what exactly? Well, they tell me that some interesting things have been happening in the United States. It seems unlikely, but I will give it a shot.

Originally published in National Review*, 3 February 2020, www.nationalreview.com/2020/02/brexit-goodbye-to-all-that-early-eurosceptic-and-thatcher-aide-looks-back/#slide-1.*

Brexit: The Movie
10 January 2020

A British film about the referendum portrays brilliantly the political currents that shocked the UK's ruling class. *Brexit*—or, in the UK, *Brexit: The Uncivil War*—is now showing on HBO. I started watching it at 12:30 a.m. two nights ago and, inevitably, I continued doing so until well after 2:00 a.m. I strongly urge even those who think they are thoroughly bored with Brexit in the real world to search for it. My own amateur view—Kyle Smith, please stop reading here—is that it is the best political movie since *The Manchurian Candidate* (1962).

Of course, it is somewhat more realistic. It has a clever and witty screenplay by one of Britain's best new playwrights, James Graham, who has made a specialty of plays and screenplays about politics and who, though neither a Tory nor a Brexiteer, is not possessed by the vitriolic hatred of both groups that disables most minds in theatre and television. Its director, Toby Haynes, moves it along at a cracking pace that is nonetheless never confusing. And it contains mostly good and some outstanding performances, in particular Rory Kinnear (familiar from Bond movies) as the Remain campaign's chief strategist, Craig Oliver, and Benedict Cumberbatch as the Leave campaign's presiding genius, Dominic Cummings, now installed at 10 Downing Street as Boris Johnson's main adviser.

Their rivalry is played out in several scenes that show how Cummings's discovery through data mining of a new kind of voter—one alienated from politics who has not voted before—gradually undermines Oliver's strategy of appealing to blocs of regular voters with known preferences and more-predictable reactions. Cummings arouses the sleeping abstainers, who feel that political parties ignore and despise them, with a message that they can recover the democratic power they once had by bringing it back from Brussels to Westminster. His slogan is a brilliantly simple one: 'Take Back Control.'

Two fictional scenes in particular show this. In one, Cummings is listening to voters tell of how their district has fallen into decay as its industries moved away when he hears their complaints in his head as if they were a loud subterranean sound growing in volume. Sensing something important and trying to grasp it, he gets up, leaves the house, walks into the street, and puts his head wonderingly to the roadside. It lacks only the proper soundtrack. In the second scene, a frustrated Oliver intervenes in a focus group to explain to one of Cummings's alienated voters that she does not understand what is really at stake, only for her to break down, experiencing his arguments as the familiar condescension of political elites deaf to her feelings and opinions.

As these scenes suggest, *Brexit* the television movie greatly (and necessarily) simplifies the ball of wool tangled with a spider's web that was the Brexit campaign in real life. By narrowing its vision to the battle between the two official campaigns and their leading figures, it either ignores or downgrades the importance of the main political figures on both sides and the influence of the print and broadcast media. Among those who get short shrift from the movie are Prime Minister David Cameron (he is there as a voice on the phone), Boris Johnson, Michael Gove, Daniel Hannan, and Nigel Farage—the last two in particular could sue for libel. Both played brave and important roles, first in getting a Brexit referendum called, then in pushing it over the finish line (or lines, since others were drawn after the result). In this telling they are reduced respectively to an amiable sidekick of the Cummings campaign and a loudmouthed and bigoted clown on the sidelines. But that is less wounding than it might be, since all the characters play second or even third fiddle, either to Cummings or to Oliver.

Their relationship to each other is a more subtle one. Cummings is the winner of the referendum and the hero of the screenplay. Played by Cumberbatch as a flamboyantly autistic loner, he dominates the movie whenever he is on the screen. The scene where he is summoned by the Leave campaign board to be fired, only to reverse the coup and fire the campaign chairman instead, is a political anorak's daydream (an anorak, named after the type's favourite garment, is someone who is obsessive and anti-social). Oliver is played by Kinnear with a kind of decent but baffled charisma that reflects the screenplay's own sympathies—not altogether surprisingly, since he was the film's technical adviser. Oliver may lose the referendum, but he wins its interpretation here. In a fictional scene, the two men meet just before voting day over a drink. Both agree that Cummings has aroused spirits from the vasty deep that now rampage through the land with, as Oliver warns, dangerously unpredictable results. A final scene apparently endorses that warning. Appearing before an investigative committee of some kind, Cummings concedes that the referendum has unleashed political chaos, disorder, and irresponsibility but blames it on the failure of the politicians to make good use of the popular (and populist) energies now in politics.

Since I am about to argue that *Brexit: The Uncivil War* gets one very important thing wrong, let me begin by mentioning two things (missed by most political commentators at the time) it gets damn right, and one it gets half-right. First, it clearly identifies the essential clash in the referendum: Remain argued that Brexit would mean economic disaster; Leave argued that rejecting Brexit would definitively entrench Britain's loss of sovereignty to Brussels. It was prosperity versus sovereignty—as simple as that—and sovereignty won. The voters took back control. That result was unexpected in part because the media shared the Remain view that sovereignty was a fake issue and were as slow as Oliver in reacting to it. Neither they nor Remain ever developed an effective counter to Take Back Control. It proved to be a crucial weakness. Second, the film realizes as it follows Cummings's own voyage of discovery that the Brexit outcome was the result neither of an internal Tory manoeuvre to keep its Eurosceptic backbenchers happy nor of Russian cyber-warfare, nor even of mysterious data manipulation financed by American billionaires (though it flirts with the last temptation). That outcome had been gradually building for decades. When I looked at opinion-poll surveys from the first Euro-referendum onward, I found that voters who wanted to leave the EU had been a settled, substantial minority all the time from 1975 to 2016, rising in later years to a plurality. Cummings did not invent the alienated voter; he discovered how numerous that voter was and set out to contact him. Given the 52–48 split result between

Leavers and Remainers, the millions of forgotten voters provided more than the winning margin.

But the third point—which is also the movie's endpoint, where Cummings concedes that he has stirred up dangerous passions leading to irresponsible and unstable politics—is an accurate picture of the situation except in two respects: it misidentifies the impassioned mobs creating chaos and mistakes a short period of political realignment for a permanent political disorder.

It is, in a word, dated. That is not a sneer but a precise criticism. The film's seemingly final outcome describes Britain's politics from July 2017, when Theresa May lost the Tory majority in Parliament, to December 12, 2019, when Boris Johnson won a majority of 80. In those 29 months, the MPs in all parties who privately opposed Brexit—a shifting majority, larger or smaller depending on circumstance and how far party discipline had broken down — gradually came to think that they could dilute or defeat Brexit by parliamentary tactics and legal manoeuvres. They were supported in these aims by a majority of the House of Lords and, outside Parliament, by the BBC, industry, the City of London, the labour unions, the universities, *The Economist*, the *Financial Times*, *The Times*, *The Guardian*, most pundits and political correspondents, and a large majority of the Great and Good in establishment bodies. And the expectation in all these circles—the Remainer narrative, you might say—was that this impressive coalition was likely to prevail and to restore a more civilized order to politics. It was during these months that the film was written, produced, and in January 2019 released in the UK.

But what happened as 2019 proceeded turned these expectations on their heads. Turmoil, instability, the breaking of rules, and a bonfire of precedents occurred almost daily, but it was on the Remainer side that these unruly passions held sway. The Commons speaker openly abandoned impartiality and issued rulings hostile to Brexit that his expert clerk advisers warned strongly against. With his connivance, a shifting cross-party coalition of backbenchers seized control of the parliamentary agenda to compel government actions for which they were not constitutionally accountable. Cabinet ministers voted against government measures, thereby violating the rule of collective responsibility, but remained in office. The House of Lords threw aside its deference to the democratic lower house and blocked Brexit legislation. If there was a mob to be seen, it was one clad in ermine robes and lawyers' wigs. The net effect was a growing public dissatisfaction with a 'Remainer Parliament' that seemed to promise parliamentary chicanery and political instability without end—or at least until an election, which most MPs fearfully opposed.

How did the sweaty masses on the Leave side respond to this? They remained impressively stable and responsible in their commitment to leaving the EU. The opinion polls registered only minor shifts between the two voting blocs. And their specifically political reactions were a model of democracy from Civics 101. On the Tory side, junior ministers resigned from office, 118 Tory backbenchers voted no confidence in Theresa May, and activists in the country responded to the May government's proposed withdrawal agreement by passing resolutions calling on ministers to change policy. Labour's Leave minority, mainly in blue-collar constituencies, had fewer effective means of protest in a party drifting toward Remain. They resisted the drift, resenting especially that their party was opposing a democratic mandate, but Labour was leaving them socially and ideologically.

Then Nigel Farage gave Brexiteers in all parties a vehicle for protest when he founded the Brexit party and won the largest vote share in the European elections, reducing the Tories to 8 per cent and Labour to a hardly much better 17 per cent. All these developments unsettled "tribal" party loyalties and speeded up what was starting to look like a realignment. Threatened by a national Tory vote of no confidence, May resigned. Boris Johnson then won the Tory leadership, formed a government united on a Brexit platform, expelled hardened anti-Brexit rebels, and demanded a general election to overcome the parliamentary stalemate. Jeremy Corbyn was dragged, equivocating heroically, into endorsing a second referendum and losing the workers. And, yielding in part to a public desire to get Brexit over (as much as done), Labour and the Lib-Dems capitulated to pressure from Boris and voted for an election that the Tories won handsomely.

All the events listed in the two paragraphs above happened after the Brexit film was released. They paint a slightly different picture from the film's conclusion; for starters, rather than responding grumpily to a committee of political critics, Dominic Cummings is sitting in Downing Street drawing up plans for the reorganization of the civil service. Instead of an atmosphere of chaos and instability, there is a widespread sense (which may turn out to be illusory—we cannot foresee the future) that the period between the 2017 and 2019 elections was not turbulent without meaning but the start of a necessary political realignment: the new wine of Leave and Remain is being poured into the old bottles of Tory and Labour (where the old wine increasingly tasted complex but sour).

A strong democratic impulse, liberated by the Brexit surprise, has defeated a ruthless antidemocratic resistance without resorting to its opponents' procedural trickeries. And the size of that victory has persuaded all but the most fanatical of those opponents to accept their defeat while seeking to make it as tolerable as possible for them and their causes. As a result, we have a very paradoxical situation: a stable Tory government with a strong majority presides with apparent comfort over a politics in ferment—workers going right, lawyers moving left, 'Blue Labour' theorists seeing the Tories as the party of labour (which Labour has abandoned to embrace workless welfare instead), democracy ceasing to be everybody's favourite goddess since we no longer agree on what she looks like, nationalists in Scotland demanding to be ruled from Brussels because London is too remote to care, bitter battles between "traditional" feminists and transgender activists … and any number of other novelties.

To these post-Brexit political trends I will return. But you can find a thorough discussion of Boris's victory and its likely consequences between Tim Montgomerie, the founder of the website *Conservative Home,* and me at www.youtube.com/watch?v=rPAgn7iFjBc.

Meanwhile, as Wolcott Gibbs concluded his *Time* magazine parody in *The New Yorker*: where it all will end, knows God.

Originally published in National Review, *10 January 2020,* *www.nationalreview.com/2020/01/brexit-the-movie/.*

'Rule Britannia!'—For the BBC
It Is Not a Song of Praise
29 August 2020

In my Thursday column on the many faces of revolution, there is a walk-on part for 'Rule Britannia' which is at present provoking Britain's progressive establishment into one of its periodical fits of Woke morality. These fits are occurring more frequently these days both because more and more traditional institutions from the British Museum to the National Trust are falling into Woke hands, and because ordinary people are noticing that their culture and entertainments are being made to conform to progressive priorities and expressing an opposite irritation in response. On this occasion a row burst forth when it was announced that the traditional performance of 'Rule Britannia' on the 'last night of the Proms'—i.e., the BBC's annual summer Promenade Concerts—would not take place because its lyrics were boastful, xenophobic, vulgar, etc., etc.

Now, the first thing to be said about this row is that when clever people do silly things, they contrive to be far sillier than any normal bloody fool could manage naturally. The second—and vitally important—thing to say is that the BBC can claim a matchless record of musical excellence in supporting and staging the Proms at the Albert Hall (and other musical venues in London) since 1927. Originally founded by Sir Henry Wood in the 1890s, the concerts are six weeks of great music by fine orchestras at cheap prices in London's late summer. Wood himself was a great conductor who founded the Proms on the following principle: 'I am going to run nightly concerts and train the public by easy stages. Popular at first, gradually raising the standard until I have created a public for classical and modern music.'

He succeeded brilliantly. He had some distinguished predecessors, including Sir Arthur Sullivan (of whom more later), but Wood managed to keep his concerts a permanent summer fixture with the help of a string of private benefactors until in 1927 the BBC stepped in to provide them with a permanent benefactor too. Ever since, scrupulously titling them the 'Sir Henry Wood Promenade Concerts,' the BBC has done English music, indeed all music, proud.

Now, what went wrong here? It is hard to be precise, because most of the discussion has been conducted via anonymous leaks to the press, some of which are then retracted anonymously when they prove to have misread the public mood. It was shamefully put about, for instance, that the Finnish lady conductor, Dalia Stasevska, who was to conduct the Last Night had objected to 'Rule Britannia' on the grounds of its inappropriate patriotism and requested it be dropped. That inspired indignant media articles and angry messages to her private email address (probably on the lines of 'Go Back to Finnishry'), whereupon it was re-leaked that she had raised no objection at all. No one else has stepped forward to claim authorship of the decision, and there may be some justice in that. It sounds like one of those decisions, common in corporate life, that are taken by osmosis:

> 'This social distancing thing ... might be a good way of, er, reforming the Last Night of the Proms.'
> 'Reforming? Ah, I see what you mean ... no audience participation ... all done virtually ... No, er ...'
> 'No singing ... no flag-waving ... no Rule ... yes, that sort of thing.'
> 'Purely for medical reasons, of course.'
> 'Of course, we don't want to be irresponsible.'
> 'Well, we seem to be agreed. No need for a vote, wouldn't you say? Next item, that documentary proposal on did Jane Austen have her own slave ... isn't this rather old hat?'

Some support for this view of things is provided by Catriona Lewis, the producer of the BBC's Sunday night programme of hymns and religious music, *Songs of Praise*. She wrote an indignant tweet about the song 'Rule Britannia' which ran: 'Do those Brits who believe it's OK to sing an eighteenth-century song about never being enslaved, written when the UK was enslaving and killing millions of innocents, also believe it's appropriate for neo-Nazis to shout, "We will never be forced into a gas chamber."' And she added, 'Slavery was Britain's holocaust.'

Context is needed here. 'Rule Britannia' was written in 1740 when slavery was a near-universal institution worldwide. It had not existed in England since the thirteenth century, but Britons were frequently captured by raiding Barbary pirates, with Devon and Cornwall especially badly hit, and sold as slaves in the vast slave markets of North Africa. More than one million Europeans were enslaved in this way over 200 years. It was a major political topic in the countries concerned; charities were founded to buy back their enslaved compatriots; and both Britain and the United States launched raids to free captives and punish pirates. All this went on fitfully until 1824 when a British fleet bombarded Algiers and 1830 when the French conquered Algeria.

Slavery was not just something that the Brits, like everyone else, did, it was also something that they suffered too. So it was natural that they should celebrate the fact that as a nation with growing power 'they never, never, never shall be slaves.' That helped to feed a growing national sentiment that slavery was a great evil rather than simply a profitable business and that Britain's participation in the slave trade was accordingly a great disgrace.

Abolitionism was the great idealistic cause of British politics in the eighteenth and nineteenth centuries, fuelled by a mixture of Protestant Christianity and national pride. In 1777, Lord Mansfield ruled that a slave visiting England (as it happens, from America) became free by breathing English air and could not be forced back into servitude. Pitt the Younger, as prime minister, was an early political ally of the Abolitionists, urging that since Britain had dominated the Atlantic slave trade, so it had a special duty to outlaw it. The Anti-Slavery Society in London ran what was the first human-rights campaign in history by distributing a medallion that showed a black man in chains and the words 'Am I not a Man and a Brother?' It was worn on lapels, as bracelets, and as a blend of declaration and decoration, it spread the message of abolition throughout the world. At the Congress of Vienna in 1815, Lord

Castlereagh, the British foreign secretary, insisted on a clause in its treaty committing all the signatory powers to end slavery. That itself was a major step in international law. Meanwhile, successive Acts of Parliament from 1807 to 1833 ended slavery throughout the British Empire, and as the Empire kept expanding in the nineteenth century in Africa and the East Indies, it brought slavery to an end in those countries too. Above all, the Royal Navy's West Africa squadron was established in 1808 to patrol the Atlantic and to halt the slave trade by military force. Between its foundation and 1867, it seized 1,600 slave ships and freed 150,000 Africans. An estimated 1,587 sailors died on what was a notoriously dangerous posting between 1830 and 1865.

So the Brits delivered more than 'Rule Britannia' promised: it was not only Brits who never would be slaves but anyone living under British rule or on the high seas. It was, moreover, a peculiarly *national* achievement. In order to buy the slaves their freedom peacefully, the British government raised 20 million pounds sterling in a loan on the money markets. That is 2.4 billion in today's money. The British taxpayer finally paid off the last instalment of the loan on 1 February 2015.

My conclusion is that Ms Lewis's comparison of Brits singing 'Rule Britannia' with neo-Nazis singing about being forced into gas chambers is so wide of the mark that it makes me wonder what on earth they are singing on *Songs of Praise* these days. But the malady seems to be a collective rather than an individual one. Such opinions—it would be generous to call them ideas—are almost compulsory in Wokerati circles inside and outside the BBC. And they seem to have become both acute and chronic in the last few years.

I blame Brexit. It has unsettled Remainers in the media so severely that they see threats, insults, and dangers in the lightest expression of contrary taste or opinion—jokes, songs, concert programmes, or eighteenth-century drinking songs. It has been a long time since anyone sang 'Rule Britannia' with any serious imperialist intent. Ditto 'Land of Hope and Glory.' The Last Night of the Proms is only half a serious concert. Its second half is a jolly end-of-term romp at which a succession of conductors—most famously Sir Malcolm Sargent ('Flash Harry' to his admirers) and Sir Andrew Davis—ham it up with closing speeches and the promenaders (i.e., the cheap standing seats) play games such as clapping against the grain in order to throw the orchestra off the beat.

'Rule Britannia' itself is a cheerful, rousing, quite unaggressive, popular song from a different age sung by an audience out to enjoy a good time. Is it sung ironically? No, there is an edge of hostility or subversion to irony, which is not present in the kind of pantomime atmosphere on the Last Night. Is it then patriotic? Well, it is not actually hostile to the country, which may be why it has irritated the BBC mandarins in ways they cannot quite explain. That may also be the reason why on a recent post-Brexit Last Night, some people in the audience turned up to wave European Union flags at the finale. They were mentally cancelling Brexit as best they could, by annoying those they thought were Brexit supporters. For myself I would say 'Rule Britannia' is a song of comic self-congratulation akin to a pastiche rather than a satire.

That is why the event is pretty popular with foreigners. I remember one occasion when I was a guest of Charles Crawford, the British Ambassador to Poland, at a Last Night of the Proms beamed into the concert hall from Kensington to Cracow. The mainly Polish audience, equipped with Union flags, bowler hats, and other emblems of Britishness such as umbrellas, all sang along, half-knowing, half-reading the lyrics, and waving their flags at what they guessed were appropriate intervals. After which Charles made a witty speech in praise of Polish plumbers and we all departed peacefully into the night. If you doubt something like that can happen, there is a German version of the same thing—except that this concert is not being beamed in from Kensington but performed at the Music Festival Potsdam Sanssouci where Deborah Hawkesley knocks 'em dead with zest, sex appeal, and patriotic brio.

My congratulations to Ms Hawkesley … and to her audience.

If you want a song that makes its lyrical and musical intentions, which are satirical, clear but when those intentions have themselves been subverted into purer comedy by time and events, here is 'For He Is an Englishman' from Gilbert and Sullivan's *H.M.S. Pinafore*. Gilbert's lyrics are a satire on the complacent jingoism of the Victorian middle class at a time when Britannia really did rule the waves and the Brits maybe had got a bit above ourselves. Sullivan's music satirizes the kind of musical jingoism that the BBC thinks it hears in 'Rule Britannia.' There is a version on the internet where it is sung by Australians—so you know they do not really mean it. Enjoy!

Originally published in National Review, *29 August 2020,* *www.nationalreview.com/2020/08/on-musical-jingoism/.*

From Fighting Irish Diplomat to Burke's Heir: The Brilliant Journey of Conor Cruise O'Brian

A Review of *Memoir: My Life and Themes*
by Conor Cruise O'Brien
1 December 2000

Clarissa Eden, the Prime Minister's wife, once complained during the 1956 crisis that the Suez Canal flowed through her drawing room in 10 Downing Street. Far more turbulent waterways—the Bann, the Liffey, and the Shannon—coursed through the parlour and dining room of the distinguished Irish family into which Conor Cruise O'Brien was born in 1917. As the first chapters of his memoir reveal, the young Conor was very early made aware of the gulfs separating some Irishmen from others. These naturally included the antagonism between Catholic nationalists and Protestant Unionists. But the divisions within Catholic nationalism were perhaps at least as powerful and probably more bitter. Dr O'Brien's family was divided in particular by two deep gulfs: that between constitutional nationalists and "physical force" republicans, and that between nationalists who welcomed Catholic social power and those who resisted it.

His maternal grandfather, David Sheehy, was a leading figure in the dominant Irish Parliamentary Party in the British House of Commons from 1885 until 1918. And both of his parents were firmly in the same camp of constitutional nationalists. During the 1916 Easter Rising in Dublin, however, a deranged British officer murdered his uncle, Frank Sheehy-Skeffington, a pacifist with strong republican sympathies who had come to the aid of a Catholic youth returning from Mass. Thereafter, Frank's formidable widow, Hanna, became both a symbol and propagandist for Irish republicanism, touring the United States after 1916 and lecturing on 'British Imperialism as I have known it.'

As Dr O'Brien dryly notes, this lecture probably did not include the contextual details that her father was sitting in the Imperial Parliament at the time and that her brother was legal adviser to the governor of St Kitts in the West Indies. In the independent Ireland that emerged from the Troubles, however, the fact that the Irish had been 'among the ruling peoples of the Empire' was conveniently forgotten. Constitutional nationalism was the first of many post-imperial losers. It was Hanna's republican side of the family that enjoyed social prestige and closeness to power, and the constitutional nationalists like the young Conors parents who were out in the cold.

As if that were not enough, O'Brien's father was an agnostic who specified that his son be educated in non-Catholic schools—a stipulation that his Catholic mother faithfully carried out after her husband's early death. With the Irish Catholic Church busily reshaping society in its own stern image at the time, the young Conor found himself twice suspect in unsmiling Irish eyes—once as insufficiently nationalistic, the second time as dubiously Catholic. And since his Catholicism was indeed dubious and destined to become more so, it was all the more important to him to assert his nationalism. So at his school and at Trinity College (institutions both Protestant in their foundation and Unionist in their sympathies), he went in for such gestures of Irish patriotism as remaining firmly seated when 'God Save the King' was played.

There was scant relief from such ideological turmoil at home. The young Conor seems to have been more plagued by aunts than any man since Bertie Wooster. His devoutly Catholic Aunt Mary sought to save his soul, hinting that his mother might be prolonging her husband's stay in Purgatory by educating Conor in accordance with his wishes, and his devoutly republican Aunt Hanna sought to direct his political loyalties into republicanism. Both influenced his upbringing, Hanna especially, but there seems to be a rooted impulse in O'Brien to react against any strong influence and in particular against any strong intellectual influence. As a result, the adult Conor emerged from these family quarrels neither in thrall to his aunts' fiercely held views, nor neurotically torn between them and the more tolerant nationalism of his parents, but with an independent-minded political outlook that combined a clear commitment to modern political liberalism with an analytical curiosity about the interests and justifications that all parties, not excluding liberals, bring to any dispute.

The main aspect of this outlook consisted of a hostility to arbitrary power together with a suspicion that any excessive power is likely to degenerate into the arbitrary kind. (Surely not coincidentally, such hostility was the theme that animated Edmund Burke in Dr O'Brien's thematic biography of the statesman.) But a regime that places chains on power needs to be defended where it exists or established where it is resisted. That implies a willingness either to conciliate or crush its enemies and, for either purpose, an ability to understand them and the powers at their disposal. Thus a liberal regime should not disdain the help of authority, or of tradition, or of religious belief, or of prudence, or of any of the ideas and interests that are usually supposed to rest at the right end of the political spectrum. It will always respect such aids, since they may well be rooted ultimately in popular opinion, and it will sometimes seek to seize them from the hands of its opponents.

De Valera's Ireland—that is, Ireland from about 1937 to about 1960—was not exactly hospitable to this brand of politics. Politically the country was a fledgling democracy that took peaceful changes of government for granted remarkably soon after a revolution and civil war; socially it was a quietly repressive society because the political victors (and most of the vanquished) wanted an avowedly Catholic republic that would be distinguished from liberal bourgeois England; and economically it was a Celtic dormouse. If the central reality of Irish life was the overwhelming power of the Church, however, this could not be admitted since it would confirm the Unionist slur that Home Rule would be Rome rule. The effect was a kind of limited democracy in which very lively political disputes took place within boundaries silently marked out by the bishops. Even the most radical Irish politicians presented themselves as good Catholics and manoeuvred for Episcopal approval. As the novelist Honor Tracey said about a cosmopolitan, womanizing ex-revolutionary whose baubles included the Lenin Peace Prize, 'Ireland is a country in which Sean MacBride goes to Mass.'

This was a state of affairs that O'Brien was almost designed to subvert. He had emerged from Trinity as a kind of European literary intellectual on the James Joyce model, a Catholic at best *croyant* and certainly not *pratiquant*, who undoubtedly struck his colleagues as a very exotic bird indeed when he arrived in the Finance Department in 1942 and, shortly afterwards, in the Department of External Affairs. Yet his depiction of de Valera's Ireland (and of de Valera himself) is far kinder than would be given by almost any modern young Irish liberal. He sees it the way Orwell saw wartime Britain: as a family with the wrong members in control. Although the quiet repression had real victims— poor Protestants, Catholic orphans, unmarried mothers—many a blind eye was turned to sin and heterodoxy. Under the facade of Catholic decency, even the civil service had interstices in which dissidents and bohemians were given shelter. In the Europe of the forties and fifties, it was a haven of easy-going virtue.

Besides, as a rising young bureaucrat, O'Brien had to confine his resistance to Catholic power to private practical jokes and literary essays published under a pseudonym. And his nationalism, though liberalish, still conformed sufficiently to the authorized version to facilitate his running of such sallies of nationalist diplomacy as the Anti-Partition campaign in the United States and the establishment of an Irish news agency to replace reliance on Britain's Press Association. In these years, accordingly, he was present at the creation of two transformations in Irish foreign policy.

The first, which he merely observed as a junior official, took Ireland from its policy of official wartime neutrality, embarrassing after 1945, to one of broad support for a US-led anti-communist West. This reflected Irish interests and its Catholic hostility to Soviet communism, but it was less effective than it might have been because the Irish government, while remaining outside NATO, insisted to the Americans that Britain was letting the West down by holding on to Northern Ireland.

The cracks in this policy were too gaping for mere diplomacy to conceal. Still, it succeeded domestically to the point where O'Brien, seeking entry into Ireland for Hungarian refugees in 1956, was told that they could not be admitted because they were from a communist country.

He explained that the refugees were anti-communists. 'I don't care what kind of communists they are,' replied the official. 'They're not coming in.'

As a senior member of Ireland's delegation to the United Nations, Dr O'Brien played a more influential role in the second transformation of Ireland's movement in the late fifties from its pro-Western position, which implied almost automatic support for American policy, to a more neutral stance coupled with marked sympathy for the Third World. And although he was obeying a political directive from Frank Aiken, the Irish foreign minister, he was also following his own inclinations: to win more influence for Ireland internationally by gaining friends among the newly independent post-colonial states, and—that theme again—to place some check on the overwhelming power of the United States both at the UN and internationally. As it turned out, O'Brien's connection of Irish nationalism to Third World internationalism was a prescient move later followed by many an Irish left-winger. It naturally won him admirers in the UN's 'Afro-Asian bloc.' It led to his transfer to the UN secretariat. And it made him internationally notorious when he was sent by the UN to represent its interests in the Congo crisis.

The Katanga story is grippingly told here. To simplify, O'Brien saw "independent" Katanga as a neocolonial fraud ruled by Belgian economic interests and local white settlers, and, interpreting an admittedly ambiguous UN resolution, initiated military action to end its secession from the Congo. This action only half succeeded, provoked opposition in the Security Council, was effectively disowned by the UN secretariat, and eventually led to O'Brien's retirement from UN diplomacy. In retrospect, as at the time, he fingers the British government as the villain of this piece on interesting and plausible grounds: because it was then hoping to foist its own white-ruled neocolonial fraud, namely, the Central African Federation, on Nyasaland and the two Rhodesias, it wanted neither contagious disorder nor the successful overthrow of white rule next door.

There is no reason to doubt the facts in this account. And in opposing the arbitrary rule of white Rhodesians, O'Brien is being perfectly consistent. But is he applying his other tests and estimating the forces ranged against black majority rule in Central Africa in 1960? The British government not only had to calculate the risks of violence spreading—a prudential duty for any government—but it also had to know that a quarter of a million whites controlling all the levers of power could only be dislodged either by a British military invasion or a prolonged guerrilla war. If London was not prepared to invade (and it was not), then it had to finesse the situation—which meant creating a new multiracial polity in which the black majority had limited democratic rights, in the hope that this would evolve over time into majority rule.

This attempt failed, in part perhaps because Katanga's secession was ended and O'Brien vindicated. But was it either unreasonable or dishonourable? After all, the consequences for Central Africa were exactly what London feared: a strong push for immediate black majority rule, the rise of the Rhodesian Front arguing for undiluted white supremacy, the Unilateral Declaration of Independence, fifteen years of sanctions and guerrilla war, an eventual settlement that rewarded the most extreme party, and a government that has impoverished the country and murdered large numbers of its citizens. The outcome might perhaps have been still worse if the British had succeeded in keeping Katanga afloat; but it is hard to imagine how.

Whatever the historical might-have-beens, O'Brien emerged from the Katanga crisis widely misunderstood as a Third World revolutionary and settled enemy of Western interests. This reputation increased throughout the rest of the sixties, when, as a professor at New York University, he was among the first demonstrators against US policy in Vietnam and, later, was appointed chancellor of the University of Ghana by Kwame Nkrumah. In fact, the headlines were somewhat misleading. As he anti-heroically tells the story, O'Brien prudently retired from demonstrating when a New York cop kicked him hard on the shin for 'going limp.' And he disappointed the more extreme members of the Third World lobby by bravely defending the independence of the University of Ghana and academic freedom against both the insidious pressures of the president and the outright thuggery of his supporters. Nonetheless, O'Brien still enjoyed the reputation (and some of the reality) of an international socialist when he returned to Ireland to enter politics for the Irish Labour Party in the late sixties.

This made him some predictable enemies and some surprising friends. As O'Brien points out, Ireland was until recently the only nation in the world where an accusation of communism was the cover for a more serious charge—namely, being a bad Catholic. When the influence of religion is not avowed openly, its warnings have to be expressed politically, though not necessarily subtly. Thus, he tells the story of a priest who, giving a pre-election sermon, began with a brisk denunciation of Communists and then went on to warn his parishioners about Socialists. They were, he said, worse than Communists; they were a breakaway sect of Communists; you might almost say a Protestant variety of Communists! O'Brien's political opponents, mainly in Ireland's natural governing party, Fianna Fail, were only too ready to exploit such themes against him.

What is interesting is that the IRA and its supporters, then in a Marxisant phrase, found him simpático on the same grounds. Because O'Brien had enough nationalism left in him, and because Stormont then plausibly represented the arbitrary power that invariably arouses his opposition, he flirted briefly with a left-wing version of republican politics. The flirtation quickly collapsed when IRA sympathizers called on the Labour Party to demand the release of "political prisoners." Were they, he asked, to regard men who planted bombs in pubs as political prisoners? And with that question, he began tearing away the veil of republican rationalizations for murder.

In the thirty or so years since then, Conor Cruise O'Brien has become the principal opponent of IRA terrorism in Irish politics—as a Labour Party spokesman, a minister in coalition governments, a journalist, and an editor. As a writer of such works as *States of Ireland*—the single best explanation of what the Irish conflict is about—he has painstakingly demolished the official myths of the Irish state that continue to persuade young men to die for Ireland and, of course, to kill for Ireland, too. In playing these various roles, he has revised a major element of his own thought, moving from moderate constitutional nationalism to support for Unionism, on the democratic argument that this is what Northern Irish majorities repeatedly vote for.

Events, however, seem to have been moving in the other direction. He was gently chided in a recent *The New York Times* review of his memoir for opposing the 'peace process' on the above lines. Yet he can point out in reply, drawing on themes that thread through his life and thought, that insofar as the peace process succeeds, it does so by erecting an arbitrary power over the people—an administration that the voters cannot throw out in elections, since all parties with votes above a low threshold have an automatic right to ministerial posts. This arbitrary power is imposed by a political compromise with terrorism because democratic governments in London and Dublin fear that private armies will otherwise bomb their capitals. The political compromise with these armies allows them to retain their weaponry, while requiring that the British Army and the Royal Ulster Constabulary be partially disarmed and reduced in size and authority. And to keep the show on the road, the two governments have decided not to treat the maiming and murder of coreligionists as breaches of the ceasefire but, in the chilling jargon of Whitehall, as 'internal housekeeping,' thereby validating the rule of the gun in sectarian ghettos, Catholic as well as Protestant. If these arrangements have been extorted over democratic opposition by a few hundred terrorists armed with yesterday's weapons, it can only be because, pace Mr Gladstone, the resources of civilization have finally been exhausted. It hardly seems a rational calculation of the real social interests at stake—or a solid basis for political progress.

In the South the picture is only a little better. Under the impact of economic growth and European liberalism, Catholic power has imploded with astonishing speed, to be replaced not by a liberal democratic humanism, however, but by the usual social ills of prosperity and—among intellectuals and much of the media—by terrorist chic and the romance of the gun. It is even speculated that Sinn Fein (whose members were interned by the de Valera government) might enter the next government if today's Fianna Fail needs its votes to attain a majority. O'Brien's nostalgic respect for 'Dev' is readily explicable on political grounds as well as those of personal friendship.

If this autobiography is sometimes naturally andante, as all lives are, it is invariably told allegro con brio. There are wonderful jokes, witty asides, undiplomatic stories of the diplomatic life; there are also moving personal tales, inevitably neglected in a largely political review, of O'Brien's family life and his love for his wife, Máire, which flowered improbably against the exotically risky background of the Katanga crisis; and there are brilliant pen portraits of such ornaments of recent history as Sean MacBride and Dag Hammarskjšld.

Finally, neither O'Brien's life nor the Troubles have come to an end. Even as I write, the peace process is creaking loudly. He may be writing—and making—Irish history for some years yet.

This review of Conor Cruise O'Brien's Memoir: My Life and Themes *(New York: Cooper Square Press, 2000), 488 pp., was originally published in* The National Interest, *1 December 2000, https://nationalinterest.org/bookreview/subverting-kant-820.*

When the Wokerati Came for the Literati: *Harper's* and Carpers

20 July 2020

The narrator of the following modest domestic but morally significant moment in 1935 is the late and much-lamented Sidney Hook in his 1985 memoir *Out of Step: An Unquiet Life in the 20th Century*. The two men, Marxists of different kinds at the time, were dining in Hook's New York apartment.

> It was at this point that he [Bertolt Brecht, German playwright and refugee from Hitler] said in words I have never forgotten, 'As for them [the doomed defendants in Stalin's show trials], the more innocent they are, the more they deserve to be shot.' I was so taken aback that I thought I had misheard him.
>
> 'What are you saying?' I asked.
>
> He calmly repeated himself, 'The more innocent they are, the more they deserve to be shot.' …
>
> I was stunned by his words. 'Why? Why?' I exclaimed. All he did was smile at me in a nervous sort of way. I waited, but he said nothing after I repeated my question.
>
> I got up, went into the next room, and fetched his hat and coat. When I returned, he was still sitting in his chair, holding a drink in his hand. When he saw me with his hat and coat, he looked surprised. He put his glass down, rose, and with a sickly smile took his hat and coat and left. Neither of us said a word. I never saw him again.

Brecht's remark was an expression of his determination to remain loyal to the Soviet Communist Party through all its murders while affecting small "ironic" displays of independence from it. It has the form of an epigram and the reality of corrupt subservience. Hook's straightforward moral decency cuts through the irony, and his genuine independence of mind puts an uneasy Brecht to flight.

Though that moment is a heaven-or-hell one, I do not believe I had thought of it for years. But it has been running through my head in recent days as I have read some of the critical responses to the *Harper's Magazine*'s 'Letter on Justice and Open Debate,' signed by 153 intellectuals including Fareed Zakaria, Martin Amis, Stephen Pinker, Noam Chomsky, and J. K. Rowling. The statement itself seems to me to be a good one. It accurately describes the growing hostility to freedom of speech we all sense as a drive for 'ideological conformity' that produces 'an intolerance of opposing views, a vogue for public shaming and ostracism, and the tendency to dissolve complex policy issues in a blinding moral certainty.' It proposes an admirably sensible response to disagreements and disputes: 'The way to defeat bad ideas is by exposure, argument, and persuasion, not by trying to silence or wish them away.' Both description and prescription suit me.

Inevitably, I found a few reasons for mild annoyance in it. For instance, there was the ritualistic claim that threats to free expression come from both Left and Right. Perhaps right-wingers would like to threaten free expression, but their social power to do so in universities, the media, publishing, Big Tech, and wherever else these conflicts are raging is so minuscule that they are being cancelled with greater ease and less publicity than are liberals and moderate leftists. But that is a quibble, because the principles defended in the letter are ideology-neutral and would protect heretics of all kinds. On first reading, my sense was that the letter was written in a way that made it very hard to raise objections to it.

That was, of course, a rash error. Angry and indignant objections have been raining down on its authors' heads since the day after publication. A handful of signatories have withdrawn their support for it; other collective letters have been organized to dispute its arguments; and columnists have been denouncing its authors as little better than privileged right-wingers.

Now, I have not made an exhaustive study of these responses, but I have read a good number and I think I detect three themes that run through them.

The first dismisses the authors' concerns for free thought and free speech as almost eccentric interests at a time when a pandemic is raging and mass social protests for racial justice are spreading through America. That invites the retort: if that is so, why are you taking an equal amount of trouble to sign a counter-petition or write a column questioning their set of priorities? Why are you not taking up nursing or handing out Black Lives Matter petitions on street corners? They might be doing those things, to be sure; but so might the signers of the *Harper's* letter. Considered coolly, moreover, the objection is a silly one: a claim that you cannot defend freedom and chew gum at the same time. Its intent, though, is more sinister. It hints that some discreditable motive prompted their letter. What might that be?

Well, the second theme is that the *Harper's* authors are protecting their own positions and ability to write what they wish rather than helping lesser-known writers from disadvantaged social groups, including some who have been blocked or persecuted, to gain access to good jobs in literature or journalism. But the principles advanced in the letter, if they were generally accepted, would go a long way to achieving those ends. Protection of free speech is more important to striving newcomers than to established authors or scholars. For the writers who are least likely to be subject to cancellation in practice are those who are wealthy and popular enough to defy Twitter mobs and corporations nervous of Twitter mobs—i.e., writers like those who signed the *Harper's* letter. In defending free speech, they were acting altruistically at least as much as selfishly and giving greater protection and opportunities to others.

That is so even though there is no obligation on someone entering a trade or profession to demand its reordering to create jobs for applicants from particular social groups, let alone make personal sacrifices to do so. That might be a virtuous thing to do. And there are in fact any number of prizes, scholarships, and special programmes for young, minority, and women writers in publishing and the media. But it might also be a quixotic enterprise if the group is less represented because most of its members are not particularly interested in working in that trade. You do not find many Norwegian-American hip-hop artists, for instance, and a special recruitment programme would probably either fail to recruit any or encourage worse hip-hop. Just so when it comes to getting and keeping a writer's job. It is not enough to be young, a member of a minority, a woman, a trans person, or a radical progressive; you should have talent too.

The third theme is, quite simply, that there is no such thing as 'cancel culture' and no threat to free speech except the failure of the mainstream media to provide more employment to minority, female, and radical voices. Charles Blow of *The New York Times* gives it straight: Anyone is free to write what he wishes, and if he voices conservative views, his disgusted readers quite properly have the right to stop reading him. Sure, he will have to go into another line of work—but that is accountability.

Except that is not quite how it works, and if it is accountability, to whom is the writer accountable? Kevin Williamson was not driven out of *The Atlantic* by appalled readers. They did not have the chance to reach a verdict on his literary skills or political views because he was driven out of the magazine by a grim regiment of feminists among the junior staffers who took exception to pro-life views he had expressed elsewhere earlier. Since the editor had hired Williamson because he wanted a provocative writer of a conservative disposition, it is reasonable to conclude that his hand was forced when he fired him. Bari Weiss resigned her position as an editorial-page editor on *The New York Times* semi-voluntarily in a dignified letter to its publisher that made it clear she had been subject to intimidation and bullying by her colleagues in what was plainly a hostile working environment. And Andrew Sullivan resigned in his last column for *New York Magazine*, giving a rather grand (and entirely justified) version of the song 'I've Been Thrown out of Better Joints Than This' as he left the building, announced the revival of his blog, *The Dish*, and saw its readership rise gratifyingly.

All three are writers of talent—the criterion I mentioned above—but their employment was made subject to the approval of a Jacobin editorial collective which itself made compliance with left-wing Woke ideology the main condition of employment. And the signs from corporate America are that enough members of its managerial elite have imbibed

Wokeness at good schools and colleges that they too will enforce this same condition of employment—call it Revolutionary Correctness—on both its workers and job applicants. My one difference with Ms Weiss is that I see Twitter less as an agent than as an internal system of corporate communications in James Burnham's managerial revolution. Its effect nonetheless is to impose an industry-wide and nationwide system of left-wing ideological conformity.

It should be clear from what I have written so far that I regard the contributors to the *Harper's* letter as right in detecting and opposing a cancel culture that threatens freedom, and their critics as wrong in raising false, sinister, and absurd objections to them—and I have not mentioned some of the most ridiculous complaints. If it really is the case that journalists on papers and magazines such as *The New York Times* and *New York Magazine* are made ill by the presence of Ms Weiss and Mr Sullivan, who might well be thinking odious liberal thoughts only a few desks away, then either they are unsuited to journalism, which often involves things much more rough-and-tumble than that, or they are themselves hiding other and more worrying thoughts of their own. And that is why the remark of Bertolt Brecht came into my mind as I was reading them.

One could not avoid noticing that in addition to the specific objections to the *Harper's* letter, its critics were animated by an unusually strong, almost personal, animus to the letter-writers. They constantly brought up the fact that they were wealthy, popular, liberal, and non-minority—even when they were not. Much of it was ideological hostility, of course, but it seemed also to be allied to a kind of class hatred, and perhaps to a sense of inferiority of some kind too. There is a long and impressive tradition of rhetorical viciousness on the Left; Marx himself had a real talent for invective, and Brecht too. Eventually I thought I sensed what they were saying behind the formal arguments: *the more talented they are, the more they deserve to be silenced.*

There were variations on this theme, of course: the more successful they are, or the wealthier they are, or the more liberal they are—liberal being sometimes attached to some idea of higher status. But all these things were mixed up together, and they were mostly driving emotionally to the same urge: *the more they deserve to be silenced.*

It is hard to know where this mentality comes from. In the case of Brecht, my speculation is that Hook confronted him with a choice: he could continue to live a life of communist privilege as the servant of an imperial ideology with a license to jest, or he could choose truth and liberty. Making the right choice would have meant a public humiliation at the hands of his fellow Communists at the very least. He therefore made the wrong choice and lived in comfortable corruption thereafter. But he left 'uneasy' that night in 1935. And one wonders if that uneasiness ever lifted.

Many of those who have embraced the imperialism of Wokeness must sense that they are making the wrong choice too—after all, they are usually well-educated in a formal sense—and they know where that choice led in Russia after 1917, Germany after 1933, Poland, Czechoslovakia, and Hungary after 1945, China, Cuba, Vietnam, etc., etc. So they shout louder, demand more aggressively, and condemn more harshly in order to signify their revolutionary correctness and perhaps to quell their own doubts and even their own fears that talented liberals will not be the last to be silenced or bullied into pleading forgiveness and begging to be re-educated.

How will it end this time? I doubt Wokeness will triumph in the United States or anywhere in the English-speaking world where democratic and liberal traditions are deeply rooted, if at present very far from flowering. Those traditions will almost certainly be strong enough to contain a Woke regime long enough for an election to punish its preordained chaos, failure, and authoritarianism. But we can already glimpse what the ideological control of writing by collectives and commissars is likely to produce in imaginative writing (plays, novels, poems, screenplays) from what it is already producing in journalism. From *The New York Times*'s 1619 Project through the mainstream media's ruthless downplaying of violent rioting across America to the pushing of Williamson, Sullivan, Weiss, and others away and into the still-free enclaves of opinion (which are themselves starting to be threatened too), we see that Woke journalism elevates revolutionary correctness and/or partisan political interest over truth in the most basic journalistic sense: who did what, where, how, and to whom when? You cannot trust what such journalists write—and increasingly, the public does not.

As for the consequences of *literary* correctness, we know exactly what that would mean for writers *and* readers from an old Soviet joke (told to me by the historian Tibor Szamuely):

> A regional commissar in the Union of Soviet Writers was delivering his annual report on the rising production of literature in his province.
>
> 'I am proud to announce,' he said, 'that this year's literary output has been outstanding. We have no fewer than 385 novelists working full-time for the proletariat whereas in backward Czarist times, we had only one.'
>
> 'Leo Tolstoy.'

Given what the critics of the *Harper's* letter think about its contributors, however, they might not get the punch line.

Originally published in National Review, *20 July 2020, www.nationalreview.com/2020/07/harpers-letter-left-attacks-defense-free-inquiry-debate/.*

Prequel to an Outrage—And I Was There
23 July 2019

In 1985 in New York I was asked, well told really, 'Why don't you go back where you came from?' by the distinguished historian and chronicler of the Kennedys, Arthur Schlesinger Jr. This occurred at an otherwise very pleasant dinner party in the course of a debate-turning-into-a-quarrel between Schlesinger and me over the nomination of Edwin Meese III to be attorney general.

Schlesinger was waxing indignant over the alleged sins of Ed Meese which made him spectacularly unfit to be attorney general and I was arguing that Meese was innocent of those sins and that, even if he had occasionally jaywalked, Democrat attorneys general had committed the same sins and far worse.

It was a standard row at many dinner parties that season, but this time it was not really a fair fight. I had arrived at the party hot from the task of writing a *New York Post* editorial on the Meese nomination that took the unfashionable pro-Meese position whereas Schlesinger was simply sounding off in the confident expectation that everyone at the party would agree with him.

I was stuffed to the gills with arguments and precedents; he was trotting out the conventional clichés of local liberalism. And in a clash between the conventional wisdom and an unexpected challenge to it, the smart way to bet is on the challenger because he is the one who knows the other side's arguments.

At any rate, it was not going well for Arthur. He was losing to some nobody from a New York tabloid. He became increasingly irritated until, eventually, he burst out with the fatal words: 'Why don't you go back where you came from?'

A great hush at once descended on the room. It really did. For about fifteen seconds (though it seemed more like an hour) no one said a word.

Then another distinguished historian, who was also a former US ambassador, said quietly: 'Really, Arthur, I think that goes too far.' This gentlemanly intervention came from a moderate Democrat who probably agreed with Schlesinger on the substance of the argument, and it was promptly echoed by most of the other diners (of mixed but mainly Democrat partisan loyalties) around the table.

'Yes, really ... Arthur, that's too bad of you ... please re-consider.' And so on. For the moment, though, Arthur glowered and stood firm. And sulky.

As best I now recall, I was surprised by the remark but slightly less indignant than my defenders. Schlesinger and I had been in combat only seconds before; I was buoyed up by the fact that I seemed to be scoring good points; and I expected some sort of angry riposte—just not that one.

Besides, anyone who takes part in serious debate knows that no one—*no one!*—is proof against losing his temper. In a famous parliamentary exchange during the Boer War, David Lloyd George from the Opposition benches listed all the Boer casualties claimed by the British Army and pointed out that they added up to more people than the entire Boer nation, men, women, and children. Arthur Balfour, then a cabinet minister, later prime minister, was a famously witty politician, usually detached from partisan anger. His great work was titled *A Defence of Philosophic Doubt*. But Lloyd George's sally aroused him to the point that he cast doubt and philosophy aside, rose from the front bench, shook his fist at Lloyd George, and shouted 'Cad!'

By comparison, I got off pretty easily.

I was meanwhile trying to think of some clever retort that also would make light of the matter. Since I actually come from Liverpool, I wondered if I might say: 'Did you say the same thing to John Lennon?' But that struck me as a weak joke requiring a long prior explanation and so no use at all. Besides, no one there knew I was a Liverpudlian. Schlesinger was almost certainly thinking not of Liverpool when he struck the blow but of Fleet Street, then regarded by New York liberals as a den of iniquity from which tabloid pirates had conquered and transformed their beloved liberal *Post*.

Also, it is one thing to be told to go back where you came from by some drunk in a bar, but quite another when the distinguished liberal chronicler of the Kennedys, Arthur Schlesinger Jr, says the same. Then, it has a comic side. It is sort of funny, and distinguished, and therefore memorable, the stuff of later anecdotes at other fashionable dinner parties. It was not all downside.

While my dinner-party companions were still uttering soft impeachments to the effect that Arthur should apologize, therefore, I murmured things like 'not at all,' 'It's not important,' 'I really don't think an apology is called for,' and 'let's all just get along.' In the face of these appeals from his fellow liberals and my display of nobility, Arthur eventually caved and apologized. I said something appropriately magnanimous, and we parted almost friends.

Was Arthur's remark racist? Of course not, unless you regard the Liverpool Irish as a different race—and not even then really. Was it snobbish? Well, that is a harder question. I think it was *intellectually* snobbish, a kind of assertion of superiority by Harvard over Fleet Street, but that must be put in the context that he was losing an argument he thought he should be winning. He reached desperately for an undoubted symbol of his authority and came up with the wrong one: He was an American, I was not, and so what did I know? Was that nativist? I do not (and did not) think so, and I would not have minded much if it had been. But he probably feared it was immediately after saying it. That was why he was so angry with himself and reluctant to say 'Sorry, I screwed up.'

None of those hundred-dollar-word explanations is needed. The problem with what Arthur Schlesinger said was that it was crass. He could have come up with a better riposte to me if he had paused and thought about it. But he acted on impulse.

And that is the problem with President Trump's remark about the four congressional ladies now known as the 'Squad.' He wanted to point out that they express hostility to America and its institutions almost every time they talk on such matters. Sure, they claim to want to make America a better country, but their picture of its history and present is one of unrelieved racism, oppression, and shame. And everything they have so far proposed would make it worse.

He could have said: 'I can't tell the Squad to go back where they came from—because for 75 per cent of them, that's America even if they think it's hell. But I can tell them they should go where they want to take America—because that's a real hell called Venezuela. And then they'll learn there's a difference.' Instead, Trump acted on impulse and said something crass.

Unfortunately, the two main flaws in the Trump presidency are acting on impulse and saying crass things. They outweigh the great deal that is sensible and sound in his policies. And they could lose him the next election to a Democratic Party under the sway of the Squad.

And that would be very different from a 1980s liberal dinner party.

Originally published in National Review, *23 July 2019,* *www.nationalreview.com/corner/postscript-to-an-outrage/.*

Dateline, Greeneland:
The Politics of the Intelligence Thriller
A Review of *The Foreign Correspondent: A Novel*
by Alan Furst
Winter 2006

William L. Shirer, one of the great foreign correspondents in the great era of foreign correspondents, was standing near a woman on the balcony of the Crillon Hotel in Paris on 6 February1934, when she suddenly fell down. She had been shot in the head. She and Shirer were in a group watching the Stavisky riots from what they doubtless assumed was the safety of a grand hotel. Both fascists and Communists, some armed, were rioting that night. Gunfire rang out; a random shot found her.

This unknown woman was not the night's only victim. Edouard Daladier, the moderate Left politician, who had just been sworn in as the latest prime minister of the Third Republic, resigned the next day. In his resignation letter he told the president that he was unwilling to order troops to fire on armed rioters who were trying to bring down his government.

These events are recounted on pages 5–7 of Shirer's justly renowned *Berlin Diary* (republished in 2002 by the Johns Hopkins University Press). They occurred about three weeks after he arrived in Paris to work for the *New York Herald-Tribune*. It must have seemed to him that this was an extraordinary baptism of fire and the rest of his journalistic career would be dull by comparison. In fact this random killing captured the essence of the next 11 years as he witnessed them: the feebleness of democratic leaders (Daladier returned as prime minister to sign the Munich Agreement), the ruthlessness of the two totalitarian extremes, a European atmosphere of growing violence, anxiety and suspicion, and political murder reaching from the streets to strike down the safest and most comfortable members of the bourgeoisie.

We feel we know this world because it has been described for us not only in histories of the period but also, more atmospherically, in the thrillers of Eric Ambler (*A Coffin for Dimitrios, Journey Into Fear*), the "entertainments" of Graham Greene (*Orient Express, This Gun for Hire*), and films like *Casablanca* and *Arch of Triumph*. It is a world of secret policemen and spies, frontier incidents and concentration camps, refugees and collaborators, honest journalists and corrupt newspapers. It is outwardly civilized—it boasts piped water, fast cars, and the radio—but there are Vandals and Visigoths under the smart suits and Balenciaga dresses.

Alan Furst is the latest and most scrupulous writer to describe this world for us. His is a very distinctive approach, closer to Greene than to Ambler, less the well-made thriller than a picaresque journey through Purgatory. A typical Furst story takes up a minor character at some moment of crisis—a Polish officer after the 1939 conquest of Poland, a liberal Hungarian diplomat around the time of Munich—introduces him to the demi-monde of secret intelligence, follows his progress in that world for some years, then abandons him a few years later just before or during the Second World War.

Furst has been rightly praised for getting both the "feel" and the details of the period right. In some respects his novels are like those BBC serials in which the dress and set designers are as important as the scriptwriter. They are richly atmospheric.

Furst also gets the "feel" of the period right in a deeper sense by leaving his characters still struggling in a world where the Nazis are an ever-present threat. No one makes Victor Laszlo's promise in Casablanca: 'Welcome back to the fight. This time I know our side will win.' These characters do not know they will win the war and for most of the period they feel uneasily that they are very likely to lose it. Even the reader forgets that D-Day, Liberation, Glenn Miller, and Lucky Strikes are just around the corner. They belong to a very different world. And this amnesia gives Furst's novels a dark undertone of foreboding that crystallizes the period more exactly than any research.

All these virtues granted, Furst's novels have been criticized for lack of narrative drive. There is something to this criticism, which naturally sticks to the picaresque. People who would be main characters in more conventional thrillers drift in and out of the action without much happening to them. In *The Foreign Correspondent*, Furst's latest book, the head of Italy's fascist intelligence network sets the plot in motion with a political murder. Thereafter he is glimpsed occasionally through the windows of his limousine. He gets neither a medal nor his come-uppance and at the novel's end is presumably still cruising the Paris streets to ensure that his murders are successfully carried out. A traitor in the circle of Italian anti-fascist exiles is unmasked. But this happens in a conversation after the circle has broken up for other reasons. Neither the traitor nor most of his dupes realize that he has been discovered. All that happens is that another member of the circle vows to bring him to justice once fascism has been overthrown—a relatively empty threat in 1939, when it is uttered. In short there is no neatly resolved plot that brings a series of events to a satisfying climax and in which each of the characters is punished or rewarded according to his deserts.

This criticism of narrative aimlessness is less valid in relation to *The Foreign Correspondent* than to Furst's earlier novels. Previously, their central character—invariably an anti-fascist of some kind—is simply abandoned in mid-espionage. He may have just been given a new mission by London, like the Polish officer, but essentially, he is still engaged in the struggle against Appeasement or the Axis. Furst's latest protagonist, however, is the "hero" in a self-contained story as well as a man of courage. Carlo Weisz is an Italian exile in late 1938 Paris where during the day he works for a British news agency and at night edits a small anti-fascist magazine which is then smuggled into Italy. His character is the familiar blend of idealism and cynicism we recall from Greene and Ambler. Not quite a burnt-out case, he is emotionally dry and stunted—something traceable to his sex life which is quite extensive but loveless. He is jolted back into genuine feeling, however, when he meets a former mistress on a journalistic mission to Berlin and promptly falls deeply in love with her.

Christa von Schirren is the anti-Nazi wife of a decent German aristocrat and a member of the nascent resistance to Hitler. The Gestapo seems to be aware of her activities and is closing in on her. Weisz decides that he must get her out to Paris. His chance arrives when British intelligence, foreseeing that it may shortly need to strengthen the Italian resistance to Mussolini, recruits Weisz and offers to build his modest magazine into a serious force. Weisz has the usual idealistic qualms about selling out and being used; he and his fellow exiles see the British as equivocal allies because realpolitik may dictate that they woo Mussolini to detach him from Hitler. But he takes the king's shilling (and risks returning to Italy to recruit a larger distribution network for the magazine) in return for London's rescue of his girlfriend from under the Gestapo's nose. The novel ends with Carlo and Christa reunited happily in his small Paris apartment.

It is a happy ending of sorts, more Ambler than Greene. But since the reunion of lovers occurs only a few months before the invasion of Poland, it is hardly a conclusive ending. If they stay in Paris, Christa and Carlo will soon be interned by the French as enemy aliens and then handed over to the Germans after the fall of France. More likely, they will leave very shortly for London to work for Carlo's new friends in British intelligence. The struggle continues.

This story is told with Furst's invariable skill. The writing is crisp, the period details accurate, and the atmosphere suitably full of foreboding. Real events are woven unobtrusively into the narrative. One of the advantages of making a foreign correspondent your hero is that he can be plausibly present at real historical events such as Hitler's seizure of Prague in early 1939—vividly pictured here. The total effect is persuasive: events like this really happened, people like this really existed; a nightmare was experienced in our own lifetime.

But how did this nightmare establish itself? Who worked for it? Who opposed it? And why? One standard feature of such stories was noticed some years ago by the Hungarian-Canadian writer and critic, George Jonas, in his critique of the film *Sunshine*. I quote from memory: 'The fascist thugs in such stories are simply thugs, but the Communist thugs are figures of intriguing moral complexity.' This is not here a complaint of political bias. None of the major figures in *The Foreign Correspondent* is a Communist. And Furst's bias is for civilization and against barbarism. Even so, we are given very little insight into such characters as the fascist intelligence chief whose assassination policy sets events in motion. Nazism, fascism, and their various offshoots were among the most powerful currents of modern history. They had a shattering impact on lives in all of Europe and half the world. But with a few exceptions—Irwin Shaw in *The Young Lions*, Arthur Koestler in *Arrival and Departure*—novelists have not sought to depict the interior life of Nazis or fascists.

It is easy to understand why. No one wants to give a sympathetic account of political mass murderers, and anyone who gives a realistic one risks being misunderstood at best. The portrait of Hitler in the film *Downfall* was denounced because it showed that the Führer had a human side to his personality as well as a demonic one. But the result of such nervousness, as Jonas pointed out, is that we get cardboard villains in black uniforms. That cannot be a satisfactory way of accounting for ideas and emotions that recruited both street barbarians and over-civilized intellectuals to make war on mere civilization. Such ideas and emotions may hibernate; they rarely die altogether.

If we cannot entirely understand the villains in Furst's world, we can identify them easily enough. But who are the heroes and what is 'our side'? Some in Carlo's anti-fascist circle pass muster, but in addition to the fascist spy, there are doubtless some Communist ones. Being loyal to another totalitarian creed, they are on a third side to both ourselves and the Nazis. The British are equivocal because—remember, appeasement ends only with the seizure of Prague—they might be prompted by *raison d'etat* to join the wrong side. So they are potentially on both sides. And as for America, that was summed up by Humphrey Bogart as Rick Blaine in *Casablanca*: 'I bet they're asleep in New York. I bet they're asleep all over America.' Since Rick was speaking in the small hours, Americans were not sleeping at all but eating dinner, listening to Benny Goodman, and laughing along with Jack Benny. In other words, the Americans were on no side. And, indeed, there is not a single American in *The Foreign Correspondent*. 'Our side' is simply a handful of decent but understandably disillusioned liberals in all countries, including Nazi Germany.

Not long afterwards, however, the British and the Americans (soon to be christened 'the Anglo-Americans' by perceptive Vichy propaganda) were struggling to end the nightmare. Though the state is (as de Gaulle said) 'a cold monster' and though there is an irreducible minimum of realpolitik in the foreign policy of even the most idealistic nation, the moral atmosphere of both countries made their joining a struggle against Nazism likely and their joining an anti-communist crusade alongside the Nazis an impossibility. Both were essentially liberal countries—and in the world described by both Shirer and Furst that distinguished them from continental Europe. The rules and restraints that constitute civilization had been breaking down across the channel under pressure from harsh new doctrines of violence, realism, and "action" since the mid-nineteenth century.

The result was described, interestingly enough, by Eric Ambler in his thriller, *Background to Danger*. He put into the mouth of a British commercial traveller this trenchant cultural analysis:

> People come over here for a fortnight's holiday and see a lot of pretty chalets and chateaux and schloesser, and say what a fine place it is to live in. They do not know what they are talking about. They only see the top coat. They do not see the real differences. They do not see behind the scenes. They don't see them when their blood's up. I have seen them all right. I was in sunny Italy when the fascisti went for the freemasons in twenty-five. Florence it was. Night after night of it with shooting and beating and screams, till you felt like vomiting. I was in Vienna in thirty-four when they turned their guns on the municipal flats with the women and children inside them. A lot of the men they strung up afterwards had to be lifted on to the gallows because of their wounds. I saw the Paris riots with the garde mobile shooting down the crowd like flies and everyone howling 'mort aux vaches' like lunatics. I saw the Nazis in Frankfurt kick a man to death in his front garden. After the first he never made a sound. I was arrested that night because I had seen it, but they had to let me go. In Spain, they tell me, they doused men with petrol and set light to them.

Nice chaps, aren't they? Picturesque, gay, cleverer, more logical than silly us.

Some allowance must be made here for chauvinistic exaggeration (the commercial traveller's, not Ambler's). But the sting in the tail really does sting. It was the rise and dominance of political "logic" in Europe that smoothed the path to torture and murders. Doctrines that argued all relationships were essentially about power, and that civilized restraints were therefore either sentimentality or hypocrisy, led naturally to a kind of logical brutalism. It was "illogical" not to press home power over opponents to the fullest possible extent because of restraints that were really their power in disguise.

Furst's world is the result. His Italian fascist spymaster cruising Paris to superintend his political murders has mastered the theory. In the end, of course, the theory failed. The struggle was won by "silly us" even though it took all of fifty years to defeat both sets of logicians. Odd to think that today a liberal professor of literature and media studies would probably be sitting alongside the spymaster, giving directions.

This review of Alan Furst's The Foreign Correspondent: A Novel *(New York: Random House, 2006), 273 pp., was originally published in the* Claremont Review of Books, *Vol. VII, Number 1, Winter 2006/07, https://claremontreviewofbooks.com/datelinegreeneland/.*

Selling America Short, Nasty, and Brutish

A Review of *Through a Screen Darkly: Popular Culture,*
Public Diplomacy, and America's Image Abroad
by Martha Bayles
Summer 2014

There are many variations on this story: an American diplomat/academic/journalist listens patiently to his counterpart from Europe or the Middle East roundly denouncing the United States for every imaginable sin, foreign, and domestic. When the recitation is over, he asks mildly: 'Have you got your green card yet?' 'Bastard!' the man replies.

In many cases, as almost certainly in that case, the explanation is simple hypocrisy. Getting a green card is an excellent career move, and so is spouting anti-American invective. Why not do both? For most foreigners, however, an admiration for the liberties guaranteed by the US Constitution is combined quite sincerely with a strong distaste for American culture and for what the foreigner believes to be the patterns and practices of everyday American life. That seeming contradiction— and how it came about and what to do about it—is the subject of Martha Bayles's *Through a Screen Darkly: Popular Culture, Public Diplomacy, and America's Image Abroad.*

As Bayles establishes at once, this contradiction is a problem, indeed a massive one, but not a mystery. Very few foreigners reject the political mores embodied in the Declaration of Independence and the US Constitution. Those who do are generally either authoritarian rulers and their servants, or believers in doctrines (radical Islamism, Marxism) incompatible with political freedom. These latter groups have some influence on their fellow countrymen when they trace the violence, sexual libertinism, drug taking, and self-indulgent consumerism of American life to the nation's founding ideas of freedom and political equality. Arab governments allied to the US famously encourage anti-Americanism in political debate to distract attention from their own failings. In the main, however, ideological anti-Americanism is an elite obsession.

Most adults (especially most parents) in countries across Asia, Africa, and Europe dislike and disapprove of America because of the vices and disorders of its citizens as depicted in exports of American popular culture—violent Hollywood action movies, Jerry Springer-type celebrations of moral disorder via satellite, sexually-exploitative rap music videos, etc., etc. Most adult Americans dislike and disapprove of these things, too. But Americans live in America and they know that, despite real social problems such as family breakdown and its consequences, the great majority of their countrymen live in a society characterized by stable families, widespread religious observance, a strong work ethic, social tolerance, an explosion of voluntarism, safe cities, neighbourly small towns, and rapidly declining crime.

* * *

Not everything in this reality is perfect or comforting. Nevertheless, the real America is plainly better than the one refracted through US pop-cult exports, which is too often a blend of underclass crime and upper-class decadence, with the rough-hewn middle-class decency in between largely omitted. Foreigners cannot know that because they encounter only the export version of America—or what Bayles calls the distorting 'fun-house mirror' America. When they meet ordinary Americans either in the US or in their own countries, they are struck by how different these pleasant and helpful people are from the amoral egotists in movies—and how much more like themselves and their own families (mutatis mutandis, of course). When former White House speechwriter Peggy Noonan asked an Iraqi military officer what he had learned about Americans from working with them, he replied: 'You are a better people than your movies say.'

Of course, the full picture is more complex than a simple stark contrast between a vicious fictional America and a virtuous real one. American popular culture is technically and artistically superb overall. It is also full of brilliantly imaginative depictions of kindness, decency, altruism, self-sacrifice, and repentance—consider the 1993 comedy *Groundhog Day* in which a misanthropic Bill Murray relives the titular day over and over until he has learned his lesson. Its darker treatments of social evil are usually exaggerations for dramatic purposes rather than outright libels. Some movies and sitcoms, designed to challenge social prejudices for the sake of greater tolerance, inevitably outrage people in countries where such prejudices are entrenched. And deep-dyed villains such as J. R. Ewing in the 1980s primetime soap *Dallas* and many imitators since him are, well, cartoon villains not to be taken seriously, certainly not to be seen as accurate portraits of corporate misbehaviour. Americans can put most of these threats in a context that de-fangs them. J. R. comes from a long, entertaining tradition of uncomplicated wickedness going back to the Victorian stage, and such villains always come to a sticky end so that crime will not pay. But more remote audiences may mistake them for real life. Then there remains Jerry Springer, MTV, "reality" television, et al.

* * *

These are deep shallows, and treacherous ones. Fortunately, Martha Bayles is a sure-footed, sensible, and knowledgeable guide to them. A lecturer in the Arts and Sciences Honors Program at Boston College, and author of the 'Shadow Play' feature in these pages, she is a cultural critic of depth and subtlety. Her earlier book, *Hole in Our Soul* (1994), explored the way in which American popular music, once a wonderful vehicle for the heart's longings, had cast aside tenderness and wit to become a crude expression of aggression and lust. She knows therefore that the worst is often a corruption of the best. And as she documents here, America's broader popular culture with all its technical virtuosity has been gradually corrupted by the counter-culturalism of the 1960s, which rejected all the rules—from sexual modesty to simple grammar—that used to shape culture high and low.

For the moment, that popular culture is the most powerful influence on the world's view of America. That is not wholly accidental. After the Cold War, the US government largely sub-contracted cultural diplomacy to Hollywood and the music industry, which were enjoying some unusual political prestige because rock 'n' roll had apparently helped to bring down communism. Hollywood accepted this diplomatic role, but it is of two minds about it. It is flattered by the implied tribute to its cultural influence but reluctant to show America in a favourable light. Not for nothing did a distinguished Turkish film critic slyly describe *Valley of the Wolves: Iraq* (a Turkish thriller showing US troops harvesting the organs of Turkish soldiers for transport to Tel Aviv) as 'the most anti-American movie ever made outside the United States.'

Good and bad, however, this popular culture is not the only way in which America shapes its image abroad. Other influences—all available still, some growing more influential—include old-fashioned cultural diplomacy conducted by government; US international broadcasting through Voice of America (VOA) and such surrogate broadcasters as the Russian-language Radio Liberty; cultural exchanges involving concert orchestras, museums, art exhibitions, and visits by literary celebrities; the rise of the overseas campus and the increase in American students spending a year studying abroad; the spread of aid agencies and NGOs which employ secular American experts in poorer countries; and the revival of American religious missions offering social and medical help with the Gospel thrown in as an optional extra. In the course of tracing America's cultural footprint, Bayles has spoken to everyone from jihadist leaders in Indonesia to Christian missionaries in Africa, and examined every aspect of American cultural influence from Britney Spears to 'Gospel tourism.' The result is a fascinating cultural travelogue—richly detailed, fairly argued, and highly readable.

* * *

Bayles acknowledges the specific good things done by many of the people and institutions she has studied. But she is not starry-eyed about them, and she can be quite sharp in pointing out the unintended consequences and mild hypocrisies of their work. The overseas campus, for instance, is often a device for authoritarian regimes to ensure that their young people get a first-class American technical education without being exposed to the subversive liberal ideas of an actual American campus. The colleges and academics get very high rewards in return for avoiding certain lines of research. As for the beneficial cultural effects of study abroad on young Americans, these will be slight if they spend all their time with each other, partying, binge drinking and, not coincidentally, reinforcing the negative message about America that the locals have already picked up from television and the internet. None of this need be so, but it often is the case.

An important chapter of *Through a Screen Darkly* is devoted to the neglected topic of US international broadcasting—VOA, Radio Free Europe and Radio Liberty (RFE/RL), etc. Bayles argues persuasively for greater resources for US international broadcasting when Russia, China, Iran, and others are ramping up their own propaganda output, in much more sophisticated disguise, moreover, than during the Cold War. The Ukraine crisis has since strongly reinforced her argument. She also takes the side of those who want US-funded radio stations such as Radio Liberty to concentrate on news and current affairs programming aimed at elites rather than mixing pop music with hourly news bulletins to attract larger and younger audiences. There is no particular reason for the US taxpayer to fund a stream of pop music; it is not in short supply. And an Israeli commercial radio station has been providing the same mix of pop and hourly bulletins for decades without noticeably changing the political attitudes of young Arab people. She is finally right in demanding that USIB's (US International Broadcasting's) news and current affairs programming observe the high standards of accuracy and impartiality that have been developed within American journalism. This aim inevitably requires a struggle when reporters and editors are recruited from more than twenty countries with very different journalistic traditions; in my time at RFE/RL it was a constant preoccupation at all levels of the radios—never fully achieved but tantalizingly ever closer.

* * *

Bayles is perhaps too purist in rejecting satire as a legitimate device in current affairs programming. Admittedly, satire must be sharply distinguished from news itself. Like anti-communist jokes in the Cold War, however, satire is a subversive way of telling the truth and negating propaganda. It undermines authoritarian regimes by making them funny. Some of the RFE/RL language services, coached, and encouraged by visiting satirist John Bloom (a.k.a., Joe-Bob Briggs), have used it to great effect. Truth is the best propaganda, but mockery comes a close second.

Maybe the most needlessly distressing trend observed by Bayles is the decay of formal cultural diplomacy and, in particular, the apparent lack of interest among young US diplomats in promoting elite (i.e., classical) culture: concerts, exhibitions, lectures, etc. This is sad because it means that people in the countries to which they are posted will have less access to music, painting, and novels that are beautiful in themselves, that convey the spirit and grandeur of the United States, and that refute the common European notion that "American culture" is an oxymoron. But the reason for this reluctance, intuited by Bayles, is sadder still: it is that this kind of cultural exchange 'is now deemed ineffective and politically incorrect.'

If her intuition is right, then US cultural diplomats are almost comically wrong. One of the most important cultural trends of the last few decades is the enormous and growing popularity of Western classical music in the non-Western world, including China. This is reflected in the names and nationalities of many young soloists. But a personal experience may make the point more sharply. When I visited Hanoi eight years ago, I attended a symphony concert at which a local composer played his own piano concerto. The concert's second half was devoted to a series of Viennese waltzes by Strauss and Lehár. Except for a handful of tourists, the audience in the packed hall was composed entirely of young Vietnamese. They greeted all of the items, but especially the waltzes, with passionate enthusiasm, cheering the orchestra, and dragging back the conductor to play encores time after time. They also cheered the local CEO of the multinational company that had sponsored the concert. Some patriotic Austrian enterprise perhaps? No, Yamaha.

* * *

Like the negative trends excoriated by Bayles, this timidity of public diplomacy illustrates how America's cultural overtures are repeatedly crippled by the nation's internal culture wars. She cites gifted, independent-minded Americans in all the areas above who take successful initiatives to promote America and Western culture, but they seem to be the exceptions. Most cultural initiatives, including US popular culture when it is not offending people by its vulgarity, are constrained by a kind of multicultural masochism that prevents simple expressions of patriotic pride—or what Bayles calls the 'American ethos.' A cultural civil war—which is what the culture war is—means that two patriotisms are contending for the nation's soul. Until one or the other side wins, America's cultural outreach will be at war with itself and so likely to be uneasy, half-hearted, ambivalent, and unpersuasive.

Bayles is more than aware of this; it is a major leitmotif of her work. And though she sometimes strikes an above-the-battle pose in her occasional allusions to 'the culture warriors' of both sides, there cannot be much doubt throughout the book either that the cultural Left is responsible for most of the damage done to America's cultural image or that Bayles is firmly on the side of its more moderate conservative critics. Unfortunately, there is no sign that the cultural Left is losing the war; quite the contrary. So despite her very sensible proposals, in a last chapter, to improve America's cultural diplomacy, its basic weaknesses will likely persist.

But America's rivals in the international culture wars—Russia, China, Iran, etc.—have greater weaknesses. And they must worry about their images not only internationally but also among their own citizens. If America is threatened by a false picture of its social reality, moreover, their governments are threatened by the truth about every aspect of reality. They cannot compete in a world of free information. Hence all three countries try to keep information from their peoples by jamming radio stations and erecting internet firewalls. Michael Horowitz, my colleague at 21st Century Initiatives, points out the enormous significance of this: in the global war over information America has very serviceable weapons in the form of technologies that leap over firewalls, cut through jamming, cost far more to block than to install, but that once installed make every religion, political party, international agency, NGO, theatre company, pop group, and common-or-garden dissident America's allies even despite themselves. With such allies, even a divided America cannot really lose.

This review of Martha Bayles's Through A Screen Darkly: Popular Culture, Public Diplomacy, and America's Image Abroad *(New Haven– London: Yale University Press, 2014), 336 pp.*, was *originally published in the* Claremont Review of Books, *Vol. XIV, Number 3, Summer 2014, https://claremontreviewofbooks.com/selling-america-short-and-nasty/.*

Still the Best of Enemies, but Who Won the War?

March 2023

The ghosts of 1968 continue to hover over the West's divided and masochistic civilization. That makes for bad politics and worse culture overall, but it makes for excellent theatre. Over the recent Christmas season, the hottest ticket to the London theatre was a play about one of the early signs of this prolonged and sputtering crisis: the clashing television commentaries between the left-wing playwright and novelist Gore Vidal and the conservative columnist and editor, William F. Buckley that the ABC Television News tacked onto its coverage of the 1968 Republican and Democrat Conventions in Miami and Chicago in an apparently desperate attempt to raise its ratings. The exchange of insults that concluded their final debate created a great stir at the time and never entirely vanished down the political world's memory hole. Recollections of it were refreshed by a well-done 2015 documentary film by Morgan Neville and Robert Gordon on its significance, *Best of Enemies*, which inspired a play of the same name on the London stage in 2022. Given its provenance—a play inspired by a documentary about late-night television debates seventy years ago—the play looked unlikely to be a hit. But in addition to packed audiences for several months, *Best of Enemies* also got rave critical reviews across the politico-cultural spectrum and attention on the op-ed pages for its unexpected popularity and even topicality in the age of Black Lives Matter.

One reason for its impact is undoubtedly its author, James Graham, English theatre's current wunderkind, who in the last decade has established a record for versatility—he has written plays, films, teleplays, and musicals—for his tackling a wide range of subjects, including politics, and above all for his fair-mindedness (given that the stage has been a Tory-free zone for more than a generation). His 2013 play, *This House*, about the honourable relations between the Labour and Tory Whips offices in the dying days of the Callaghan administration even included a rare friendly reference to Margaret Thatcher. That did not stop it from becoming first a sleeper hit, then an early revival, and finally an export shown outside Britain as well as in the provinces.

How fair was Graham in the *Best of Enemies*? That is a tough test because his play is a series of debates between two figures, both early practitioners of cultural politics, whose exchanges were taking place at the very moment when new social forces were emerging in US politics and changing the two political parties and their voters culturally as much as politically. That was more evident in Chicago than in Miami, because Richard Nixon conciliated the insurgent conservatives in order to preserve party unity whereas the Democrats were openly and irremediably split and their disputes erupted into violence in the streets. As the play proceeds, the intellectual duel between Vidal and Buckley on successive nights mirrors the growing tumult outside the studio. It starts not good-humouredly but at least restrained by formal good manners, but it gradually becomes testier, and eventually it erupts into a bitterly hostile exchange ending in the famous exchange of slurs: 'Crypto-Nazi' and 'You Queer.' Given that the conflicts which emerged in 1968 still divide us, fair-mindedness is hard for anyone with even mildly-held opinions to maintain throughout.

My judgement, however, is that Graham succeeds pretty well. He is fair in dealing with the two duellists. His real ire, expressed in both satiric and raucous comedy, is reserved for the ABC executives who are shown prostituting their integrity as journalists to stop the fall in their ratings—more on this below—and for the Democratic mayor of Chicago, Richard Daley, who is shown as a foul-mouthed authoritarian thug who turns a blind eye to police violence against rioters (who, however, are themselves violent). Admittedly, it is impossible to defend Daley's conduct during the Chicago Convention. That is not the whole truth about Daley's largely competent and racially balanced conduct of the mayoralty, as a comparison with Chicago today will confirm, but in 1968 and in the context of this play, he is unavoidably collateral damage.

Both Buckley and Vidal, meanwhile, are treated as morally and intellectually serious people who detest each other on grounds of principle at the beginning and, alas, at the end of their battles too. Vidal sees Buckley as the advocate of a fading American empire that at home is racially unjust, sexually bigoted, devoted to greed, and heading for trouble; Buckley treats Vidal as someone whose essentially frivolous advocacy of cultural and sexual revolutions—unless it is sharply challenged—will undermine what is essentially a decent civilized country, warts and all. To underscore his argument, he cites Vidal's gender-bending novel, *Myra Breckenridge*, then a best-seller, as the kind of 'pornography' that will bring about the demoralization of America in every sense.

Who wins this ten-round debate? Until the final climactic slurs, honours in both the play and the documentary record strike me as even. Vidal had prepared very carefully for it; the documentary filmmakers found that he had conducted major 'Oppo' research on Buckley's journalism and composed a long list of ready-to-use witticisms; Buckley took a vacation to rest and relax as debate preparation. As a result, Vidal inflicts some wounds at the cost of sometimes smelling of the midnight oil; Buckley sounds more spontaneous at the cost of being sometimes caught off-guard. Vidal approached the debates as a way of destroying Buckley as a cultural leader; Buckley took more seriously his ABC News brief to discuss the Conventions. Vidal is incisive, scornful, needling, and waging a culture war; Buckley employs his debating technique of analysing the flaws in Vidal's statements to make partisan political points.

In the scenes between the debates—which are obviously Graham's major original contribution—we get a very skilled presentation of how each duellist learns that his initial contempt for his opponent was mistaken and how he must adapt his own debating technique to match or outwit the other's style. These scenes are cleverly written to reflect (or rather forecast) the actual debate transcripts which, for instance, show Vidal's personal jabs getting under Buckley's skin until he returns in the next debate with a determined equanimity that throws Vidal off his form.

That said, the backstage scenes have more to say about Vidal than about Buckley. In part that is because Buckley's debates with his 'handlers,' wife Pat and *National Review*'s literary editor Frank Meyer—who himself crafted conservative 'fusionism' to unify the respectable Right—are straightforward strategy sessions in comparison to Vidal's anguished doubts underneath the jagged sophistication. They discuss sensible political adjustments to Bill's approach; they contain some wonderfully characteristic put-downs from Pat Buckley to her husband; and they had a real impact on improving his performance. But Bill showed no sense then or later that he needed to make any fundamental change in the case he was making. His defence of America was sincere and self-confident. And though Graham places, in my view, a little too much stress on Bill's evocation of his earlier debating performance at Cambridge—it was a triumph for both Bill and his opponent, the African-American novelist James Baldwin, whom Graham brings onto the stage at points as a Greek chorus on racial justice—Bill did not need to pump up his morale. Until the end, both men thought they were winning. And there was enough in both performances to justify their admirers in agreeing with them.

Vidal by contrast undergoes a crisis that blends the personal and the political as the play proceeds. He is at first breezily contemptuous towards Buckley and the GOP and confident of victory over both. However, when the Republicans select Nixon as their presidential nominee, he frets that they have chosen a 'professional' at a time of Democratic disarray. Then, having earlier been dismissive of Buckley's rhetorical skills, he reads a line from a *National Review* article—'Though liberals do a great deal of talking about hearing other points of view, it sometimes shocks them to learn that there *are* other points of view'—and reflects his task is going to be harder than he thought. To unsettle him still further, Vidal holds a reluctant conversation with a young aide who wonders if he should not be down on the streets fighting with the students and the poor rather than debating with their enemy in the suites above. All this serves both to undercut Vidal's revolutionary pose, to hint at the Democratic Party's future evolution, and to prepare the ground for an encounter at least as dramatic as the debates themselves.

In a surrealist succession of scenes depicting the riots and the reactions of various characters to them, Vidal runs into Mayor Daley who as a fellow-Democrat congratulates him on 'flying the flag' for the party and none too subtly invites him to resume a conventional political career in the US Senate. Vidal attempts to distinguish his kind of Democratic politics from the Mayor's but too feebly to sustain his self-respect. Fired by some shame at that failure, he goes back into the final television debate, which is inevitably dominated by the riots and especially the violence shown by the Chicago cops to the rioters, in a mood of intense, even febrile, determination to choose the right side of history and expose Buckley as the smooth face of brutalist reaction.

There has been an interesting controversy in the British media about the decision to have Bill Buckley played by a black actor (the activist actor, David Harewood, who traces his heritage to a slave plantation owned by the royalty-connected Harewood family). This casting conforms to the modern theatre's belief in 'non-traditional casting.' But it has also been argued by sympathetic critics that it was done to subvert any prejudices a liberal English theatre audience might have against a white American making conservative arguments on racial questions. Given what I have written about Graham, that is a plausible motive but probably not the actual one since Graham has defended this casting justified by the limited opportunities that Britain gives to black actors and by extension to black people in general.

Whatever the motive, I think the decision was an artistic mistake. Depicting historical figures whom living people remember should never be merely impersonation. But some element of impersonation is surely inseparable from a convincing performance. Both principals here are strong. Zachary Quinto was Vidal to the life—witty, snobbish, brilliant, self-absorbed; David Harewood gave a good performance as Buckley, and delivered arguments he probably disliked with brio, but he simply did not have the oddly impish spontaneity of the mercurial man he was playing. Was that because he did not look like Bill? Or because the part as written did not quite catch Buckley's personality? I cannot be certain, maybe a mixture of both, but unless I am the only critic asking this question, it is a fair one.

On the other hand, it is worth making the point that if the purpose of this casting decision had been to render Bill's opinions less offensive to an English liberal audience, then maybe it was necessary (something I have changed my mind about since first writing this essay). In the key scene in which Vidal and Buckley debate the conduct of the Chicago police, Buckley insisted on distinguishing between the violent behaviour of individual cops and the general conduct of the police in Chicago *and America*. Vidal insisted equally strongly on blurring that distinction. Graham depicts the debate over that distinction without loading the dice.

Nearly sixty years later, however, that same distinction is still fought over—and largely on the basis of false statistical impressions. Several recent studies have established that the opinions of almost all Americans, liberals especially but not solely, greatly exaggerate the numbers of unarmed black men killed by police. More than half of 'very liberal' respondents believe the number is between 1,000 and more than 10,000. For 'liberals' that same figure is 38 per cent. Careful estimates by among others *The Washington Post* put the actual figure at, variously, 12, 22, and 27 people. Police officers 'feloniously killed' number several times those figures, fluctuating between about 55 and 76. Murders *of* cops are currently rising not only because of lesser crimes that go wrong, but also because of deliberate ambushes intended to murder the police. Buckley's distinction is certainly not weakened by these figures, but a middle-class London audience is likely to be 'very liberal' on this topic and so unlikely to be either aware of the statistics or inclined otherwise to doubt Vidal's stance of unqualified condemnation of America as a police state. But it is not Graham's job to quarrel with what happened on the night of the debate because of wider and later information.

At the time Buckley knew, like everybody else, that he had lost the overall debate when in response to Vidal's angry accusation of 'Crypto-Nazi,' he responded with 'You Queer' and a (not very convincing) threat of violence. We see Buckley distressed by his own loss of control, striding quickly through the technicians to his dressing room to get away from it all, while Vidal rejoiced. Buckley tried to recover some ground in a later essay for *Esquire,* but he would probably have done better to admit simply: I lost my temper—half the world would have sympathized—while Vidal delighted in playing videotapes of the incident as after-dinner entertainment for his guests down the years.

Is that the end of the matter? Probably it is, though when the 2015 documentary came out, Hendrik Herzberg in *The New Yorker* delivered an ingeniously revisionist interpretation: Vidal *was* gay but Buckley was not a Nazi, crypto, or otherwise. Besides, cultural change had altered the meanings of both terms: 'To call someone "queer" is merely to accuse him of embracing a fellow-human being. Vidal won the fight in 1968, but he loses it in 2015.' It is a nice ploy, but despite Herzberg's verbal jujitsu, the slur 'Nazi' is now applied recklessly and, alas, often effectively to anyone who is *not* an authoritarian left-wing racist. Those falsely accused feel damaged but unable to complain lest the police arrest them.

Rather than embark on such revisionist second thoughts, Graham's play changes course and becomes a lament for the degeneration of journalism of which the Buckley–Vidal debates were supposedly the *fons et origo*. My response is that this flatters the self-regard of pre-Woke journalists, whose bias was just more subtly cloaked, and it somewhat exaggerates the influence of these debates. But if we endorse, as we should, the play's request for media that take time to explore and discuss serious questions with serious people without anger and hostility, should we not also recall that William F. Buckley ran a television programme, *Firing Line*, that did exactly that and won public service awards for doing so for thirty years after 1968? Surely, that achievement should be part of any plea for the Buckley–Vidal debates to lead to something better than endless ideological slugfests.

But the question remains: if Vidal won the battle, who won the wider war? As it happens, one of the documentary filmmakers gave an illuminating answer to it: Buckley had won the war for the next thirty years which saw the election of Ronald Reagan, the recovery of America's economy and self-confidence, and the West's victory over communism in the Cold War. But events since then had reversed that verdict, and Vidal now seemed to be the irreligious prophet of an omnivorous sexual revolution and racial reckoning that had swept America's institutions, even its corporations, and converted them to a new secular religion of—among other novelties—Woke androgyny and radical transgenderism. It is hard to dismiss this interpretation when you leave the London theatre that hosts *Best of Enemies*, walk half a block past newspaper placards heralding sex changes for adolescents without medical approval (in Scotland!) to the box office of the Garrick Theatre where *Orlando*, an adaptation of Virginia Woolf's picaresque novel about a hero(ine) who changes sex among other things while travelling through several centuries of English literature, is playing to more packed houses and making Emma Corin (who played a luminous Princess Diana in *The Crown*) a poster-boy-girl-boy for androgyny.

That surely merits an Olympic Gold in the Dubious Achievement stakes, but it also compels Vidal to share his guru reputation with Buckley. Watching his play, I had wondered if Graham was not placing too much emphasis on Bill's apparent obsession with *Myra Breckenridge*, Vidal's own early satirical take on trans-sexuality, as we then called it. But his insight was correct. Like Vidal's crisis of political conscience, *Myra* may have fuelled Bill's uncharacteristic outburst. He had read it for the purposes of debate preparation between the two Conventions, and it had deeply alarmed him. He took it seriously. He read it as the high road to Sodom and Gomorrah, and not in Gore's hopeful frame of mind. And the semi compulsory progress of radical transgenderism through the fabric of American life, above all education at all levels, would surely have strengthened him in his belief that this was a fight worth fighting.

None of these battles are over as yet, moreover. As Morgan Neville and Robert Gordon observed, Vidal has a strong lead at this point. But history is a game of musical chairs that only ever stops for a moment. It resumes continually, and when it does, the lead often changes. At present we can see both the dominance of the Woke revolutionaries—and the growing resistance of parents, doctors, lawyers, scientists, voters, and almost anyone of independent mind to it. We cannot know the final outcome which, however, will be signalled by the lack of controversy over a new settled status quo.

But we can already see one historical irony that would delight Gore Vidal if it were not at his expense. His brave new world of untrammelled sexual libertinism has seemingly arrived and for the moment holds the field. But how could Gore who never acknowledged he was 'a friend of Dorothy' and shrank from organized homosexuality as from a dull sentence have foreseen that this victory would take place under the management of the same kind of grim doctrinaire puritan academic scolds he disliked almost more than he disliked Republicans.

Originally published in the Hungarian Review, *Vol. XIV, No.1, March 2023, https://hungarianreview.com/article/issue/volume-xiv-no-1-march-2023/.*

Remembering Robert Conquest
September 2015

The opening line in most obituaries of Robert Conquest, who died on 3 August, described him as a 'historian and poet.' That would be a capacious enough description for most men of letters. In Tom Stoppard's *The Invention of Love*, Charon keeps A. E. Housman waiting on the banks of the River Styx for a second arrival since he is expecting two people, 'a poet and a scholar,' until Housman says shyly: 'I think that must be me.' In Bob's case Charon would have been waiting for a historian, a poet, a novelist, a satirist, a critic, a diplomat, a strategist, a soldier, a social and political theorist, a limerickist, and of course a scholar—and I have almost certainly left out some of Bob's other professional identities. Charon probably brought along a second boat.

It is well-nigh impossible to do justice to a life of such varied achievement. Most of Bob's obituaries rightly focused therefore on the most important aspects of his public achievement (in particular his histories, *The Great Terror* on Stalin's purges, and the *Harvest of Sorrow* on Stalin's forced Ukrainian famine). They made clear that his accounts of the dictator's crimes (in particular, the number of his victims) had first been challenged and later vindicated; they attributed a major change in the world's opinion of Soviet communism at least in part to his work; they gave lesser but still important standing to his literary achievements; and they gave a general impression of a life devoted to truth and crowned by honours. With the exception of a *Guardian* obituary that hinted so many faults and hesitated so many dislikes (to paraphrase Alexander Pope) that it revealed its overwhelming animus, they were all both (largely) accurate and highly favourable. Their main conclusions need not be further developed here.

For the other half of Bob's public achievement was his life in literature. That too was extremely varied, and it went very deep. He was a major poet and critic who in 1956 launched the 'Movement' poets—including Philip Larkin, Kingsley Amis, Thom Gunn, and Donald Davie—in the anthology *New Lines*. Much ink has been spent arguing that the Movement poets were no such thing and soon went their separate ways. That seems overargued. Poets of their nature do not remain in formation. What is surely more significant is that the Movement included many poets who in retrospect are among the most-read British poets of the post-war years, that the country's single best-loved poet, Philip Larkin, was among them, and that their work *did* exhibit certain common traits, notably concern for technique and formal perfection, avoidance of rhetorical and romantic excess, strong dislike of pretension, and belief that poetry should be intelligent as well as moving or powerful. Bob himself, having called for a renewed attention to the 'necessary intellectual component in poetry viewed from a common-sense standpoint,' was clearly the moving spirit as well as the anthologist of the Movement. And his own poetry met that (and most other) criteria.

Is it so necessary
For a wild memory
To fade and blur
Before the full charge
Of an old love or rage
Can really register?

With a life's long perspectives
The changed picture gives
More depth and scope
As twisted faces shrink
To little more than pink
Blobs on its landscape...

A passion, sharp and hot,
Might once have seized the heart
To rip or scald.
So far as this can be
Recalled in tranquillity
It's not recalled.

A strong dislike of pretension, accompanied by a happy delight in puncturing it through satire and parody, is also a major element in his literary criticism. His demolition of Ezra Pound is especially effective because, as a classical scholar and linguist, he is able to establish that many of Pound's most admired technical effects are in reality simple errors of grammar or translation. Some of his satires even merit the judgement 'too perfect.' His essay 'Christian Symbolism in "Lucky Jim,"' which appeared in the *Critical Quarterly* of 1965, was a parody of the then-dominant literary criticism and contained such absurdities as seeing Jim as a Christ figure because his surname Dixon—read it Di(e)xon—was centred on an X on which a man might die. After Eng Lit professors started getting its arguments in their students' essays, the *Quarterly* published a note to readers that the essay was in fact satirical. Read today it is a masterpiece of dry irony. These and other essays in criticism, originally scattered through several journals, were collected in the 1979 book *The Abomination of Moab*, which will serve well as a manifesto of Bob's literary common sense. In response to the charge of philistinism levelled by the academic and transgressive critics of popular or traditional literature, he hurls back the charge of Moabitism. Just as the Philistines were the enemies of the children of light, the Moabites were their false friends who set them 'whoring off after strange doctrines.' Most literary and artistic intellectuals are, in short, the false friends of art and damage it by their support. Bob transferred this insight from literature to the wider arena of education as a whole in the 1970s 'Black Papers' lamenting, with Kingsley Amis and others, the decline of schooling and cultural standards generally. This criticism of progressive education made him a 'controversial' right-winger, as the media understand these things. Few other conventional critics of modern education, however, could have matched this criticism—a parody of one of Bob's favourite nineteenth-century light versifiers, Winthrop Mackworth Praed:

'Those teach who can't do' runs the dictum,
But for some even that's out of reach:
They can't even teach—so they've picked 'em

To teach other people to teach.
Then alas for the next generation,
For the pots fairly crackle with thorn.
Where psychology meets education
A terrible bullshit is born.

In addition to his writings on Soviet history, critical articles, 'Black Paper' polemics and columns for *The Daily Telegraph*, Bob wrote two novels, a study of science fiction (with Kingsley Amis again), a constant stream of poetry, and the limericks of which he is widely regarded as a master. Philip Larkin admired this skill without reserve and declared that Bob's version of the seven ages of man had leapt over one major hurdle for deserving the approval of posterity: instant memorability. All these different activities came together in his now celebrated limerick:

There was a great Marxist called Lenin
Who did two or three million men in.
That's a lot to have done in
But where he did one in
That grand Marxist Stalin did ten in.

Much more can and should be written on the works, but Bob has also left behind some autobiographical sketches that fill gaps in our knowledge of the life too. Not incidentally in such a life, they amuse and enlighten us about equally on a range of twentieth-century topics. Seeing the Communists taking over Bulgaria, first as a soldier, later as a diplomat, he writes, would have made anyone a firm anti-communist. The tortures they inflicted on a secretary to a democratic politician will lead him in time to produce studies, now known to be accurate, of Soviet behaviour for the Information and Research Department of the British Foreign Office and later to write *The Great Terror*. Immediately, however, he helps Bulgarians under threat to escape to the West.

Back in England in the literary wars there is his strong and (to my mind) conclusive defence of Philip Larkin against his biographer's charge of pornophilia and general nastiness (and tore but lesser charges against himself). Simply put, it was not pornography as we now understand the genre but the equivalent of modern ads for bras. But this parody of one of Philip's most famous poems may serve as an *hors d'oeuvre*:

They fuck you up, the chaps you choose
To do your Letters and your Life.
They wait till all that's left of you's
A corpse in which to shove a knife.

How ghoulishly they grub among
Your years for stuff to shame and shock:
The times you didn't hold your tongue,
The times you failed to curb your cock.

To each of those who've processed me
Into their scrap of fame or pelf:
You think in marks for decency
I'd lose to you? Don't kid yourself.

And there are lighter episodes on every other page—as when, acting as a liaison officer to the local churches in Scotland, he told the Free Kirk pastor that there did not seem to be much difference in theology between them and the Church of Scotland and was informed: 'Aye, there are not many differences but there is one important one: we go to heaven and they go to hell.' Or when, acting as diplomatic host at a cocktail party in Sofia, he asked the Exarch of the Bulgarian Orthodox Church upon entry, 'Manhattan or Martini, Your Beatitude?' (Manhattan, replied the prelate instantly). Bob remained calm, balanced, decent, and good-humoured through the best and worst of times, except when faced with cruelty and lying.

Several obituaries wondered hopefully whether Bob was 'a Man of the Left.' That does not seem to me the most interesting question to ask about him, but he certainly described himself in those terms, adding that he had voted Labour in every election until 1979 when he switched to Mrs Thatcher's Tories. At school and university, Bob had been a free-spirited bohemian, famous for girl-chasing and pranks (such as placing chamber pots on the college roof to mark the Coronation) at least as much for his fling with communism. He found Oxford Conservatives such as Edward Heath priggish. Though he had proved to be an effective soldier, six years in the Army had not made him more conventional. As he later reflected: 'In most ways ... it strengthened and clarified my dislike of authority and organisations in general, and an attachment to the principles of personal and civil liberty (reinforced, also, by seeing what happened to the Balkans in the successive totalitarian grips).' So he was a strong supporter of Labour during the war and afterwards he was enthusiastic about working with Labour ministers such as Christopher Mayhew who headed the Information Research Department. He also drafted speeches for (and with) the fiery red-headed left-wing minister, Barbara Castle, at the United Nations, finding her very attractive along 'Susan Hayward lines' as well as firmly anti-Soviet. As long as the Left was anti-totalitarian in foreign policy and liberal in domestic politics, he was comfortable within it.

None of these tastes and attachments changed at all seriously for the rest of Bob's life. But as other people have found, the scenery moved sideways while he remained wedded to his original ideas. As the political Left diluted its opposition to the Soviets, so Bob criticized their appeasement; as the academic Left replaced the idea of making art and literature more available to people with that of deconstructing them and reconstructing them as transgressive politics, he mocked them. Over time that resulted in his becoming an adviser to Margaret Thatcher and, in the partisan terms of the day, a conservative. In a longer-term perspective, however, as others became radicals, he remained a liberal. Whether a liberal is a man of the Left today, however, is another matter.

Much of what I have written here is drawn from a friendship with Bob that began in 1972, when I was invited to join the 'fascists' lunches' at Bertorelli's. Two years later, both our marriages having recently ended, I moved into his Battersea apartment to share the rent. My one additional contribution was to introduce Bob to Margaret Thatcher which led to the first 'Iron Lady' speech and, more important, to their becoming lifelong friends. Otherwise I was overwhelmingly the beneficiary of this arrangement, enjoying lunch with Senator Scoop Jackson, a birthday party for Philip Larkin (not at all a gloomy occasion), several other literary parties fuelled by champagne and kedgeree, and the easy-going education of watching Bob work on anything from a translation of a Solzhenitsyn poem to a new limerick.

One summer evening I returned to the flat to find Bob looking out at Battersea Park and drinking a gin and tonic. He offered me one, and then said, 'Hang on a minute; I've just thought of something.' He sat down and, after what seemed to me a few pencil strokes, read out this:

My demands upon life are quite modest,
They're just to be decently goddessed.
Astarte or Isis
Would do in a crisis,
But the best's Aphrodite, unbodiced.

Those lines met Larkin's test of instant memorability as far as I am concerned. I have recalled them without difficulty ever since. They also seem to me now to express Bob's demands upon life at the time quite accurately. By the mid-1970s, he already enjoyed a secure reputation as the historian who had revealed the truth about Soviet communism. Full vindication, other achievements, and other honours would follow. But while he was attractive to women—my then-girlfriend described him as 'like a lovely Teddy Bear left out in the rain overnight'—and had several companionable former girlfriends to escort around town, he had ultimately been unlucky in love over two marriages and cursed by tragedy in another. In 1975, he was still a single man in want of a wife.

Three years later, Aphrodite walked into a party following one of Bob's poetry readings, and a little later mislaid her bodice. A happy marriage lasting thirty-six years and a life that continued to produce fine work at the rate of a book a year to the very end on 3 August were the results. He was lucky to have her; we were lucky to have him. RIP Robert Conquest.

Originally published in The New Criterion, *September 2015,* *https://newcriterion.com/issues/2015/9/remembering-robert-conquest.*

The Incomparable Frank Johnson
—A Conservative despite Himself
22 December 2006

One Monday morning in the early summer of 1973 when I was returning by train from a weekend with friends, I opened my copy of *The Telegraph* to scan the editorial page. I had a fierce semi-proprietary interest in its contents. Only six months before, I had joined the paper as a parliamentary sketch-writer and leader-writer. Frank Johnson had come on board the same week in the same combination of jobs. Together with Michael Harrington, an editorial writer who enjoyed six months seniority over us, we made up the "Young Turks" who were supposedly pushing *The Telegraph* towards a more libertarian conservatism. In any event, we three were agreed on the need for a more combative conservative 'line,' and with the passionate suspicion of young men, we watched for any deviation from it.

The big issue of the moment was the Watergate crisis. Not even Michael, Frank, and I were agreed on that last. Frank had declared early on that Nixon was plainly guilty; Michael and I were sticklers for constitutional due process and the presumption of Nixon's innocence. So far our side had prevailed. But Frank was alone on leader-writing duty that weekend.

I opened the paper with some trepidation. My fears were confirmed: an editorial titled 'An American President' listed a long catalogue of crimes of which the president had been 'plausibly' accused: burgling the offices of his opponents, misusing the security services for partisan warfare, overriding the Constitution, etc., etc. The editorial was appalling, a clear breach of collegial etiquette, an outrage. Something would have to be done.

Then I turned to the second paragraph. It read something like this: 'Yes, Salvador Allende of Chile has been accused of all these crimes—and not without reason or evidence.' This was a very good example of Frank's editorial writing. It was witty, indirect, wove two different themes together to illuminate both, and it was deeply conservative. Not many Fleet Street journalists then or later were brave or principled enough to take on the saintly left-wing Allende. But Frank managed to do so while leaving the Left few grounds either for responding effectively or for denouncing him. When I rang to congratulate him (and to admit that I had risen to his bait), he laughed, confessed that he had written the leader with me partly in mind, and said: 'But when I pulled the rug out from under you, I also pulled it out from under the Left—but from the opposite direction.' He was quite right. His conceit had made it hard to complain about the attack on Allende without exonerating Nixon too.

Most of the obituaries for Frank, excellent though they have been, have played up his sense of mischief. But they have either ignored or underplayed the stern unbending quality of his conservatism, his anti-Allende side. That is understandable. To be sure, his conservatism shifted back and forth between different schools of thought depending on events, the topic under discussion, or his guru of the moment. Sometimes he was the Tory cynic, a follower of Maurice Cowling, who thought that all politics was about the next by-election and that principles were an irrelevant distraction. On other occasions, he was helping Peter (later Lord) Bauer to hone his economic critiques of foreign aid. Frank was a curious journalist exploring current controversies not a professor of philosophy seeking the reconciliation of all his values (which professors of philosophy now tell us is impossible anyway). Almost always, however, he gravitated to the conservative side of any argument, and on the great political issues of his life, he was a devout monetarist and a firm Cold Warrior.

After a 1975 meeting with Milton Friedman in America, Frank emerged dazed: the great man had answered all his objections before he had had a chance to raise them. Because he was known to hold such opinions, he was consulted by Keith Joseph about the establishment of the Centre for Policy Studies in 1974. When Keith was preparing his famous 'Preston' speech that formally signalled the breach between the Heath leadership and its monetarist critics, he asked Frank to play the part of a hostile journalist interrogating him at a press conference. Frank thought this the greatest fun and he became a regular attendee at the lunches of the Centre for Policy Studies where the Thatcherite agenda was first sketched out. No one present when the TUC's Len Murray attended one of Bill Deedes's *Telegraph* drink parties could have doubted that Frank had digested the full Thatcherite creed. Murray was arguing that the workers in a failing company deserved financial compensation because they had 'invested their lives' in it.

'I would be a little wary of that argument, Lord Murray,' I said politely, 'because if that were so ...'

'When the company went bankrupt, the workers would all drop dead,' interjected Frank.

In those days too, a heated conversation in the press gallery tea room was likely to be about the Vietnam War. Frank was one of a small band who supported the South Vietnamese and their US allies. He had read widely in the classics of anti-communism—it was Frank who recommended *Witness* by Whittaker Chambers to me—and he predicted the horrors that followed the victories of Hanoi and the Khmer Rouge. Such horrors had, after all, attended almost every other communist takeover.

Nor was Frank a warrior in theory only. Days after Ted Heath lost the second election of 1974, the Sunday papers all produced stories saying that Ted would stand down and back Willie Whitelaw as leader to stop Keith Joseph. None of the stories (which reflected a Central Office briefing but which foundered on Ted's refusal to resign) contained any response from Keith. Frank rang me in a panic that Keith would be defeated unless he got some sort of press operation going. We contacted Keith who invited us around to the CPS the following morning. Admitted and given a cup of coffee, we were surprised when the door opened and Mrs Thatcher (whom neither of us knew well) came in and said: 'I am Sir Keith's campaign manager, gentlemen. What can I do for you?'

Well, as we know, the campaign developed rather differently. But Frank remained loyal and on board with only one small hiccup: at a small Reform Club dinner a few days before the first leadership vote in 1975, Frank asked Mrs Thatcher what she would do after the election.

'I shall be leader of the Tory Party, Frank,' she said.

'No, I mean really,' said Frank.

'Frank,' she replied, 'if I didn't think I could win, I wouldn't run. I don't take on losing battles.'

Maybe we should have listened to her words more carefully. At any rate, Lady Thatcher, Frank and Virginia, Ken Minogue, and I reminisced about these early battles of Thatcherism over a long weekend lunch at Brown's restaurant this spring. It may have been the last time they met. If so, it was a fond farewell. Frank went on from 1975 to be involved somehow or other in every Tory leadership struggle, always backing the right-wing runner—notably last year when he was a firm if despairing supporter of David Davis.

Why has Frank's conservatism been underplayed? Well, Frank was a wit and comic writer. He often compared himself to a court jester who has to be prepared to offend both King and Barons. His parliamentary sketches assailed both establishments with brilliant raillery but also gave credit to independent spirits like Denis Skinner whom he christened 'the Beast of Bolsover.' Frank's wit was Tory wit throughout, and it gave heart to ordinary conservatives around the nation. But because some of his victims were Tories, he inevitably struck the more conventionally minded as 'not a team player.'

They were right about that. As one obituarist observed, Frank hated to be 'one of a gang'—especially a victorious and complacent gang. He had been keen to rally to the Thatcherite standard in the embattled seventies but once it had triumphed, he wanted to demonstrate his independence. He was not only a believer in individualism; he went to the extreme length of being an individual. The purely political aspect of this individuality was that he liked to distinguish himself from any conservative orthodoxy. Again, however, he usually found respectably conservative grounds for doing so.

(And there was a simple cure that we more orthodox figures could employ to draw him back into our ranks—namely, to arrange for Frank to attend a left-wing gathering. His (and my) friend, the feminist writer Yvonne Roberts, once invited him to a party given by John Pilger. The next day Frank was sounding off like Dostoevsky in one of his gloomier moments or Gordon Brown on a good day.)

Then again, like a good individualist, Frank was many-sided. He loved music, opera, ballet, literature, history, good food, and conversation from long before he arrived in Fleet Street. He devoted more time and thought to these pursuits as time went on. The shift of emphasis in his later writing towards opera, history, etc. occurred in part because the great political battles of the 1970s and 1980s had been resolved in favour of liberty. He had fought the good fight. The lesser battles interested him much less. Now, quite logically, he was using the liberty he had defended to explore and enjoy the good life.

That good life was completed by a late and entirely happy marriage. Virginia Fraser created around him that rare thing in London—a political salon—with a foreign branch in his house in southern France. At his table, you would find a Tory leadership hopeful, an opera singer, a newspaper editor, a New Labour peer, a veteran of the Thatcher years. The conversation was history, politics, music, literature, and wonderfully complicated jokes—Virginia had created for Frank the kind of high Edwardian table that as young men in Fleet Street we had long ago fantasized about. Still, as with high Edwardian tables, a good deal of Tory plotting went on around it.

It sounds odd to say so, but the last years of Frank's life, though plagued by cancer, were tranquil and happy. The restlessness and striving of his Fleet Street days had left him. He was delightfully happy in his marriage. He had become what he wanted to be since his secondary modern schooldays in Shoreditch (and what in reality he had been all along): a genuinely civilized man. And he leaves behind a large body of writing characterized by wit without malice.

At his death, his friends have learnt that we loved him more than we knew. We will miss him more than we can say.

Originally published in Conservative Home, *22 December 2006,* *www.conservativehome.com/platform/2006/12/john_osullivan_-2.html.*

A Tribute to Owen Harries
28 June 2020

Harries was walking down the Strand in 1955 when he saw an advertisement that changed his life. His life at the time did not seem to need much changing. Having served two years 'national service' in the RAF, he had recently graduated from Oxford, where his teachers included Sir Isaiah Berlin, and made a happy marriage with a new wife.

But even though his personal prospects were good, he found the atmosphere of post-war Britain stultifying and unadventurous. He thought life should offer more. And at the end of the Strand there was a large advertisement outside the Australian High Commission that showed a couple entering a sunny landscape and offered emigration to Australia for the bargain price of just 10 pounds. He and Dorothy Harries signed on and arrived in New South Wales a few months later as 'Ten Pound Poms.'

Within a short time, Harries was climbing the ladder of academic achievement at the University of Sydney and the University of New South Wales. His combination of sharp mind, judicious temperament, hard work, crisp logic in writing or speaking, and adamantine anti-communist principle brought him to the attention of conservative opinion and Liberal party leaders. He became one of the 'Cold War' intellectuals around *Quadrant* magazine—Australia's own *Encounter*—and a reliably effective representative of the conservative and anti-communist side in national debates.

At a time when Australia was moving leftwards under the impact of the Vietnam War, he was the foreign policy intellectual who could make the strongest case for Australian intervention in the war on America's side. It made him that rare thing—a foreign policy celebrity. Though Owen was to be sharply critical of US foreign policy in the post-Cold War world—he strongly opposed the Iraq War and the Bush Doctrine, for instance—he never retreated from his conviction that communism was an oppressive evil and the Vietnam War a necessary resistance to it.

When Malcolm Fraser became Prime Minister in 1975, he invited Owen to serve as an adviser on foreign policy in his Liberal-County coalition government. As director of policy planning in the Department of Foreign Affairs and as speechwriter for Fraser and Foreign Minister Andrew Peacocok, he laid the groundwork for Australia's foreign policy and in particular its continued alliance with the United States in the post-Vietnam world.

It is fair to say that Harries set a course for Australia in the world that has been profitably maintained until the recent disenchantment with China. Harries never forgot the debt he owed to Fraser, who lost power in 1983, for his generous patronage. He repaid it by being a great public servant.

But what could he do for an encore? In fact, Owen went on to have almost as many encores as Dame Nellie Melba.

One afternoon in the early 1980s, I walked into my office at the Heritage Foundation to find Robert Conquest who introduced me to his companion, saying 'This is Owen Harries. He should be a Fellow here.' Not long afterwards he *was* a Heritage Fellow, and one with a mission. Having served as Australian Ambassador to UNESCO in Paris in 1982 as his last diplomatic task, he had emerged with the firm opinion that it was a corrupt, wasteful, anti-Western agency that should either be reformed or abandoned. Such ambitions, though often reasonable, are almost never achieved. But Owen waged a sustained intellectual campaign in both Washington and London (where his debate with UNESCO's former Assistant Director-General Richard Hoggart degenerated into almost complete agreement) that resulted in both the Reagan and Thatcher administrations pulling out of the discredited agency—and as Harries urged, starting the momentum to reform it.

That scalp made Harries a celebrity in Washington too, especially among neoconservatives who were happy to see a UN agency taken down a peg. So it was natural that when Irving Kristol set out to establish a foreign policy magazine that would foster serious debate on international affairs, he should ask Harries to serve as co-editor alongside

Robert Tucker, a long-time academic devotee of the 'realist' tradition in foreign affairs. Most commentators expected that anti-ideological Tucker would be the Yin to Harries' neoconservative Yang on *The National Interest*, and that together they would produce enlightening clashes of opinion and strategies among first-class minds. As long as the Cold War lasted, that happened. And when the Cold War ended and ushered in a completely new set of foreign policy issues, the clash of serious opinion on such issues, far from abating, intensified with such contributors as Samuel Huntington, Francis Fukuyama, Henry Kissinger, Conrad Black, Charles Krauthammer, Eliot Cohen, Jeane Kirkpatrick, Fareed Zakaria, Josef Joffe, Daniel Patrick Moynihan, and many others of equal or near distinction debating furiously on everything from the expansion of NATO to the end of history.

For more than a decade, *The National Interest* was the most important international relations journal in the world. Readers actually got impatient for its monthly appearance. When had that last happened to a foreign policy journal? The reason for this, however, was not because Harries and Tucker represented conflicting traditions in foreign policy. As Tom Switzer—Owen's frequent collaborator and close friend in later years—has pointed out, the end of the Cold War produced its own change in Owen's thinking. Not that he repented one iota of his anti-communism but that he thought it was simply less relevant to a world in which Soviet communism had suffered a historic reverse. In Owen's own words, quoted by Switzer:

> 'If we spend 40 or 50 years saying the Cold War was a tremendously important event, a critical life-and-death struggle, then for Christ's sake, the end of the Cold War must also be important,' he told *The Sydney Morning Herald* in 1997. 'You can't say, "Well, it's finished but that doesn't mean much; the world goes on pretty well as it is." When life-and-death struggles end, it is supposed to make a very large difference, and I think it has.'

Harries and Tucker were therefore on the same realist wavelength after 1989, and the intellectual liveliness of *The National Interest* arose not from their clashes but from their personal qualities of originality and imagination. Though Harries never spoke of Tucker with anything other than great respect, I and most external critics would mainly credit Harries with the astounding flair with which the magazine was edited. He was in my view a born editor, full of strong editorial ideas, a brilliant talent-spotter of writers and junior editors (Jacob Heilbrunn, Gideon Rose, Adam Garfinkle, Scott McConnell, Michael Lind), a first-rate critical eye when evaluating prose or argument, a mischief-maker who enjoyed creating controversies (especially among highly distinguished people), and an intellectual with a touch of the tabloid in his make-up. I think he realized all these things about himself when once he sat in the editorial chair and started having the time of his life.

Owen's slow turn towards foreign policy realism after the end of the Cold War reflected his conservative concern that America was forgetting the natural limits to the power even of a superpower. He found himself understanding why Burke had dreaded his country being too much feared, and this sense was reflected in his 'discovery' of contributors like James Kurth who brought a tough sceptical, sometimes religious, criticism to the pursuit of national power.

His odyssey continued after he left *TNI* and returned to live happily in Sydney, spend more time with his family, to cultivate his garden and his friendships, which were extensive and deep and not confined to political life. His last great service to controversy was his delivery of the Boyer Lectures—Australia's equivalent of the Reith Lectures—which caused a sensation in Liberal and Conservative circles and a breach with his old political patrons. For he sharply attacked both President George W. Bush's 'doctrine' of preventive war and its first implementation in Iraq which they supported. It was an amusing sign of the respect in which he was generally held that it was not Owen but the Liberal leaders who desperately tried to heal the breach. I do not think he changed his mind about Iraq, or preventive war, or the risks of our being too powerful, but those dangers have now been superseded by greater ones. And all quarrels end at the grave.

Both as a Cold War anti-communist and a post-Cold War sceptical realist, Owen was chary of talking in moralistic terms. But he was a moralist all the same. His speeches and writings are marked throughout by what Pascal called 'the first principle of morality—thinking clearly.' He judged political and diplomatic decisions not by whether they advanced noble ideals but by whether they made life better for most people without imposing undue burdens on some. One of the reasons why he was a quiet but serious Australian patriot is that as he once told me, he believed the British working class had built as decent a society as we can hope for in this world on Australia's distant shore. He was happy to have his place in the sun there.

Was it raining on that day in London's Strand in 1955? If not, it should have been.

Originally published in The Critic, *28 June 2020, https://thecritic.co.uk/ a-tribute-to-owen-harries/.*

Printed in the USA
CPSIA information can be obtained
at www.ICGtesting.com
JSHW010902260324
59777JS00003B/4/J